Fundamentals of Emergency Management: Preparedness

Norman Ferrier

2009
Emond Montgomery Publications
Toronto, Canada

Emond Montgomery Publications Limited
60 Shaftesbury Avenue
Toronto ON M4T 1A3
http://www.emp.ca/college

Printed in Canada.
Reprinted December 2018.

We acknowledge the financial support of the Government of Canada through the Canada Book Fund for our publishing activities.

Acquisitions and developmental editor: Tammy Scherer
Supervising editor: Jim Lyons
Copy editor: Claudia Forgas
Permissions editor: Nick Raymond
Proofreader: Cindy Fujimoto
Text designer and typesetter: Tara Wells
Indexer: Paula Pike
Cover designer: David Gee

Library and Archives Canada Cataloguing in Publication

Ferrier, Norman
    Fundamentals of emergency management : preparedness / Norman Ferrier.

Includes index.
ISBN 978-1-55239-298-0

    1. Emergency management.   I. Title.
HD49.F47 2008   363.34'8   C2008-903455-4

To my late mother, Barbara Ferrier, who always believed in me, and to my wife, Jennifer, without whose constant support and encouragement my career goals would never have been achieved.

CONTENTS

PART II   HAZARD, RISK, AND VULNERABILITY

PART III PREPAREDNESS

PART IV   EMERGENCY MANAGEMENT EDUCATION AND FUNDING

Preface

Fundamentals of Emergency Management: Preparedness was created for use in college- and university-level emergency management programs. It was also created to provide a practical reference for emergency management practitioners, whether they are new to the field and have not received the benefit of formal training or whether they are experienced. Indeed, any reader with an interest in disasters or emergency management may find this book useful.

This book has a practical orientation because most of its readers are adult learners who typically will learn best by doing. As a result, in addition to presenting theoretical knowledge, each chapter provides opportunities for readers to apply what they have learned in practical ways through case studies and assignments.

This book is organized into four parts: "Emergency Management and Communities," "Hazard, Risk, and Vulnerability," "Preparedness," and "Emergency Management Education and Funding." Each part provides a comprehensive overview of a different core element of the emergency management process.

Each chapter includes the following sections:

▶ **Learning Objectives:** This section describes in general terms the information that readers are expected to understand upon completion of the chapter and its associated assignments. It is intended to provide readers with a guide to getting the most out of the content.

▶ **Key Messages:** This section presents a clear and concise description of the most important concepts contained in the chapter. It does not eliminate the need to read the chapter. The main body of the chapter provides the detailed explanations, discussion, and examples necessary for a complete understanding of the concepts being studied.

▶ **Introduction:** As its title suggests, this section introduces the concepts contained in the chapter and outlines the areas to be covered. It provides readers with a roadmap with which to direct their reading.

▶ **Purpose:** This section describes how the information obtained through the reading of the chapter is used, why this information is important, and what makes it relevant to the practice of emergency management.

▶ **Conclusion:** This section summarizes the key information contained in the chapter, and also draws certain important conclusions regarding that information's application to the practice of emergency management.

▶ **Key Terms:** Each time a new term of particular importance appears in the text, the term is highlighted. Readers will find definitions for these key terms in the glossary. These terms are in common usage in the field of emergency management and, to some extent, represent the jargon of the field. As such, they are important terms for readers to know, understand, and be able to use comfortably in their daily practice.

▶ **Learning Check:** Close to the end of each chapter there is a series of 20 multiple-choice questions related to the chapter content. These questions allow readers to self-test their level of knowledge after reading the chapter. Readers should take the time to consider each question carefully, and, in all cases, should select the *best* answer. The answer to each question appears in the answer key at the end of the book. Readers should be able to answer at least 16 questions out of 20 correctly (80 percent). If they cannot, it is recommended that they re-read the chapter. This section provides readers with a valuable review of key information, and may also be of use as a study tool when preparing for state/provincial or International Association of Emergency Managers (IAEM) certification examinations.

▶ **Case Studies:** Each chapter contains two case studies. Each case study places readers in the position of a working emergency manager, and provides them with initial exposure to the practical application of the chapter material in planning and problem solving.

▶ **To Learn More:** This section provides readers with relatively simple assignments that they can undertake to better understand the concepts contained in the chapter. In most cases, these assignments will not take more than an hour or two of a reader's time. Most of them are to be undertaken by readers at a local level to provide them with a broader exposure to emergency management as it is practised in their own community, and to make the information obtained locally relevant.

▶ **Notes:** This section provides readers with additional resources in the form of readings or websites with relevant information. Notes present resources that refer to a specific concept discussed, provide a supporting example, or discuss a concept in greater detail. No reader can learn all that there is to know about any subject by reading a single book, and these notes are intended to provide readers with a broader spectrum of information. Taken collectively, the notes from all chapters may provide readers with a useful collection of research sources for additional work assignments given in class.

The end of the book includes the following sections:

▶ **Glossary:** The glossary is intended to more fully and concisely explain key terms that appear in the main body of the book. These terms include jargon that is common to the practice of emergency management, and that the reader must know, understand, and be able to use appropriately.

▶ **Answer Key:** This section provides the correct answers for each chapter's "Learning Check" questions.

Acknowledgments

No book is ever the result of a single person's thoughts. A long list of people, both colleagues and mentors, have made some contribution to the content of this book, whether they realize it or not. While these people are too numerous to mention individually, I would like to express my thanks to each of them—they know who they are. I would also like to thank the staff and administration of the Toronto Emergency Medical Service, who have constantly supported and encouraged my career aspirations, providing me with perspectives, opportunities, and experiences that helped make this book what it is. Finally, I would like to thank my editor, Tammy Scherer, whose thoughtful insights and sense of humour kept me focused and helped take this book from an idea into reality.

Introduction

All communities are challenged from time to time by unforeseeable disasters that are a result of natural events, technological accidents, and, in some unfortunate cases, deliberately planned events. The ability to respond to such events quickly and effectively is a central part of community safety, and just as important in its own right as the emergency services (such as Emergency Medical Services [EMS], fire protection, and policing) that we normally take for granted. The ability to respond well can mean the difference between safety and misery, and may even affect the community's ability to survive the event. Despite the importance of this priority, communities large and small are routinely challenged to find both the physical and monetary resources as well as the expertise to prepare for such events effectively.

Emergency management and preparedness are the mandate of an emergency manager. Increasingly, this critical role is becoming formalized and evolving into a profession in its own right, complete with educational requirements, standards, and a required knowledge base.

It is clearly impossible and impractical to attempt to put everything that one might need to know about emergency management into a single book. With this in mind, *Fundamentals of Emergency Management: Preparedness* is intended to be the first in a series of three books on the subject of emergency management. Subsequent books in the series will focus on community response to emergency events and on the community's recovery from emergency events. The process of mitigation will be a recurring theme in all three books, in much the same way that it recurs in real-life emergency management.

This book is divided into four parts, with each addressing a different aspect of preparedness. Part I deals with the history and evolution of emergency management as a process, its role within governments and organizations, the evolution and composition of communities, and land-use issues. Part II explores and explains the nature and evolution of hazard, risk, vulnerability, and resiliency, how they affect communities and organizations, and how they may be evaluated in a meaningful way when creating a preparedness process for the community or organization. Part III addresses the processes, procedures, and issues involved in writing a meaningful and effective emergency plan for a community or organization. Finally, part IV explores preparedness activities, including the testing of emergency plans through exercises, the role of public education, the education of key decision-makers, and the funding of preparedness projects through municipal funding and alternative sources.

The practice of emergency management is rarely identical in any two communities. At a local level the process will be affected by the local reality and priorities, the availability of resources, and legislated mandates. This book presents the general principles behind the practice of emergency management, and draws on examples from a variety of countries and jurisdictions, each with its own priorities, realities, and good ideas. It also presents readers with assignments that will not only help them better understand how emergency management is practised in their local context, but also give them the opportunity to apply the general principles of emergency management in their own locale.

Modern emergency managers are not specialists, but sophisticated generalists. Knowledge is required from not only the field itself but also a broad range of academic disciplines. The formal education of emergency managers is an essential step in the process of preparedness, and will come from a variety of sources, and a variety of mentors, all with their own experiences. No single source will ever prepare emergency managers for their role. Educated emergency managers create communities that are truly prepared for emergencies, and prepared communities are usually more resilient to the effects of any disaster that might befall them. This book is intended to contribute to that process of education.

PART I
Emergency Management and Communities

Source: www.CartoonStock.com.

THE NEED FOR EMERGENCY MANAGEMENT

Communities are complex organisms. They are much more than a collection of bricks and mortar; they are our homes. Communities are the result of a convergence of factors including topography (physical features), resources, wealth generation, and transportation routes. The relationships among these factors are not always obvious to the casual observer, but they are real nonetheless. One of the most important factors is people, who are, after all, the reason communities exist in the first place. They provide workplaces, raise families, and interact socially with one another, ideally in a safe environment.

Communities are vulnerable organisms as well. They are exposed to the unpredictable forces of nature, affected by our activities, and, occasionally, when we become careless or even greedy, subject to the results of our own folly. Our communities and their residents need to be protected, whether from the ravages of weather and the movement of earth or water; failed industrial processes and other forms of human carelessness; or even poor planning. Communities must have mechanisms in place to reduce the incidence or effect of untoward events, and plans in place to address the effects of such events, should they occur, and the immediate needs of residents. Developing such mechanisms and plans is the role of the emergency manager.

In order to be effective, emergency managers require a detailed knowledge of how communities operate and which events might affect them. They need to understand a community's history, topography, land use, wealth-generating processes and other human activities, human composition, and risk exposures. Emergency managers are not specialists, but sophisticated generalists, with knowledge in a variety of areas. Although this knowledge may not be comparable with that of a subject expert, it should exceed that of the ordinary citizen, and perhaps even that of many community decision-makers. Part I focuses on the history of emergency management and the role of the emergency manager, and on the complex factors that make up all communities—factors that must be understood, and in some cases acted upon, before any emergency actually occurs. Chapter 1 describes the nature and history of emergency management. Chapter 2 focuses on the role of government in the protection of its citizens. Chapter 3 explores the manner in which communities have evolved and the factors that have influenced that evolution. Chapter 4 considers the human element, particularly the role of community composition in the creation of emergency management strategies. Chapter 5 considers the role that land-use issues play in the field of emergency management.

CHAPTER 1

The History of Emergency Management

LEARNING OBJECTIVES

On completion of this chapter, you will

▶ Understand the evolution of the practice of emergency management, under its various names, from prehistory to the present.

▶ Understand the key factors that have influenced the development of emergency management.

KEY MESSAGES

1. The primary role of emergency managers is to protect communities.

2. As communities change and evolve, the hazards to which they are exposed change and evolve.

3. There is a direct connection between human activity and hazards.

4. Community safety functions tend to evolve based upon genuine need, and on the availability of the resources required to support them.

5. Emergency management, like most public-safety services, has its origins in the military.

6. Contemporary emergency managers are not specialists, but sophisticated generalists.

Introduction

Professional emergency managers are charged with making arrangements to guarantee the safety of communities, both before untoward events occur, and during their occurrence. Their responsibilities include identifying and analyzing potential community safety issues, formulating strategies to reduce or eliminate potential **hazards**, preparing a community for **response** to hazards that cannot be **mitigated**, and assisting with the direction of a community's response, should the untoward event occur. The goal of emergency managers is to make a community and its residents as safe as possible from untoward events, and as **resilient** as possible to their effects.

This concern about safety is not new; it is one of the primary reasons humans have banded together in communities throughout time. Initially, the issue of safety was addressed by community leaders; then it was delegated to those with the greatest knowledge; later it became the responsibility of those who could draw upon the knowledge gathered by people working in related fields; and, finally, it became a profession in its own right, complete with a body of knowledge and standards of practice. Today's emergency managers are not specialists; they are sophisticated generalists who must possess at least a preliminary knowledge of many different fields—and as society becomes more complex, that knowledge requirement is growing. This chapter examines the evolution of the practice of emergency management, from prehistory to the present, and highlights key factors that have influenced the development of the profession.

Purpose

It is not mandatory to understand the history of emergency management in order to be an emergency manager; one does not have to understand how to build a car in order to drive one. Nevertheless, knowledge of the history of emergency management will help you make sense of why some elements of emergency management function the way that they do, and help you practise emergency management more effectively.

The History of Community Safety

Early History

As previously stated, concern about safety is one of the primary reasons that humans have chosen to live together in communities. Other issues, such as trade and access to resources, also influenced the decision to live in communities (see chapter 3), but invariably safety was the foremost consideration. For primitive humans, the world was a dangerous place, particularly when they were alone. The climate was harsh, nature was poorly understood, or not understood at all, and in the quest to hunt and gather food, it was probably not uncommon for human predators to become prey for other hungry creatures, and even for other humans.

Primitive humans learned quickly that there was safety in numbers, and so the first bands of humans, probably extended family groups or clans, appeared. Primitive humans were probably for the most part nomadic hunters, migrating to follow their supplies of food through a fixed range that was driven by the seasonal migration of their food supply. Both agriculture and permanent settlements were still a long way into the future; useful plants were gathered rather than cultivated.

Safety was often a matter of trial and error; when something was done incorrectly, people were injured and sometimes died. As a result of this process of trial and error, knowledge about the environment began to grow, usually among the oldest and most experienced members of the group, and was passed on to future generations by oral tradition. To illustrate, the elders of the group might remember that in the past it was safe to cross a river at one particular place and unsafe at other locations, or that one place was safer to camp than another. Over time, these memories likely evolved into an analysis of the environment by individuals. Eventually, certain individuals could look at the physical characteristics of one river and determine its safety, based on their past experiences with other rivers with similar characteristics. It is unlikely that such individuals were actually in charge of the group—leadership was more often a matter of physical prowess and hunting skills—but they did function as advisers, and were often revered for their knowledge.

Permanent Settlements

The **Neolithic period** emerged, and with it came the domestication of animals, the development of agriculture, and the use of stone tools. As a direct result, the first permanent human settlements began to appear. The first settlements were probably just a few families, who put down roots in the most advantageous locations: near hunting grounds, agricultural land, water supplies, and trade routes.

As the hazards posed by continual migration disappeared, new hazards related to permanent settlement arose. For the first time, humans began to stockpile food and other resources, and the stockpile locations were relatively easy to find. Concentrations of food and resources were a temptation for both predatory and scavenging animals, as well as for other bands of humans, who might simply wish to take the accumulated resources or displace the occupants of the site by force. As a result, stockades became a common feature of late Neolithic and early **Bronze Age** settlements, and one could argue that they are one of the earliest examples of **critical infrastructure**.

Leadership in communities continued to be a function of the strongest; those able to exert control and influence over the community became tribal chieftains. Activities related to public safety remained focused on rendering the community less vulnerable to external attack. Most of the knowledge regarding community safety resided with the elders and shamans.

Safety has always been a consideration in community planning. Note the palisade constructed to protect the village from wild animals and marauding intruders.

Source: Venita Roylance, <http://homepage.mac.com/venitar/home.html>.

As settlements grew and developed, a number of neighbouring communities formed alliances (or, in some cases, one neighbouring community conquered another). Technological know-how was progressing, making trade easier and more attractive, and increasing productivity. More humans also became specialists. The specializations of hunter and healing/religious practitioner (shaman) had long existed, but other specialists began to appear, including farmers, bakers, brewers, and metal workers.

War and Military Intervention

At this time, before recorded history, people lacked the science required to understand natural events; natural calamities were seen as divine intervention and inevitable acts of God. By contrast, they did understand war. Threats to the community were generally viewed as external, which led to the debut of another type of specialization: the military. In the past, defence had been the province of the hunters, but, increasingly, tribal chieftains began to employ individuals for the specific purpose of providing defence and preserving safety and order for the community. In addition to being soldiers, these individuals almost certainly were used to impose the directives of the chieftain upon the community's residents and to maintain order; arguably the first policing function. By having these individuals under their direct control, chieftains centralized and solidified power over their communities, and the first "kings" began to emerge. Sustaining these forces was not inexpensive, and so it is not surprising that one of the next specialists to appear was the tax collector. Communities had generally cooperated among their own members where local safety was concerned, but, for the first time, some of the surplus resource production of the community began to be used to address community safety.

Government and Community Services

As communities developed, so too did increasingly stronger central governments. In tandem with these changes was the move toward more formal community safety services. For example, at the time of ancient Rome, two new innovations arose. The first innovation was the use of aging centurions, no longer capable of fighting, to transport and care for the wounded as a specific function; arguably the world's first formal ambulance service. The second innovation was the organization of the world's first formal fire brigade, consisting of slaves under the control of military officers. Such services were provided both in Rome and in provincial capitals, such as London. By serving in a fire brigade for seven years or by rescuing a prominent Roman, a slave would be granted freedom and citizenship.

These innovations, while useful, would die with the fall of the Roman Empire, and, for the most part, would not reappear again for more than a thousand years. Some notable exceptions to this occurred during the Crusades (circa AD 1000), with the Knights of St. John of Jerusalem, who would provide battlefield ambulance service, and in 13th-century Paris, where municipal fire watches were organized. The public safety services that we recognize today as police, firefighters, and ambulance service would not re-emerge in an organized way until the beginning of the 19th century.

Throughout the Renaissance (from the 14th to 17th centuries), community safety arrangements, where they existed, remained largely the responsibility of the military, and the public continued to perceive **disasters**, apart from war, as inevitable and the result of divine will. This is hardly surprising, since at that time almost no one in society, apart from the military and the very rich, had sufficient resources to even consider the problem. In 14th-century Europe, a new type of disaster emerged: the **Black Death**. This highly infectious disease struck repeatedly over the course of some 300 years, and is estimated to have killed between one-third and two-thirds of Europe's population.[1] Government, trade, and commerce were virtually destroyed. The disease's attack on London at the start of the 17th century killed an estimated 38,000 Londoners in a population of just 200,000.[2]

The Black Death is probably the first well-documented public health **emergency**, and one of the few in which the role of the military was minimal. In spite of a lack of understanding of disease and modern medicine, officials managed to implement one of the first public safety measures related to public health: **social distancing**. It was noted that the disease spread far more quickly among groups, and so public gatherings were banned. Among other measures, London's theatres were closed for several years, prompting William Shakespeare to write what is perhaps the first formal reference to emergency management in English literature:

> What plagues and what portents, what mutiny,
> What raging of the sea, shaking of earth,
> Commotion in the winds, frights, changes, horrors,
> Divert and crack, rend and deracinate
> The unity and married calm of states[3]

In 1666, the Great Fire of London, in the absence of fire protection, managed to destroy nearly 70 percent of the city. Supposedly starting in a bakery in Pudding Lane, the fire raged for days until the military finally intervened. The Duke of York's troops, using black powder explosions to create a fire break, eventually succeeded in bringing one of the worst fires in history under control. Afterward, as an early example of mitigation, building regulations were changed: the construction of wooden buildings was banned and the replacement of the then-common thatched roofs with more fire-resistant slate tiles was mandated. Also following this event, fire protection was offered by some insurance companies, but only to subscribers; it would be another 150 years before universal fire protection was available in most communities.

Modern Emergency Management

The First World War

Modern emergency management began in England in the 1920s, with a concept called **civil defence**. During the First World War the devastation experienced by London as a result of aerial bombardment, first by German Zeppelins and then by Gotha bombers, had been substantial, with an estimated 121 **casualties** per ton of bombs dropped.[4] Concern about protecting civilians led to the creation of the Air Raid Protection Committee in the United Kingdom. The committee emphasized that any aerial bombardment of London in the future would result in massive casualties and widespread public panic (and these casualty estimates were regularly revised upward), but this information was largely ignored until the Second World War loomed on the horizon.

The Second World War

In 1938, with another war appearing to be inevitable, the British government created the Air Raid Precautions service. The fledgling service initially recruited about 2,000 volunteer air raid wardens, but this number would grow to more than a million in just a year. Air raid wardens were charged with enforcing night-time blackout regulations for British cities, constructing prefabricated bomb shelters, supervising overnight bomb shelters created in the deep tunnels and stations of the London subway system, and providing initial assistance to **victims** following a bombardment.

Air raid wardens were trained in basic firefighting, light rescue, and first aid, in many ways foreshadowing the creation of the community emergency response teams found in many communities today. Each air raid warden had an assigned post, built from sandbags, and containing much of the same equipment now suggested for personal emergency kits. Training of air raid wardens by the Home Office was regular, usually consisting of exercises conducted in conditions that simulated bombardment or exercises using tabletop scale models of community buildings. Many aspects of the air raid warden program formed the foundation of modern emergency management programs.

As one of the earliest known modern efforts at public emergency education, Imperial Tobacco, in cooperation with the British government, created a series of air raid precautions information cards,[5] circa 1939, that were inserted into the company's cigarette packages, one to a pack. Remember that at the time the connection between smoking and health issues had not been made, and that the majority of adults smoked cigarettes. Each card in the 50-card set provided useful information on one aspect of personal preparedness for air raid attacks, and, collectively, the set's instructions were comprehensive. Each card contained written instructions on one side and a colour illustration on the other; and each was self-adhesive, so that it could be affixed into an album, which was available for a penny from any local tobacconist's shop, complete with an introduction by the Home Secretary.

Air raid wardens, ordinary citizens with special training, formed the foundation of modern emergency management.

Source: Brighton & Hove City Libraries, UK (n.d.).

The majority of members of the Air Raid Precautions service were volunteers. Many were ex-military personnel too old to serve, or those who held "essential" occupations that precluded them from military service, such as police officers and firefighters. A great number of air raid wardens were women; following the United Kingdom's lead, the United States, Canada, and Australia also appointed women as air raid wardens. In the United Kingdom, the Air Raid Precautions service was disbanded in 1946 and replaced by the volunteer Civil Defence Corps in 1948.

The Cold War

The lessons learned in the Second World War and the intensifying Cold War in the 1950s created a renewed interest in civil defence as a community responsibility in many parts of the world. Communities began to employ staff, primarily those with a military background, whose primary function was civil defence. Officers retiring from military service and looking for ways to apply their skills in civilian life often found this to be an attractive career option, and many of them continued to serve their communities until the late 1990s.

The primary focus of civil defence from 1950 to 1965 was the protection of communities against nuclear attack; for many, as political tensions increased between the United States and the then-Soviet Union, such an attack was considered to be inevitable. Nuclear fallout shelters began to appear in most major centres, relatively affluent governments at all levels began to create their own shelters to ensure the continuity of government, and people were provided with instructions on how to create their own personal fallout shelters.[6] Public education efforts were largely directed at providing citizens, including schoolchildren, with instructions on how to survive nuclear fallout; children's instructional films, such as *Duck and Cover*,[7] were a regular feature for those attending school from 1950 to 1980. Such efforts were based on an obviously faulty assumption that a nuclear blast was a survivable event; they were probably largely intended by governments to alleviate public fear and panic.

It was not until the 1960s that the emphasis in civil defence began to shift from war-based scenarios to natural and technological disasters occurring in the community. With this change in emphasis came a change in terminology, from civil defence to *emergency measures* or *emergency planning*. The transition process was a slow one; emergency planners from military backgrounds did not all possess the same level of knowledge regarding potential civil emergencies, and communication with those in academic and research circles was sporadic at best.

As a result, the approach developed to respond to disasters was largely generic; a single set of community contingency measures were produced and ready to apply, regardless of the type of emergency. The phrase "**all-hazards approach**" was coined, and local officials worked diligently to create a single framework called *emergency response* into which all disaster events, regardless of their nature, were expected to fit. The emphasis was almost exclusively on **preparedness** and response, while **recovery** and mitigation were seldom considered. Although the development of emergency plans was certainly recommended and encouraged within communities, it was not mandatory in most jurisdictions. Consequently, emergency plans rarely captivated the minds of key decision-makers, and in the face of competing priorities, emergency plans were almost always considered to be projects rather than processes.

Emergency planners continued to rely on their military skills for community preparedness activities. Training, if it occurred at all, usually focused on full-scale **exercises**; essentially dress rehearsals for a disaster event. This approach to training was drawn from the military, where simulated battles, or "war games," were a common training tool. Another approach, also drawn from the military, was the table-top exercise, in which emergency response resources were deployed and moved across a scale model of the community in a simulated disaster scenario, in much the same manner that generals planned battle strategies. Both of these approaches continue to be used by emergency planners in communities today.

Perhaps the greatest shortcoming of early emergency planning also has its origins in the military, and this is the concept of **lessons learned**. In the military, it is quite common for officers to prepare for a coming battle by studying what occurred in previous battles, and in that context, it is an effective technique; one is comparing battles to battles. In the civilian world, however, there are different types of disasters, many of which are unrelated to one another. As a result, attempting to prepare for the next disaster (a chemical spill) by studying the last disaster (a flood) sharply limits the amount of learning that is possible, and the translation of that learning from one event to another can be challenging. The other challenge with this approach is that in many cases the same "lessons" recur repeatedly after each emergency and exercise, and so it may be more appropriate to identify these as "lessons identified but not resolved."

By the late 1960s federal governments around the world began to take interest in the field, which was by then widely referred to as *emergency planning*. Inconsistencies in the knowledge and practices of emergency planners as well as their relatively poor understanding of enabling legislation were identified as systemic problems. In response, federal governments established formal training programs and centres in Australia (Mount Macedon), Canada (first Arnprior, then Ottawa), the United Kingdom (Easingwold), and the United States (Silver Spring). With some exceptions, most notably in the United States, these training programs and centres were operated by the federal department or ministry of national defence. This made a certain amount of sense, since in most cases these federal agencies were responsible for disaster-related issues.

Initially, the emergency planning training conducted by federal governments was limited, focusing on basic preparedness, exercise design, site management, and operations centres. Most courses were short (a week or less), and in the earliest stages students were required to travel, usually at government expense, to the training centres, as these were the only places where training was offered. Attendance at such courses was generally restricted to those already employed in the field, and to senior staff from traditional emergency services. Demand for courses was high, budgets were tight, and, as a result, the competition to gain a seat in the classroom was often stiff. A candidate might wait months for a space to become available. Eventually, state and provincial emergency measures organizations began to offer courses as well, which eased the training burden somewhat.

The focus of emergency planning began to change in the early 1970s. Communities realized that while the spectre of nuclear annihilation remained at least a theoretical possibility, natural and technological disasters occurred somewhere almost every day. Emergency planners began to turn their attention from preparing the population for war to ensuring that plans were in place for floods, forest fires, hurricanes, train derailments, plane crashes, and so on. Many of the skills used to produce these new plans remained unchanged, as indeed did most of the practitioners. The generic "all-hazards approach" also persisted. In most cases, all that really changed was the type of disaster being prepared for, although disasters were prepared for with better and more consistent training.

By the 1970s, a growing number of scientists and academics—particularly those in the earth sciences, social sciences, and psychology—started to study the subject of disasters. Distinguished scientists Thomas Drabek and Enrico Quarantelli created disaster research centres at the University of Colorado and the University of Delaware, respectively. These scientists, along with many others, conducted disaster research and published contributions that are among the foundational works of contemporary emergency management. Meanwhile, direct communication and interaction between academics and practitioners remained sporadic at best, primarily because the majority of practitioners did not understand the need for such contact.

By the 1980s, the original full-time emergency managers were reaching the end of their careers. These "cold warriors" began to be replaced by a new breed of practitioner. Often these individuals were drawn from the traditional "red light" emergency services, such as police and fire services, and from the professional emergency medical services. They understood the response function well; they were frequently experienced, command-level officers within their organizations. However, they lacked much of the knowledge in planning and logistics that their predecessors had brought with them from the military. Once again, emergency management training needed to be revisited.

Present Day

As emergency management continued to evolve, exchanges between federal governments and academics specialized in the field grew, which led to the inception of formal academic training of emergency managers. Initially, emergency management academic programs spread slowly; colleges and universities first offered certificate courses only, then eventually undergraduate degrees. By the 1990s, graduate degrees in emergency management became available. One of the first institutions to offer a graduate degree was the University of Hertfordshire in the United Kingdom; it debuted its master of science in emergency planning and disaster management in 1992. Similar programs also appeared in the United States and elsewhere. Early programs were targeted to those already involved in active practice, rather than to those completely new to the growing field.

It became quickly evident that practitioners faced challenges in acquiring academic credentials; most had to deal with both work and family life, and for many the institutions offering such credentials were not nearby, adding significant expense to the list of challenges. In the United States, the **Federal Emergency Management Agency (FEMA)**, through its Emergency Management Institute, began to offer high-quality distance education programs online for those who were unable to attend a faraway university or college. Such programs offered college credit-level courses, complete with course manuals, learning checks, and final examinations, making more comprehensive education and training accessible to more and more practitioners.

The need for greater professionalism in emergency management led to the creation of the **International Association of Emergency Managers (IAEM)**. Based in the United States, the organization has grown to include membership in a variety of countries, and has chapters in the United States, Canada, Europe, and Oceania. Among the organization's achievements is a formal certification program for those practising emergency management. Certification is based on a candidate's postsecondary education, training in the field of emergency management, demonstrated work history and experience in the field, contributions to the profession, a written essay, and a written examination. Candidates may be certified, depending on their educational background, as either a certified emergency manager (CEM) (the senior designation) or an associate emergency manager (AEM). As an important distinction, CEMs are required to possess an undergraduate degree. Both CEMs and AEMs are required to renew their certification every five years.

The sad events of September 11, 2001, in the United States brought about a paradigm shift within the emergency management profession; the emphasis changed from protecting communities from natural and technological events to protecting them from deliberately planned events, or terrorism. Notably, FEMA was reorganized and became a part of the U.S. Department of Homeland Security. It is certainly true that the events of 9/11, along with others at the time, resulted in significant changes to the emergency planning priorities of federal governments. However, subsequent events made clear that while preparation for terrorist events is important, the more pressing and immediate needs of communities are, and will continue to be, protection against natural hazards and accidental human-caused events. The catastrophic destruction caused by and arguably failed response to Hurricane Katrina in New Orleans in August 2005 is a case in point.

Modern emergency managers are not specialists, but sophisticated generalists. Practitioners have found their way into this field from the traditional emergency services and a variety of other areas. While a body of knowledge specific to the field does exist, and is growing, practitioners equally require knowledge from a vast array of other disciplines, including earth sciences, social sciences, law, engineering, chemistry, marketing, education, and psychology. Having knowledge in diverse disciplines is absolutely necessary to create the programs and processes that will keep communities safe.

To illustrate, a practitioner does not need to be a meteorologist or possess an expert's knowledge of meteorology, but he or she does need to have sufficient knowledge of that field to understand what meteorologists are saying and how it will affect the community. It is a practitioner's job to take that information and make it accessible, so that the community and its key decision-makers will understand what the information means and take the steps necessary to respond to it. Emergency managers are similar to professional science writers: they take complex ideas and make them comprehensible to the general public.

Emergency managers work at all levels of government, and in quasi-public organizations such as hospitals and schools. They also work in the private sector—an area of practice that has become a discipline in its own right. Private sector practitioners, often called *business continuity planners*, protect the physical resources and business operations of corporations, large and small. It is completely appropriate to view a business entity as a specialized community, and while business continuity planners address business-related issues, the general standards of practice that they follow remain largely identical to those adhered to by public sector practitioners.

Today, emergency management focuses on four key areas: preparedness, response, recovery, and mitigation. Each of these areas has a sizable body of knowledge that merits exploration. Together, these areas are designed to ensure that our communities remain as safe as possible from the effects of any type of disaster. Contemporary emergency managers must be proficient in each of these areas.

Conclusion

Throughout history, the safety of individuals has been a primary concern and one of the main reasons for the existence of communities. Today, affording protection to communities requires both specialized knowledge and a good understanding of the issues related to hazard, risk, vulnerability, and protection strategies. Within communities of all types and at all levels of government, the field of emergency management has become the first repository of this knowledge and understanding. The primary role of emergency managers is to protect communities. As the profession has evolved, so too has its effectiveness in fulfilling its critical function.

KEY TERMS

all-hazards approach

Black Death

Bronze Age

casualties

civil defence

critical infrastructure

disaster

emergency

exercises

Federal Emergency Management Agency (FEMA)

hazards

International Association of Emergency Managers (IAEM)

lessons learned

mitigation

Neolithic period

preparedness

recovery

resilient

response

social distancing

victims

LEARNING CHECK

Take a few minutes now to test your knowledge of the history of emergency management. Select the best answer in each case. Any score of less than 16 out of 20 (80 percent) indicates that you should re-read this chapter.

1. The primary role of emergency managers is
   a. to analyze disaster events
   b. to protect communities
   c. to direct the response to a disaster
   d. both (a) and (c)

2. As communities change and evolve, the hazards to which they are exposed
   a. often disappear
   b. may be reduced
   c. change and evolve
   d. are determined by the population

3. There is usually a direct connection between hazards and
   a. human activity
   b. weather
   c. community affluence
   d. local knowledge

4. Community safety functions tend to evolve, driven by
   a. genuine need
   b. trends or fads
   c. availability of resources
   d. both (a) and (c)

5. Emergency management has its origins in
   a. the military
   b. the political arena
   c. academia
   d. fire departments

6. In primitive cultures, information regarding hazards was passed from one
   generation to the next by means of
   a. ritual
   b. oral tradition
   c. the emergency plan
   d. confidential knowledge from chief to chief

7. In the earliest cultures, knowledge regarding hazards generally resided with
   a. hunters
   b. the chief
   c. farmers
   d. elders or shamans

8. In many primitive cultures, disasters were generally believed to be
   a. the efforts of evil spirits
   b. avoidable events
   c. of divine origin
   d. scientific phenomena

9. In many primitive cultures, the one untoward event that people believed they could prepare for and protect themselves against was
   a. weather
   b. famine
   c. war
   d. an earthquake

10. Although some early advanced societies began to develop formal public safety measures, these largely disappeared following
    a. the fall of the Roman Empire
    b. the Norman Conquest
    c. the appearance of the Vikings
    d. the appearance of Christianity

11. In the 1950s and 1960s, emergency management was largely referred to as
    a. civil defence
    b. emergency planning
    c. disaster management
    d. contingency planning

12. During the 1950s, the primary focus of the field was the protection of communities against
    a. natural hazards
    b. chemical spills
    c. transportation incidents
    d. nuclear attack

13. By the late 1960s, federal governments around the world began to offer formal, short courses to emergency planning practitioners by means of
    a. community colleges
    b. night school
    c. federal training programs
    d. universities

14. Early academic interest in the field of emergency management tended to be concentrated in the academic disciplines of earth sciences, psychology, and
    a. marketing
    b. political science
    c. social sciences
    d. medicine

15. As the original full-time emergency managers with military backgrounds began to reach the end of their careers, they began to be replaced largely by
    a. academics
    b. professional civil servants
    c. those from the traditional emergency services and emergency medical services
    d. professional engineers

16. The first academic programs available to emergency managers through colleges and universities were
    a. undergraduate programs
    b. postgraduate programs
    c. doctoral programs
    d. certificate programs

17. The International Association of Emergency Managers offers two levels of certification for practitioners: associate emergency manager and
    a. professional contingency planner
    b. certified emergency manager
    c. business continuity planner
    d. professional emergency manager

18. Those certified by the International Association of Emergency Managers must renew their certification
    a. every five years
    b. annually
    c. every two years
    d. every ten years

19. Emergency managers are not specialists; they are best described as
    a. earth scientists
    b. sophisticated generalists
    c. social scientists
    d. behaviourists

20. A related discipline that essentially performs emergency management functions in the private sector business environment is called
    a. corporate emergency planning
    b. corporate emergency management
    c. certified contingency planning
    d. business continuity planning

CASE STUDIES

A. You are a modern emergency manager operating in 17th-century London. Assume that you possess all of your current knowledge. In terms of technology, you have only those tools that would have been present in Britain at the time.

1. What are the major hazards for which the city must be prepared?
2. What measures (plans, public education, etc.) can you implement in order to prepare the community for these hazards, and how can you achieve these?
3. What resources do you have to respond to each of these hazards?
4. How would you use these resources to respond to each hazard, should it occur?

B. You are an emergency planner in a North American city in 1955. You have just joined city staff after spending 15 years in the military, from which you retired with the rank of major. Emergency planning is a new concept in your community, and you are starting completely from scratch. The elected officials ask you to prepare a civil defence plan for your community.

1. Which hazard is likely to be foremost in your mind?
2. What are your general strategies to prepare the community for that hazard?
3. Which strategies can you accomplish without substantial resources?
4. Which strategies are likely to require approval and funding by elected officials?

TO LEARN MORE

1. Perform online research on some historical aspect of the practice of emergency management that interests you. Here are a few suggestions:
   a. the story of air raid wardens in the Battle of Britain
   b. civil defence during the Cold War
   c. the history of emergency management in your own country
   d. the history of disaster research

2. Visit your local community's emergency management office and speak to the emergency manager. How long has the office/position existed? Under what circumstances was it created? Who was the original emergency manager for the community? How was he or she chosen for the position? Have there been any major changes to the organization or its mandate since its creation? Has the organization ever been reorganized or re-aligned within the municipal structure? If there have been changes, what circumstances brought them about?

NOTES

1. "Plague and Public Health in Renaissance Europe," *Institute for Advanced Technology in the Humanities*, <http://www2.iath.virginia.edu/osheim>.
2. "History of London: Population," *Wikipedia*, <http://en.wikipedia.org/wiki/History_of_London#Population>.
3. William Shakespeare, *Troilus and Cressida*, 1.2.96–100.
4. "Air Raid Precautions," *Wikipedia*, <http://en.wikipedia.org/wiki/Air_Raid_Precautions>.
5. Peter Hibbs, "Air Raid Precautions Cigarette Cards," *NBCD*, <http://www.nbcd.org. uk/arp/cigarette_cards/index. asp>.
6. Kelsey-Hayes Company, *Protect Your Family in a Backyard Fallout Shelter* (1962), <http://luminiferous-aether.net/2007/09/19/protect-your-family-in-a-backyard-fallout-shelter>.
7. U.S. Civil Defence Administration, *Duck and Cover* (1951), <http://knowgramming.com/free_stuff/downloads/mp3_and_mpeg_files/Free_Mpeg4_Movies.htm>.

CHAPTER 2

The Role of Government

LEARNING OBJECTIVES

On completion of this chapter, you will

▶ Understand the basic approaches governments follow to protect citizens.

▶ Understand the overall role of government in emergency management.

▶ Understand the roles and responsibilities of different levels of government in emergency management.

KEY MESSAGES

1. Governments have a duty to provide to their citizens whatever protection is possible against untoward events that are beyond the means of individual citizens to respond to and cope with.

2. The primary responsibility for coping with emergencies lies with the individual, with an expectation that government at some level will intercede when the individual begins to exceed the ability to cope.

3. All levels of government have some responsibility for developing and facilitating emergency management, preparedness, and response activities within communities.

4. The degree to which a given level of government becomes involved in an emergency varies according to the nature and scale of that emergency.

5. The primary responsibility for government response to emergencies typically lies with the local authority.

6. Successive levels of government are generally most effective in providing guidance, funding, facilitation of preparedness assistance, and coordination of the response to large-scale emergencies.

Introduction

Governments have a duty to protect their citizens; indeed, this duty is one of the main reasons individuals submit themselves to government in the first place.[1] Citizens expect protection from obvious threats to personal safety, such as crime, fire, and medical emergencies, but they equally expect protection from the effects of disasters in the community as well. Communities provide policing, firefighting, and emergency medical services to deal with the more common threats, and many also maintain a service for response to disasters. In most Western societies, this service is typically known as *emergency management,* although some societies call it *emergency planning, civil defence,* or *civil protection.*

Emergency management is a complex process of education, planning, and acquisition of response resources. In most cases, it involves a coordinated effort among the various levels of government operating in a jurisdiction, traditional emergency response resources, volunteer agencies, and individual citizens. Emergency managers are responsible for coordinating and facilitating the different aspects of the process.

The protection of communities is achieved through a combination of governance processes. These processes include enacting legislation that provides the policy framework for emergency response. They also include funding programs aimed at making individuals, their communities, and, therefore, the entire jurisdiction, more resilient to the effects of untoward events. Emergency managers are often the primary point of contact between different levels of government on emergency issues. They are responsible for ensuring that the community is in compliance with the legislation of different levels of government, and that the response by governments occurs in a coordinated fashion—before, during, and after an emergency.

Purpose

Emergency management is, in most circumstances, a government function. Emergency managers must understand the political context in which they operate, how government functions, and how the activities of government influence the emergency management process. It is only through such understanding, and by working cooperatively and collaboratively with all levels of government, that emergency managers can succeed in fostering true preparedness, an effective response to emergencies, successful recovery efforts, and solid mitigation programs.

Government and Community Protection

One of the primary responsibilities of governments is to protect the individuals whom they serve. Citizens have an absolute expectation, apart from increased safety in numbers, that banding together in communities with central coordination will help reduce their exposure to the impact effects of untoward events.

Governments provide protection to citizens in a number of ways. First, they organize physical, financial, and human resources at the local community level to respond to the most common types of emergencies; this approach forms the rationale for the creation of the police, firefighter, and emergency medical services. Second, they create legislation, regulations, and standards aimed at ensuring that individual communities and, by extension, their entire jurisdiction will acquire and develop the plans, processes, and resources required for emergency response. Third, they provide funding for emergency response; this funding is intended to augment the limited resources of local communities who supply such services, and in many cases to "level the playing field" between large communities and small to achieve a consistent level of response. Lower levels of government achieve this consistency by using the organizational structure and resources of successive levels of government in order to coordinate and share resources among communities of all sizes, so that each can reliably provide emergency services to its own residents. Each of these approaches will be discussed in this chapter.

The Role of Government in Emergency Management

What *is* government? Perhaps the simplest explanation is as follows: government is the governing authority of a political unit.[2] Such political units may be countries, regions, or communities. Governments provide the framework by which economic welfare, social welfare, and defence of communities are delivered. They have the ability to enact laws and create regulations for the public good, adjudicate disputes between individuals and groups in the societies in which they govern, and provide centralized decision making on administrative matters. In most cases, governments also have a monopoly on the use of force to compel compliance with all of the above, in the interest of maintaining public order.

Governments can take many forms. The most common form in Western countries, such as Canada and the United States, is democracy, in which decision-makers are elected directly by citizens. Another common form is monarchy, in which the head of government rules by birthright and where the will of an individual or group is imposed on the majority without recourse to the ballot box—the United Kingdom is one example. Also prevalent is dictatorship, a type of government ruled by a dictator who has absolute power, as is the case in some developing countries. A long list of other government forms exists, although they are less widespread; this list includes theocracy, which is followed in some Islamic countries and the Vatican. The "best" form of government is a topic of considerable debate; ultimately, each form of government has its strengths and weaknesses.

Government Organization: The Three-Tiered Model

The majority of Western countries use a three-tiered model of government. The upper tier is the **federal** government, which operates at a national level and deals with both domestic and international matters such as inter-regional trade, defence, and international relations and trade. This level of government provides the upper tier of authority within any given society. The government of Canada is an example of this level of government.

The middle tier is the regional level, often called the *provincial* or *state* government. This level of government is, depending on the country in question, subordinate to the federal government to some degree, and subject to its laws and regulations. This level of government is responsible for a number of areas including resources, infrastructure (such as highways), health and social services, and the coordination of activities between the communities within its boundaries. Middle-tier governments function within smaller political units such as states, provinces, or territories of the country as a whole, and their responsibilities and authorities are often the result of extended negotiation with the senior level of government, and are frequently enshrined in the country's constitution. The Province of Ontario and the State of California are examples of this level of government.

The lower tier is the **local authority** level, consisting of individual communities, such as cities or towns. This level of government is primarily responsible for meeting the needs of the population within its boundaries, which includes providing core municipal services and community planning. Municipal or local governments operate at a purely local level, and are subordinate to the other two tiers. The cities of Vancouver and New York are examples of this level of government. Not all Western countries use the three-tiered system; some, such as the United Kingdom, use a two-tiered system that comprises the federal and local authority levels only.

In all types of governments, decision-makers receive bureaucratic support from the civil service. The civil service is typically organized into areas of specific responsibility called *departments* or *ministries*. At the federal level, civil servants might work in defence or foreign affairs; at the regional level they might work in natural resources or agriculture; at the local level, they might work in the police or fire departments, city planning, and so on. The function of emergency management appears at each level of government.

Legislation

All levels of government have the ability to enact laws and create regulations to support those laws; what varies is the jurisdiction in which the laws and regulations will operate. The laws and regulations of the federal level of government carry force in every region and local authority in the country. Those of the regional level carry force within their region alone, and have no bearing on others. To illustrate, a law enacted by the legislature of the State of Vermont has no force whatsoever in the State of Washington, and vice versa. Local authorities have the ability to enact laws (**bylaws**) and create regulations that affect their own community but not others. To illustrate, a bylaw limiting overnight parking in the City of Toronto has no force in the City of Ottawa.

In addition, a law issued by a particular level of government may have primacy over all others issued by that government. To illustrate, in Ontario, the *Emergency Management and Civil Protection Act*[3] has primacy over all other **provincial** laws, with the exception of the Ontario *Human Rights Code*.[4]

It is noteworthy that the language in which laws are crafted affects their usage. Laws are typically written in two general types of language: permissive and directive. The *permissive* type typically "permits" a given course of action, and may go to the extent of recommending that course, but the language used does not make the course of action mandatory. To illustrate, older emergency management laws, particularly those at the regional level, tend to permit communities to create emergency plans, rather than oblige them to do so. The legislative language used might be "is permitted to," "is advised to," or "is encouraged to," but there is really nothing stating compulsory compliance.

Permissive phraseology was typically used when a government wanted subordinate levels of government to do something, but was not necessarily prepared to subsidize the course of action with additional funding. More often than not communities would comply with the legislation, but the use of this type of legislative language provided an escape clause of sorts for communities that legitimately could not fund the activity in question. This is true not only of legislation, but also, in some governments, of associated regulations and directives. In the United Kingdom, for example, emergency management information frequently arrives in the form of Home Office "advice."[5]

Directive legislative language provides subordinate levels of government with a clear legislative mandate to proceed with a particular course of action. The legislative language used might be "the community must," "the community shall," or "the community is required to," thereby providing the community with clear and unequivocal direction as to the course of action being required of it. This is the more modern form of legislative language. It was adopted by decision-makers at upper levels of government who recognized the increased importance of emergency-management arrangements and, thus, elevated their priority from a "good idea" to an absolute necessity. It is not uncommon to see both types of legislative language in use, depending on the location, the level of government involved, and the importance placed on emergency management by the government in question.

Funding

The funding of emergency management activities generally occurs in three separate and distinct forms. The first of these is *program funding*. This is the annual budget provided for the operation of emergency management activities at a given level of government. This money is used to pay for emergency managers, their operating space, and expenses related to preparedness, training, and public education activities. This is baseline funding, and is typically the responsibility of the level of government operating the program, without subsidy from other levels of government in most cases.

The second type is *program enhancement funding*. This funding is intended to provide "seed" money for the development of new programs and the acquisition of additional emergency response resources, aimed at boosting local preparedness and resiliency. It often takes the form of monetary grants from senior levels of government, and goes by different names in different countries. In certain circumstances, some money for these types of activities may come from non-governmental sources, such as industry or community service groups. Program enhancement funding is not reliable or consistent.

The third type is *emergency response costs funding*. This funding comes into play only when an actual emergency occurs. It is triggered by means of a formal **declaration of emergency** by some level of government's senior officials. This funding is intended to assist communities during a disaster by absorbing some or all of the actual response costs. Often, the amount of emergency response costs funds provided is calculated according to a formula. To illustrate, in Ontario, once an emergency has been declared, the local community is responsible for the first dollar per resident of response costs, with additional response costs being subsidized by senior levels of government for the duration of the emergency declaration. In some jurisdictions, similar funding might be available to offset the uninsured financial losses experienced by individuals as well.

The Roles and Responsibilities of the Three Tiers of Government

Historically, governments have tended to embrace a top-down approach to emergency management. Directives would be issued by a senior level of government for subordinate levels, local communities, and ordinary citizens. In some locations, such as the United States, this approach is still followed to some extent. A senior level of government issues periodic guidelines and standards, and, in some cases, uses its financial power, primarily through the potential denial of grants or emergency response costs to other levels of government and communities that are non-compliant.

Many countries, including Canada, however, have opted to follow a bottom-up approach to emergency management. Individuals are expected to deal with their own emergencies, with intervention by successive levels of government occurring only when individuals, then the community, have exceeded their own ability to cope with the problem. It should be noted that this devolution of responsibility to the individual has met with some success. Individuals, and communities, that know that they will probably have to deal with untoward events are more likely to engage in preparedness activities, which fosters the growth of the emergency management sector. In countries that follow this approach, the legislative language is still very much top-down and provides a clear and mandatory set of standards, but the responsibility to comply is placed squarely on individuals and communities. It is from the bottom-up that we will examine roles and responsibilities.

The local authority level of government represents a critical area of emergency management activities. This level of government, while having fewer resources than other levels, typically owns most or all of the emergency response resources. Without this level of government, the community response to emergencies would fail before it started. It is at this level that community emergency managers operate. In advance of an emergency, local communities are expected to operate emergency management programs that include the following: the identification and assessment of hazards present in the community, the development and testing of emergency response plans, the acquisition of emergency response resources through both the budgetary process and grantsmanship, the creation of hazard mitigation programs, and establishment of both staff and public education programs. Virtually all of the efforts to prepare communities for an emergency occur at the local level.

The local authority level of government controls most of the resources that are likely to be required in the earliest stages of an emergency. In many cases, it has outright ownership of those resources, which include public safety services (such as policing and firefighting); emergency medical services; community services; and buildings such as the town or city hall, community centres, and schools. In other cases, the local authority may have influence over rather than own particular resources through licensing. Examples of these resources include local transit contractors, hospitals, and certain emergency medical services. There are other areas over which a local authority has less direct but nonetheless real influence. These areas include local businesses, service organizations, and construction companies.

When an emergency occurs, the local authority takes steps to address the issues related to that emergency and meet the urgent needs of residents. In the early stages, these activities are undertaken using wholly owned resources, such as the traditional emergency services. As the emergency evolves, resources from other wholly owned municipal departments, such as social services, come "on line" as required. Additional resources may be provided by entities that have a licensing or contractual relationship which the local authority (a construction or maintenance contractor), and by those that do not (a local merchant). In most cases, particularly when the emergency is relatively small and local, these resources are sufficient to address the issues related to the emergency, meet the immediate needs of residents, and begin to take the community toward a process of recovery.

However, when a situation exists in which the community cannot adequately address the issues related to the emergency, or normal or near-normal operations cannot be restored using local resources, other actions may be required. In many jurisdictions, this type of situation signals to senior levels of government that assistance is required by means of a formal declaration of emergency. For example, in Ontario, the declaration must be in written form, must specify the nature of the emergency and its location, and must indicate the resources required. This document must be signed by the mayor or elected head of council and sent to the provincial (regional level) government via the provincial emergency management organization.[6] The process for making a formal declaration differs somewhat in other jurisdictions, but the end result is the same.

Sending a formal declaration of emergency to the regional level of government is not, in most jurisdictions, an invitation to that upper level to come in and "run" the response to the emergency; and, in most cases, it is not treated as such. It is merely an indication that the emergency has exceeded the ability of local resources to deal with it, and that assistance is required. That assistance can take a variety of forms, including resources and financial assistance to the local community.

In the pre-emergency phase, in most cases, the regional level of government is charged with the development of regional programs intended to increase emergency preparedness, the creation of standards, the encouragement of the development of mutual assistance agreements between local authorities, and the training of emergency managers for their role at the local authority level. The regional level of government is also typically tasked with the creation of a regional emergency plan, and with the creation of the legislation required to support these efforts.

During an actual emergency, the regional level of government may support the local authority level with the provision of advice and guidance, and also with additional resources required to cope with the emergency. These additional resources may take the form of wholly owned resources, such as the provincial or state police. The wholly owned resources available will vary by jurisdiction, and by the responsibility-sharing arrangements negotiated between the regional and federal levels of government. For example, if a regional government is charged with overseeing natural resources, it could potentially provide assistance in the form of additional firefighting support. In some jurisdictions, where the regional level of government has control over the military, military resources might be used (in the form of state militia or national guard units under the control of the regional government); clearly, this would not be the case in jurisdictions where the control of the military remains the exclusive prerogative of the federal level of government.

Regional governments may also be able to provide assistance by identifying and sharing emergency response resources held by other local authorities within their jurisdiction. In some cases, there may be voluntary resource sharing, but increasingly those in the uppermost levels of emergency management in regional governments have the legislated authority to issue emergency orders.[7] For example, in certain jurisdictions, the senior level of a regional emergency management department has the authority to order other communities, privately held resources, and even individuals to provide assistance and resources to a community in immediate need. To illustrate, a senior regional emergency manager might order a community with a public transit system to provide buses to another community to assist with an evacuation. Such emergency powers can be far reaching, and are often accompanied by significant fines and even imprisonment for non-compliance.

In addition, regional governments might have resources that are too large and expensive for individual communities to own. Examples include **Heavy Urban Search and Rescue (HUSAR)** teams and Hazardous Materials Response teams.

In the aftermath of an emergency, regional levels of government may continue to provide assistance to local authorities in the form of advice and guidance, short-term loan of resources, or financial assistance with recovery efforts. This assistance may take the form of recovery grants or loans to communities for the reconstruction of lost critical infrastructure, to individuals and businesses to assist with their recovery costs, and generally includes the absorption of some portion of the response costs associated with the emergency.

When an emergency event is of a truly large scale, or affects so many communities that it exceeds the regional resource base, regional levels of government typically issue a similar emergency declaration to the federal level of government. The formal declaration of emergency provides the federal level of government with an official request to begin providing assistance. The requirements of this declaration tend to be similar to those of the declaration made at the local authority level, and produce similar results.

In the pre-emergency phase, federal governments support emergency management at the regional level. This support can take a variety of forms. The federal government can develop cooperation agreements between regional governments. It can also provide assistance with the training of emergency managers and responders; for example, the Emergency Management Institute operated by the Federal Emergency Management Agency in the United States offers emergency management programs. As well, it can supply funding to enhance emergency management programs; the Joint Emergency Preparedness Program grant funding by the government of Canada is one example.

During an actual emergency, federal governments can provide different types of assistance. For example, they can undertake inter-regional coordination, make federal resources available, and fund response and recovery efforts.

Inter-regional coordination may involve the facilitation of resource sharing between different regions, and perhaps even the coordination of international aid, including mutual assistance treaties between neighbouring countries, such as Canada and the United States.

The federal resources used most often in an emergency are military resources, but it should be noted that the further up the government hierarchy one goes, the fewer and more specialized actual response resources become. That being said, there are advantages to being able to access military resources; in most countries, they have the "heavy lift" capacity required for rapidly moving resources between regions.

The presence of an actual emergency may prompt the funding and purchase of some form of response resource that was not previously in the inventory of any level of government. As the emergency begins to wind down, the assistance provided by the federal level of government is more likely to be financial in nature. It may take the form of payments for response costs or recovery funding in excess of existing insurance coverage for communities, businesses, or individuals.

Conclusion

Responding to emergencies is a complex matter that challenges the capabilities and resource base of any government, and the demand for resources increases along with the scale of the emergency. There is an old saying in emergency management that the correct definition of a disaster is "any emergency that generates one more issue than you have the resources to deal with." By working together, the various levels of government help ensure that any community in need of assistance will receive it quickly, efficiently, and in a cost-effective manner.

KEY TERMS

bylaws

declaration of emergency

federal

Heavy Urban Search and Rescue (HUSAR)

local authority

provincial

LEARNING CHECK

Take a few minutes now to test your knowledge of the role of government in emergency management. Select the best answer in each case. Any score of less than 16 out of 20 (80 percent) indicates that you should re-read this chapter.

1. The protection of citizens from the effects of untoward events is regarded by governments as a
   a. duty
   b. recommendation
   c. non-binding concept
   d. challenge

2. The primary responsibility for coping with emergencies lies, in the first place, with
   a. the federal government
   b. the provincial/state government
   c. the local authority
   d. the individual

3. All levels of government have some responsibility for developing and facilitating emergency management, preparedness, and
   a. control
   b. response activities
   c. fire protection
   d. communications

4. The degree to which a given level of government becomes involved in an emergency will vary according to the emergency's nature and
   a. characteristics
   b. legislated mandates
   c. scale
   d. political involvement

5. The primary responsibility for government response to serious emergencies typically lies with the
   a. federal government
   b. state/provincial government
   c. local authority
   d. emergency manager

6. With respect to preparedness activities, senior levels of government are generally most effective in providing guidance, funding, and
   a. facilitation
   b. design
   c. solicitation of public support
   d. both (b) and (c)

7. Most governments have within their mandate the ability to enact laws, adjudicate disputes, and
   a. regulate the lives of individuals
   b. control the media
   c. provide centralized decision making on administrative matters
   d. operate industries

8. The most common forms of government are monarchy, dictatorship, and
   a. democracy
   b. oligarchy
   c. consensus
   d. theocracy

9. In a three-tiered model of government, the levels may be described as federal, local authority, and
   a. regional
   b. civil service
   c. town
   d. city

10. In emergency management legislation the form of legislative language used may be either permissive or
    a. coercive
    b. suggestive
    c. cooperative
    d. directive

11. One of the problems encountered with the use of permissive language in emergency management legislation is that it
    a. can be confusing
    b. fails to provide a clear mandate
    c. results in community resistance
    d. is rarely used

12. The funding of emergency management activities may take the form of program funding, emergency response costs, or
    a. program enhancement funding
    b. growth funding
    c. capital funding
    d. insurance-based funding

13. Emergency response costs funding is intended to assist the local community by means of
    a. providing grants
    b. providing taxation powers
    c. assisting with actual response costs for actual emergencies
    d. recovering response costs from insurance companies

14. In most jurisdictions, to receive emergency response cost funding, the community must
    a. apply to the senior level of government
    b. issue a formal declaration of emergency
    c. pass a bylaw
    d. apply to the regional government

15. The intervention of any level of government commonly occurs only when the individual or community
    a. contacts politicians
    b. no longer has the ability to cope
    c. incurs costs in excess of a standard formula
    d. has not engaged in preparedness activities

16. As an emergency evolves, the response to support the local authority in the emergency will typically fall to
    a. the emergency manager
    b. the local authority
    c. the regional government
    d. the federal government

17. During the pre-emergency phase, the duties of regional governments include, in most cases, development of regional programs intended to increase emergency preparedness, the creation of standards, the encouragement of the development of mutual assistance agreements between local authorities, and
    a. the provision of access to military resources
    b. program funding
    c. the training of emergency managers
    d. interaction with other communities

18. During the pre-emergency phase, in most cases, the duties of federal governments include the development of cooperation agreements between regional governments, assistance with the training of emergency managers and responders, and
    a. the provision of funding to enhance emergency management programs
    b. the establishment of local standards
    c. the provision of funding recovery efforts
    d. the activation of mutual assistance treaties

19. When considering declaring an emergency for the purpose of resource acquisition, an emergency manager should remember that the further one climbs up the government hierarchy, the more likely that actual response resources may become
    a. cost-prohibitive
    b. fewer
    c. more specialized
    d. both (b) and (c)

20. During the emergency itself, funding from the federal level of government is
    most likely to be directed to
    a. assistance with local response costs
    b. funding of recovery activities
    c. purchasing new resources
    d. both (a) and (b)

CASE STUDIES

A. You are the emergency manager for a community with a population of 50,000
   people. A senior level of government has enacted a law requiring the presence
   of an emergency program—including an emergency plan, public and staff education, and regular testing of the emergency plan by emergency-simulation
   exercises—in all communities within your jurisdiction. The law includes financial penalties for non-compliance.

   1. Describe the manner in which you would provide the information gener-
      ated by the above activities to the elected officials of the local council of
      your community.
   2. Describe the steps you would take to determine whether your community
      was compliant.
   3. Describe the measures that might be available to you to ensure compliance
      by all members of the community.
   4. Identify the other municipal (local authority) agencies with whom you
      would have to collaborate to determine and ensure compliance with the
      new law.

B. You are the emergency manager for a small community with limited resources.
   Based upon a report by you, the local elected officials have expressed serious
   concerns regarding the level of the community's potential risk exposure, and
   have asked you for a report recommending possible risk mitigation strategies.

   1. Describe a method for identifying those risks that might be amenable to
      mitigation efforts in your community.
   2. Identify a number of risks and describe a series of options that the com-
      munity might take to reduce its exposure to them.
   3. Describe any potential community partnerships that might be used to
      facilitate risk mitigation.
   4. Describe any means by which senior levels of government might poten-
      tially assist the community with its risk mitigation strategies.

TO LEARN MORE

1. A great deal of emergency management legislation from various jurisdictions around the world is available online. Select two pieces of legislation, one in which you believe the legislative language is permissive, and another in which you believe the legislative language is directive. Read both laws carefully. In each case ask yourself why you believe the legislative language to be permissive or directive. What examples can you identify in the legislative language to support your position? What do you believe is the result of the type of legislative language used? Why do you believe that this particular approach was used in each case?

2. Most local governments have a clerk's office. The town/city/county clerk is responsible for, among other things, recording and overseeing the legislative process, which can vary considerably from one jurisdiction to another. Learn about the process by which your local government creates a new bylaw or regulation. Identify the different steps, and why each step is necessary. Are there any laws or regulations issued by senior levels of government that govern the process of creating local laws and regulations?

NOTES

1. Hagen Schulze, *States, Nations and Nationalism* (Malden, MA: Blackwell, 1994).
2. <http://wordnet.princeton.edu/perl/webwn?s=government>.
3. <http://www.e-laws.gov.on.ca/html/statutes/english/elaws_statutes _90e09_e.htm>.
4. <http://www.search.e-laws.gov.on.ca/en/isysquery/e57ff5cf-5aa6-4cf1-b15b -188ee648b380/1/frame/?search=browseStatutes&context=>.
5. <http://www.homeoffice.gov.uk/security>.
6. <http://www.search.e-laws.gov.on.ca/en/isysquery/dd23352d-4e65-4c7a -866a-c710134941c9/1/frame/?search=browseStatutes&context=>.
7. <http://ogov.newswire.ca/ontario/GPOE/2005/12/15/c1054.html?lmatch =&lang=_e. html>.

CHAPTER 3

The Evolution of Communities

LEARNING OBJECTIVES

On completion of this chapter, you will

▶ Understand how communities have evolved over time.

▶ Understand the need for detailed knowledge about the composition and wealth-generating activities of communities.

▶ Understand how a community's wealth-generating activities and, at times, its physical location create risk exposure.

▶ Understand the need for community planning and design to reduce a community's risk exposure.

KEY MESSAGES

1. Communities exist to provide some measure of safety for their residents and to provide opportunities to create wealth.

2. There is often a relationship between wealth-generating activities and community safety issues.

3. The physical location of communities is generally driven by the presence of wealth-generating opportunities.

4. Communities, like individuals, place a greater priority on the generation of wealth than on safety issues.

5. Emergency managers must possess a solid understanding of the wealth-generating activities in the community to be able to identify possible areas of risk exposure.

6. Community planning and design plays a critical role in reducing a community's risk exposure.

Introduction

The primary reasons for the existence of any community, at the most basic level, are twofold. One reason is to provide opportunities for residents to have access to assets and wealth. Another is to provide residents collectively with a degree of safety from untoward events that may occur. The understanding of both reasons is extremely important to those involved in emergency planning.

The degree of importance afforded to community safety and wealth generation is generally determined by the residents of the community. Almost invariably, wealth generation (and the acquisition of assets) is given priority over issues of community safety. It is not until sufficient assets and wealth exist to meet community needs that community safety assumes a dominant place in the minds of residents. Understanding the complex relationship between these two areas will help emergency managers not only plan for emergencies but also educate and motivate the community, acquire response resources, and conduct mitigation programs.

Purpose

A complex relationship exists between the composition and activities of communities, and the risks to which they are exposed. For emergency managers, understanding this relationship is central to their preparation of communities to respond to any emergency event that may occur. The presence of such knowledge increases the likelihood that the community's emergency planning arrangements will be effective, and will meet the community's needs during a crisis.

The Creation of Communities

Nomadic Groups

From the outset, humans have banded together for two purposes. The first of these was to provide improved access to assets or wealth, whatever these individuals judged "wealth" to be. In the earliest stages of human development, what constituted wealth was probably relatively simple: a food supply. The availability of food was essential to survival, and it is likely that one of the first hazards faced by humans, apart from falling prey to larger, better-equipped predators, was probably starvation. Formal communities did not yet exist, and humans were nomadic in nature, primarily moving to follow their food supply.

Individuals quickly recognized that there were advantages to banding together in groups. Single hunters could only hunt relatively small animals with existing technologies for hunting; food supplies were erratic, depending on the success and skill of a single person. It took larger numbers of hunters, working in a coordinated fashion, to hunt larger animals, and successfully hunting larger animals meant greater food availability and a more reliable food supply. In the absence of even the most rudimentary agriculture, the presence of large groups also meant that the gathering of those plant materials intended to supplement the hunter's catch could be more organized. Such early groups of hunter-gatherers were probably composed of extended family groups, with most members of the community being related by either birth or mating.

From time to time, such groups were confronted with external attacks. Although the number of humans in most areas was relatively small, prime hunting and gathering areas were also limited, and it is likely that the competition for access to these resources was intense. Maintaining access to these resources was probably a matter of brute force in a great many cases, and it is probable that some human groups learned quickly that it was easier to take by force the food that another group had obtained than to hunt for their own. As a result, the predators that each group required protection from were not all of the four-legged variety.

Permanent Settlements

During the early Neolithic period, perhaps as early as 10,000 BC in some areas, humans discovered agriculture. The first crops that humans could grow for themselves appear to have been wheat, barley, peas, lentils, and flax.[1] The presence of more reliable local food supplies meant that humans had less need to migrate in search of food. The need to stay in one place long enough to harvest the crops that had been planted, and the production of food supplies too large to be easily transportable, led to the first permanent human settlements. Some of the earliest specializations of humans within communities is also likely to have evolved at this time, with a distinction being created between hunters and farmers. Other early specializations likely included tribal shamans (a combination of religious leader and healer), bakers, and brewers. The abundance of food also permitted other specializations, such as the creation of tools.

The permanent presence of humans in a given location likely resulted in the rapid depletion of local animals to hunt, and, thus, the domestication of animals began. Animals began to be kept in permanent proximity to communities, and food sources were further ensured. Sheep, goats, cattle, and pigs were probably the first animals to be domesticated,[2] and, eventually, based on a complex set of factors (including the ability to domesticate these animals and the potential benefits derived from doing so), would expand to approximately 14 domesticated species in common use: dogs, cats, sheep, goats, cattle, pigs, horses, donkeys, water buffalo, camels, chickens, ducks, geese, and guinea pigs. The presence of ready supplies of not only plant material, but also meat, milk, hides, etc., meant that little incentive existed for further migration.

Another direct benefit of continuous close proximity to large numbers of domesticated animals may be the development of some measure of disease resistance among humans. Historically, it has been demonstrated that when groups with domesticated animals encountered populations without, the latter group was often decimated by diseases for which they had no resistance (such diseases were often regarded as relatively minor for those in the former group). It has been speculated, for example, that, between the 15th and 19th centuries, Spanish conquistadors in the Americas overcame local resistance from Indigenous people not so much from technological superiority as from epidemics originating in the herds of pigs, which were part of their food supply, that moved with them.[3]

The Development of Government and Trade

The need to coordinate food systems and mediate conflict between individuals now living in much closer proximity to each other led to the creation of the first forms of rudimentary government,[4] probably an evolution of the pre-existing system of clans with tribal chieftains. Leadership was more often based upon physical strength, and this is important because these new communities, with their reliable food supplies and wealth, were surely tempting targets for other human groups.

While the earliest agriculture probably occurred on a subsistence basis, it was not long before surpluses in production occurred. The existence of surpluses led to two important innovations. The first innovation was the storage of food supplies for future needs (for example, in granaries), creating additional stability in the available food supply. The second innovation was trade between communities. A community that had experienced a poor harvest of one **commodity** (such as wheat) might be able to trade a surplus of another commodity (such as pigs) in order to balance supply with demand.

Early trade was probably limited by the physical ability of humans to carry resources, but the domestication of pack animals and the use of water transportation increased trade significantly. Community wealth was generated through the production of commodities, and the transport and trade of excess commodities. Although they have grown to involve more complex processes, the same wealth generators have driven the development of modern communities.

The ability of a community to protect its population from the predations of outsiders remained a consideration, and so the three primary considerations for choosing a settlement site became the availability of usable land and water, the proximity to trade routes, and the defensibility of the location. Common locations for early permanent settlements were hilltops (defence) with arable land (commodities) below, adjacent to a trade route (transportation) such as a road, a river, or a harbour. When communities failed to thrive, it was frequently because one of these factors had not been adequately provided for, or had been disrupted by some other event, such as an epidemic or other natural catastrophe.

The increased stability of communities' social structure and food supply led to population growth, and, with it, the specialization of more individuals. This specialization led directly to the creation of an artisan class in many communities. Potters, spinners, weavers, and metal workers created new commodities that both advanced their own communities and enhanced trade with others. The use of soft metals, including copper and gold, then bronze, and finally iron (in the **Iron Age**), became widespread, further advancing the technologies and living standards in human communities.

Modern Communities

Communities today have some similar features to those of the past. Modern communities still produce commodities and trade them with other communities to generate wealth. Some of the commodities have changed, and transportation technologies have certainly changed, but the production of commodities and their transportation to markets generally provide an important reason for the existence of any given community.

Issues and Risks

Several important distinctions have evolved in modern communities, however. Large communities may produce a vast array of commodities, may act as distribution hubs for goods, and may provide a variety of services. These large communities are typically the most successful, but may in fact be the victims of their very success. The coming together, or *convergence*, of humans at locations of successful wealth generation presents its own problems. Overpopulation, crime, inadequate housing, and large numbers of urban poor combine to actually increase the relative vulnerability of the very populations that the cities were created to protect. One need look no further than Mexico City or Cairo to see the problems created by runaway population growth.

Some communities, such as mill and mine towns, may have a single economic focus. In such communities, people converge around an independent industrial operation. In some cases, such planning is deliberate, with the owners of the mine or mill constructing housing, stores, and services to attract a workforce. Many communities have begun in this way, but if the community fails to diversify economically, residents remain completely at the mercy of the mine or the mill. If a mine closes, or if a fire destroys the mill, the primary reason for community existence vanishes along with it. In Canada, northern Ontario has a large number of ghost towns, where a mine or a mill once existed. Cordova Mines, Ontario, for example, was a thriving community of more than 10,000 people, with shops, a hotel, and a school, existing to service a local iron-mining operation. When the mine shut down in the 1940s, the community became a mere shadow of its former self, with a population of a few hundred, and a single shop.

In other communities, wealth might be generated by converting one commodity (for example, raw materials) into another (for example, a finished product). When such operations are truly large, employing the majority of the community's residents, they too create vulnerabilities. In this case, the production facility becomes the lifeblood of the community, with most community businesses either participating directly in the production process or providing some service intended to support it. Should the primary production facility be removed for any reason, either through economic necessity or disaster, the result is economic catastrophe for the community. The Rust Belt of the northeastern United States is dotted with towns and cities such as Allentown, Pennsylvania and Flint, Michigan whose economy depended heavily on industrial operations, but which have been economically and socially devastated as a direct result of plant closures.

Some communities exist primarily as distribution centres for commodities produced elsewhere and destined for smaller, less-concentrated communities. Such centres tend to be small in size; agricultural support communities are a good example. These communities are just as dependent on a single source of wealth generation, and while the effects of different types of natural or technological catastrophe may differ, the loss of that single source of wealth has the same net effect as an actual disaster event on the local community.

Other communities exist primarily to support the transportation networks that move commodities and people from place to place. Towns such as Newcastle, Ontario are typical examples; they were built around railway division points or on the first major highways during the late 19th and early 20th centuries. If the railway were to close or the highway be redirected, the source of wealth of these communities would disappear and leave them to either wither away or fail entirely.

The development of some communities has been strongly influenced by service and information sectors; they are often considered to be commodities for community-planning purposes. For example, the community hospital is often the centrepiece of smaller rural communities, and is often the major employer as well. The good news is that health care is one type of service that is viable in many environments and under most conditions. People will continue to require health care services, regardless of the state of the rest of the economy or the vagaries of the local marketplace. This example is certainly true in Canada and the United Kingdom, which have socialized health care systems, but it is equally true in the United States, where health care operates principally according to a market approach. In the smaller communities in which they operate, educational institutions such as universities and colleges often play a similar pivotal role in the community's economic well-being.

Transportation networks create wealth for communities, and also play a role in their vulnerability. The major highway that brings money to a community also carries one heavy truck in ten with a load of hazardous materials. The railway that transports goods to market or provides a rail yard that is important to the local economy also has some form of hazardous materials on almost every freight train. Airports bring economic growth, but also the potential for plane crashes, and seaports also have both benefits and risks. Harbours are a critical source of income for a local economy but are obvious locations of risk exposure. For example, on December 6, 1917, Halifax, Nova Scotia saw the largest non-nuclear explosion in the history of the world, when two ships, one of them carrying munitions, collided in its harbour and levelled the town.

Why do communities permit the presence of such risks in their midst? The truth is that communities may frequently see themselves as having little choice in the matter. Remember that one of the primary reasons for the existence of communities is the generation of wealth, and that safety considerations almost always receive less priority as long as wealth generation remains an issue. Communities will often make a conscious choice to accept the risk from a particular enterprise, particularly when no other source of wealth (employment) is on the horizon.

In other cases, communities may accept risk for the simple reason that they have become accustomed to it. In many cases, the original reason for risk acceptance may have disappeared, but the risk continues and is tolerated because it has always been there. The City of Peterborough, Ontario provides a good example. The original site was chosen in the 19th century to give the community access to water power from the Otonabee River in order to operate mills. This location made the community prone to periodic floods, which was accepted; one needed to be near the water in order to power the mills. In the 21st century, the community has changed and the mills have disappeared, but the periodic flooding that occurs has become a part of the "way of life" of the community. The community has developed a tolerance for that particular risk exposure.

Arguably, a mix of some or all of the above-mentioned wealth-generating factors makes for better, stronger, communities. The more diverse the mix of these factors present in any community, the more resilient that community will become to the effects of untoward events, whether physical or economic. Conversely, the more reliant a community becomes on a single factor, the greater the likelihood that the community might fail at some point. At the same time, the more diverse the mix of factors, the more diverse the potential risks.

Conclusion

An understanding of how community wealth is generated is essential for emergency managers. Knowing the wealth-generating factors of a community leads to an improved understanding of the risks that may be present, and how they operate. An understanding of the community's history may also lead to knowledge of exactly how the risks in a particular community have evolved since its origin. Many of these risks may involve infrastructure that the community regards as critical, and, as a result, a balance of sorts will need to be struck. But with this understanding, emergency managers will be better equipped to craft sound risk mitigation strategies (such as encouraging the community to reconsider and re-examine high-risk land use) and pursue the creation of legislation and regulations that can effectively reduce or eliminate risk.

KEY TERMS

commodity

Iron Age

LEARNING CHECK

Take a few minutes now to test your knowledge of the evolution of communities. Select the best answer in each case. Any score of less than 16 out of 20 (80 percent) indicates that you should re-read this chapter.

1. Communities exist in order to provide some measure of safety for their residents and to
    a. co-ordinate activities
    b. ensure effective communications
    c. provide opportunities to generate wealth
    d. provide social interaction

2. There is often a relationship between wealth-generating activities and
    a. government activity
    b. community safety issues
    c. education assets
    d. transportation resources

3. The presence of wealth-generating opportunities generally determines
    a. physical location
    b. community safety resources
    c. size of government
    d. placement of schools

4. When not confronted by community safety issues, communities will generally place a greater priority on
   a. quality of life
   b. generation of wealth
   c. continuity of governance
   d. both (a) and (c)

5. Emergency managers must possess a solid understanding of the wealth-
   generating activities in the community to be able to identify
   a. available program funding
   b. government support for programs
   c. public support for programs
   d. possible areas of risk exposure

6. A community's risk exposure may often be effectively reduced (mitigated) by
   a. community planning
   b. community design
   c. legislation
   d. both (a) and (b)

7. Among the most common risks of early human groups was
   a. external attack
   b. fire
   c. flooding
   d. earthquakes

8. The earliest development of primitive agriculture occurred in
   a. the Bronze Age
   b. the Iron Age
   c. the Renaissance
   d. the Neolithic period

9. The earliest examples of agricultural crops include wheat, barley, peas,
   lentils, and
   a. fruit
   b. lettuce
   c. flax
   d. potatoes

10. In the development of primitive communities, the primary consideration for community placement was frequently
    a. the decision of the hunters
    b. access to resources
    c. community safety
    d. agricultural land

11. The specialization of individuals in communities was probably the direct result of
    a. surplus resources
    b. decreased hunting grounds
    c. social planning
    d. individual wealth

12. The earliest example of humans becoming specialized is probably
    a. bakers
    b. hunters
    c. potters
    d. traders

13. The primary considerations for the placement of early settlements were the availability of usable land and water, the defensibility of the location, and
    a. access to trade/transportation routes
    b. nearby markets
    c. lack of pollution
    d. all of the above

14. The most common purposes for contemporary communities include
    a. the creation of commodities
    b. the distribution of commodities
    c. the provision of social focal points
    d. both (a) and (b)

15. In communities with a single source of wealth generation, such as a mine or a mill, the communities remain particularly vulnerable to
    a. market fluctuation
    b. loss of the single source
    c. inability to diversify
    d. both (a) and (c)

16. In addition to those items considered traditional commodities, modern
    communities tend to include
    a. information
    b. services
    c. imports
    d. both (a) and (b)

17. Communities that include more than one significant source of wealth
    generation tend to be more
    a. complacent
    b. resilient
    c. vulnerable
    d. prepared

18. Understanding how a community generates its wealth leads emergency
    managers to
    a. increased program funding
    b. increased political influence
    c. improved understanding of risk
    d. an understanding of community history

19. Understanding the history of a community leads emergency managers to an
    improved understanding of
    a. political processes
    b. how risk has evolved
    c. patterns of volunteerism
    d. current levels of resiliency

20. Emergency managers can pursue risk mitigation strategies by means of
    legislation, regulations, and
    a. community planning
    b. increasing response resources
    c. increasing public funding
    d. appealing to other levels of government

CASE STUDIES

A. You are the emergency manager for a medium-sized (100,000 pop.) community somewhere in the North American Midwest. The community is located beside a rather large river, which experiences periodic spring flooding. As a result, there are neighbourhoods within the community that experience flooding almost every spring, and which sometimes require evacuation. This situation has been ongoing for many years, and those in the community typically tend to regard it as unavoidable.

1. Describe the sources that are available to determine the history of flooding within your community, including the actual causes of flooding.
2. Describe the methods you could use to determine which neighbourhoods in particular are subject to the risk of flooding, and whether there are legitimate reasons why these neighbourhoods continue to be occupied.
3. Describe the methods you could use to determine who the residents of the affected neighbourhoods are, and precisely why they choose to accept the risks involved.
4. Describe the methods you could use to identify whether there are any reasons that are no longer valid for the neighbourhood's placement.

B. You are the emergency manager for a community in northern Ontario that relies on a pulp and paper mill for its wealth generation. It is almost the only local employer, and virtually all other businesses in the community rely on the income generated by the mill. You have been asked to participate in a community-development forum and to provide your expertise to ensure that future community-planning efforts result in a safer community. You are not from the community originally, and so you will need to learn more about pulp and paper mills to participate effectively.

1. Identify the risks associated with the operation of the pulp and paper mill for the community.
2. Describe how, when, why, and to whom such risks occur.
3. Provide an opinion regarding whether or not the pulp and paper mill should continue to operate.
4. Describe five methods the community could use to reduce its risk exposure from the mill, without adversely affecting mill operations.

TO LEARN MORE

1. Conduct research on the history of the founding of a nearby community. What factors determined the original placement of the community? Did any of those factors, or the selected location, generate specific risks for the community? How have those risks been addressed over time?

2. In almost every region there are examples of failed communities, or ghost towns. Select a failed community and describe the factors that determined its original placement. What factors contributed to that community's failure to thrive and grow?

NOTES

1. Daniel Zohary and Maria Hopf, *Domestication of Plants in the Old World*, 3rd ed. (Oxford: Oxford University Press, 2000).
2. Brian Hayden, "Models of Domestication," in *Transitions to Agriculture in Prehistory*, ed. Anne Birgitte Gebauer and T. Douglas Price (Madison, WI: Prehistory Press, 1992).
3. Jared Diamond, *Guns, Germs, and Steel: The Fates of Human Societies* (New York: Norton, 1999).
4. David Christian, *Maps of Time* (Berkeley: University of California Press, 2004).

CHAPTER 4

Understanding Community Composition

LEARNING OBJECTIVES

On completion of this chapter, you will

▶ Understand the relationship among community composition, vulnerability, and disaster-resource requirements.

▶ Understand where information on community composition can be found, and the variables that are of particular interest to emergency managers.

▶ Understand how demographics can be used to create better emergency plans and more resilient communities.

KEY MESSAGES

1. Communities are collections of individuals, and understanding who these individuals are is central to the process of emergency management.

2. A detailed understanding of the population to be protected—in terms of who they are, how they live, and their relative strengths and weaknesses—is at least as important as the understanding of economic activities and the community's physical location.

3. Individuals have different abilities and requirements for protection at different times in their lives. Other factors, such as socio-economic status and communication skills, also play a role in determining vulnerabilities.

4. Just as the study of land use and economic activity provide valuable information on hazards and risks, demographic data provide important information on both vulnerability and resource requirements.

5. Demographic data have long been used effectively in economics, marketing, health care planning, and community planning.

6. The art and science of demographics can play a major role in the effectiveness of community emergency plans.

Introduction

Who lives in your community? How many children, seniors, rich people, poor people? Are there people within your community whose first language is not the majority language? Is there a significant number of single-parent families? Is your community home to a large number of people with disabilities? If yes, what types of disabilities do they have and what needs do they have for daily living? Most of us have some sense of the number of people within our communities, if for no other reason than the fact that this information is usually posted on town or city-limit signs. But how many of the demographic details of our community do we actually possess?

Demographic data is crucial to emergency managers, whose primary role is to safeguard residents from the effects of any type of disaster. Yet, surprisingly few emergency managers actually monitor this type of data on an ongoing basis. Unpleasant surprises and fundamental failures in the processes and procedures that emergency managers have so carefully crafted can be the result, often at the very time when they can least afford to have them occur. Emergency managers might neglect to fully consider human factors when planning for community response to emergencies, but communities, above all, comprise people!

This chapter focuses on the art and science of **demographics** and its role in the process of emergency management. The use of demographics in other fields is discussed, as are the specific demographic variables that are of interest to emergency managers. Finally, the application of demographic data to improve specific aspects of the emergency management process is examined.

Purpose

Emergency managers must understand the inherent vulnerabilities within a community to adequately plan to safeguard vulnerable populations. Much of a community's relative vulnerability is directly tied to the well-defined characteristics of its population. Understanding how to identify and analyze these characteristics often leads to better community preparedness and to emergency plans that are well-thought-out and more functional.

Community Composition

A community is a collection of people; each person has different abilities and needs, and will be affected by a community emergency in a unique way. While it is virtually impossible for emergency managers to plan for the needs of every single individual they serve, there are, nevertheless, certain commonalities and shared characteristics among groups. When emergency managers fully understand group characteristics and apply them properly, they can make a community's emergency arrangements much more effective and better able to address the urgent needs of the individuals within the community.

Two of the primary objectives of emergency management are the continuation of government and the delivery of vital services to residents in an area affected by a natural or technological disaster. Just as every individual is different, every community, whether large or small, is also different. In order to effectively meet the needs of a community during a disaster, it is necessary to understand the composition of that community. This section examines the impact effects of demographic changes on society and the use of demographics in emergency management. It also outlines some basic demographic techniques for emergency managers and identifies some resources that can be consulted when applying demographics to an emergency management system.

Demographics is the study of human populations. It is an extremely useful resource, which is held in high esteem by government planners, health care providers, and marketers, among others. The use of demographics revolves around the assumption that individuals have very different needs and engage in different activities at different stages in their lives. The typical 40-year-old is far less likely to ride a motorcycle than the typical 20-year-old. It follows logically that if one wished to predict the number of motorcycle accidents or motorcycle sales at some point in the future, knowing the growth of the segment of the population that purchases motorcycles would be valuable.

Noted economist David Foot says that "demographics can be used to explain two-thirds of all social phenomena."[1] The two key factors that must be considered are the number of people in each age group and the likelihood of a given individual experiencing a particular need. In general terms, 20-year-olds don't have heart attacks, and 70-year-olds don't go hang-gliding. This type of general trend prediction can be extremely useful for emergency managers. Before examining the implications for emergency management, it is appropriate to briefly visit the major demographic trend that makes the use of demographics both interesting and useful.

Following the end of the Second World War, Western industrialized societies experienced a period of elevated birth rate, which was unprecedented in recorded history. This post-war baby boom is one of the most studied social phenomena of the 20th century. Those who are considered to be baby boomers were born between 1946 and 1966; it is the largest generation ever born. In the post-war period, families with four or more children were quite common, with an average of 2.4 children per family. By contrast, baby boomers are the generation with the lowest reproductive rate in recorded history, with less than two children per family. The baby-boom generation is also one of the most difficult groups to accommodate for planning purposes, particularly with respect to publicly operated services, including emergency management.

In North America, and presumably elsewhere in the developed world, a myriad of classrooms and even school buildings that were created for the baby boomers are now empty due to a sharp decline in school enrolment. During the 1950s, 1960s, and 1970s, everyone thought that the population growth would just continue. As early as the 1990s, however, it became obvious that the population growth bubble had burst. In the 21st century, it is increasingly clear that barring unforeseen social phenomena, the need for certain elements of societal infrastructure, such as schools and hospitals, that were built to accommodate the baby-boom generation is transient. Nonetheless, this generation currently requires and will require services that must be included in community planning. While many disasters cannot be predicted with any reliability, the social trends that affect our ability to respond to disasters effectively can.

Key Demographic Variables in Emergency Management

Age

A population's age is an important demographic variable in emergency management planning. Twenty-year-olds don't have the same abilities or needs as 75-year-olds. For example, 20-year-olds who can drive, bicycle, or walk to an emergency shelter may not require transportation in an emergency, but 75-year-olds likely will. Thus, prudent emergency managers would be well-advised to know whether there are enough buses or ambulances in an area to transport the elderly to safety.[2] A community with a larger proportion of elderly requires more **evacuation** transportation than a younger community. However, unless emergency managers know precisely how many seniors must be planned for, there is no real means of identifying whether such a transportation plan is adequate. Old-fashioned evacuation plans that assumed that the majority of people would simply get into their cars and leave have become increasingly unreliable as the baby-boom generation ages.

The elderly are also more likely to experience medical emergencies in an ongoing community emergency. Many of these medical emergencies will be serious in nature. Research conducted by Toronto Emergency Medical Services has indicated that of those calls identified by algorithm (a process of scripted questions used to identify specific problems or requirements) as life-threatening, 75 percent were from those over 40 years of age.[3] While plans for a first-aid station might be adequate in the emergency shelter of a younger community, more elaborate medical support might be required in the emergency shelter of a community of retirees. Understanding community demographics can help reveal medical requirements in advance of an emergency.

Similarly, small infants and children have special needs in an emergency.[4] These needs may be medical, dietary, or simply related to "entertainment." A community with a large number of children or infants may wish to stockpile or develop emergency purchase arrangements for items such as diapers and infant formula, or they may wish to ask those who have agreed to operate emergency shelters to develop a children's activity program, in cooperation with a voluntary service organization. Children also need to be counselled by specialists, if they are available, following a disaster. Emergency managers should be aware of these issues, and should be able to identify the necessary resources and services in a community's emergency plan.

Socio-economic Status

Socio-economic status is also a significant demographic variable that should be considered when planning for community emergency response. An individual or family's access to resources will play a considerable role in determining how they will respond to a given emergency. It is highly unlikely that those with significant financial or other resources will spend protracted periods in any type of emergency shelter. They will likely house themselves in hotels or with relatives rather than in an emergency shelter. The experience of Hurricane Katrina in New Orleans illustrates the fact that typically only the most economically disadvantaged will rely on emergency shelters for an extended period. Typially, extended shelter usage will only be required by about 10 percent of the affected population. This observation is supported by extensive experience in the State of Florida, which typically is subject to several significant hurricanes each year.

Disability

The needs of people with disabilities must also be addressed. Emergency managers must know how many blind or deaf people live in the community. These individuals may very well miss local emergency notification messages, and may require special help to reach safety. Similarly, people with mental and physical challenges may require special evacuation assistance, shelter arrangements, or medical support. But before emergency managers can plan for any of these needs, the size and nature of the group must be properly identified.

How many people in the community have disabilities that make them reliant on service animal companions? While there are issues related to pets in emergency shelters, service animals must be given special consideration. In many cases, people with disabilities rely on service animals to help them cope with the challenges of life. An emergency manager would never consider asking a paraplegic to surrender his or her wheelchair as a condition of admission to an emergency shelter. Is it any more reasonable to ask a blind person to surrender his or her guide dog? It should also be noted that increasingly, service animals come in a variety of shapes and species; some people with disabilities have service companions that are primates!

Of increasing concern to emergency managers is a particular group of people with disabilities: those reliant on technology-based life-support systems. With advances in medical science, more people are surviving medical problems that would have resulted in their deaths just a few decades earlier; these advances have allowed them to continue to lead meaningful and productive lives. At the same time, economic necessity has moved many people with serious illnesses from hospital-based care to community care with appropriate support. As a result of these two factors, emergency managers need to recognize that not everyone in the community is healthy and capable, and that unhealthy individuals with challenges to their abilities are not all located in hospitals and special-care facilities. There are more people than ever before with disabilities who need medical support living in communities.

The challenge is in planning for the needs of this group, beginning with simply establishing who they are. While most of these people receive support from some type of health care agency, information on them continues to be "siloed" (held in a proprietary manner, and not readily shared with other agencies), making it difficult for emergency managers to identify them. Once identified, their special requirements, such as access to emergency power, will need to be planned for. For this group and others regarded as having disabilities, information can be scarce; surprisingly few governments collect census data on such individuals.

Enlightened emergency managers recognize that people with disabilities represent a potential source of emergency response resources. The old view that people with disabilities are a vulnerable group who must be protected should be replaced with an understanding that many people with disabilities are able to assist with the community response to disasters. For example, a healthy person using a wheelchair can assist with registration and inquiry operations at a wheelchair-accessible emergency shelter. Similarly, a person who is deaf may be able to assist with the provision of emergency information to other deaf citizens. As well, a person with a particular disability might make an extremely effective post-emergency counsellor for those with a similar condition. If emergency managers don't have data on a community's people with disabilities, the potential help these people can offer in an emergency will go unused.

Length of Residency

Length of residency in a community is also an important demographic variable for emergency managers. It has been demonstrated repeatedly that, in the case of recurring phenomena such as tropical cyclones, long-time residents are far less likely to evacuate than "first timers."[5] This response generally holds true unless the community is struck by a truly catastrophic event; and then the community resumes as time and distance permit it to place the event behind them. This variable is highly significant to emergency managers because a community with a large number of new residents, or one that has experienced a recent catastrophic event, is likely to experience far more demand for shelter space than a community with a stable population.

The move to take in disaster victims is largely a cultural response, and something more likely to occur in rural than in large urban settings. For example, the people of Newfoundland hosted many stranded airline passengers following 9/11. It is highly unlikely that you would see a similar response in a large urban centre. In terms of affecting recovery efforts, the less that is taken away (that is, people evacuated), the less that requires restoration.

Ethnicity

People have become increasingly mobile since the latter half of the 20th century, a fact that has had an impact on emergency management. People have immigrated to more developed countries in search of a better life, which has altered the ethnic composition of once homogenous societies. Even if immigrants have some proficiency in speaking the majority language of their new community, it is possible that they are unable to read or write in that language. Thus, pre-emergency education in the majority language may be of little use to them.

Some immigrants, particularly older people, never master the language of their new community. Perhaps an immigrant is an elderly person who has never learned English, despite several years in the community. While we might normally tell residents to tune in to a particular local radio station for emergency instructions, of what possible use would this information be to this elderly person? In communities where there may be substantial language barriers, it is no longer enough to disseminate emergency instructions in English, and emergency managers must take into consideration the challenges of "getting the word out."

Failing to recognize and understand this element of community composition not only creates problems for emergency managers but also denies them access to potential solutions. Ethnic communities that have been identified in the pre-emergency phase can work with emergency managers to achieve a whole variety of positive outcomes with respect to both preparedness and response.

In the pre-emergency phase, conversations with the leadership of an ethnic community might lead to the volunteer translation of pre-emergency education materials to make them more accessible to that community. Community leaders might also be willing to assist with pre-emergency education efforts in the language in question. During the emergency itself, some members of the community might be prepared to provide translation services to assist emergency managers and other emergency responders. By identifying ethnic communities and meeting with their leaders in advance, emergency managers may be able not only to decrease the vulnerability of these communities but also to identify new and valuable resources that will make the community as a whole more resilient.

Clearly, if emergency managers intend to disseminate useful public education information (both in the pre-emergency phase and during the emergency itself) and plan for and provide emergency services effectively, they must understand the composition of their target audience. While not yet widely used in emergency management circles, demographics can be an invaluable tool for planning and providing well-thought-out emergency services during a disaster.

Tools of the Trade

Those in the economic and marketing sectors, among others, have used demographic data for years to reliably understand the markets in which they operate. Demographic data can be used to cost-effectively distribute advertising materials, products to be sold, and even the sites of retail outlets. To illustrate, a toy retailer considering the placement of a new store performs a demographic analysis of a community and discovers that it is home to few children. As a result and after analysis of other communities, the retailer decides to open the new store in a potentially more lucrative location whose community has a large number of children.

Similarly, community planners might use demographic data to determine the placement of a new school, commercial district, or transportation corridor. Demographic data may also drive the amount and type of new home construction, protection services, and recreation facilities offered in a given community. In health care, demographics are often used to determine the placement of hospitals and clinics as well as the types of medical services offered at those facilities; they are also used to predict future demand for services and staffing. Where then, does such critical information come from, and how can emergency managers access it?

Unfortunately, little demographic data is readily available to the public. Although corporations pay big money to produce demographic data, their data are usually tied to non-disclosure agreements. Corporations such as VISA, by contrast, have huge data stockpiles and regularly market this information to retailers. They would be happy to share their data, but the price of that data would probably be beyond the reach of most communities. Emergency managers do have access to a limited amount of demographic data through municipal-planning departments. However, the quality of the data isn't always high; some planning departments are far better than others at capturing and working with demographic data.

Census Data

In most Western countries, a **census** is conducted by government on a regular basis—usually at five- or ten-year intervals. Data is collected by community, and the result is a relatively accurate picture of the composition of each community in terms of age, gender, total population, language, ethnicity, education, and socio-economic status. In Canada, the grouping of census subdivisions in a large urban area is called a *Census Metropolitan Area (CMA)*; in the United States, it is called a *Metropolitan Statistical Area (MSA)*. Data are usually collected within predetermined boundaries called **census tracts**. The data can be used to provide emergency managers with a relatively accurate portrait of the community served. While most governments make the census data available to the private sector for a fee, many provide them to other government agencies free of charge. Census data are also often available in the reference section of most college and university libraries.

Demographic Projections

Most governments develop demographic projections of populations for planning purposes. In these projections, populations are usually lumped into five-year age groups, or *cohorts*. The increase or decrease in a population is projected by cohort for each year of a 25-year period. These projections are based on census data, and are used by governments to predict future tax revenue, and increases or decreases in the need for various types of government services. While the federal government typically conducts the census, the finance department of a regional government usually produces demographic population projections. Municipal-planning departments also produce projections to determine future service requirements. Often governments make these projections available to the private sector for a fee, but many provide them to other government agencies free of charge.

Emergency managers might consider a strategic alliance with a local university or college to produce projections—particularly with the social sciences or geography department. While emergency managers would receive research by second- or third-year students for free, the students would gain the opportunity to apply some of their skills and training to a project with real-life implications. In this manner, both emergency managers and the university or college derive benefits.

In most cases, applying these projections to resource requirements is a matter of simple arithmetic. To illustrate, an emergency manager knows that there are currently sufficient buses to evacuate the 600 people over age 65 that live in the community. If the emergency manager also knows that the number of people in that age group will increase by 20 percent over the next five years, then it logically follows that he or she will need to develop access to 20 percent more buses within the next five years, if the community's evacuation plan is to remain effective. Similar exercises can be followed in relation to emergency shelter space, emergency food stocks, and a host of other emergency commodities and services.

Census data provide emergency managers with valuable insight into the composition of a community, as well as what the current needs of that community likely are. This information is valuable for the purpose of developing the current emergency plan. Demographic projections provide information on what future needs will likely be, and permit emergency managers to plan ahead and match resources to those needs before a disaster occurs.

Using Demographic Data

Demographic data can provide other benefits to emergency managers. Once it has been collected, data on potentially vulnerable groups can be plotted **spatially** on maps, which will identify concentrations of vulnerable populations and also areas where service delivery might need to be concentrated. Emergency managers may be able to determine the need for and placement of emergency resources, such as emergency shelters, in the same manner that school-board officials decide on the location of schools.

When demographic data sets are overlaid with mapping software, the proximity of vulnerable populations to areas of hazard or infrastructure may become evident. The "layers" of data sets could include all of the demographic data, data from a Hazard Identification and Risk Assessment, surface topography, and other community-planning data. By integrating the data sets, it may be possible to see relationships between risk and vulnerability that were not immediately clear. The benefit of understanding the relationship among different variables is obvious, and the use of mapping software is growing in emergency management. Being able to map data is a highly useful skill for emergency managers, but one that is not yet widespread. The cost of mapping software may seem prohibitive, but it is still cheaper than contracting out data mapping to specialists.

Conclusion

While the occurrence of disasters cannot generally be predicted, their effects on a community often can. The key to understanding these effects is knowledge of the composition of a community in terms of key demographic variables such as age, socio-economic status, ethnicity, and disability. Certain groups within a larger community often have special needs that must be taken into account when preparing an emergency plan.

Governments routinely use demographics to identify populations and plan for future needs. Demographics is also used by health care providers throughout the world for planning purposes. The use of demographics is every bit as valid in emergency management, which seeks to determine the necessary steps to prepare effectively for an emergency.

A successful emergency strategy requires a full understanding of community composition. Once the needs of a given community are understood, it becomes possible to identify whether the community's resources are adequate to meet those needs in an emergency. Armed with this understanding, it is possible to begin a process of mitigating any shortfalls in resources, so that if the time comes when those resources are needed, the effects of the disaster on the population will be minimized—and the community will be truly prepared.

The use of demographics gives emergency managers the opportunity to identify the variables that affect community needs. Understanding these variables is as critical to the process of creating an emergency plan as hazard identification and risk assessment. Specifically, emergency managers need to use these variables to identify people who are likely to have special needs and to ensure that the resources within a community are adequate to meet those needs, now and in the future.

KEY TERMS

census

census tract

demographics

evacuation

socio-economic status

spatial

LEARNING CHECK

Take a few minutes now to test your knowledge of the application of demographics to emergency management. Select the best answer in each case. Any score of less than 16 out of 20 (80 percent) indicates that you should re-read this chapter.

1. To identify a community's vulnerabilities, in addition to understanding a community's economic activities and physical location, emergency managers must also possess a sound understanding of
   a. psychology
   b. community composition
   c. political processes
   d. communications technology

2. An understanding of community demographics can provide emergency managers with potentially important information regarding
   a. vulnerability
   b. receptiveness to education efforts
   c. disaster resource requirements
   d. both (a) and (c)

3. Demographics have long been used effectively in marketing, government planning, health care planning, and
   a. community planning
   b. firefighting
   c. school curriculum planning
   d. the manufacturing industry

4. Central to the concept of demographics usage in emergency management is the fact that individuals have different abilities and requirements for protection
   a. at different times in their lives
   b. depending on place of birth
   c. after emergency preparedness education
   d. both (b) and (c)

5. Noted economist David Foot has written that _____ of all social phenomena can be predicted through the use of demographics.
   a. one-quarter
   b. one-third
   c. one-half
   d. two-thirds

6. Socio-economic status information is important to emergency managers because it provides some potentially useful indicators on
   a. the local economy
   b. the type and amount of emergency resources required
   c. the degree of political support
   d. both (a) and (b)

7. It has been well documented that only about _____ of a given population will rely on the use of emergency shelters for an extended period during an emergency.
   a. 10 percent
   b. 20 percent
   c. 30 percent
   d. 40 percent

8. The prolonged usage of emergency shelters by a given group is most likely to be determined by
   a. age
   b. gender
   c. socio-economic status
   d. language skills

9. Failure to identify demographic variables may not only create additional, unnecessary vulnerabilities for the community, but also deny emergency managers
   a. access to useful resources
   b. community support
   c. funding
   d. both (b) and (c)

10. Among the demographic variables likely to influence relative vulnerability, emergency managers should consider age, socio-economic status, and
    a. marital status
    b. occupation
    c. communication skills
    d. place of birth

11. In most Western countries, demographic data is typically collected by means of
    a. marketing statistics
    b. universities and colleges
    c. government finance departments
    d. a census

12. Census data is generally divided into smaller geographical areas called
    a. census tracts
    b. counties
    c. polygons
    d. municipalities

13. In most Western countries, a census is typically conducted
    a. on an as-needed basis
    b. annually
    c. every five years
    d. every five or ten years

14. Data collected in the census is generally examined and projected by the finance departments of regional governments to
    a. determine community planning needs
    b. determine placement of schools
    c. predict future tax revenue levels
    d. determine the placement of transport corridors

15. Municipalities tend to use demographic data to
    a. determine future service requirements
    b. set electoral boundaries
    c. set aside agricultural land
    d. determine major issues

16. Census data is typically collected by the _____ level of government.
    a. local authority
    b. regional
    c. federal
    d. municipal

17. Census data that has been modified to make it applicable to a specific local community may be available from the finance department of a regional government or from
    a. municipal-planning departments
    b. the newspaper
    c. libraries
    d. retail firms

18. To produce projections using demographic data, emergency managers might consider a strategic alliance with
    a. retailers
    b. hospitals
    c. a local university or college
    d. national marketing firms

19. The spatial plotting of demographic data on maps can be useful because it permits emergency managers to see
    a. concentrations of vulnerable people
    b. locations of increased service requirements
    c. areas of hazard
    d. both (a) and (b)

20. The "layering" of data sets, including demographic data, on maps may give emergency managers better insight into the relationships between
    a. hazard and risk
    b. risk and vulnerability
    c. hazards and schools
    d. population and health care

CASE STUDIES

A. You are the emergency manager for a community of 100,000 people located in eastern North America. The new national census findings have just been released, and you wish to examine the potential presence of vulnerable groups within your community.

1. Where could you potentially find relevant information that has been adjusted to include your community exclusively?
2. Which specific demographic variables would you research to attempt to identify vulnerable populations?
3. What method(s) might be used to identify the specific locations of populations that are potentially vulnerable?
4. How could you correlate your data on vulnerable populations with known risk factors?

B. You are the emergency manager for a large urban centre located in eastern Canada. You know that you have a large and growing population of new immigrants, drawn from a variety of countries around the world.

1. What factors related to these new immigrants might influence emergency management operations in advance of an emergency?
2. What factors related to these new immigrants might influence emergency management operations during an emergency?
3. How would you identify the presence of these factors?
4. What strategies might you pursue to mitigate the effects of these factors in the pre-emergency phase?

TO LEARN MORE

1. Speak to your local planning office and attempt to obtain data on your community's composition by age. If possible, determine where the concentrations of the elderly and very young are in the community, and plot these on a map. Do any patterns emerge? Are elderly people or children more concentrated in specific area(s) of the community? Next, add the locations of known hazards to the map. Is there any relationship between potentially vulnerable residents and known hazards?

2. Speak to your local planning office and attempt to obtain data on community composition by socio-economic status. If possible, determine any concentrations of the economically disadvantaged, and plot these on a map. As a

next step, add the locations of all public buildings, such as schools, recreation centres, and arenas, to the map. Are there specific public facilities in proximity to these populations that might be used as emergency shelters?

NOTES

1. David Foot, *Boom, Bust and Echo: How to Profit from the Coming Demographic Shift* (Toronto: Macfarlane, Walter & Ross, 1996).
2. James Hanna, *Guidelines for the Planning and Operation of Emergency Reception Centres and Shelters* (Ottawa: Emergency Preparedness Canada, 1996).
3. Norman Ferrier, *Beyond 2000: A Demographic View of the Future of Toronto's E.M.S. System* (internally circulated) (Toronto: Toronto E.M.S., 1998).
4. Emergency Management Australia, *Disaster Recovery—Australian Emergency Manual Series* (Dickson: Emergency Management Australia, 1996).
5. Paul Beaulieu and Jean-François Marchand, *Evacuation Procedures in Densely Populated Areas: A List of Planning Responsibilities* (Ottawa: Emergency Preparedness Canada, 1996).

CHAPTER 5

Land-Use Issues

LEARNING OBJECTIVES

On completion of this chapter, you will

▶ Gain a preliminary understanding of the concept of community planning and its history.

▶ Understand the relationship among community planning, risk, and vulnerability.

▶ Understand the role of community planning in emergency management.

▶ Understand the role of emergency management in influencing community planning to reduce risk exposure and mitigate the effects of hazards.

KEY MESSAGES

1. There is a clear relationship between the physical location of both people and infrastructure, and the exposure to risk from human-created events and processes that potentially generate hazards.

2. There is a clear relationship between the physical location of both people and infrastructure, and the exposure to risk from some types of naturally occurring events.

3. People in communities may choose to accept a risk exposure when living in its proximity is absolutely necessary for the generation of wealth.

4. Some communities that initially accepted exposure to a risk, driven by the need for access to a given location or process, may eventually find that the need to live in proximity to that risk has disappeared, even though the risk remains.

5. Emergency managers may be able to reduce community risk exposure through the planned relocation of populations and infrastructure away from unnecessary areas of hazard.

6. Emergency managers may be able to influence modern community-planning processes and decisions, so that potential risk exposure is not created in the first place.

Introduction

Most human settlements are subject to some sort of planning process. This process can range from simple choices on where to locate required structures, to elaborate plans for specific land uses (**planned communities**). Since the earliest settlements, the two major factors that influence planning processes are access to the resources and means used to generate wealth for the community and community safety. While community safety is a consideration when planning communities, it may, too often, take a "back seat" to proximity and access to wealth-generating resources. Sometimes the result is the unnecessary proximity to risks for the community and its residents.

Some of the risks communities face may be related to wealth generation, such as industrial processes and transportation corridors. To illustrate, a community's risks might be created by the presence of a much-needed factory containing potentially hazardous production processes. For example, in Nobel, Ontario the principle industry during the First and Second World Wars was the production of explosives; a major highway crossed the town, through which hazardous materials were carried. Or, a community's risks might be created by the location of community resources and structures in proximity to once important wealth-generating resources that are now gone. The previously accepted risks remain, but for no good reason. By working together with mainstream community planners and understanding their function, emergency managers can play a significant and effective role in community risk reduction.

Purpose

A clear relationship exists between a community's location and risk, particularly with respect to proximity to hazards. Today, emergency managers must understand the motivating factors and processes that influence land-use decisions. With such knowledge, emergency managers can influence community planning to prevent potential exposure to risk and mitigate the effects of hazards that are already present in vulnerable populations and infrastructure. While historically the influence of emergency managers in this type of planning has been minimal, it is now growing, particularly in communities that see the benefits of emergency management. Still, in all cases, the economic needs of the community will be weighed against potential risk exposure, and trade-offs will often be required.

The History of Community Planning

Humans have always attempted to choose their settlement sites carefully. In the earliest communities, one of the primary considerations was ready access to assets, such as hunting grounds. As civilization evolved, this consideration was overshadowed by the availability of agricultural land, pastoral spaces for livestock herding, and access to the resources required for early specialization, such as appropriate stone and metal for tools, clay for pottery, and so on. In all such settlements, the presence of a water supply was also important; water was required for survival, carried away waste, and provided power for the earliest industrial processes, such as milling and tanning.

The security of the population was also an important consideration in choosing the site of a community. Early communities tended to be placed in locations that were easily defensible; often on hilltops or surrounded by water. There are many documented examples of Iron Age settlements in northern Europe whose houses were constructed on stilts in water, and only joined to land by a narrow causeway. This concern for defence can still be seen in many towns of the northern Mediterranean; they were constructed on hilltops with few entrances and narrow, easily defensible streets. Defensibility, however, was rarely the foremost consideration of a community when selecting a site; access to resources needed for wealth generation was typically viewed as more important.

As civilizations evolved, so did trade. Access to trade routes, whether land- or water-based, also influenced community placement. Many communities were established adjacent to converging roads, along waterways, and at harbours. The increasing wealth of communities made them tempting targets for outsiders, and additional defence considerations, such as town walls, began to appear (these were probably among the first public works projects).

Community Configuration

The earliest examples of formally planned communities include cities in the Indus valley of northern India and those along the Tigris and Euphrates rivers in the "fertile crescent"—these communities are considered by many to be the birthplaces of civilization.[1] They had roads laid out in grid patterns and houses positioned, it seems, to gain protection from noise, odours, and thieves. Among early examples of planned communities, the most rational were those of the ancient Romans. Sites were often selected straddling a river, so that drinking water was available and waste was carried away, even in times of siege. A city was laid out around a central forum that housed the market and administrative buildings, and roads followed a grid pattern that is very similar to many cities and towns today.

Roman tenement blocks, called *insulae*, were bounded by roads and were 80 yards (73 metres) square. Local residents were assigned spaces in an *insula* in which to build their own houses. The entire community was surrounded by a wall for defence purposes, with one or two gates to regulate the comings and goings of people and resources. Agricultural land was located outside the community's walls, and any particularly noxious industrial processes, such as leather tanning or fabric dyeing, were usually located outside the walls and downstream.

After the fall of the Roman Empire, grid-patterned cities disappeared, and communities tended to develop in a radial pattern around some point of interest or wealth—typically a church or cathedral, or the fortress of a noble. Growth of the community was often organic in nature; "rings" (resembling the growth rings of a tree) were added to the existing community as required.

By the time of the Norman Conquest of England (AD 1066), communities had become more specialized; local nobles, always eager for new sources of revenue, began to issue charters to towns for markets.[2] In England, market towns were spaced approximately 30 miles (50 kilometres) away from one another; or about the distance that a person could walk in a day. The intent was to ensure that a person could walk to, or carry goods to, a market within one-third of a day, spend one-third of the day in the market, and then walk back home at the end of the day. By placing such practical restrictions on the development of market towns, competition among nearby communities was reduced. Examples of this type of town can still be found all over Europe.

During the Renaissance, rational community planning re-emerged, with the star-shaped city. Urban roads radiated outward from a central point, and specific economic activities tended to be concentrated in separate areas. For example, one street might contain all of the fishmongers, another all of the butchers, another all of the greengrocers, and so on. In many European cities today, the names of streets and neighbourhoods reflect this largely vanished planning practice.

Occasionally, communities were reconstructed. The need to rebuild might derive from a variety of causes, including exhaustion of resources, war, plague, or the worst enemy of any community, fire. Large-scale fires were common; many cities, from those in ancient Rome to those in contemporary North America, have experienced their version of the "great fire." Such events represented not only an economic challenge, but also an opportunity for mitigation; many of these fires led to the creation of protective measures that we now take for granted. For example, the Great Fire of London (1666) resulted in not only the complete reconstruction of the central part of the city (and possibly the end of the plague) but also the creation of some of the first formal building standards, including a ban on thatched roofing and the construction of buildings from anything other than stone.[3]

Transportation Considerations

Early settlements in North America tended to develop along trade routes. In the relatively complete absence of roads, these early settlements appeared around harbours and water routes such as rivers, particularly in the northern part of the continent. In Ontario, for example, the first settlements were established along the shore of Lake Ontario, and then spread along navigable rivers.[4] The earliest roads were muddy affairs that were usable for about six to eight months out of the year, so water transportation was crucial to the movement of both people and goods. Settlements in the southern part of the province supported the transport of agricultural goods produced by the settlers. For example, long before roads or railways, Newcastle had a busy harbour that shipped barley produced by local farmers to breweries located on the south side of Lake Ontario in the United States. In northern Ontario, the presence of other natural resource industries, such as the fur trade, mines, and logging, determined the location of communities.

Prior to the advent of the railway, water provided the most convenient and efficient means of transporting large quantities of goods from one location to another. Societies used not only coastal shipping and navigable rivers, but many actually augmented those routes by creating artificial waterways or canals for shipping both raw materials and finished products in bulk. These canals became commonplace across England, Europe, and the eastern part of North America, and many examples still exist today,[5] although their use for shipping has declined dramatically.

Railways began to appear in the late-18th century with local, horse-drawn railcars; the first steam-powered locomotives appeared in the early 19th century. By 1869, the first American transcontinental railway spanned the continent, allowing the movement of people and goods westward. Communities began to arise along the railway, in much the same manner that they had previously arisen along rivers, and for the same reasons. In Canada, having a transcontinental railway was considered of such economic importance that its construction was a condition of several provinces for joining Confederation. Heavy dependence on the railway would continue into the 20th century, until the development of the automobile, airplanes, and modern, paved roads. Even with the appearance of new modes of and advances in transportation, railways continue to be a major factor in the movement of goods to market, and are of tremendous economic importance to many communities. While the use of rail transportation for long-distance movement of people has decreased, regional transportation, such as commuter trains, continue to influence where people live and work.

Contemporary Communities

Almost all communities, until well into the 20th century, developed as the result of a convergence of people around points at which wealth could be generated. Admittedly, wealth on a grand scale existed for a privileged few: those who were the owners of the means of wealth generation. For most people, however, wealth generation occurred in the form of employment. As a result, the average person sought to locate his or her home and family in a location where employment in a factory, a mine, a mill, or a transportation system was possible, or where the provision of services, either to the facility in question, or to its employees, was possible.

Risk Tolerance

In the absence of modern transportation, living physically close to a source of wealth is extremely important; people could not spend half the day travelling to and from their place of employment and still hope to make a living. As a result, many communities remained relatively small, and many tolerated the risks generated by those wealth-generating processes because they were considered necessary for continued employment. This concept is known as **risk tolerance**.

In some cases, risk tolerance for a community's location continues even when the reason for accepting the risk has disappeared. To illustrate, a mill is constructed on a river to exploit the available water power. People settle in the vicinity of the mill, even though the area is somewhat flood-prone, to have access to employment at the mill and associated businesses. As time passes, the situation changes, either because the mill closes or switches from water to electrical power, making the location of the operation less important than it was originally. But in many cases people remain, having purchased homes and established relationships, and having found other employment in the more developed and advanced community. In this case, people continue to live with the risk, although the reason for its existence is gone.

Today, access to affordable transportation means that it is no longer necessary for workers to live in the shadow of a factory, close to the risks generated by its operating processes. In most societies, the local authority level of government has the legislated authority to determine both where and how new community features will be constructed, primarily through building permits and zoning regulations.[6] Ultimately, this authority covers the creation of formal community plans. In modern society, community planners tend to develop communities on the basis of sectors or zones, which they seek to make both safe and livable for residents.

Industrial processes may be approved for placement only in designated areas, with commercial districts and housing occupying other zones. Areas of potential risk may be "buffered" to reduce their proximity to housing and human populations. Such buffering may consist of low-risk industrial processes, commercial districts, parkland, or some combination of these, and may be defined by either transportation corridors or surface features. This approach, where it is practised, provides an improved quality of life for a community's residents.

Modern Planning Issues

While transportation is an important consideration in community planning, other issues must also be addressed. Not the least of these is economics. The presence of both people and businesses has an economic impact on communities, and most must live within their means, which is to say that they must sustain growth from their own property tax base, development fees levied by communities and paid by property developers to fund the creation of supporting infrastructure, and other revenue streams that they have access to, such as billing for municipally owned utility services. The presence of industry in a community often dictates the number of occupied dwellings, and, as a direct result, the number of property-tax dollars the community can raise. Those involved in community planning must make decisions carefully because industry, housing, and tax base are interdependent upon one another.

To illustrate, the creation of a new industry in a community is expected to generate new housing starts and a greater number of taxpayers. Thus, the new industry would generate more revenue for the community, but it would also create a demand for additional resources and services, including water, sewer systems, electrical and other utility services, and roads and transit. More community-operated resources, such as policing, fire protection, emergency medical services, schools, and libraries, may also be needed. The new population will also create new services, enhancing the quality of life in the community, making it more attractive and raising real estate values. In many modern societies, real estate values determine the amount of property tax that can be levied on individual homes and businesses. An influx of new residents may increase the community's tax base. However, initially the additional resources and services required will need to be paid for by the community, either by existing taxes or from development fees; without these resources and services, the new housing construction cannot proceed. Without new housing, the new industry may not be able to attract a sufficient pool of skilled workers, and may have to consider establishing itself elsewhere. The relationship among industry, housing, and tax base is complex.

The Role of Emergency Management

Emergency management is, in large measure, an attempt to manage a community's exposure to risk. As has been discussed previously, risk frequently arises by both wealth-generating activities and by the transportation corridors required to do business. Such risk exposure is occasionally the result of new community development, one of the easiest types of risk exposure for emergency managers to address because the risk hasn't actually occurred yet. Working closely with community planners, emergency managers can often readily and economically address the risks generated by new residential, commercial, and industrial developments. The objective is to keep the human populations as far away as possible from any areas of risk.

The ability to address risk exposure in new communities is not always foolproof, however. Local authorities frequently experience significant pressure from property developers, who are in the business of new-home construction, and who prefer few barriers to their profit-making. It is not uncommon for a property developer to select a parcel of land that might be visually pleasing and contribute to quick sales, but that has inherent exposure to risks that are not well understood. Risks might include the potential for wildland fires, flooding, landslides, or even the subsidence, or collapse, of the land surface into sinkholes. The unenlightened local authority might be tempted by the prospect of higher tax revenues and succumb to pressure from developers, but the result might be a community disaster that need not have occurred.

Sometimes individuals construct homes in areas of risk exposure as well. In some parts of North America, there is a recurring problem with the construction of housing in areas that are prone to wildland fires or other natural disasters. Someone who is eager to escape urban life is attracted to a rural site that is visually appealing. Perhaps a person is given a permit to build a house in the middle of a forest, which is subject to wildfires. Or perhaps a person is given a permit to build a house on a hillside that has become prone to landslides during heavy rain because of deforestation related to construction. Although such sites may be beautiful, they have hazards associated with them. Each year, emergency services must respond to urgent calls that are a consequence of well-known hazards related to the natural life cycle of an area.

Often overlooked is the relationship among land use, socio-economic status, and risk. It is not uncommon for the less affluent and socially marginalized members of a community to be pushed by housing costs to the least desirable, and frequently most dangerous, areas of a community. As a general rule, prudent emergency managers should remember that people will almost always choose access to wealth over personal safety in terms of priorities. As communities develop and individuals acquire personal wealth, they often move to better living locations at greater distances from industrial processes and transportation corridors. Only those with the fewest resources, and fewest options, will remain in an undesirable area, and only the poorest will continue to live in the shadow of a factory indefinitely.

Marginalized people tend to live in a community's least desirable areas in developing countries and, to some extent, in developed countries. The poorest tend to exist on land that no one else wants. People sometimes live in areas of risk primarily because they have few other options. While the problem of addressing community poverty may be beyond the scope of emergency managers, it should not be forgotten. Be aware of where the least-affluent people in the community reside; this knowledge can help point to areas of potential risk, and will, at a minimum, identify those most likely to require assistance during an emergency.

Emergency managers should also consider the risk exposure related to elements already present in the community. A railway may be important to a town's economy. It may have been placed in the centre of the town to facilitate passenger services that no longer exist, or the town itself may simply have "grown up" around the railway in its early days. When one considers that in North America virtually every freight train carries some form of hazardous material, is it still absolutely necessary for the railway to run right through the middle of the community?

The community can play a major role in mitigation efforts. For example, even when a railway cannot be relocated, for a variety of reasons, is it prudent to make the problem potentially worse by continuing to create housing developments immediately adjacent to the rail corridor, just because "we have always done so"? While rethinking past approaches may not eliminate exposure to risks, it can be effective at limiting them. As another example, while the main highway may run through the middle of a community, with one heavy truck in ten carrying some form of hazardous materials, might a separate hazardous materials road corridor on the outskirts of the community be an effective and appropriate method of reducing risk exposure?

Emergency managers must also understand the mechanisms by which a community delivers services to its residents, both individual and commercial. By possessing at least a basic understanding of how the community delivers utility services such as water or electricity, or uses transportation services such as roads, emergency managers are in a better position to judge exposure to risks. Those risks may derive from the disruption of the delivery of services or may exist in the physical means of service delivery. Emergency managers should have a level of understanding that is sufficient for planning purposes.

Conclusion

Land use and the policies that surround it play a significant role in the safety of communities, and the concepts of safety and affluence are not mutually exclusive; both objectives can be achieved simultaneously. These areas can and should be addressed concurrently in effective community planning. Safe communities require a partnership made up of all of the community's stakeholders. To achieve these objectives, emergency managers must understand why each element of a community is placed where it is, and how it contributes to or reduces the community's overall risk exposure.

To help create safer communities, emergency managers can participate in community planning by acting as educators to elected officials and other planning professionals. They may also need to educate and solicit cooperation from other levels of government, the general public, and community businesses. Emergency managers must understand the needs and priorities of each of these groups to create a culture of community safety, where the consideration of risk exposure issues becomes automatic, each time a new development or redevelopment is considered.

KEY TERMS

planned communities

risk tolerance

LEARNING CHECK

Take a few minutes now to test your knowledge of land-use issues. Select the best answer in each case. Any score of less than 16 out of 20 (80 percent) indicates that you should re-read this chapter.

1. There is a clear relationship between potential risk exposure and the proximity of both people and infrastructure to human-created
   a. factories
   b. rivers
   c. areas of potential hazard
   d. schools

2. There is a clear relationship between potential risk exposure and the placement of
   a. areas of human settlement
   b. forests and reforestation projects
   c. commercial areas
   d. municipal resources

3. People in communities may choose to accept a risk exposure when living in its proximity is absolutely necessary for
   a. the generation of wealth
   b. access to schools
   c. political purposes
   d. satisfying density requirements

4. In some cases, it may be found that the original reasons for community placement have disappeared, but the associated
   a. population will not move
   b. risks remain
   c. politicians are resistant to change
   d. both (a) and (c)

5. The planned relocation of populations and infrastructure away from unnecessary areas of hazard has the potential to result in
   a. improved socio-economic status
   b. longer commutes
   c. reduced risk exposure
   d. political issues

6. By working with community planners, emergency managers may be able to influence how land is allocated for usage, thereby
   a. improving tax revenues
   b. reducing transportation needs
   c. reducing needs for municipal services
   d. preventing risk exposure from occurring

7. In contemporary communities, development is ideally a balance between safety from risk exposure and the growth of
   a. economic activity
   b. political power
   c. quality of life
   d. tax revenues

8. The two primary motivating factors influencing the placement of early communities included
   a. transportation routes and trade
   b. resources and defence
   c. arable land and trade
   d. proximity of hazards and trade

9. The use of grid system based roads began with communities in the
   a. Indus valley
   b. Renaissance
   c. Roman Empire
   d. settlement of North America

10. Following the Norman Conquest of England, one notable example of community planning involved the creation of
    a. castles
    b. harbours
    c. market towns
    d. roads

11. The calamities that beset early communities, such as fire,
    a. reduced population pressures
    b. provided mitigation opportunities
    c. eliminated other social problems
    d. stimulated economic growth

12. As a general principle, regardless of type, the development of communities will typically first follow
    a. transportation corridors
    b. traditional homelands
    c. access to resources
    d. government direction

13. As new areas of land opened up, development would typically occur first near
    a. primitive roads
    b. water routes
    c. airports
    d. castles

14. In the pre-Modern era, communities often used water-based transportation because
    a. it was safer from attack
    b. it was easily accessible
    c. large volumes of goods could be moved
    d. both (a) and (b)

15. Most contemporary communities regulate community growth by means of community planning and
    a. development of services
    b. increasing tax base
    c. zoning regulations and building permits
    d. political pressure

16. In many contemporary communities, the risks arising from human-caused events are typically focused on industrial facilities and
    a. schools
    b. hospitals
    c. transportation corridors
    d. community preparedness

17. As communities develop and personal wealth grows, individuals typically
    a. remain in and enhance existing homes
    b. move to areas more distant from risk exposure
    c. insist on the relocation of the risk exposure
    d. move closer to areas of wealth generation

18. Emergency managers must possess a knowledge of how communities deliver services to understand the potential for the disruption of such services and
    a. the vulnerabilities within delivery systems
    b. how to exploit those services in an emergency
    c. how the funding for such services occurs
    d. the potential availability for program funding

19. When planning for the safety of communities, emergency managers must understand that
    a. any growth is good for the community
    b. safety and affluence are not mutually exclusive, they should be addressed concurrently
    c. industrial development means jobs for the community
    d. government intervention will eliminate hazards

20. The safest communities are the result of a partnership between
    a. all levels of government
    b. business and commercial interests
    c. emergency managers and community planners
    d. all stakeholders within the community

CASE STUDIES

A. You are the emergency manager for a small (under 20,000) suburban community that is adjacent to a large metropolitan area. Housing pressures in the metropolitan area are creating interest among property developers in the creation of "bedroom" communities in your area. The local elected officials are enthusiastic, as this will mean both business growth and increased tax revenues for municipal services. The initial development, "Old Mill Estates," is currently being considered for a site near the local river. This development would not only provide new housing in the community but also ensure the preservation of a beautiful old historic mill, around which the town was originally founded (some 600 metres from the existing structure), at the bottom of a scenic valley.

   1. What factors would you wish to research to determine any potential risks that might be inherent in the chosen site?
   2. Where might you seek the information that you require?
   3. What is your role in this project, as the community's emergency manager?
   4. What measures might the community take to reduce or eliminate any potential risk exposure that might be identified?

B. You are the emergency manager for a small (20,000) rural community that is primarily focused on support of the prime agricultural area that surrounds it. The town is located at the bottom of a valley, immediately adjacent to a fairly large river. The town was founded in this location to exploit the river's water power to run a large mill operation in support of local farmers. The mill itself burned to the ground in an unfortunate incident about 30 years ago and was never replaced and, since then, all milling has occurred at a more distant commercial operation. Every spring, for at least the past 100 years, ice dams have formed in the river, resulting in the flooding of a sizable portion of the town and, occasionally, even the town's evacuation. The community regards the flooding as a part of life, even organizing sandbagging "parties" each spring.

1. How would you begin to assess the issues surrounding the annual flooding?
2. From what sources would you draw your information?
3. What options might you recommend to local officials, in order to mitigate the annual flooding problem?
4. How would you attempt to justify the expenditures required for any of the proposed mitigation measures? What factors will need to be satisfied to achieve approval for the proposed mitigation measures?

TO LEARN MORE

1. Most jurisdictions have a formal building code. Often, this code identifies both construction standards for various types of buildings and also where the buildings can be located. While the technical standards for construction may be somewhat difficult to understand, there are other provisions that are of considerable interest to emergency managers. Look up the building code for your jurisdiction and become familiar with it. If you experience difficulty in understanding the code's provisions, visit your local planning office and talk to your community's planners.

2. Many communities have an official plan, providing details for both current and anticipated land use. Examine the official plan of your community and talk to local planners to learn the process by which it was created. Having a conversation with a property developer about the official plan may provide an interesting, if different, perspective.

NOTES

1. Jacquetta Hawkes, *The First Great Civilizations* (New York: Knopf, 1973).
2. Eleanor Smith Morris, *British Town Planning and Urban Design* (Singapore: Longman, 1997).
3. Neil Hanson, *The Dreadful Judgement: The True Story of the Great Fire of London* (New York: Doubleday, 2001).

4. J.M. Bumsted, *The Peoples of Canada: A Pre-Confederation History* (Toronto: Oxford University Press, 2004).
5. Charles Hadfield, *World Canals: Inland Navigation Past and Present* (New York: Facts on File, 1986).
6. Ivar Holm, *Ideas and Beliefs in Architecture and Industrial Design: How Attitudes, Orientations, and Underlying Assumptions Shape the Built Environment* (Oslo School of Architecture and Design, 2006).

PART II
Hazard, Risk, and Vulnerability

Source: Emergency Canada Preparedness.

IDENTIFYING HAZARDS AND
UNDERSTANDING RISK

Central to the process of emergency management are the interrelated activities of identifying potential hazards that may be present in a community or organization, evaluating and understanding the level of risk that they represent, and assessing the community or organization's vulnerability to those hazards. To effectively plan responses to all types of adverse events, it is essential for emergency managers to possess a clear understanding of the types of risk exposure that may come into play. In the past, emergency management in communities tended to embrace an all-hazards approach to planning. This generic approach, while functional, was not without its problems. Modern emergency management is risk based: it focuses on those untoward events that have the greatest likelihood of occurring and the greatest potential impact. As well, it seeks to ensure that, wherever possible, a community or organization is prepared to respond to those events.

Part II focuses on the methodologies of hazard identification and risk assessment for use in the development of emergency preparedness programs. Chapter 6 explores the nature of critical infrastructure, and how it can be identified by emergency managers. Chapter 7 provides an introduction to basic risk theory, including how and why risks occur. Chapter 8 focuses on Hazard Identification and Risk Assessment (HIRA) and the steps involved in this process. Chapter 9 explores the concept of vulnerability as a feature in communities, and how emergency managers can both identify and assess it. Chapter 10 focuses on the steps involved in promoting resiliency to the effects of disasters in communities.

CHAPTER 6

Critical Infrastructure

LEARNING OBJECTIVES

On completion of this chapter, you will

► Understand what constitutes "critical infrastructure."

► Understand the nature and types of criticality, the characteristics that influence criticality, and why some elements of infrastructure are more critical to community survival than others.

► Understand how critical infrastructure elements can be interconnected in their vulnerability.

► Understand how to scan the community to identify elements of critical infrastructure, determine their relative vulnerabilities, and incorporate them into the emergency management process.

KEY MESSAGES

1. Some elements of community infrastructure play a greater role in the survival and economic success of a community than others.

2. Critical infrastructure categories include critical services, communication systems, transportation systems, and economic elements.

3. Elements that provide products or services from multiple locations (redundancy) are less critical than those that represent a single source.

4. Elements of critical infrastructure are frequently interdependent, and a full understanding of each element and how it functions, including time to critical loss, is required.

5. Vulnerabilities in critical infrastructure must be mitigated whenever possible.

6. One of the leading causes for the outright failure of a community is the loss of one or more elements of critical infrastructure.

Introduction

A community comprises three key elements: its people, its physical environment, and the built environment and resources contained within it. Each of these elements must be examined separately and in detail. Knowing who and what are present in the community is insufficient, though; emergency managers must also understand how each of those elements interact with one another. If one's goal is to ensure the continued functioning of the community during and following a disaster event, it is absolutely necessary to understand how elements work in the first place, their relationship with one another, and how they interact.

When studying the community and the potential effects of any disaster upon it, emergency managers will quickly conclude that some elements of infrastructure play a more critical role in the welfare and prosperity of communities than others. The loss of some elements may represent an inconvenience for residents, while the loss of others is catastrophic. Without a complete understanding of how the community functions, determining which elements are critical is difficult at best.

Once they identify critical infrastructure elements, emergency managers must also understand how, when, and why the vulnerability of those elements occurs. To illustrate, it is insufficient to know that a single major grocery store is present in the community; one must also understand how, when, and why that store receives new inventory to understand both its criticality and its vulnerability. This chapter examines the nature of community infrastructure, and the reasons why it becomes critical to the community's welfare or, in some cases, its survival. Methods for identifying how, when, and why such infrastructure becomes vulnerable are also examined.

Purpose

Those elements that are absolutely necessary for a community's ongoing operation or survival are key factors in its vulnerability. Communities may experience critical vulnerabilities in a variety of areas, and in a multitude of ways. Some of the more obvious critical elements in the face of a disaster event may be government facilities and emergency response resources, but the criticality of elements may not be immediately obvious. Emergency managers require a process for examining and studying all of the elements of a community: infrastructure, transportation systems, communication systems, service delivery, economic activities, supply chains, quality of life, and emergency response. Without a detailed understanding of these elements, how they work, and how they interoperate, a truly effective emergency management program is not possible.

What Is Critical Infrastructure?

Over the past decade or more, critical infrastructure has become an area of increasing attention among those charged with emergency management and homeland security. Formal critical infrastructure programs currently exist in the United States, the United Kingdom, Canada, and Germany, and are under development in other jurisdictions as well. In 1996, the United States was among the first to develop such a program, under the direction of then-president Bill Clinton.[1] This program was expanded and enhanced by President George W. Bush in 2003,[2] partly in response to the events of September 11, 2001. In the United Kingdom, the Centre for the Protection of National Infrastructure[3] was created as an interdepartmental organization;

it has resources from a number of government departments including Britain's national security service (MI5), operates under the provisions of the *Security Service Act* (1989),[4] and reports to the director general of the Security Service. In Canada, critical infrastructure was seen as so important that Public Safety Canada,[5] the country's leading federal agency for emergency management, was briefly renamed the Office of Critical Infrastructure Protection and Emergency Preparedness.

What constitutes critical infrastructure at a national level varies greatly among countries. It ranges from the broad-brush approach of the United States and Canada to the more detailed approach of Germany, in which the primary emphasis is on the resiliency and security of telecommunications infrastructure. In Australia, using a broad-brush approach the working definition of *critical infrastructure* at the federal level is

> those physical facilities, supply chains, information technologies and communication networks that, if destroyed, degraded or rendered unavailable for an extended period, would significantly impact on the social or economic well-being of the nation or affect Australia's ability to conduct national defence and ensure national security.[6]

Similarly, what constitutes critical infrastructure varies at the provincial/state and local levels. It may be fair to say that what each level of government views as critical infrastructure is influenced to a certain degree by the areas of activity covered by its mandate. At the local level, critical infrastructure may be best defined as those elements of a community without which the community's survival might prove difficult. All communities possess critical infrastructure in one form or another. The nature of critical infrastructure is relative, and can be determined to some extent by the size of the community and its location, and the nature of the infrastructure element and its availability in the community.

Determining Criticality

The size of a community influences both what constitutes critical infrastructure and which factors generate relative criticality. In a larger community with more than one infrastructure element of a particular type, the individual infrastructure elements may be less critical to the community if lost. To illustrate, in a larger community with three gas stations, the loss of a single gas station has completely different implications for community operations than would be the case in a small community with a single gas station. On the other hand, larger communities tend to have infrastructure elements, such as hospitals, that could not be maintained by a smaller community; it is these types of elements that are more likely to constitute critical infrastructure.

The relative isolation of a community also plays a role in determining which infrastructure is critical. Communities in densely populated areas with well-developed communication and transportation systems tend to have less truly critical infrastructure than isolated communities, primarily because they have greater options for alternative delivery or provision of services located within a reasonable distance. Consider the small community in northern Canada or rural Australia with a single supermarket. That element of infrastructure is more likely to be viewed as critical, because its loss would force residents to travel long distances to purchase food. In a less-isolated community with a single supermarket, which is located close to other communities that have supermarkets, that single supermarket is likely to be viewed as less critical. Its loss would constitute an inconvenience, but not a critical blow to the community's survival.

The nature of an element of infrastructure will also influence its relative criticality. An infrastructure element that delivers products or services that are desirable but not essential is less likely to be viewed as critical. One that delivers essential services to the community is more likely to be viewed as critical. To illustrate, in a small town, the single gas station is viewed as critical, while the local cinema is not. As much as the community might value entertainment, it is a luxury item, and one that the community could cope without during a crisis.

To determine relative criticality, emergency managers must consider each infrastructure element individually. The following questions must be answered.

What Role Does This Element Play in the Life of the Community?

An infrastructure element upon which the community relies for daily operations is much more likely to be critical. There are some elements of community life, such as the education of children, which are typically viewed by residents as absolutely mandatory. Whether or not elements are actually "critical" over the short term is usually non-negotiable for residents.

Does the Element Provide an Essential Service or Access to an Essential Resource?

To understand what constitutes "critical," one must first consider how essential the service or resource actually is to community welfare. This is a decision that will, more often than not, be made by the community itself. There are obvious elements that would be viewed as essential, such as emergency services, hospitals, and many government facilities. Other essential elements might not be immediately obvious, but are vital nonetheless, and many of these are elements of economic infrastructure such as a major highway, rail line, or airport. If a community has a major employer, such as an auto-assembly plant that provides work for 40 percent of local residents, the loss of that plant would be an economic catastrophe for the community. It plays an essential role in the economic welfare of the community, and may therefore be judged to constitute critical infrastructure.

How Many Elements Providing Similar Services or Resources are Available in the Community?

The relative redundancy of an individual element of infrastructure clearly plays a role in determining whether or not that element is critical to community welfare and operations. The availability of a resource or service from multiple sources within the community typically tends to make each individual element less critical. To illustrate, if a community is large enough to support two hospitals, and one of those hospitals had to cease operations for a period for any reason, residents would still be able to obtain medical services at the other hospital. The result might be inconvenience for residents, but not a critical loss.

Are Other Options for Providing Services or Resources Available Nearby?

Isolated communities tend to have more critical infrastructure elements than communities that are not isolated. Once again, this fact speaks to the issue of redundancy reducing vulnerability in communities. The presence of a bank branch within a community is generally seen as important, but when nearby communities also have bank branches, the loss of a single branch for whatever reason constitutes an inconvenience, not a critical blow to community survival.

Are These Elements Directly or Indirectly Dependent on Other Community Elements for Their Operation?

A community is a complex organism. Very little that happens to one element of a community occurs in isolation. Most elements of a community are to some degree interdependent. To illustrate, how long could a major employer, such as a manufacturing facility, continue to function without either a road or rail network to bring in raw materials for use in the facility, and to ship finished goods to market?

Determining Vulnerability

Once critical infrastructure elements have been identified, emergency managers must attempt to determine their vulnerability. Issues such as proximity to potential hazards and the effects of the loss of each element on the vulnerability of the community as a whole must be understood. While maps and diagrams are useful, a physical visit to the site will provide the emergency manager with information that is more complete. The following questions must be answered.

Where Are These Elements Located in the Community? Is Proximity to Potential Sources of Hazard Events an Issue?

There is often a direct relationship between proximity to a source of hazard and the relative vulnerability of the infrastructure element to loss. In some cases, the vulnerability may be adequately addressed by means of careful community planning. To illustrate, during Hurricane Katrina (in 2005) the City of New Orleans learned a painful lesson about permitting the construction of hospitals in areas located below sea level. When the levees broke, not only were these hospitals unable to provide medical services to the hurricane's victims, but they were also charged with the monumental task of evacuating their facilities; some of the hospitals in question have not yet re-opened their doors.

If the Element in Question Were Unavailable, What Impact Would There Be on the Community? How Soon?

This question presents an interesting opportunity for the determination of the criticality of virtually any community element. Simply remove the element and determine what the results would be. In some cases, the impact may not be immediate, as with the loss of a school building during summer holidays. In other cases, the impact on the community is immediate and dramatic. To illustrate, consider a community divided by a large river, for which there is a single bridge. The next nearest bridge is some ten kilometres away. At first glance, one might conclude that the loss of the bridge would be inconvenient, but not critical. Now consider that all of the town's emergency services (such as police, fire fighters, **Emergency Medical Services [EMS]**) and the hospital are located on one side of the river. The critical nature of that bridge becomes clear the first time a fire or heart attack occurs on the other side of the river.

How Long Could the Community Continue to Function Normally Without the Presence of the Element?

The answer to this question helps clarify criticality and vulnerability in a general way. It helps to determine both the priority for replacement and the time to critical loss. In most cases, the loss of the element in question will result in significant changes in how the community operates, but in some cases, it may involve the life and death of the community itself. There are often elements whose loss will result in an immediate failure of the community. Most frequently, these elements of critical infrastructure are likely to be economic in nature. Consider the town that relies on a single mine, mill, or factory for its livelihood, and what might happen if that element suddenly ceased to exist. Almost every jurisdiction has its ghost towns—places where the loss of an element of critical infrastructure resulted in the outright failure of the community (see chapter 3).

The vulnerability of a given element of critical infrastructure may also be event driven or influenced by the presence or absence of previous mitigation measures. For example, in an area-wide electrical failure, the local hospital, although critical, may be affected to a much lesser extent than the community at large because emergency generators will allow it to continue to operate.

Critical Infrastructure Elements

Elements of the Supply Chain

Many critical infrastructure elements relate to the community's supply chain. Most communities normally operate with a seven-day supply of critical resources, such as food and fuel, within their boundaries. The removal of these critical resources, particularly for an extended period, has the potential to fundamentally change the nature of the community, and in some cases may even jeopardize its survival. To illustrate, a community has a single gas station that is a substantial distance from any other gas station; the presence or absence of that gas station is just as critical to the successful operation of the community as a petroleum tank farm would be to a large urban centre. Other supply chain elements that might be considered critical include electrical service, natural gas systems, heating fuel delivery, water supply, and sewer systems. The interruption of any of these would likely have an immediate effect on the community. See figure 6.1 for examples of supply chain elements that are critical to the successful functioning of a community.

⬤ **FIGURE 6.1   Critical Infrastructure:**
          Elements of the Supply Chain

- Food supplies
- Heating fuels
- Raw materials (for industry)
- Electricity
- Vehicle fuel
- Pharmaceuticals
- Water supply
- Sewage system

Economic Elements

Not all disasters involve howling wind, pouring rain, trembling earth, or the release of dangerous substances; some community disasters are economic in nature. One of the primary reasons for the existence of a given community is to generate wealth. People tend to live in a given locale for a reason, and if that reason is removed, either through disaster or a planned event, there is a good chance that the people in that locale will leave as well. Economic infrastructure is often critical because greater assets often equal greater resiliency, and access to assets will play a direct role in recovery.

The presence of a single employer, such as a mill or factory, could constitute a critical economic element. Other elements worth consideration include the proximity of the community to major transportation corridors. Many communities exist to provide services to corridors such as major highways and railways, and the relocation of a corridor can have a potentially catastrophic impact on the community. North America has been home to many communities that once thrived but utterly failed after a major road or railway was relocated, or when the factory or mine that was the community's principal employer closed. See figure 6.2 for examples of economic elements that might be the reason for the existence of a community.

Elements That Affect Quality of Life

A community is not driven solely by economics. Other elements of infrastructure affect the quality of community life, and thus are considered critical, including a wide variety of day-to-day services that are often taken for granted. Consider how the loss of a fire or police station, the town hall, a hospital, retail stores, a bank, or a school might influence the willingness of a community's residents to remain. Would people be as willing to live in a community that was governed at a distance, in a community where children had to be bused 30 kilometres each way for their

---

⚫ **FIGURE 6.2   Critical Infrastructure: Economic Elements**

- Major employers
- Major railways
- Airports
- Mines
- Factories
- Roads
- Major highways
- Ports
- Universities/colleges
- Mills
- Banks
- Bridges

education, where the nearest emergency department was 30 kilometres away, or where there was no immediate fire or police protection? All or most of the elements required to provide such services can be viewed as critical; without them, the quality of life in a given place would be degraded. See figure 6.3 for examples of essential elements needed to provide residents with the quality of life necessary for a community to grow and thrive.

Emergency Response Elements

Emergency response elements are also considered critical infrastructure. These include the obvious elements, such as police, fire department, EMS, and hospitals, as well as those that might not be immediately obvious. Elements in this latter category include telecommunications systems, such as telephone lines. To illustrate, a major ice storm occurred in 1998 that affected the area from eastern Ontario to southern Quebec. Many communities were profoundly affected, as much by the failure of the telephone system and the ability to call for help, as for any other reason. In all, some 66 communities declared a state of emergency, but were unable to communicate that fact to the outside world because of the telephone system failure. As a result, more than two weeks passed before some communities began to receive emergency assistance. See figure 6.4 for examples of essential elements needed to provide efficient emergency response to abnormal events and promote community safety.

⊛ **FIGURE 6.3 Critical Infrastructure: Elements That Affect Quality of Life**

- Hospitals
- Town/city hall
- Fire stations
- Retail sector
- Schools
- Police stations
- EMS stations
- Garbage removal

⊛ **FIGURE 6.4 Critical Infrastructure: Emergency Response Elements**

- Dispatch facilities
- Police vehicles
- Ambulances
- Public works
- Public health
- Emergency operations centre
- Firefighting apparatus
- Transit resources
- Social services
- Hospitals

Conclusion

When considering the vulnerability of a community, emergency managers require a complete understanding of the community elements that constitute critical infrastructure. It is necessary to understand why each element is critical, how it is vulnerable, and what the short-term and long-term effects of its loss might be. To achieve that understanding, research is required not only on how the elements interact but also on how and why the vulnerability of those elements occurs in each type of hazard event under consideration. This research is an essential component of understanding hazard, risk, vulnerability, and resiliency.

Emergency managers generally have access to publicly held information on critical infrastructure. The old view of the emergency manager as a barrier to development is disappearing as more communities become conversant with the concept of risk management and aware of real-life incidents of failure to manage risk (such as the fallout from Hurricane Katrina in New Orleans). Gaining access to privately held information may be more of a challenge. However, an enterprise's reluctance to share information can be overcome once its owners understand that the information will be used for planning purposes and will not be publicly disclosed.

KEY TERMS

Emergency Medical Services (EMS)

LEARNING CHECK

Take a few minutes now to test your knowledge of critical infrastructure and its role in the community. Select the best answer in each case. Any score of less than 16 out of 20 (80 percent) indicates that you should re-read this chapter.

1. Critical infrastructure may be defined as those elements in a community that
   a. play a major role in normal operations
   b. are essential to community welfare or prosperity
   c. are seen by the community as quality-of-life elements
   d. would result in inconvenience if lost

2. Critical infrastructure categories include elements associated with the supply chain, quality of life, emergency response, and
   a. economic components
   b. secondary municipal services
   c. large retail outlets
   d. libraries

3. In general terms, the more a single type of resource is present in the community,
   a. the more likely a single resource is to be critical
   b. the less likely a single resource is to be critical
   c. the more the public would be concerned about its loss
   d. both (a) and (c)

4. One method emergency managers use to assess the relative criticality of a particular element of infrastructure is
   a. time to critical loss
   b. public perception
   c. political advice
   d. both (b) and (c)

5. When they examine elements of critical infrastructure, emergency managers often discover that these elements are
   a. capable of functioning independently
   b. interconnected
   c. completely unconnected with one another
   d. low-vulnerability elements

6. One of the most common reasons for the outright failure of a community is
   a. the general effects of a disaster event
   b. the failure of government
   c. the loss of one or more elements of critical infrastructure
   d. failure to plan for emergencies

7. When determining the criticality of any infrastructure element, emergency managers should also consider the result of the element's loss in terms of
   a. impact on the local community
   b. impact on its corporate structure
   c. the subsequent impact on other communities
   d. impact on the national economy

8. Economic infrastructure is often critical because
   a. greater assets often equal greater resiliency
   b. access to assets will play a direct role in recovery
   c. it affects the municipal tax base
   d. both (a) and (b)

9. When assessing the vulnerability of critical infrastructure, emergency managers must understand
   a. how vulnerability occurs
   b. when vulnerability occurs
   c. why vulnerability occurs
   d. all of the above

10. In a small town, an example of an element of critical economic infrastructure might be
   a. the presence of several bank branches
   b. the local gas station
   c. a major employer
   d. the municipal-planning office

11. The less redundancy that exists with a particular element, resource, or service, the more likely that element, resource, or service is to be
   a. critical
   b. non-critical
   c. desirable
   d. both (b) and (c)

12. Infrastructure elements not physically located within a community may nonetheless constitute critical infrastructure because
   a. of their role in the community supply chain
   b. they pose some type of hazard to the community
   c. they prevent community resources from being overwhelmed
   d. both (b) and (c)

13. In isolated communities, transportation corridors may constitute critical infrastructure for manufacturers because they provide
    a. access to raw materials
    b. a means of sending finished goods to market
    c. access to a head office
    d. both (a) and (b)

14. One of the most common causes of vulnerability for elements of critical infrastructure that emergency managers must consider is
    a. previous mitigation measures
    b. proximity to potential hazards
    c. lack of community support for emergency management
    d. political pressure

15. When assessing time to critical loss, emergency managers may find that critical loss effects occur
    a. immediately
    b. over the short term
    c. over a longer term
    d. all of the above

16. Examples of critical infrastructure elements not physically located within the community might include
    a. petroleum tank farms
    b. food distribution centres
    c. hospitals
    d. all of the above

17. The two primary reasons for the creation of any community are the protection of residents and
    a. the availability of land
    b. proximity to transportation
    c. access to health care
    d. the generation of wealth

18. Ecomonic elements of a community's infrastructure that might be critical include
    a. roads
    b. bridges
    c. factories
    d. all of the above

19. When considering the relative vulnerability of a particular element of critical infrastructure, it is generally best for emergency managers to
    a. rely on the opinion of its owner
    b. rely on public opinion
    c. physically visit the site
    d. rely on maps and diagrams

20. Other elements of a community's infrastructure that might be critical include the town hall, emergency response resources, and
    a. hospitals
    b. libraries
    c. community centres
    d. all of the above

CASE STUDIES

A. Research the critical infrastructure in your own community. Identify and locate all police, fire, EMS, hospital, and major government buildings. Do not forget to include dispatching locations and the Emergency Operations Centre, whether these are combined or separate entities. Create a list of all such elements. Visit and examine their sites. Consider each one and answer the following questions:

   1. Is the element unique in the community, or does it provide services from multiple locations?
   2. Is the element dependent upon any other element of infrastructure for its function?
   3. Is the element located in proximity to any potential hazard event?
   4. What would be the immediate, short-term, and long-term result to the community if the element were lost?

B. Research the critical infrastructure in your own community. Identify and locate all major employers, food stores, fuel distribution outlets, pharmacies, schools, and major retail locations. Create a list of all such elements. Visit and examine their sites. Consider each one and answer the following questions:

1. Is the element unique in the community, or does it provide products or services from multiple locations?
2. Is the element dependent upon any other element of infrastructure for its function?
3. Is the element located in proximity to any potential hazard event?
4. What would be the immediate, short-term, and long-term results to the community if the element were lost?

TO LEARN MORE

1. Take the elements presented in figures 6.1 to 6.4 and create a list of all of the examples of each within a given community. Who "owns" each element, and how can that person be accessed?

2. Looking at your list, does each element generate or mitigate risk? Explain how and why this is the case. Are there any immediate steps that might be taken to reduce the potential vulnerability of each element?

NOTES

1. William Clinton, *Presidential Decision Directive PDD/NSC-63* (Washington, DC: The White House, 1996), <http://www.fas.org/irp/offdocs/pdd/pdd-63.htm>.
2. George W. Bush, *Presidential Homeland Security Directive HSPD-7* (Washington, DC: The White House, 2003), <http://www.whitehouse.gov/news/releases/2003/12/20031217-5.html>.
3. *Centre for the Protection of National Infrastructure* website, <http://www.cpni.gov.uk>.
4. *Security Service Act*, 1989, <http://www.opsi.gov.uk/acts/acts1989/Ukpga_19890005_en_1.htm>.
5. "About Critical Infrastructure," *Public Safety Canada*, <http://www.securitepublique.gc.ca/prg/em/nciap/about-eng.aspx>.
6. "About Critical Infrastructure," *Trusted Information Sharing Network for Critical Infrastructure Protection (Australia)*, <http://www.tisn.gov.au>.

CHAPTER 7

Basic Risk Theory

LEARNING OBJECTIVES

On completion of this chapter, you will

▶ Understand hazard, risk, and vulnerability and how they interrelate.

▶ Learn about past approaches to understanding hazard and risk, and their effects on communities.

▶ Understand the important differences between the all-hazard and risk-based approaches to emergency planning.

▶ Understand the purpose of and need for the Hazard Identification and Risk Assessment (HIRA) process in community emergency management programs.

KEY MESSAGES

1. An understanding of the interaction of hazard, risk, and vulnerability is central to effective emergency management.

2. Risk management should be based on facts, not assumptions.

3. The presence of a given hazard and the distribution of its resulting risk is neither universal nor equitable.

4. The distribution of hazard and risk can be **temporal** as well as spatial.

5. The assessment and management of risk is a dynamic process.

Introduction

All communities experience risk to some degree, and from a variety of sources. From the perspective of emergency managers, it can be argued that communities are largely risk management devices. The distribution of risk is neither universal nor equitable, whether among communities or within groups in a given community. Investigating hazard, risk, and vulnerability, and how they operate and interrelate within a community, can be likened to journalism. What type of disaster event is likely to occur? Why? Where in the community is it likely to occur? Why? When and how often is it likely to occur? Why? What impact will likely result? Why? Who is likely to be affected? Why? Are there some groups more likely to be affected or more likely to experience more severe effects than others? Why?

One of the roles of emergency managers is managing risk—before an adverse event occurs, while it is ongoing, and during the community's recovery phase. This role should include fostering mitigation measures to eliminate exposure to an adverse event or, when this is not possible, to minimize the effects associated with its occurrence. To fulfill this role, emergency managers must possess a thorough understanding of hazard, risk, and vulnerability.

Purpose

Armed with a comprehensive understanding of hazard, risk, and vulnerability, emergency managers are in a unique position within a community. This knowledge helps emergency managers set priorities for community planning. It also helps them develop public education and staff training programs, emergency exercises, and other educational activities directed at preparing the community for crisis. As well, it helps emergency managers create the business cases frequently required to justify the acquisition of much-needed response resources. Finally, this knowledge can help emergency managers gain approval for mitigation measures related to reducing the potential effects of an emergency, and, in some cases, even help them contribute to community planning.

Understanding the Basics

Hazard

A *hazard* is an event that has the potential to cause adverse effects within a community, organization, or some subset of the population. The types of hazards present in communities are not universal; an urban community will be confronted by hazards that are substantially different from those experienced by a rural community. Hazards are generated by a variety of factors, including the physical location of the community, its composition, and the activities within that community. Hazards can be created by nature, technology, and humans (accidentally or deliberately). See figure 7.1 for a few examples (there are many more).

Risk

Risk is the likelihood that a particular hazard will cause adverse effects within a community, an organization, or some subset of the population. Risk is determined by the nature of the hazard, its frequency of occurrence, and the probable magnitude of the event, should it occur.

⚠ **FIGURE 7.1   Types of Hazards**

Natural

Flood	Earthquake
Wildland fire	Hurricane
Drought	Tornado
Ice storm	Blizzard
Severe summer storm	Microburst
Epidemic/pandemic	Landslide/subsidence

Technological

Plane crash	Train derailment
Major fire	Hazardous materials
Highway accident	Radiation release
Water pollution	Air pollution
Utility failure	Dam break
Pipeline break	Shipwreck

Human Caused (Accidental or Deliberate)

Labour disruption	Terrorist act
Industrial sabotage	Gun shooting
Supply chain disruption	Negligence
Military action	Major plant closing
Effect from distant event	Computer virus
Bank/economic failure	Community isolation

Frequency

Frequency is the incidence of an event in a community, an organization, or some subset of the population, based on information on the community's history. How many times has "Event X" occurred in this community in the past? How often? How recently? Usually, such information can be drawn from sources such as university research studies, formal historical accounts, community archives, local newspaper "morgues" and other types of media reporting, and local historians.

Magnitude

Magnitude indicates the likely size of an event, should it occur within a community, an organization, or some subset of the population. Generally, emergency managers express magnitude in terms of a worst-case scenario, since it is invariably better to plan to over-respond to a given event than to under-respond and then have to adjust the response. The magnitude of impact will be driven by such issues as the nature of the event, land use, community composition, and proximity to the event in question.

$$\text{Risk} = \text{Frequency} \times \text{Magnitude}$$

Vulnerability

Vulnerability is the susceptibility of a community, an organization, or some subset of the population to the adverse effects of a given event; should that event occur. Vulnerability can be driven by such factors as proximity to a hazard, community composition, other activities and resources in the community, and prior efforts to mitigate the hazard in question. It can have a number of results, including loss of life, injuries, loss of resources, financial loss, and even damage to reputation.

Resiliency

Resiliency is the relative ability of a community to absorb the effects of a hazard event and quickly return to normal or near-normal operations. This concept is generally viewed as the opposite of vulnerability. Its presence or absence is driven by the presence or absence of an effective emergency-response plan, by the availability of resources, by the level of community education, and by the success of previous mitigation efforts.

History of Emergency Planning

Over the last 30 years, emergency planning has been largely reactionary, with planners basing most new planning efforts on the "last bad thing" that happened. Unfortunately, since no two events are ever exactly alike, and few are relatively even similar, the plan that resulted was never able to adequately respond to the "next bad thing." A personal exploration of this problem, and indeed, the work of many other practitioners, has led in recent years away from an all-hazards approach to emergency planning toward an approach that is more **risk based**.

While a risk-based approach is more effective, and is currently in vogue, it too fails in some critical respects. Although risk itself can be calculated or estimated to some degree, and much risk-based work has been published (including that of this author[1]), this approach does not address the actual issue: the *degree of vulnerability* in a community, organization, or subset of the population.

Like risk, vulnerability is relative. It is not a constant, it is not static, and it is not equally distributed throughout a community. When examined closely, many assumptions regarding the vulnerability of a subset of a population can be easily disproved. This point is important because assumptions can provide an incorrect basis for planning. According to Piers Blaikie and colleagues, "It is imperative to accept that vulnerability involves something very different from simply dealing with hazards through mitigation, prediction or relief."[2] It logically follows that a plan based on assumptions rather than facts is likely to be ineffective in meeting the needs of the community that it is intended to serve.

As already stated, until recently, emergency planning has been largely an exercise in hindsight—an exploration of the issues generated by the last major incident or exercise to attempt to prepare for the next major incident. This approach was followed throughout the Cold War. At that time, most of those involved in emergency planning or its predecessor, civil defence, were ex-military personnel. Their learning and analysis process evolved from military science, and was perfectly reasonable within its original context. Since battles were essentially alike, it seemed rational to look at the last battle to prepare for the next. The result was a generic type of emergency planning referred to as the *all-hazards approach.*

Unfortunately, when taken out of its original context, the all-hazards approach failed in some fundamental respects to deliver the type of dynamic process required in a community. This is hardly surprising when one considers the potential difficulties associated with attempting to prepare for a flood by analyzing the outcome of a train derailment. One adverse event might provide some generic lessons for others, such as identifying the need for specific improvements in response capacity, but each event is so different that the transferability of most lessons from one event to another is simply impossible. Nevertheless, enough knowledge was transferred that the emergency-planning system began to document its progress in terms of "lessons learned."

Anecdotally, the lessons were only rarely actually *learned*; one can study **after action reports** over the last 50 years and find the same generic problems (for example, perimeter control, communications) identified, but seldom actually corrected. Indeed, given that the problems identified are so seldom practically resolved, one might almost consider the term *lessons learned* to be an oxymoron of sorts. Perhaps "lessons identified but not resolved" would be a more accurate description.

More recently, emergency managers have focused on developing emergency plans based on identified risks. As indicated earlier, risks are the product of frequency of occurrence multiplied by the relative magnitude of the event. In most cases, identifying risks becomes a ranking exercise for emergency managers attempting to set priorities for training and resource acquisition. The models used to identify risk have become more elaborate, factoring in social consequence, because of the increased public awareness of risks and the political will to mitigate risks that have been identified.

Past modelling[3] expressed the event as a convergence of physical effects (such as frequency and magnitude) and socio-economic effects (such as social consequence and population vulnerability) combined with an initiating event. According to this model, mitigation is a critical factor whose presence or absence affects outcome (see figure 7.2).

The risk-based approach strives for mitigation and resiliency within the community. It is founded largely on the principles of resilient systems developed by Aaron Wildavsky[4] (see figure 7.3). Wildavsky essentially views a community in the same manner that one might view a production line or a machine of sorts, with the purpose of the machine being the generation of assets and the reduction of vulnerability. Wildavsky's approach deals primarily with the throughput of resources, and the control of their use. More resources and control result in greater community assets, and therefore greater resiliency, while less resources or poor control result in fewer assets and vulnerability, and must therefore be mitigated.

Types of Risk Modelling

Indeed, there are several major schools of thought on risk modelling. Piers Blaikie and colleagues propose two models on vulnerability to disasters: the pressure and

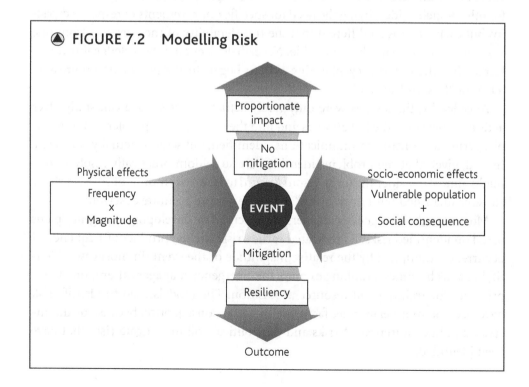

△ FIGURE 7.2   Modelling Risk

◬ FIGURE 7.3   Wildavsky's Principles of Resilient Systems

The homeostasis principle: Systems are maintained by feedbacks between component parts which signal changes and can enable learning. Resilience is enhanced when feedbacks are transmitted effectively.

The omnivory principle: External shocks are mitigated by diversifying resource requirements and their means of delivery. Failures to source or distribute a resource can then be compensated for by alternatives.

The high flux principle: The faster the movement of resources through a system, the more resources will be available at any given time to cope with perturbation.

The flatness principle: Overly hierarchical systems are less flexible and hence less able to cope with surprise and adjust behaviour. Top-heavy systems will be less resilient.

The buffering principle: A system which has capacity in excess of its needs can draw on this capacity in times of need, and so is more resilient.

The redundancy principle: A degree of overlapping function in a system permits the system to change by allowing vital functions to continue while formerly redundant elements take on new functions.

Source: Mark Pelling, *The Vulnerability of Cities: Natural Disasters and Social Resilience* (London: Earthscan, 2003), p. 8.

---

release model and the access model. The pressure and release model considers that vulnerability proceeds in a linear fashion through several stages. The first stage involves root causes, such as limited access to power and resources. The second stage deals with dynamic pressures, such as a lack of local institutions and rapid population growth. The third stage is unsafe conditions, such as a fragile environment or local economy. As vulnerability progresses through these stages, it generates increasing pressure until it collides with the forces of some calamity, whether natural or human caused, at which time the pressure is released and the cycle begins again (see figure 7.4).

The access model examines how vulnerability is affected by the economic and political processes that allocate resources, assets, and income. This model is essentially cyclical, with subsistence progressing to surplus, surplus providing access to additional resources (such as better farmland), greater surplus creating access to more resources (such as better housing), ultimately leading to access to social, political, and economic assets before the cycle begins again. Each stage of the cycle generates additional vulnerability to the effects of a disaster, and the interruption of progress through the cycle defines and may even increase vulnerability (see figure 7.5).

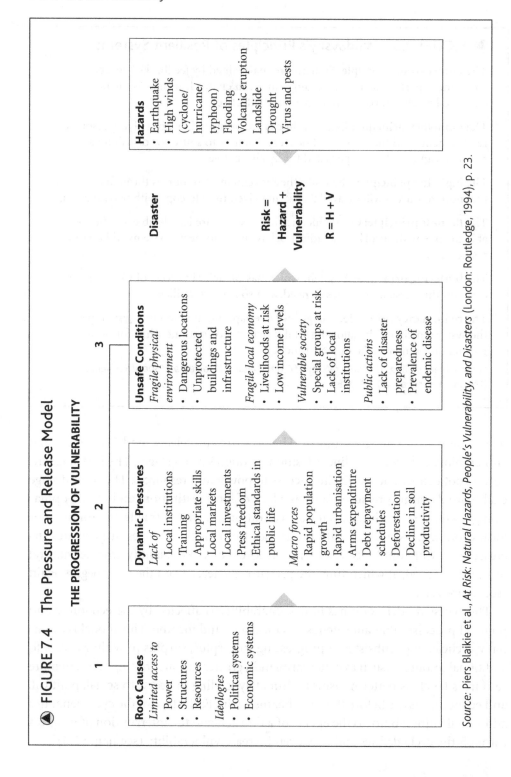

● FIGURE 7.4   The Pressure and Release Model

THE PROGRESSION OF VULNERABILITY

1

Root Causes

Limited access to
• Power
• Structures
• Resources

Ideologies
• Political systems
• Economic systems

2

Dynamic Pressures

Lack of
• Local institutions
• Training
• Appropriate skills
• Local markets
• Local investments
• Press freedom
• Ethical standards in public life

Macro forces
• Rapid population growth
• Rapid urbanisation
• Arms expenditure
• Debt repayment schedules
• Deforestation
• Decline in soil productivity

3

Unsafe Conditions

Fragile physical environment
• Dangerous locations
• Unprotected buildings and infrastructure

Fragile local economy
• Livelihoods at risk
• Low income levels

Vulnerable society
• Special groups at risk
• Lack of local institutions

Public actions
• Lack of disaster preparedness
• Prevalence of endemic disease

Disaster

**Risk =
Hazard +
Vulnerability**

R = H + V

Hazards
• Earthquake
• High winds (cyclone/ hurricane/ typhoon)
• Flooding
• Volcanic eruption
• Landslide
• Drought
• Virus and pests

Source: Piers Blaikie et al., *At Risk: Natural Hazards, People's Vulnerability, and Disasters* (London: Routledge, 1994), p. 23.

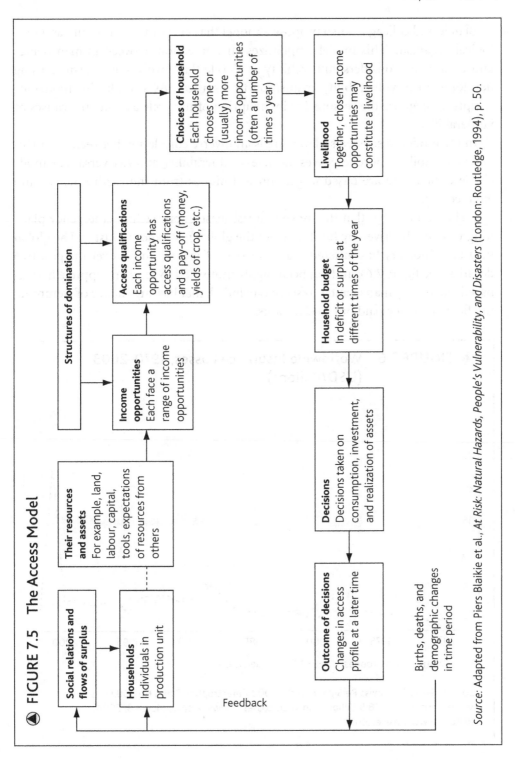

⬤ **FIGURE 7.5   The Access Model**

Social relations and flows of surplus

Households
Individuals in production unit

Their resources and assets
For example, land, labour, capital, tools, expectations of resources from others

Structures of domination

Income opportunities
Each face a range of income opportunities

Access qualifications
Each income opportunity has access qualifications and a pay-off (money, yields of crop, etc.)

Choices of household
Each household chooses one or (usually) more income opportunities (often a number of times a year)

Livelihood
Together, chosen income opportunities may constitute a livelihood

Household budget
In deficit or surplus at different times of the year

Decisions
Decisions taken on consumption, investment, and realization of assets

Outcome of decisions
Changes in access profile at a later time

Births, deaths, and demographic changes in time period

Feedback

Source: Adapted from Piers Blaikie et al., *At Risk: Natural Hazards, People's Vulnerability, and Disasters* (London: Routledge, 1994), p. 50.

Blaikie and colleagues also propose a model that views the community as a biological organism. This model emphasizes an interaction between human beings and nature and considers vulnerability as a cycle that involves an ever-increasing development of vulnerability acquisition to resources. As a result, this model attempts to diagnose the reasons for interruption of the cycle as potential causes of vulnerability.

In the models discussed so far, there is an inverse correlation between resources and vulnerability: more resources mean less vulnerability, and vice versa. The models described here are based largely on techniques from the earth sciences and engineering.

It should be noted that the move to a risk-based approach to emergency planning was largely driven by funding from the global insurance industry. The global insurance industry has suffered year after year of insured losses over the past two decades (see figure 7.6), and has been highly motivated to fund any approach, risk-based emergency management research included, that has any chance of stemming the flow of money paid out to claimants.

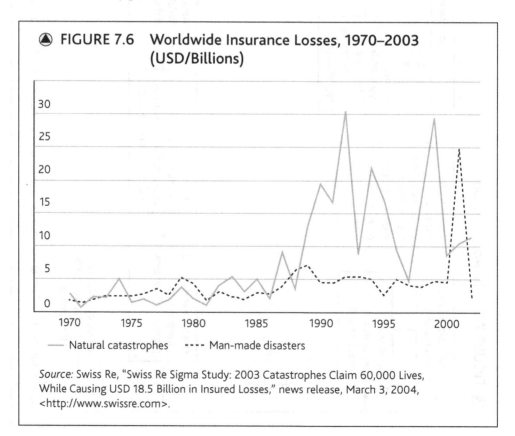

● FIGURE 7.6   Worldwide Insurance Losses, 1970–2003 (USD/Billions)

— Natural catastrophes   ---- Man-made disasters

Source: Swiss Re, "Swiss Re Sigma Study: 2003 Catastrophes Claim 60,000 Lives, While Causing USD 18.5 Billion in Insured Losses," news release, March 3, 2004, <http://www.swissre.com>.

Unfortunately, this approach provides very little attention to either vulnerability as a social phenomenon or the reduction of the loss of human life. As cynical as this observation may appear, the insurance industry also controls most pension funds, and since life insurance and pensions are already hedged against each other, the insurance industry has little to gain from any research that focuses on the human cost of disasters.

While the risk-based approach is clearly superior to and more cost efficient than the all-hazards approach, it is limited in its effectiveness. One flaw in such an approach is that it continues to be based on faulty assumptions and, to some extent, neglects the fact that the mitigation of the physical phenomena of disasters is not always possible. Its use also precludes any great interest in the social aspects of vulnerability, "responding to individual sectoral risks, so that ameliorating social vulnerability to environmental risk is divorced from vulnerability to economic or socio-political risks."[5] This approach does consider vulnerability but, without any real interest in establishing cause, provides little possibility of mitigation.

Philip Buckle, Graham Mars, and Syd Smale propose another approach to identifying vulnerability.[6] This approach is more people centred and attempts to identify specific subsets of the population that are most vulnerable to loss in a disaster event (see figure 7.7). While the intent to identify people who are most vulnerable so that steps can be taken to reduce their vulnerability is clearly good, the work is based largely on assumptions and generalizations, and may actually mislead those performing a vulnerability assessment.

It can also be argued that Buckle, Mars, and Smale's approach, in addition to potentially stigmatizing people, is factually inaccurate. Consider the urban homeless, often assumed to be at an increased level of vulnerability during a large-scale electricity failure. For them, electricity and those conveniences powered by it (such as lighting, air conditioning, refrigerators, televisions, and radio) are not an integral part of everyday life. The opposite is true for those in the "mainstream" population; they would have to learn to cope without electricity and stave off increased vulnerability due to its loss.

In the past, other efforts have been made to identify groups at increased risk, particularly with respect to evacuation requirements, that are now considered questionable. Consider the following: "the most obvious generalization to be drawn is that women and children (and most especially mothers) were principal candidates for evacuation, and logically so, since these groups are normally deemed by society most physically helpless and vulnerable." The same authors also state that "another category of residents particularly likely to be evacuated was the incapacitated, those who were ill or injured before or during a disaster, and perhaps already

---

⚠ **FIGURE 7.7   Subsets of the Population That Are Most Vulnerable to Loss**

1. Aged (particularly the frail)
2. Very young
3. Disabled (mental and physical)
4. Poor/people with limited resources to meet essential needs
5. Non-English (majority language) speakers
6. Indigenous peoples
7. Socially isolated
8. Physically isolated
9. Seriously ill
10. People dependent upon technology-based life support systems
11. Large families
12. Single-parent families
13. Workers at risk from machinery/equipment failure
14. People with limited psychosocial coping
15. People with limited financial resources
16. People with inadequate accommodation
17. People on holiday and travelling (particularly those in tent and caravan resorts)
18. Tourists from overseas
19. People living close to areas of hazard (e.g., floodplains, chemical-processing plants, areas of potential landslip)
20. People affected by the impact of a hazard (e.g., people who are trapped, people made homeless)

Source: Philip Buckle, Graham Mars, and Syd Smale, "New Approaches to Assessing Vulnerability and Resilience," *Australian Journal of Emergency Management* 15, no. 2 (2000): 8–15.

---

hospitalized."[7] This point can be considered a generalization as well, since many hospitals will "shelter in place" in most situations of emergency.

The research of the past has provided valuable contributions to the study of hazard, risk, vulnerability, and resiliency, but it is deficient in several respects. Communities comprise people; as such, any research with a primary focus on infrastructure and the built environment is likely to inadequately address the human cost of a disaster. Research that has focused on the human factor has provided insight that may be useful in some cases, but because it is based on assumptions, it can be misleading. Moreover, this research, while of great academic interest, provides few practical tools for practitioners who must be able to accurately assess and evaluate the hazards and risks that occur in a community. What is required is an approach to emergency planning that is both risk based and people centred.

Contemporary Risk Modelling

Over the past ten years, there has been a paradigm shift in the field of emergency management. Practitioners have moved away from the old all-hazards approach toward a risk-based approach. The latter approach, which will be discussed in greater detail in chapter 8, is often referred to as Hazard Identification and Risk Assessment (HIRA). Emergency managers who use the HIRA process constantly research, collect, and update information regarding the nature of each type of event and its incidence of occurrence, as well as the evolution of the population and infrastructure of the community under review. They also perform a series of ranking exercises, using various methodologies. First, the individual event types are ranked in terms of frequency and magnitude. Once this has been done, emergency managers rank all events likely to occur within a community to establish priorities for planning, training, resources, and mitigation efforts.

HIRA is currently viewed as the "state-of-the-art" approach to emergency management, and certainly meets the most immediate needs of practitioners. It is relatively comprehensive, and provides even the least-trained emergency manager with a process that is immediately usable in their assessment of risk exposures. As research in this field continues, it is hoped that even better tools for the mitigation of the human costs of disasters will emerge.

Conclusion

While older models of risk identification and analysis were useful in the emergency-management process, they were often based on faulty assumptions. Contemporary emergency managers must achieve a solid understanding of how, when, and why risk occurs, and how it affects people within a community. This knowledge forms a major part of the basis upon which community-emergency plans are created. Understanding the nature of risk is essential to effective emergency management, and this understanding must be based on fact. An approach to risk that is fact based is more likely to meet the real needs of a community during a disaster without wasting time and resources than one based on information that may be inaccurate.

KEY TERMS

after action reports

frequency

magnitude

resiliency

risk

risk based

temporal

vulnerability

LEARNING CHECK

Take a few minutes now to test your knowledge of hazard, risk, and vulnerability. Select the best answer in each case. Any score of less than 16 out of 20 (80 percent) indicates that you should re-read this chapter.

1. The distribution of a given risk in a community is neither equitable nor
   a. probable
   b. limited
   c. definable
   d. universal

2. A sound understanding of hazard, risk, and vulnerability may provide emergency managers with information that can be used to set planning priorities, develop public education and staff training programs, develop mitigation measures, and
   a. alert the local government
   b. acquire response resources
   c. develop media management plans
   d. develop grant funding for programs

3. An event that has the potential to cause adverse effects within a community or an organization is called
   a. a risk
   b. a hazard
   c. a vulnerability
   d. an exposure

4. The likelihood that a particular hazard will cause adverse effects within a community, an organization, or some subset of the population is called
   a. a risk
   b. a hazard
   c. a vulnerability
   d. an exposure

5. When conducting research on the frequency of occurrence of a given type of event, likely sources of information for emergency managers would include
   a. formal historical accounts
   b. community archives
   c. local newspaper "morgues"
   d. all of the above

6. In emergency management, the risk from a given event equals frequency times
   a. probability
   b. vulnerability
   c. magnitude
   d. exposure

7. The susceptibility to the adverse effects of a given event is called
   a. a risk
   b. a hazard
   c. vulnerability
   d. an exposure

8. An emergency planning approach that creates a generic response for a variety of disaster types is called
   a. a risk-based approach
   b. an all-hazards approach
   c. a multiple hazards approach
   d. a generic approach

9. A major problem with basing planning on "lessons learned" from past events is that
   a. the next event may have little in common with the last
   b. resources are likely to be tied up unnecessarily
   c. there is little chance of the last event occurring again
   d. staff already understand the last event

10. Past attempts to model disaster events typically expressed the event as a convergence of the physical effects of the disaster event with effects that are primarily
    a. political
    b. socio-economic
    c. psychological
    d. philosophical

11. In Wildavsky's principles of resilient systems, the principles that foster increased resiliency to the effects of a disaster include homeostasis, omnivory, high flux, and
    a. flatness
    b. buffering
    c. redundancy
    d. all of the above

12. Wildavsky's observations were based on work primarily done in the sector of
    a. manufacturing
    b. information technology
    c. government
    d. retail

13. Piers Blaikie and colleagues proposed two major models on vulnerability to disasters: the pressure and release model and
    a. the access model
    b. the cause-and-effect model
    c. the input model
    d. the organic model

14. In the Blaikie models, the increased availability of resources means that vulnerability is
    a. increased
    b. constantly fluctuating
    c. decreased
    d. static

15. Buckle, Mars, and Smale identified specific subsets of the population who may be at increased risk from disasters. One problem with this approach is that the groups are identified based upon
    a. socio-economic status
    b. assumptions that may be inaccurate
    c. limited samples for research
    d. all of the above

16. When examining vulnerability in populations, one problem with the use of generalization is that
    a. it may not be universally true
    b. vulnerability may vary by circumstance
    c. individuals and groups may be unfairly stigmatized
    d. all of the above

17. Much of the past research on the nature of hazard, risk, and vulnerability has focused on the physical effects of disasters on infrastructure and the built environment. This is problematic because
    a. the political effects are often overlooked
    b. the effects on responders are often overlooked
    c. the effects on people are inadequately addressed
    d. all of the above

18. Contemporary approaches to Hazard Identification and Risk Assessment are research based, and they are essentially exercises in
    a. command and control
    b. ranking
    c. information distribution
    d. public education

19. As a first stage in a HIRA exercise, emergency managers consider the
    a. political climate
    b. overall risk exposure
    c. risk from individual events
    d. available budget

20. When evaluating hazard, risk, vulnerability, and resiliency, emergency managers require a process that is both risk based and
    a. people centred
    b. politically correct
    c. fiscally responsible
    d. complex

CASE STUDIES

A. You are the emergency manager for a medium-sized city (pop. 50,000) in the US Midwest. You have been asked by the mayor and city council to prepare a briefing report on the risks posed to the community by tornadoes.

1. List the basic types of information that should be included in the briefing report.
2. Describe each type of information in as much detail as possible.
3. Identify three potential sources for each type of information.

B. You are the emergency manager for a city of 100,000 people located on the eastern seaboard of North America. The city council has decided to revise the existing emergency management bylaws and regulations. As part of the discussion, the need for specific provisions for residents with disabilities has been raised. You have been asked to prepare a briefing report for city council on the presence of people with disabilities in the community, and their specific needs during a disaster.

1. List the basic types of information that should be included in the briefing report.
2. Describe each type of information in as much detail as possible.
3. Identify three potential sources for each type of information.
4. Prepare a brief statement on the vulnerability of people with disabilities in disasters, for inclusion in the report.

TO LEARN MORE

1. How did emergency management evolve as a formal process in the area where you live? Talk to local practitioners and write down the history of emergency management in your own community.

2. Emergency management can be found in almost every country in the world, although it may be called another name, such as civil defence, civil protection, or emergency planning. Find an emergency-management system in another

country and compare how its operations, priorities, and features differ from those of the system in your country.

NOTES

1. Norm Ferrier, "Demographics and Emergency Management: Knowing Your Stakeholders," *Australian Journal of Emergency Management*, Spring 1999; and Norm Ferrier and Emdad Haque, "Hazards Risk Assessment Methodology for Emergency Managers: A Standardized Framework for Application," *Journal of Natural Hazards* 28, no. 2-3 (2003): 271–90.
2. Piers Blaikie et al., *At Risk: Natural Hazards, People's Vulnerability, and Disasters* (London: Routledge, 1994).
3. Norm Ferrier and Emdad Haque, "Hazards Risk Assessment Methodology for Emergency Managers: A Standardized Framework for Application," *Journal of Natural Hazards* 28, no. 2-3 (2003): 271–90.
4. Aaron Wildavsky, *Searching for Safety* (London: Transaction Books, 1988).
5. Mark Pelling, *The Vulnerability of Cities: Natural Disasters and Social Resilience* (London: Earthscan, 2003), p. 9.
6. Philip Buckle, Graham Mars, and Syd Smale, "New Approaches to Assessing Vulnerability and Resilience," *Australian Journal of Emergency Management* 15, no. 2 (2000): 8–15.
7. Wilbur Zelinsky and Leszek Kosinski, *The Emergency Evacuation of Cities* (Savage, MA: Rowman and Littlefield, 1991), pp. 20–21.

CHAPTER 8

The Risk Assessment Process

LEARNING OBJECTIVES

On completion of this chapter, you will

▶ Understand the methods for identifying risk and the need for the Hazard Identification and Risk Assessment (HIRA) process.

▶ Understand the HIRA models, and how the choice of model can influence the information yielded by the process.

▶ Understand the role of the HIRA process in prioritizing planning, public education, resource acquisition, and mitigation activities.

▶ Be able to complete a basic HIRA process for a community or an organization.

▶ Understand the options available for managing risk.

KEY MESSAGES

1. A clear understanding of risk exposure is central to effective emergency management.

2. Risk is the product of frequency × magnitude.

3. Ranking exercises permit emergency managers to effectively compare risks from very different sources.

4. The ability of the HIRA process to differentiate among risk exposures is governed to some extent by the model used.

5. The HIRA process can be adapted to address the specific needs and concerns of communities and organizations.

6. The HIRA process is an effective tool for setting priorities for planning, public education, resource acquisition, and mitigation activities.

Introduction

To plan an effective response to all types of adverse events, it is essential for emergency managers to possess a clear understanding of the types of risk exposure to which a community or an organization is subject. In the past, emergency managers tended to embrace an all-hazards approach to planning. This approach, while functional, was not without its problems. Modern emergency management is risk based; it focuses on those events that have the greatest likelihood of occurrence and the greatest potential impact, and ensures that, wherever possible, the community or organization is prepared to respond to those events.

This chapter focuses on the methodology of **Hazard Identification and Risk Assessment (HIRA)** for use by communities and organizations in support of their emergency preparedness programs. It also describes HIRA models, the steps in the

HIRA process, sources for the information required in this process, additional models for more comprehensive assessments, and options for managing risk.

Purpose

A clear understanding of risk exposures is central to the process of emergency management for both communities and organizations. Since risk is neither universal nor equally distributed, an understanding of how, where, when, and why risk occurs plays a major role in the preparation of a community or an organization to cope with its effects. The HIRA process permits emergency managers to differentiate between the risks posed by disparate types of events. The process allows emergency managers to rank and prioritize risks so that each can be address appropriately, in order of severity. See figure 8.1 for a general overview of the emergency management process of risk identification and assessment.

Categories of Hazards

Any community or organization faces hazards from a variety of sources. To plan effective preparedness, response, recovery, and mitigation measures, emergency managers are expected to be aware of all types of hazards and risks. Traditionally, there have been three categories of hazards: natural, technological, and human caused (accidental or deliberate). Examples of these hazards are presented in chapter 7. There is, however, another approach to categorizing hazards—one in which hazards are considered according to their general effect in a community or an organization. In this approach, hazards are placed into one of three categories: (1) events that generate a surge in demand for services, (2) events that interrupt supply chains, and (3) events that disrupt normal business operations. Each category generates its own impact on and issues for planning.

Events That Generate a Surge in Demand for Services

These events may be the result of natural events, such as severe weather (for example, heavy snowfall, blizzards, ice storms, violent thunderstorms, lightning strikes, tornadoes, microbursts, and in-line wind), floods, earthquakes, or epidemics. They may also be the result of human-caused events, whether accidental or deliberate, including transportation incidents (for example, large motor vehicle accidents, plane crashes, and train crashes), major fires, hazardous materials releases, or even terrorist events. These lists of examples are by no means exhaustive; emergency managers will need to carefully assess which hazards might occur in their location.

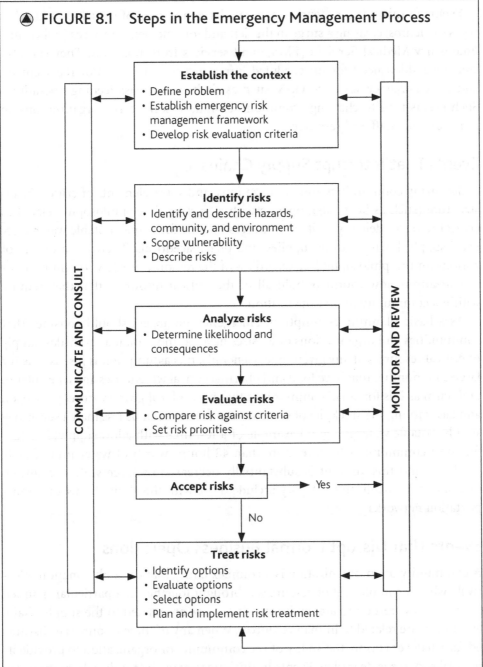

⊛ FIGURE 8.1   Steps in the Emergency Management Process

Source: Alan March and Susan Henry, "A Better Future from Imagining The Worst: Land Use Planning & Training Responses to Natural Disaster," *The Australian Journal of Emergency Management* 22, no. 3 (August 2007): 20.

Events in this category tend to generate large numbers of casualties and other types of victims, creating a **surge** in the demand for emergency services (police, fire, Emergency Medical Services [EMS]) and services from hospitals. They can also create a sudden need for unscheduled infrastructure repair and/or replacement, and for emergency social services, such as shelter and mass-feeding operations. Such events tend to challenge communities and, in some cases, organizations, in terms of both staff and resources.

Events That Interrupt Supply Chains

Today, many communities and organizations, and some elements of critical infra-structure (such as hospitals), operate with a "just-in-time" philosophy related to critical resource delivery. Critical resources include food, fuel, potable water, electrical supply, linen, medical supplies, and pharmaceuticals. There are a variety of reasons for this philosophy, but, regardless of the reasons, very few communities or organizations now routinely hold all of the critical resources that they require within a community or an organization.

As a basic planning assumption, emergency managers should consider that communities and organizations of all sizes have no more than a seven-day supply of critical resources at any given time. Generally, this assumption is just as true for large communities that have food and pharmaceutical warehouses and a petroleum tank farm as it is for small communities that have a local grocery store, pharmacy, and gas station. The stockpile of some resources may even be less than a seven-day supply. Potable water is a good example of a resource with a low supply; it is rare for most communities to have more than 48 hours' worth of water immediately available, and this amount is substantially decreased by large-scale firefighting operations. Events in this category include those with the ability to disrupt trans-portation networks.

Events That Disrupt Normal Business Operations

A community or an organization is a complex entity that can only function effec-tively when a complex set of resources is brought together in a particular manner. Some of these resources are environmental, some are related to the supply chain, and others are related to human resources. When any of these resources is disrupt-ed for whatever reason, the ability of the community or organization to provide its normal services is degraded. Events in this category include utility disruptions (in electricity, water, sewage systems, or heat), communication-system failure, critical infrastructure damage (such as the loss of the only bridge in a community), loss of access to essential equipment or workspaces, or labour disruptions.

HIRA Models

The HIRA process is intended to permit emergency managers to evaluate and quantify risk exposures from all types of hazards. As already discussed, hazards come in a variety of types, and each generates its own particular risk exposures. The HIRA process is an effective tool for understanding hazards and the risks that they generate, and for comparing risk exposures from very different types of events to set priorities for planning and other activities related to an emergency response plan.

Virtually all HIRA models are **ranking exercises.** These ranking exercises are not difficult and involve some simple math; there is really no need for formal probability analysis. There are a variety of models available for assessing hazard and risk. Some are for communities, while others are for organizations. Each has been developed in a specific location or organization, based on local needs. Thus, all models do not meet the needs of all communities or organizations (see figure 8.2).

HIRA models compare different types of hazards and risks. With this in mind, emergency managers should use the model that provides the most useful results. Some HIRA models are simple—using very short ranges of ranking for frequency and magnitude—while others are complex. Although emergency managers might

---

⊛ FIGURE 8.2   The Ontario Ministry of Health and Long-Term Care Risk Assessment Model

Risk assessment is based both on probability (likelihood of occurrence) and consequence (impact on province). The ministry scored the hazards identified above on a scale of 1–4. The scale is shown below:

Probability/Likelihood:

1. Low
2. Moderate
3. High
4. Extreme

> The probability scale was based on the level at which a hazard may occur within the province, and its ability to overwhelm local resources and require provincial coordination from the MOHLTC.

Consequence/Impact:

1. Minor
2. Severe
3. Extensive
4. Catastrophic

> The consequence scale was based on potential casualties and societal disruption as well as the level and nature of provincial involvement, including information sharing, resource coordination, and funding.

Source: Ontario Ministry of Health and Long-Term Care, *Emergency Response Plan*, 2005, <http://hdl.handle.net/1873/620>.

be tempted to choose the simplest model, they should consider how well the results will serve their purposes. To illustrate, if one uses a ranking scale of 1 to 4, there are only 16 possible ranking outcomes. Often, very different types of events with very different risk exposures end up achieving identical **risk scores**. Such a model may not always differentiate among various types of hazards and risks sufficiently. A similar technique, without the numeric values, was developed by the University of Western Australia[1] for use in evaluating risk. Some departments, such as the Health and Safety Executive of the United Kingdom,[2] do not suggest the use of numeric values in evaluating risk at all.

While some HIRA models are better than others at differentiating types of hazards and risks, they may be more complex than is required for the task at hand. For example, the HIRA model used by the Auckland Local Authority Hazard Liaison Group in New Zealand[3] does not assign numeric values to frequency or magnitude, but does assess the frequency of a given event by calculating its return period. This type of model can be somewhat complicated and challenging to use. Clearly, the ideal model sits somewhere in between; differentiating hazard and risk sufficiently, without being too onerous or time consuming.

The HIRA Process

Getting to Know the Community

The first step in the HIRA process is gaining a full understanding of the community (or organization) to be served. A comprehensive gathering of information involves getting to know the community in detail; effective emergency managers understand the community at least as well as any other resident and hopefully more so. This information comes from a variety of sources, some of which are formal (such as historical records or local experts) and some of which are informal (such as personal observation). Both types of information contribute to an overall understanding of the community and its inherent hazards and risk exposures.

Topography

Take a walk or drive around the community. Examine the topography. Are there rivers that might flood? Are there areas that are prone to landslides? If you work in a mining community, has subsidence ever occurred? Are there forests or large wooded areas adjacent to the community? What types of industrial facilities exist in the community? What types of transportation routes? Once potential problem sites have been identified, where are these located in relation to residential areas, schools, hospitals, and other elements of critical infrastructure?

Weather

Gain an understanding of local weather patterns, and when you do so, think of the bigger picture. A few months of good weather does not indicate a local climate that is completely benign. What are the prevailing wind patterns and directions? What are the normal precipitation patterns on a month-by-month basis? Is the community located in an area that historically receives heavy snowfalls, hurricanes, ice storms, or other types of severe weather? Has heavy rainfall presented a problem in the past? Is the community subject to cyclical periods of drought? Does the community experience tornadoes periodically?

History

Search historical records to determine what hazards have affected the community in the past. Has the community ever been subject to earthquakes? Have major transportation or hazardous materials incidents occurred in the past? Have major fires occurred in the past? Have major business failures occurred in the past; if yes, why? This information may be obtained from civic, local-planning, and emergency-service officials; community archives; local newspapers; and local historians. If you are fortunate enough to be in a community with a college or university, prior research on events in the community may exist.

People

Get to know the composition of the community; a community comprises people. The ethnic origin of residents and the languages they speak are of interest. In some circumstances, religious beliefs may also be significant. The socio-economic status of the community may also be important; are there disproportionate numbers of poor or wealthy individuals? The population distribution by age and gender is also significant for purposes of emergency planning; communities with large numbers of elderly people or small children represent different types of risk exposures than those with a more balanced population distribution. Such information is often readily accessible from a variety of sources, including census departments; state or provincial finance departments (who typically use and monitor census data to predict tax revenue); and municipal planning departments, which may use census data for community planning.

Business and Infrastructure

Understand what makes the community "tick." All communities exist to some degree for the purpose of generating wealth for their residents. How is wealth generated in the community? What elements of the community are critical to that wealth-generation process? Which elements of infrastructure are essential to the continued operation of those elements? These, along with the community's normal supply chains, represent critical infrastructure. Has the community experienced plant closures or major economic setbacks at any time in the past? How robust is local wealth generation currently? Talk with those in the community who own assets that are critical for wealth generation, and determine any points of vulnerability that they have identified. Also talk with local civic officials, including those responsible for elements of critical infrastructure (such as bridges or hospitals), and try to determine any areas of vulnerability that they have identified. Once a comprehensive understanding of the community has been achieved, it is time to begin to examine hazard and risk in more detail.

Identifying Hazards

Emergency managers should begin this step by listing all the hazards that they can think of. Include everything; having items on your list that initially seem ridiculous is less important than inadvertently omitting a hazard that later turns out to be significant. The list should be as comprehensive as possible. Ask civic officials, emergency-service officials, and senior civic officials to comment on the list in terms of errors or omissions. No one is perfect, and it is likely that some other person with a long history in the community or special knowledge may identify a risk of which an emergency manager was previously unaware.

Next, emergency managers should vet their list, eliminating those hazards that have little likelihood of occurring. A variety of hazards can be safely eliminated for a number of reasons. The physical location or topography of the area may preclude the occurrence of a particular hazard; for example, "flooding" could be eliminated from a list for a community built on high ground with no substantial body of water nearby. Local weather and climate conditions may eliminate other hazards, such as "heavy snowfall" for a community in the American South. Community activities and infrastructure may eliminate other hazards; "radioactive spills" could be eliminated from a list for a community not located near a major transportation corridor and without any local processes that use radioactive material.

In all cases, emergency managers must ensure that the elimination of any listed hazard is the result of fact, and is not subject to popular misconceptions. To illustrate, Toronto, Ontario, was struck by a major hurricane in 1954 that was considered a "freak" event. In reality, an examination of the local historic records reveals that the city has been affected by two to three hurricanes per century since its existence. The hurricane in question was not an isolated event, but an infrequently occurring event. Thus, for Toronto, it would be inappropriate to eliminate "hurricanes" from the list of hazards.

It may be helpful at this point to categorize the remaining hazards according to type. Emergency managers may choose to use the traditional "natural, technological, human-caused" categorization of hazards, the hazard effects approach, or a combination of the two. Strictly speaking, neither approach is indispensable to the HIRA process. The point of this step is not so much to categorize the lists in a particular way as it is to make the workload manageable.

Creating Hazard Profiles

Until now, emergency managers have undertaken only a general review of the community and the hazards that have affected it in the past. However, to achieve a thorough HIRA, they must create a well-researched profile for each type of hazard on the list that they generated.

A **hazard profile** is a research-based summary of the major characteristics of the hazard in question, the type of impact it may have, and its rate of occurrence locally, regionally, and elsewhere. It describes points of vulnerability within the community in general terms, and the possible effects of the event on the community. Finally, it describes any resources that might be required at the local level to manage such an event, and any public education or mitigation strategies that might prove useful. The information included may come from a variety of trustworthy sources. Any information included in the document should be cited individually to permit emergency managers and others to retrieve that information at a later date, if required.

Each profile should be created as a separate document, and all should be retained indefinitely. Many jurisdictions, such as the State of Maine,[4] use a specific format for the hazard profile. However, the format used is less important than the accuracy of its information and consistency of its presentation. In later risk assessment efforts (such as regular review), a researched and validated hazard profile can save emergency managers a substantial amount of additional research and time; the existing profile can be updated as necessary, rather than recreated from scratch.

More important, hazard profiles help emergency managers and the community demonstrate **due diligence**, if need be, following an emergency. Hazard profiles demonstrate that the HIRA and, by extension, the emergency response plan are based on research and facts, and that the best information available was used to prepare the community for the emergency. They also show that emergency managers and other civic officials took all reasonable measures available in advance of the event. Once emergency managers complete a profile for each hazard on the list, it is time to proceed to the actual HIRA.

Ranking Frequency

The process for evaluating frequency of occurrence of an event is straightforward. Each event is researched to determine the number of times it has occurred in the past in the community or organization under review, as well as regionally, nationally, and elsewhere. It is important to determine how recently the event has occurred; circumstances can change, and an event that occurred with some frequency in the distant past may no longer be as likely to occur because of changes in procedures, land use, or technology. To illustrate, the crash of a train carrying hazardous materials would be unlikely to affect a community that has experienced such an event in the past because the community's train service has been discontinued. Ranking frequency allows emergency managers to better understand the actual probability of each event, given the circumstances that exist today. Each event is assigned a numeric score, based upon the best estimate of probability of occurrence in the current set of circumstances (see figure 8.3). The event is ranked on a scale from one to ten, with ten being the worst outcome.

▲ FIGURE 8.3   Ranking Frequency

Score	Characteristics
1	An event that has occurred somewhere in the world, or at least has some realistic potential for occurrence in your community/organization.
2	An event that has occurred somewhere within your country, at some point in the past, and has at least some potential for occurrence in your community/organization.
3	An event that has occurred somewhere in your country within the past ten years, and has at least some potential for occurrence in your community/organization.
4	An event that has occurred within the past ten years somewhere in your region of your country.
5	An event that has occurred within the past five years somewhere in your region of your country.
6	An event that has occurred within the past year somewhere in your region of your country.
7	An event that has occurred within the past ten years in your community/organization.
8	An event that has occurred within the past five years in your community/organization.
9	An event that has occurred within the past year in your community/organization.
10	An event that occurs with great frequency (weekly or monthly) within your community/organization.

Ranking Magnitude

Next, emergency managers attempt to estimate the magnitude of impact on the community or organization, should the event in question occur. In each case, a worst-case scenario should be used, since it is always more prudent to over-prepare and over-respond, sending unneeded resources away, than to under-prepare and under-respond, having to wait for needed resources to arrive while the incident continues to evolve. As with frequency ranking, events are ranked on a scale from one to ten, with ten being the worst outcome, using the characteristics included in the list in figure 8.4. In many cases, there are multiple characteristics associated with each ranking score; only one characteristic must be present to receive that ranking. When characteristics of the event are found in more than one score level, the highest-ranking score level should be used.

⚠ **FIGURE 8.4   Ranking Magnitude**

Score	Characteristics
1	Results in no injuries. No property damage.
2	Results in some minor injuries. Isolated property damage.
3	Results in widespread minor injuries. No major injuries. Homes or local business areas are damaged, but are not unsuitable for habitation or use.
4	Results in widespread minor injuries, some major injuries. Small number of homes or local business areas in a single neighbourhood are seriously damaged. Interruption of municipal services and/or utilities in a single neighbourhood.
5	Results in widespread major injuries. Large amount of damage to private property in individual neighbourhoods and locales. Localized interruption of municipal services and utilities. Some homes or business areas in individual neighbourhoods are unfit for habitation or use.
6	Results in the loss of a single life. Widespread damage to private property. Major interruption of municipal services and utilities. A large number of homes or business areas are unfit for habitation or use.
7	Results in the loss of less than five lives. Loss of private property. Damage to public infrastructure. Financial loss for the community or organization beyond normal response costs.
8	Results in the loss of five to ten lives. Some loss of private property, public infrastructure. Substantial financial loss for the community or organization. Localized interruption of normal business.
9	Results in the loss of ten or more lives. Loss of large numbers of homes, public infrastructure. Loss of public confidence in the local government. Interruption of normal business across the community or organization. Formal declaration of emergency is required.
10	Results in widespread or large-scale loss of life. Creates financial losses from which the community or organization cannot recover.

Scoring Risk

Once scoring for both frequency and magnitude have been completed for an event, these two scores are multiplied together to arrive at a *total risk score* for that event. When using the suggested model, this risk score will be somewhere in a range from 1 to 100. Once this score has been calculated, it will fall into one of four scoring ranges, as shown in figure 8.5.

FIGURE 8.5   Categories of Risk

100	90	80	70	60	50	40	30	20	10
90	81	72	63	54	45	36	27	18	9
80	72	64	56	48	40	32	24	16	8
70	63	56	49	42	35	28	21	14	7
60	54	48	42	36	30	24	18	12	6
50	45	40	35	30	25	20	15	10	5
40	36	32	28	24	20	16	12	8	4
30	27	24	21	18	15	12	9	6	3
20	18	16	14	12	10	8	6	4	2
10	9	8	7	6	5	4	3	2	1

80–100 score: A regular occurrence with potentially serious and damaging impact. Should be viewed as a top priority. Requires immediate mitigation and planning for emergency response.

50–79 score: Infrequent but serious, or frequent but relatively less serious cumulative impact potential. Should be addressed for mitigation and resource planning from highest to lowest score, as funding and resources are available.

20–49 score: Low impact event, potentially. Assess mitigation and preparedness cost in relation to other priorities.

1–19 score: Infrequent event with minimal or no significant potential effects. The lowest priority for mitigation and planning purposes. Planning activities could be deferred but should not be ignored.

Risk scores place a **quantitative** value on risk from different types of **hazard events.** Events are ranked, based on their total risk score, to assist with setting priorities for planning, public education, acquisition of response resources, and mitigation efforts. An example of this ranking exercise is illustrated in figure 8.6 (the lists are for demonstration purposes and are by no means exhaustive). It is essential to include in this ranking every potential hazard event on an emergency manager's list.

▲ **FIGURE 8.6   Risk Scores: City of Toronto**

Natural Hazards

Event	*Rating*
Flooding	72
Heat waves	63
Extreme cold event	56
Extreme snow event	56
Microbursts	42
Ice storm	35
Tornado	35
Severe storm (non-winter)	32
In-line wind phenomena	32
Epidemic/pandemic	30
Ex-tropical storm (hurricane)	27
Earthquake	21
Drought	8

Technological Hazards

Event	*Rating*
Air pollution	100
Aircraft incidents	80
Railway incidents	70
Hazardous materials (transport)	60
Shipping incidents	60
Hazardous materials (fixed site)	56
Widespread electrical failure	50
Terrorism	49
Mass transit incidents	49
Water quality	15
Radiation (transportation)	12
Radiation (fixed site)	6

Source: Norm Ferrier, *Creating a Safer City: A Comprehensive Risk Assessment for the City of Toronto* (internal document) (Toronto: City of Toronto, 2000).

More Comprehensive Risk Modelling

From time to time, emergency managers may need to undertake more comprehensive risk modelling. This need may arise in communities where it is difficult to gain approval for emergency management activities. It may also arise in businesses, quasi-governmental organizations, or non-governmental organizations (NGOs). Each of these entities may have special requirements or concerns that must be addressed by the HIRA process. To meet these needs, special models can be added to the HIRA process that yield greater information on the location and nature of risk exposures. These models do not replace the HIRA model; they enhance it.

Social Consequence Model

The social consequence model was created by the author and Emdad Haque in 2004 as part of the National Assessment of Natural Hazards in Canada. It is intended to address the role of public perception (as expressed by both the general public and elected officials) in the risk assessment process. Recognition of risk, and the presence or lack of public will to prepare and mitigate, can play a significant role in the relative risk exposure of a given community. The failure to recognize a hazard or prepare for and mitigate against its eventual occurrence can be a key influence on the impact experienced. To illustrate, it has been well documented that the government of France failed to recognize the potential hazard of a heat wave that occurred in Paris during 2003. With no response plan prepared for this type of event and the prolonged recognition time for the hazard, Paris suffered more than 14,700 deaths in a six-week period; nearly five times the impact suffered by nearby jurisdictions affected by the same event.[5]

This model builds on the previously described ten-scale model, adding a ranking score for the **social consequence** factor. The scale for social consequence is reversed, however, so that communities that exhibit low public perception of risk or little political will to prepare for or mitigate against a given event will achieve a higher score (see figure 8.7). First the HIRA process is conducted, then it is followed by a measurement of the perception of risk and hazard by the general public and elected officials. This measurement usually takes the form of a simple, questionnaire-type survey, and is conducted by emergency managers to gauge the hazard and risk perception and "will" to prepare for and mitigate against all of the hazard types under review. As a result, the basic equation for estimating risk is changed to risk × frequency × magnitude × social consequence, and results in a risk score with a maximum of 1,000 instead of the customary 100 used in a conventional HIRA.

> ### ⬕ FIGURE 8.7   Social Consequence Evaluation
>
> | Score | Characteristics |
> |---|---|
> | 10 | Event may be infrequent and community may not approve a high-cost response or prefer a deferment of mitigation and preparedness actions. |
> | 9 | Event may be infrequent and/or damage potential is limited; community prioritizes this at a very low level. |
> | 8 | Very limited damage is expected from the event and response activities should be compared with other social needs. |
> | 7 | Limited social consequences are expected from the event but some forms of response are preferred. |
> | 6 | Some degree of social consequence is expected from the event and mitigation and preparedness actions are needed. |
> | 5 | Community recognizes as low–medium damage potential from the event and prefers gradual mitigation and preparedness-related actions. |
> | 4 | Community recognizes as modest damage potential from the event and prefers a mix of immediate and gradual mitigation and preparedness-related actions. |
> | 3 | Community recognizes the event as potentially damaging and prefers immediate mitigation and preparedness-related actions. |
> | 2 | Community recognizes the event as having potentially serious and damaging consequences. |
> | 1 | Community recognizes the event as having potentially most serious and devastating consequences. |
>
> *Source:* Norm Ferrier and Emdad Haque, "Hazards Risk Assessment Methodology for Emergency Managers: A Standardized Framework for Application," *Journal of Natural Hazards* 28, no. 2-3 (2003): 271–90.

The social consequence model allows emergency managers to estimate the impact of public perception and the will to mitigate against the potential effects of different types of hazards. This information is useful to the emergency management process. For example, let's say that an emergency manager calculates risk scores for both tornadoes and a hazardous materials incident, and determines that their rankings are 50 and 40, respectively. Measurement of the social consequence factor, however, reveals that the general public in the community perceives tornadoes to be a more immediate risk than a hazardous materials event, and are much more likely to support acquisition of resources to deal with a potential tornado than a hazardous materials spill. The community is, as a result, much more likely to be prepared for a tornado than a hazardous materials spill. Consequently, the risk from tornadoes is scored at 100, while the risk from hazardous materials incidents is scored at 320. The risk from a hazardous materials incident scores higher because the community is less likely to have preparedness or mitigation measures in place. This model demonstrates the importance of community preparedness and the role that public perception plays in it. It is also useful in identifying areas in which public education is required.

Organizational Risk Model

The organizational risk model operates in precisely the same manner as the ten-scale model previously described. It is effective in identifying risk for communities and can also provide greater information on risk for organizations and quasi-public organizations, such as schools, airports, and hospitals. While other models identify and quantify risk, this model is useful for the categorization of risks by type, some of which are more applicable to organizations than to communities. Following the process of ranking frequency, each event is then examined in terms of its potential effects on the community, should the event occur. A worst-case scenario is used, since it is always more prudent to over-prepare and over-respond to a given emergency, as mentioned earlier. The five major types of risk exposure (loss of life, degradation of service, loss of physical plant, financial loss, and damage to reputation) should be considered and ranked independently, using the impact ranking scale (see figure 8.8). As can be seen in figure 8.8, each type of risk exposure has a corresponding impact characteristic for the impact score. These are identified as follows:

1—Loss of life

2—Degradation of service

3—Loss of physical plant

4—Financial loss

5—Damage to reputation

Arriving at different scores for each type of risk exposure during this ranking exercise is not only normal, it is expected. To illustrate, a significant fire might rank highly in terms of impact in the "loss of life" category in a hospital, but have a significantly lower rating in the "financial loss" category, because of the hospital's fire-insurance coverage. For this model, individual risk scores for each type of risk exposure may be treated independently, or they may be added together to produce a final score.

▲ **FIGURE 8.8**   Impact Ranking Scale

Score   Characteristics

1   (a) There are no deaths or injuries. (b) Critical services remain uninter-
        rupted. (c) Minor clean-up of affected areas is required. (d) There are no
        financial losses. (e) There is no damage to the community's/organization's
        reputation.

2   (a) There are small numbers of minor injuries, with no lost-time
        incidents. (b) The operating procedures for critical services may require
        adjustment, but will not be interrupted significantly. (c) Extensive
        cleanup of affected areas by staff is required. (d) Financial losses are less
        than $1,000. (e) Staff and public complaints begin to be made.

3   (a) An increased number of minor injuries, with some lost-time incidents.
        (b) Critical services may be disrupted for a day or two, but will continue
        to function. (c) Professional cleanup services are required for affected
        areas. (d) Financial losses are less than $10,000. (e) Staff and public
        complaints begin to escalate.

4   (a) One or more serious injuries occur. (b) Critical services are disrupted
        for a week or more. (c) Replacement of furniture or other daily-use items
        is required in addition to clean up. (d) Financial losses are less than
        $100,000. (e) Staff and public complaints result in grievances and/or
        local news media coverage.

5   (a) Less than ten serious injuries occur. (b) Critical services are disrupted
        for two weeks or more. (c) Minor physical repairs are required, in
        addition to clean up and furniture replacement. (d) Financial losses are
        less than $500,000. (e) The local news media begin to take serious notice
        of the "problems" in the community/organization.

6   (a) Ten to 20 serious injuries occur. (b) Critical services are disrupted for
        a month or more. (c) Major reconstruction of a single area is required,
        or a single piece of critical infrastructure must be replaced. (d) Financial
        losses are less than $1,000,000 and are covered by insurance. (e) Local
        media coverage escalates and/or local elected officials begin to express
        serious concern about the community's/organization's operations.

7   (a) There are no deaths, but a large number of people are seriously
        injured. (b) The ability to provide a critical service will be lost for more
        than three months. (c) The community/organization will require
        reconstruction of a single key service delivery area or a single element of
        critical infrastructure. (d) While recovery of financial losses will occur, it
        may take a year or more to settle lawsuits, insurance claims, etc. (e) Media
        coverage at a national or regional level creates public avoidance in the
        community and difficulty in attracting business lasting more than three
        months.

8   (a) One to four people are killed. (b) The ability to provide a critical
        service will be lost for more than six months. (c) The community/

organization will require reconstruction of multiple key service delivery areas, or multiple elements of critical infrastructure. (d) While recovery of financial losses is possible, it may take a year or more to achieve. (e) Media coverage at a national or regional level creates public avoidance of the community and difficulty in marketing lasting more than six months.

9   (a) Five to ten people are killed. (b) The ability to provide a critical service will be lost for more than one year. (c) The community/organization will require extensive reconstruction to provide services at pre-event levels. (d) The community/organization will sustain financial losses from which it will be difficult to recover. (e) Media coverage at a national or regional level creates public avoidance of the community and difficulty in marketing lasting more than one year. The name of the community/organization is nationally associated with the event.

10   (a) More than ten people are killed. (b) The ability to provide a critical service will be permanently lost. (c) Some critical element of community infrastructure, or an organization's entire physical plant will be destroyed. (d) The community/organization will sustain financial losses on a scale from which it will be impossible to recover. (e) Adverse media coverage at a national or international level results in long-term public avoidance. The name of the community/organization is associated with the event internationally.

Source: Norm Ferrier and L. Hales, *Incident Management System Toolkit* (Toronto: Ontario Hospital Association, 2007).

Graphic Modelling

Emergency managers could also consider using a graphic display of risk assessment findings. As previously discussed, risk distribution is not equal, nor is it universally distributed. Risk exposure may have temporal or spatial components. Different areas of a community may experience different levels of risk exposure from a given hazard, and a graphic display can show affected areas clearly. To illustrate, since the greatest risk of a plane crash occurs during takeoff and landing, residential areas adjacent to the end of an airport runway have a much greater risk exposure to a plane crash hazard than other neighbourhoods. Similarly, a community may have no sites that use hazardous materials, but if two trains that carry hazardous materials pass through it daily, there is a temporal component to risk exposure from a hazardous materials event. The risk is present when the trains are present, and greatly reduced when they are absent.

People typically have varying degrees of difficulty in processing information from large tables of numbers, but this difficulty can be overcome relatively easily by means of graphic display. By performing separate risk assessments for the various elements of a community (political wards, for example), it is entirely possible that the differing exposures identified can be plotted spatially, like a map. Temporal and quantitative elements of risk exposure may also be plotted graphically, using charts and graphs. Prudent emergency managers will acquire the skills necessary to use spreadsheet and database software, such as Microsoft Excel and Access, and mapping software, such as ArcView and MapInfo, or will know where to access these skills within the community.

Managing Risk

Once emergency managers have successfully identified and assessed all of the risks posed by the various hazards affecting a community or an organization, a risk management plan must be developed. There are a variety of options for managing risk, including risk avoidance, mitigation, transference, and acceptance. The effectiveness of each option must be determined, based on the event characteristics, its likely impact, and community or organizational resources. All of these options, and their implications, require careful assessment by the community before a risk management choice is made. Each of these options is discussed briefly below.

Risk Avoidance

With the **risk avoidance** option, a community or an organization makes a decision not to participate in the activity that generates the risk exposure. To illustrate, a community receives a planning application for the construction of a chemical-manufacturing facility, and decides not to permit the construction of that facility within the community. In this manner, the risk of a hazardous materials spill from a chemical-manufacturing facility is avoided.

Risk Mitigation

With the **risk mitigation** option, a community or an organization engages in activities that are directed at preventing the occurrence of the event generating the risk exposure, minimizing the effects of that event should it occur, and making the community or organization more resilient to the effects of the event. This option may take the form of changes to policies and procedures to minimize risk impact or the probability of occurrence. To illustrate, a community may be able to significantly mitigate against flooding through the use of land-use policies that prevent the construction of residential, commercial, and industrial sites, or critical infrastructure on a known flood plain. This option may also lead to the creation of multiple layers of redundancy of equipment and technology used on a daily basis. For example, a community that is replacing fire trucks may elect to hold the replaced equipment in reserve, against the possible risk of loss of the new equipment through some untoward event. As a result, the community retains its ability to provide some level of service, albeit at a reduced level, even in the face of the permanent loss of the new equipment.

Risk Transference

With the **risk transference** option, a community or an organization recognizes the potential risk exposure from an event, and makes arrangements to transfer that risk exposure to another location or entity. Transferring the risk exposure might entail the construction of a completely separate physical space for the storage of large quantities of potentially hazardous materials that is away from the main production facility, or limiting the use of potentially hazardous materials within the main facility to small quantities only. As another example, every community is potentially exposed to the risk of fire. That fire could destroy critical equipment or service-delivery sites and, in some cases, entire buildings. A fire could result in a very large financial liability for a community in terms of the cost to replace equipment and buildings. By purchasing adequate fire-insurance coverage, the community transfers that financial risk exposure, for a fee, to an insurance company.

Risk Acceptance

With the **risk acceptance** option, a community or an organization recognizes the potential risk exposure from an event, concludes that there is no legitimate method of mitigating or transferring that risk exposure, and chooses to live with it. Moreover, the community or organization considers that the activity generating the risk exposure is too important to its welfare to be interrupted. As a result, the community or organization decides to proceed with the high-risk activity because discontinuing it would be damaging in some other way. To illustrate, a community's sole employer is in the business of manufacturing high explosives. All of the approved safe handling and storage measures are in place and being complied with, so that no meaningful opportunities for further mitigation measures exist. Without that production facility, no primary employment would thrive in the community, and secondary businesses, such as shops and restaurants, would fail. As a result, the community, while aware of the potential risk exposure, elects to continue to permit the operation of the high-risk facility, because not doing so would create a greater hardship for the community.

Conclusion

A community's or organization's response to risk must be both generally effective and cost effective. The all-hazards approach to emergency planning has failed to achieve these objectives for several reasons. Modern emergency management is risk based, and relies on the best possible information on the community or organization, its people, and the types of hazard events that it might experience. Hazard Identification and Risk Assessment is the cornerstone of modern emergency management, and an essential skill for any practitioner.

KEY TERMS

due diligence

hazard events

Hazard Identification and
  Risk Assessment (HIRA)

hazard profile

quantitative

ranking exercises

risk acceptance

risk avoidance

risk mitigation

risk scores

risk transference

social consequence

surge

LEARNING CHECK

Take a few minutes now to test your knowledge of Hazard Identification and Risk Assessment. Select the best answer in each case. Any score of less than 16 out of 20 (80 percent) indicates that you should re-read this chapter.

1. The HIRA process provides an effective means of prioritizing planning, and also
   a. public education activities
   b. resource acquisition
   c. mitigation activities
   d. all of the above

2. As a general hazard category, events such as fires, earthquakes, and tornadoes, may be described as
   a. events that generate a surge in demand for services
   b. events that disrupt supply chains
   c. events that disrupt normal business operations
   d. technological hazards

3. As a general hazard category, events such as the destruction of a fuel pipeline or petroleum tank farm may be described as
   a. events that generate a surge in demand for services
   b. events that disrupt supply chains
   c. events that disrupt normal business operations
   d. natural hazards

4. As a general hazard category, events such as labour disruptions or the loss of an element of critical infrastructure may be described as
   a. events that generate surge in demand for services
   b. events that disrupt supply chains
   c. events that disrupt normal business operations
   d. natural hazards

5. The elements essential to understanding a community are topography, weather, history, and
   a. people
   b. infrastructure
   c. business
   d. all of the above

6. Information for the HIRA may be obtained from a variety of sources, including
   a. community archives
   b. local historians
   c. civic officials
   d. all of the above

7. Hazard profiles should be retained by emergency managers
   a. until the next risk assessment
   b. indefinitely
   c. for at least six months
   d. for at least one year

8. The HIRA process must be ongoing, or, at a minimum, regularly reviewed by emergency managers because
   a. it is a legislated requirement
   b. community composition changes
   c. risk exposure changes
   d. both (b) and (c)

9. The creation of the hazard profile assists emergency managers by providing a concise overview of each type of hazard event, and by
   a. enabling demonstration of due diligence
   b. providing background information for the media
   c. providing a comprehensive listing of resources
   d. indicating the precise severity of impact

10. An additional advantage of a properly executed hazard profile is that it can help demonstrate that
    a. the emergency manager is competent
    b. there is community support for the emergency plan
    c. the emergency plan is based on the best information available
    d. compliance with local regulations has occurred

11. One problem with the use of smaller number scales in the HIRA ranking process is that
    a. risk differentiation is poor
    b. they are ineffective
    c. they always yield the same result
    d. both (b) and (c)

12. The organizational risk model may be of special interest in some circumstances because it addresses
    a. the specific risk exposures of businesses
    b. the specific risk exposures of quasi-governmental agencies
    c. the specific risk exposures of non-governmental agencies
    d. all of the above

13. The social consequence model may be useful because it identifies the relationship between
    a. media reporting and risk
    b. preparedness and risk
    c. public perception and risk
    d. pubic perception and preparedness

14. In the social consequence model, risk is expressed as the product of
    a. frequency × magnitude
    b. frequency × public will
    c. magnitude × public will
    d. frequency × magnitude × social consequence

15. In addition to providing insight into community risk exposure, the social consequence model may
    a. identify the need for public education
    b. identify the need for response resources
    c. suggest mitigation measures
    d. provide increased preparedness

16. In the organizational risk model, the specific risk exposures examined include loss of life, loss of physical plant, financial loss and
    a. loss of key personnel
    b. damage to reputation
    c. devaluation of share prices
    d. loss of market share

17. In the organizational risk model, the individual risk scores for each type of risk exposure may be treated independently, or they may be
    a. added together to produce a final score
    b. multiplied by one another
    c. added then divided to produce an average
    d. plotted spatially

18. The graphic plotting of data can help emergency managers understand risk because
    a. trends and patterns can be more easily seen
    b. legislation requires it
    c. temporal data is more visible on a map
    d. spatial data is more visible on a chart or diagram

19. The relative ability of a community or an organization to experience the effects of a hazard event and return to normal or near-normal operations is called
    a. vulnerability
    b. resiliency
    c. preparedness
    d. mitigation

20. The major options for managing risk available to a community or an organization are risk avoidance, mitigation, acceptance, and
    a. transference
    b. forecasting
    c. public education
    d. evaluation

CASE STUDIES

A. Trillium is a medium-sized town (pop. 9,600) located in southern Canada, on the banks of the Central River, and immediately adjacent to a reforestation area of several thousand hectares. The town began as an agricultural support centre, and has since evolved to include a variety of light industries, including a plastic-fabrication plant. The town is located at the juncture of two major highways, and is also served by a main railway line with daily freight service, but no passenger service. A train derailment and fire at the plastics plant resulted in a major fire and the evacuation of the entire town about 30 years ago. Also present in the town is a small, general aviation-type airport, which, over its 50-year history, has experienced several light aircraft crashes.

Throughout its history, the town has experienced cyclical periods of drought, as is the case for most agricultural communities. Winter usually lasts from December to mid-March, and snowfall accumulations of 10 centimetres are common, with truly large snowfalls (30 to 35 centimetres) occurring about every five years. The area is also subject to ice storms, which have typically occurred every two to three years. Every two to three years in the early spring, the Central River is subject to ice dams, which result in the flooding of low-lying areas. The area is subject to two to three small (cat. F-1) tornadoes per year, with one large (cat. F-4) tornado having struck within the past ten years. None of these have actually struck the town itself.

1. Given the history provided, prepare a list of all possible hazards for Trillium.
2. Categorize the causes of these hazards by origin as natural, technological, or human.
3. Using the 1 to 4 scale described in this chapter, identify the frequency ranking for each hazard listed.
4. Using the 1 to 4 scale described in this chapter, identify the magnitude ranking for each hazard listed.
   a. Rank each type of hazard according to its risk score.
   b. Decide which three hazards represent the highest level of risk to the community and determine immediate priorities for preparedness and mitigation.

B. You are the emergency manager for a medium-sized community located on the Eastern Seaboard of the United States. The community has an emergency-response plan and has done substantial work on risk assessment in the past. At one time the primary business of the community was manufacturing. However, over the last 20 years various manufacturers have moved their operations offshore, which has resulted in an economic downturn and significant unemployment for the community. Your federal government has just announced that, in cooperation with a local major railway, it will be performing substantial upgrades to your commercial port facilities. In cooperation with this venture, the railway has announced that it will be creating a new marshalling yard, along with an intermodal freight transfer facility that will be tasked with moving steel shipping containers between railcars and commercial ships. This news is welcome in the community, because the new facilities will create several hundred new jobs. The media are reporting that the new facilities will lead to an economic renaissance in the community. You are tasked with the creation of a revised risk assessment for the community.

1. How are the announced changes in the community likely to affect the hazard profiles that have already been developed? Explain how these changes to risk exposure will occur.
2. What types of potential risk exposure in the community are the new facilities likely to generate? How and why are the new risk exposures likely to occur?
3. How will you go about determining the opportunities for new risk mitigation measures?
4. How will you go about determining the need for new emergency-response resources?
5. How will the community's vulnerability to potential risk exposures be affected by the new facilities? Will the results be positive, negative, or both? Why will the community's vulnerability change?

TO LEARN MORE

1. Visit the emergency management office in a local community and ask to review the work that has been done on Hazard Identification and Risk Assessment. Learn the process that was used to create this information. Does the community's risk assessment appear to be reasonably informative, thorough, and comprehensive? Why? Does the process for Hazard Identification and Risk Assessment used for the community appear to be effective? Why?

2. In a local community, select a single business for review. It may be large or small, but a smaller business will make the project more manageable. Create a detailed profile for that business, answering the following questions: Do business activities generate any type of risk for the community? Of what

type(s)? How, where, when, and why does risk occur? Which risk management strategy does the community appear to be following with respect to that business? Why? Is the business itself vulnerable to specific types of hazard events? How, where, when, and why does vulnerability occur? Does the business have specific strategies for reducing vulnerability? How do these work? Do they appear to be effective? Why?

NOTES

1. "Risk Management Matrix," *University of Western Australia Safety and Health*, 2002, <http://www.safety.uwa.edu.au/forms/risk_management_matrix>.
2. Health and Safety Executive, "Five Steps to Risk Assessment," *United Kingdom, Health and Safety Executive*, 2006, <http://www.hse.gov.uk/pubns/indg163.pdf>.
3. Auckland Local Authority Hazard Liaison Group, "Hazard Identification and Risk Assessment for Local Authorities," *Auckland Regional Council*, 2002, <http://www.arc.govt.nz/shadomx/apps/fms/fmsdownload.cfm?file_uuid =966864A4-027F-A6B2-CB34-C030594A0392&siteName=arc>.
4. Maine Emergency Management Agency, "Hazard Identification and Risk Assessment for Schools," *State of Maine*, 2006, <http://www.maine.gov/mema>.
5. Eric Klinenberg, "The Politics of Heat Waves: Victims of a Hot Climate and a Cold Society," *International Herald Tribune*, August 22, 2003, <http://www.iht.com/articles/107276.html>.

Assessing Vulnerability

Introduction

In an effective emergency management process, understanding the hazards experienced by a community or an organization and the risks that they pose is insufficient. Contemporary emergency managers must have a detailed understanding of the factors that operate, and sometimes combine, to generate risk. The Hazard Identification and Risk Assessment (HIRA) process identifies the "when? how? and how badly?" of disasters; but to be effective, the process must address the "who? what? and why?" of disasters as well. This chapter examines the paired concepts of vulnerability and resiliency. For example, why are some facilities or population groups more vulnerable to the effects of a given event than others? It also discusses critical infrastructure and the role it plays in community or organizational vulnerability, recovery, and resiliency. As well, it describes **root cause analysis**, a tool for understanding the causes of disaster events. Finally, it describes how root cause analysis can contribute to both preparedness and mitigation efforts, making communities and organizations more resilient as a result.

Purpose

Chapter 8 examined HIRA, the process for identifying, evaluating, and ranking hazards, along with its contribution to community or organizational preparedness and mitigation efforts. For their preparedness and mitigation efforts to be effective, emergency managers must possess a detailed understanding of how and why potential hazards, and their resulting risks, occur. Key to this understanding is the ability to effectively gauge the risks posed to elements of the community's critical infrastructure as well as to the people who live in the community.

Determining Vulnerability

Critical Infrastructure

To determine vulnerability, emergency managers must possess a comprehensive understanding of the community's or organization's critical infrastructure, how it operates, and which factors or events might make that infrastructure vulnerable to any type of hazard event. This process involves a "scan" of the community or organization to determine exactly what critical infrastructure is present. The elements that constitute critical infrastructure (see chapter 6) play a major role in determining the community's or organization's relative level of vulnerability.

How Does Vulnerability Differ Among People?

Before the vulnerability of the victims of any disaster or serious event can be assessed, the term *vulnerability* must be defined. Piers Blaikie and colleagues describe vulnerability as "characteristics of a person or group in terms of their capacity to anticipate, cope with, resist, and recover from the impact of a natural hazard."[1] This definition is good, although one could argue that it should not be limited to natural hazards and also include hazards created by technology and humans (accidental or deliberate). Mary P. Anderson and Peter J. Woodrow contrast *vulnerability* with the term *capability*—"the ability to protect one's community, home and family, and to re-establish one's livelihood."[2] Both definitions are useful to a full understanding of vulnerability. Indeed, the notion of capability as an objective is key to vulnerability assessment.

One may logically conclude, to some extent, that the disaster event itself will determine who might be vulnerable. However, just like risk, the distribution of vulnerability is neither equitable nor universal. Vulnerability to one type of disaster event may not automatically result in vulnerability to another. Any attempts to label populations as vulnerable based on assumptions must be challenged. Consider the following example. In Australia, during the early 1990s, a fuel shortage was assumed to pose a greater risk for senior citizens, who were dependent upon transportation. In fact, it was found that those same seniors, who had survived the oil embargo of the Second World War, were actually able to teach coping strategies to their offspring.[3]

In a recent article, Jeff Arnold, an American emergency physician, attempted to identify some of the causative factors that generate increased vulnerability in populations. "The factors tending to generate vulnerabilities to hazardous events include population growth, ageing populations, poverty, maldistribution of populations to disaster-prone areas, urbanization, and marginalization of populations to informal settlements within urban areas, cultural tribalism, and structural vulnerabilities."[4] One might reasonably argue that physical impairment, cognitive impairment, language skills, and non-residency could be added to this list. The list is by no means exhaustive. Even so, this type of list might be based on assumptions that are erroneous. There is nothing, for example, to lead one to conclude that being elderly automatically predisposes one to greater vulnerability to all types of hazard events.

Others, particularly those in the fields of sociology and the social sciences (most notably Philip Buckle, Graham Mars, and Syd Smale[5]), have sought to find some reasonable method of identifying subsets of a population who would be at increased risk from disaster events. However, the attempt to label subsets of a population at increased risk often leads to faulty assumptions and to resistance to such labelling within the populations themselves. While the objectives of such efforts are clearly good (identifying and locating those who might require additional information, education, resources, or protection to increase their resiliency), the identified group may have a negative reaction to the labelling that could close off all possibility of effective communication and information sharing.

When examining the impact of emergencies on people, it becomes quickly evident that the playing field is not level. Emergency managers require a method for identifying groups with specific vulnerabilities, so that the needs of such groups can be effectively planned for and met. By identifying *the specific causes of vulnerability*, those causes may be addressed, reduced, or even eliminated. The result will be a subset of the population with reduced vulnerability and increased resilience, and corresponding effects in the community as a whole. However, the method for identifying groups with specific vulnerabilities must be based on facts rather than assumptions or generalizations. The vulnerability assessment framework in figure 9.1 uses measurable factors that can help emergency managers make judgments about the vulnerability of populations. Just as emergency managers must plan to mitigate against the physical effects of hazard events on the built environment, they must also plan to deal with the "human cost" of disasters, or *social mitigation*.

Root Cause Analysis

In a broader approach to the identification of issues relating to vulnerability, it may be more useful to simply avoid labelling subsets of a population as being at increased risk and instead examine the actual social factors that create and reduce vulnerability. Emergency managers may never be completely successful in mitigating away the effects of recurrent natural phenomena. Therefore, it may be preferable to identify those subsets of a population that are more vulnerable and attempt to mitigate their level of vulnerability. One process that has the potential to achieve this goal is root cause analysis. Root cause analysis, originally called *failure mode analysis*, has been used in the industrial engineering sector since the 1960s, and was modified for use in the health care sector during the 1980s as a tool for investigating medical errors. It continues to be part of both health care risk management[6] and industrial safety processes.

Root cause analysis is a structured, step-by-step technique that focuses on finding the cause of a problem, rather than continuing to deal with its symptoms. It is used to ascertain and analyze the causes of problems so that methods of solving or preventing them can be developed to achieve a permanent solution. Just as one thinks of performing a Hazard Identification and Risk Assessment to be able to mitigate against the effects of physical phenomena, it is reasonable to consider performing a root cause analysis to be able to mitigate against the social causes of vulnerability to a given hazard event.

Root cause analysis is similar to the process used in medicine for diagnosing the disease causing a patient's symptoms. For health care providers, simply alleviating symptoms is regarded as insufficient. One must undertake a thorough examination and rule out the potential causes of the symptoms to establish the actual cause of the disease, which can then be treated (this process is called a *differential diagnosis*). For example, physicians, paramedics, and many first-aiders will have memorized a

▲ FIGURE 9.1   Vulnerability Assessment Framework

Key factors	Less vulnerable 1	2	3	More vulnerable 4	5
A. Factors operating at individual/household level					
A1. Association with hazard prone area	1	2	3	4	5
a. Location of residence					
b. Suitability of residence					
c. Location of livelihood					
A2. Coping capacity					
a. Financial resilience/susceptibility					
b. Knowledge of appropriate protective behaviour					
c. Capability to undertake appropriate protective behaviour					
d. Health					
e. Social network					
B. Factors operating at community/local government level (internal)					
B1. Public safety service provisions	1	2	3	4	5
a. Community planning processes					
b. Mitigation measures					
c. Response/recovery capability					
B2. Social infrastructure resilience					
a. Lifelines					
b. Items of economic significance					
c. Items of environmental and/or cultural significance					
C. Factors operating at community/local government level (external)					
C1. Public safety service provisions	1	2	3	4	5
a. External government planning processes					
b. Mitigation policies					
c. Response/recovery support capability					

Note: This tool identifies key factors which can be easily measured and provide necessary and sufficient information to inform judgments about vulnerability.

Source: Adapted from Ken Durham, Michael Cawood, and Roger Jones, "The Application of Risk Management Principles to Municipal Emergency Management Practice," *Australian Journal of Emergency Management* 11 (Winter 2001).

differential diagnosis for unconsciousness through the initialism AEIOUTIPS, which stands for the causal factors in order of likelihood (alcohol, epilepsy, insulin or other metabolic disorder, overdose, uremia, trauma, infection, psychoses, sepsis). Such a diagnosis is required to provide definitive care as quickly as possible. While one can simply maintain the patient in the found state until arrival at a hospital, it is highly unlikely that the patient's condition will improve significantly until the underlying cause of unconsciousness is determined and addressed.

Similarly, without the use of root cause analysis in emergency management, all other activities (such as mitigating risk) will reflect symptomatic treatment instead of an accurate diagnosis and definitive care. Emergency managers must get to the root of the problem. Until the cause of the problem is diagnosed, true corrective action is difficult to achieve.

The Process of Root Cause Analysis

The process of root cause analysis is based on the **Logic Tree**.[7] This diagrammatic approach is helpful because it presents a logical progression from identifying the issue to identifying its root causes (see figure 9.2). The entire process demonstrates the relationship between cause and effect.

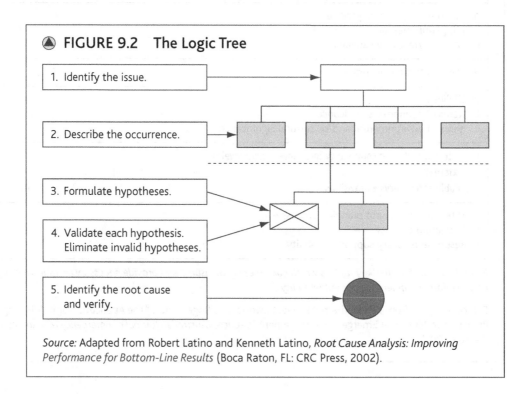

▲ **FIGURE 9.2   The Logic Tree**

1. Identify the issue.

2. Describe the occurrence.

3. Formulate hypotheses.

4. Validate each hypothesis. Eliminate invalid hypotheses.

5. Identify the root cause and verify.

Source: Adapted from Robert Latino and Kenneth Latino, *Root Cause Analysis: Improving Performance for Bottom-Line Results* (Boca Raton, FL: CRC Press, 2002).

Identify the Issue

Root cause analysis begins with a single fact. It must be stated emphatically that the process *must begin with a fact* rather than conjecture or assumption. To illustrate, let's say an emergency manager is assessing the vulnerability of a particular neighbourhood in a small town that has been flooded. It might be tempting to immediately identify the ice dam at the mouth of the river beside the town as the issue. This conclusion is an assumption, and is incorrect in the process of root cause analysis. To quote Robert and Kenneth Latino, "there is a propensity to act on assumptions as if they were facts. This assumption and subsequent action can lead an analysis in a completely wrong direction. The analysis must begin with facts that are verified; conventional wisdom, ignorance, and opinion should not be accepted as fact."[8] In this case, the real issue is the fact that the neighbourhood is flooded, and while the ice dam may or may not be a contributing cause, it would be premature to identify the ice dam as the root cause. It might be tempting to assume that the nature of a problem is understood at the outset, but the pursuit of assumptions might easily lead emergency managers on a false tangent.

Describe the Occurrence

In the second stage of this process, the facts surrounding the event are identified in as concise a manner as possible. Again, it must be stressed that only facts and not assumptions must be used. To continue with the analogy of the flooded neighbourhood, it is necessary at this stage to identify the possible factual causes for the flooding of the neighbourhood. One might conclude that the relevant facts are that it has been raining heavily, there is an ice dam at the mouth of the river, and the neighbourhood is situated on a flood plain beside the river. All of these causes are factual, and one or more may contribute to identification of the root cause of the flooded neighbourhood. Other identified causes might be contributing causes, but they are not the root cause.

Formulate Hypotheses

In the third stage of this process, each of the identified causes is examined, and one or more hypotheses is formulated as to the root cause. Once the hypotheses have been made, it is necessary to perform objective research to either validate or invalidate each hypothesis. In the case of the flooded neighbourhood, one might begin with the hypothesis of the heavy rainfall. On the one hand, if it can be demonstrated that the neighbourhood floods after each heavy rainfall, the information could potentially support a direct correlation between the heavy rainfall and the flooding, and help establish the rainfall as a root cause of the flooding. It should be stated that the heavy rainfall is not necessarily the only root cause, and therefore the process of examination and validation of each hypothesis must be continued. On the other hand, if it can be demonstrated that there have been many occurrences of heavy rainfall in the past that did not result in the flooding of the neighbourhood, then the heavy-rainfall hypothesis must be either discarded or relegated to the status of a contributing cause.

The second potential hypothesis involves the ice dam at the mouth of the river. If research reveals that the flooding only occurs when the ice dam is present, then there may be a direct correlation between the ice dam and the flooding, and it might be considered as a candidate for the root cause. However, if research leads one to discover that the river floods the neighbourhood at other times in the year when no ice dam is present, then there is no direct correlation, and this hypothesis must also be discarded.

A single hypothesis is left for examination: the flood plain. This is not necessarily the root cause; one may conceivably find that after examination it too fails to be a valid cause, and the entire process must begin again. However, the fact that the neighbourhood is constructed on the flood plain may have some validity. In conducting this research, it has already been established that this particular neighbourhood is constructed on the flood plain and experiences flooding, while other neighbourhoods in the same town are built on higher ground and do not experience flooding with any historical regularity. Moreover, research also reveals that other communities built on flood plains are subject to periodic flooding as well. In this case, the hypothesis is valid. It is not yet, however, a root cause.

Identify the Root Cause and Verify

The final stage in this process is called **discoverability**. The discoverability process consists of subjecting the hypothesis to the questions how? and why? and repeating this process for as long as is necessary to arrive at a satisfactory root cause. "We can generally answer the series of 'why' questions about five times before we do not know the actual answer. This is discoverability—[at each stage] questions only lead to more questions. On the logic tree, discoverability is expressed from level to level when we ask 'how can something occur?' The answer only leads to another 'how can' question."[9] In each stage, the answer to this question must be supported by the appropriate research.

Once again, assumption is not a valid method of analysis. To illustrate, if one were to ask the question, "Why is this neighbourhood built on a flood plain?" the required research may yield one or more results. One might conclude that there is some historical basis for remaining in that location; perhaps the original reason for the establishment of the neighbourhood was to access water power for the purpose of milling, or some other industry. If the industry still exists and still requires water power (as may be the case in some developing countries), then one may be led to conclude that the residents have chosen to accept the risk of flooding, considering it to be less important than the economic assets that proximity to employment provides.

Past research in the field of social sciences tends to support this theory. "The urban poor use their location as a base around which to organise livelihood activities ... . If the structure of land ownership and rent means that the closest they can get to economic opportunities is a hillside slum, people will locate there, regardless of the landslide risk."[10] Similarly, if one discovers through research (using real estate price indices, for example) that the neighbourhood in question has very low property values due to flooding, and that the residents have substantially lower incomes than other neighbourhoods in the same town, one might be led to conclude that the root cause for the suffering of this particular group of residents is a lack of economic assets that precludes them from finding safer housing.

The root cause of this particular example of vulnerability has been established, in a direct chain of cause and effect. This deterministic approach to vulnerability is based on human behaviour: "People are determinable within a broader range than equipment, because of the variability of the human race. If we subject humans to a specific stimuli, they will react within a certain range of behaviours."[11]

The Rules of Root Cause Analysis

Root cause analysis embraces five basic rules, generally referred to as the *rules of causation* (see figure 9.3).

⬆ FIGURE 9.3   Rules of Causation

Rule 1: Causal statements must clearly show the "cause and effect" relationship.

Rule 2: Negative descriptors (e.g., poor, inadequate) are not used in causal statements.

Rule 3: Each human error MUST have a preceding cause.

Rule 4: Each procedural deviation MUST have a preceding cause.

Rule 5: Failure to act is only causal when there was a pre-existing duty to act.

Source: National Center for Patient Safety, US Department of Veteran Affairs, "Using the Five Rules of Causation" (emphasis added), <http://www.va.gov/ncps/CogAids/Triage/index.html>.

Demonstrate a "Cause and Effect" Relationship

When describing why an event has taken place, it is necessary to establish a clear relationship between the root cause and the outcome. To illustrate, when describing a heat emergency, a statement such as "private residences lacked suitable air conditioning" is inadequate because it doesn't indicate how and why the event happened. Cause and effect, which is truly the test of validity, must be demonstrated. Cause and effect statements can be simple, but they MUST be definitive. If one can read the statement and come up with another who? why? or how? question, then root cause has not been successfully described. If such statements cannot demonstrate a direct connection between the causal factor and the outcome, they do NOT demonstrate root cause.

Avoid Negative Descriptors

Negative descriptors (such as negative words or judgments) are often used as "short cuts" in describing inadequacies in processes. The issue with negative descriptors is twofold. First, they do not adequately describe the findings of the research. Second, with human nature as it is, those responsible are far more likely to be receptive to and amenable to fixing a problem when the problem does not commence with an assignment of blame. There is a vast difference between saying "government agencies failed to act in an appropriate fashion" and saying "in the absence of mitigation, long-standing social conditions (isolation) persisted. This situation made the victims particularly vulnerable to this emergency, and resulted in most of the loss of life that occurred." The first statement would immediately put the government agencies on the defensive, while the second identifies a root cause that might potentially be repaired, as well as a benchmark for judging the government's performance on the issue.

Identify the Cause of Human Error

Any process that involves humans involves errors. One cannot simply attribute a problem to human error; the underlying cause for the human error must be identified (the same is true for each human error identified in the causal chain). Human errors can be process related (such as using instructions with a missing step on how to transfer chemicals from a railway wagon to a truck). Or, human errors can be behaviour based (such as choosing to work from memory, even though an appropriate checklist is readily available). It does little good to attribute a problem only to human error, when the intent is to identify and repair the underlying cause of an incident. Although it is difficult to mitigate human error, faulty processes and risky behaviours that lead to human error can be fixed.

Identify the Cause of Procedural Deviation

The best procedures only work when they are followed. Like human error, procedural deviation always has an underlying cause. To illustrate, a city might operate a series of emergency cooling centres for dealing with extreme heat emergencies. The guidelines for setting up and opening a cooling centre may be adequately described in a written procedure. However, if past practice has left the arrangements for cooling centres up to the discretion of the local manager, and the guidelines have been allowed to be violated, then the application of the guidelines is the root cause rather than the decisions made by the local manager.

Interestingly, in Canada, the court recognizes a distinction between operational and policy decisions in relation to local authorities. Municipalities can be held accountable for operational decisions, but they are immune for the most part from civil action with regard to policy decisions. This distinction stems from the notion that all levels of government are representatives of the Crown, so that suing them would be the equivalent of suing the Crown. However, there is a trend in which the distinction is regarded as a "legal fiction," where the courts will decide whether something represents a policy or operational decision, based on the decision that the court wishes to render.[12]

Examine "Failure to Act" as a Root Cause

While various people and agencies might be seen as having a moral duty to act in an emergency, unless there is a statutory or procedural duty for them to do so, failure to act may not be established as a root cause. To illustrate, in the United Kingdom local authorities have no statutory duty to warn the residents of their community about an impending flood. Failure to provide such a warning would not be considered an acceptable root cause for the community's vulnerability to such a flood.

Root Cause Analysis Applications in Emergency Management

Root cause analysis can provide emergency managers with special insight into the vulnerabilities within a community. This new insight will be based upon hard fact and the actual experiences of other communities, instead of assumptions and generalizations. Vulnerability in the local community may operate differently from that in the subject community, and, armed with a logic-based tool, emergency managers should be able to identify and understand these differences.

Root cause analysis is equally applicable to an examination of the vulnerabilities of critical infrastructure elements as well as areas of social vulnerability. When assessing the vulnerabilities of critical infrastructure, emergency managers examine similar infrastructure failures that have occurred elsewhere. When assessing social vulnerability, emergency managers study the event itself and identify the social effects and vulnerabilities, along with their causes. The process is sufficiently adept at identifying information that it is likely that any attempt to identify root causes for one element of vulnerability will identify issues arising from the other as a part of the same process.

It is hoped that the root cause analysis will be incorporated into emergency managers' quests to understand hazard, risk, vulnerability, and resiliency. If the process is applied consistently to all hazard events, it may lead the planning process in new directions. The key to fixing a problem is complete understanding. As a result, emergency managers who are able to examine the events in other communities effectively may be able to identify additional opportunities for preparedness and mitigation, particularly in relation to the social costs of emergencies.

Conclusion

Every community requires an effective emergency plan. To be effective, that plan should have a sufficiently generic (all-hazards) approach so that it is flexible enough to respond to various types of events. The plan should also realistically evaluate the risks to which the community is exposed from all sources to ensure that the community's response resources are acquired in a responsible and cost-effective manner. In many communities, emergency plans already meet these standards, and the trend is growing.

More important, an effective emergency plan should address the composition of the community; the distribution of population and assets; how and why social, economic, and political assets are generated; and how these factors affect the vulnerability of the community and those who live and work in it. The plan should also identify how and when that vulnerability operates in each case. "The most important root causes that give rise to vulnerability (and that reproduce vulnerability over time) are economic, demographic, and political processes. These affect the allocation of resources between different groups of people."[13] Until now, emergency management has focused on the concepts of hazard identification and risk assessment. Like any other dynamic process, the emergency management process must continue to move forward.

In assessing the potential impacts of disaster on a community, just like a journalist, an emergency manager requires answers to six key questions: who? what? where? when? why? and how? Who might be affected? What effect might occur? Where is the event likely to occur? When is the event likely to occur, and if there is a return cycle, how often? Why is the event likely to occur, and why would it affect particular groups? How might the people, the landscape, and the infrastructure be affected, and how can one respond when the vulnerability of each is challenged? Hazard Identification and Risk Assessment does address what, where, and when questions. However, it fails to adequately address why? and how? and often fails to fully address who? It largely overlooks the fact that people live in the community in question. This situation must be corrected.

It may be appropriate to characterize the emergency management process as a two-pronged response to the potential effects of a disaster in a community. The two prongs are (1) the study and mitigation of the physical effects of a disaster, and (2) the study and mitigation of the social consequences of a disaster. If one accepts this characterization, it becomes clear that for a great many years much emphasis has been placed on and energy expended on the study and mitigation of physical effects, while there has been only limited interest in social consequences. More attention must be given to social consequences if a balanced approach is ever to be achieved.

Understanding risk by itself is insufficient; emergency managers must also understand the true nature of vulnerability, toward which root cause analysis may prove useful. In many cases, it is clear that the mitigation of the root cause of vulnerability may be a more effective response to the potential for calamity than attempts to mitigate the effects of the event after the fact. Just as cost-efficiency justifies risk mitigation, it could be argued that it is less expensive for a community to identify potential vulnerabilities and, where possible, eliminate them before they begin to operate and generate additional response costs. However, without an intimate understanding of the community, a pre-emptive emergency response plan may never become truly attainable.

Until emergency managers begin to embrace this concept of risk- and vulnerability-based planning and actively mitigate the social issues that promote vulnerability in subsets of a population, current efforts to foster a proactive type of emergency management may fail. This profession was created to serve the community, and communities are not limited to landscape and infrastructure; the presence and activities of people are central to the whole concept of community. Emergency management should be about the needs of the population, and not solely about the phenomena that create disasters.

Clearly, mitigation is the most cost-effective response to any type of disaster, and the preferred approach, where possible. While identifying and reducing the level of a given risk is clearly mitigation, it can also be argued that reducing the overall vulnerability of a community or population, and thereby increasing its resiliency, is also a highly effective form of mitigation. An emergency plan is not a project, but, rather, a process; thus the development of such plans must be process based and forward looking. It may very well be that with further research and validation, root cause analysis, a tool borrowed from the industrial engineering and health care fields, will become integral to vulnerability assessment and instrumental in changing how the profession views the community.

KEY TERMS

discoverability

Logic Tree

root cause analysis

LEARNING CHECK

Take a few minutes now to test your knowledge of vulnerability assessment, critical infrastructure, and root cause analysis. Select the best answer in each case. Any score of less than 16 out of 20 (80 percent) indicates that you should re-read this chapter.

1. For emergency managers, the study of hazards and risks is incomplete without a comprehensive understanding of how and why _____ occurs.
   a. communications
   b. vulnerability
   c. continuity of governance
   d. all of the above

2. For emergency managers, vulnerability is a concept that must be continuously paired with the concept of
   a. hazard
   b. risk
   c. resiliency
   d. command and control

3. A better understanding of the vulnerabilities experienced by subsets of a community's population has the potential to lead to an increase in
   a. community resiliency
   b. emergency management funding
   c. legal liability
   d. community welfare programs

4. The analysis of the vulnerabilities of subsets of a population may help emergency managers identify additional opportunities for
   a. community dialogue
   b. funding
   c. community education
   d. mitigation

5. Central to an emergency manager's understanding of the community's vulnerabilities to hazard events is _____ they occur within the community.
   a. how
   b. where
   c. why
   d. both (a) and (c)

6. In smaller communities, in contrast to larger communities, a factor that constitutes critical infrastructure is
   a. airports
   b. major local employers
   c. sewage systems
   d. all of the above

7. The loss of which of the following directly affects a small community's vulnerability?
   a. major transportation corridors
   b. agricultural areas
   c. parkland
   d. both (b) and (c)

8. The fewer of any given infrastructure element (for example, gas stations) found in a community, the more likely they are to be
   a. unnecessary
   b. critical
   c. privately held
   d. publicly held

9. Critical infrastructure includes those elements of the community without which community survival would be unlikely, and also
    a. theatres, convenience stores, and video outlets
    b. elements without which emergency response would degrade
    c. parks and playgrounds
    d. nursing homes

10. Which of the following items would be considered to be critical infrastructure?
    a. hospitals
    b. emergency services facilities
    c. the town hall
    d. all of the above

11. Which of the following items would be considered to be critical infrastructure?
    a. fire trucks
    b. the telephone system
    c. the local public swimming pool
    d. both (a) and (b)

12. The process of root cause analysis has its origins in the _____ sector.
    a. industrial engineering
    b. health care
    c. information technology
    d. retail

13. The root cause analysis process was originally called
    a. industrial failure analysis
    b. failure mode analysis
    c. differential diagnosis
    d. transactional analysis

14. Central to the process of root cause analysis is the use of the
    a. problem solving chart
    b. hazard/risk matrix
    c. Logic Tree
    d. organizational chart

15. In root cause analysis, any hypothesis presented for examination as a potential root cause must be based on
    a. opinions from the operator
    b. facts only
    c. reasonable speculation
    d. conventional wisdom

16. The _____ process subjects a hypothesis to questions to arrive at a satisfactory root cause for an event.
    a. green-lighting
    b. conjecture
    c. discoverability
    d. elimination

17. To identify a root cause, each hypothesis is subjected to a series of _____ questions, until no logical follow-up question of the same type is possible.
    a. how?
    b. why?
    c. where?
    d. both (a) and (b)

18. Instead of being root causes, candidate hypotheses may also be identified as
    a. mitigating factors
    b. contributing causes
    c. indications of responsibility
    d. uncontrollable variables

19. The discovery of a root cause should not automatically end the process for an emergency manager, because
    a. finding more than one root cause is possible
    b. the process requires finding at least two root causes
    c. finding contributing causes may add to understanding
    d. both (a) and (c)

20. Root cause analysis may be useful to emergency managers for the identification of areas of social vulnerability and
    a. shortfalls in the emergency response process
    b. reasons for critical infrastructure failure
    c. failure of governance
    d. required legislation

CASE STUDIES

A. During July and August of 2003, a major heat wave occurred throughout western Europe, but no one location was more profoundly affected than Paris, whose residents experienced more than 14,700 deaths during this period. While other locations experienced the same effects, the resulting number of deaths they experienced was substantially lower.

   1. Perform a literature search on this event, focusing primarily on Paris. Gather as much information as you can from all available sources—in print and on the Internet.
   2. Identify the group(s) of people primarily affected by this event.
   3. Identify any potentially causal factors that might have contributed to the resulting emergency.
   4. Identify similar events that may have occurred elsewhere, or at other times. Are any similar causal factors immediately evident?

B. Using the information gathered in Case Study A, continue the process of root cause analysis to identify the actual causes of this event.

   1. Prepare a Logic Tree for the event.
   2. Identify the potential root causes and list them in the Logic Tree.
   3. Subject each potential root cause to the discoverability process to determine which of these were actual root causes and which were contributing causes.
   4. Examine your own community and determine whether any of the root causes identified operate in your own community, and which group(s) are likely to be affected in a similar scenario.

TO LEARN MORE

   1. Select for study a disaster event that has occurred within the past three years. Gather as much information as you can about that event. This information may be drawn from after action reports, scholarly papers in journals, or media reports. Following the process described in this chapter, perform a root cause analysis based on the Logic Tree to determine the actual root cause(s) of the disaster event. What measures might be taken to reduce the incidence of each particular root cause? How would these measures affect vulnerability? What are the obstacles to the implementation of these measures? How would you attempt to overcome them?

2. Select a high-ranking (frequency and magnitude) hazard event in your local community. Determine which risk management strategy the community is currently using to address the risk exposure. Does that strategy appear to be effective? Why? How is local vulnerability affected by the risk management strategy in use? Why? Are there other potential strategies that might better reduce community vulnerability? What are they? What are the obstacles to their implementation?

NOTES

1. Piers Blaikie et al., *At Risk: Natural Hazards, People's Vulnerability, and Disasters* (London: Routledge, 1994).
2. Mary B. Anderson and Peter J. Woodrow, *Rising from the Ashes: Development Strategies in Times of Disaster* (Boulder, CO: Westview, 1989).
3. Philip Buckle, Graham Mars, and Syd Smale, "New Approaches to Assessing Vulnerability and Resilience," *Australian Journal of Emergency Management* 15, no. 2 (2000): 8–15.
4. Jeffrey L. Arnold, "Disaster Medicine in the 21st Century: Future Hazards, Vulnerability, and Risk," *Prehospital and Disaster Medicine* 17, no. 1 (January–March 2002).
5. Philip Buckle, Graham Mars, and Syd Smale, "New Approaches to Assessing Vulnerability and Resilience," *Australian Journal of Emergency Management* 15, no. 2 (2000): 8–15.
6. Hirsch, K., Wallace, D. and Osborne, D. *The Theory, Philosophy and Justification for Root Cause in Health Care Risk Management*, <http://www.sentinel-event.com/theory.php>.
7. Robert Latino and Kenneth Latino, *Root Cause Analysis: Improving Performance for Bottom-Line Results* (Boca Raton, FL: CRC Press, 2002).
8. Ibid., p. 97.
9. Ibid., p. 107.
10. Jorge E. Hardoy, and David Satterthwaite, *Squatter Citizen: Life in the Urban Third World* (London: Earthscan, 1989).
11. Supra note 7, at p. 107.
12. Andrew Roman, Municipal Liability, speech to the Canadian Institute, February 22, 2002.
13. Supra note 1, at p. 24.

CHAPTER 10

Fostering Resiliency

LEARNING OBJECTIVES

On completion of this chapter, you will

▶ Understand the relationship between vulnerability and resiliency.

▶ Understand the principles used to foster resiliency in both communities and organizations.

▶ Understand the reasons why fostering resiliency takes primacy over emergency response plans in the emergency management process.

▶ Understand the strategies that can be used to foster resiliency in communities or organizations.

KEY MESSAGES

1. Vulnerability and resiliency are paired concepts. There is a direct inverse relationship between the two concepts.

2. Communities or organizations that have resiliency measures in place are less susceptible to the effects of any hazard event than those communities or organizations that do not.

3. Resilient communities or organizations may suffer less from the effects of a given hazard event, and typically recover more quickly.

4. Resilient communities may experience lower response and recovery costs from a given hazard event.

5. Fostering resiliency should be emergency managers' first line of defence against any type of hazard event.

6. A variety of strategies can be successful in enhancing community/organizational resiliency.

Introduction

Fostering resiliency should play a key role in any emergency management process. All communities and organizations experience some level of vulnerability to the effects of various types of hazard events. While the degree of that vulnerability may vary by community or organization, and by event, there is almost always the opportunity to address at least some of those areas of vulnerability in advance of the occurrence of the event in question. There is a direct and inverse relationship between the concepts of vulnerability and resiliency; communities that have greater resiliency have less vulnerability, and vice versa. When a hazard event occurs, communities or organizations that have a high degree of pre-existing resiliency will typically recover more quickly from the event and experience lower response costs than those that do not.

This chapter focuses on the strategies that can be used by emergency managers to create and foster a more resilient community or organization. Aaron Wildavsky's six fundamental principles for fostering resiliency in communities and organizations are explored in detail, along with their application to the emergency management process. Also, the process for identifying opportunities for increasing resiliency in communities and organizations is examined. Finally, setting priorities for resiliency measures and obtaining support and approval for them are discussed.

Purpose

In chapter 9, the nature of vulnerability and the means of identifying its presence in terms of both critical infrastructure and human costs were examined. As a general principle in emergency management, a practitioner identifies and evaluates risks and vulnerabilities, repairs (mitigates) vulnerabilities where possible, and plans for those hazard events and vulnerabilities where repair is not possible. This chapter focuses on the principles and practices used to effectively mitigate vulnerabilities identified within communities or organizations.

Vulnerability, Resiliency, and Human Behaviour

Emergency managers understand that the primary reason for the existence of any given community is human need. An appreciation of human behaviour will help emergency managers understand how to create and foster resiliency. The human-need factor is real whether the community is a village, town, or city, or whether the community is an organization (after all, organizations can be viewed as specialized communities). People place priorities upon their various needs, and these needs are well understood. Early social theorists such as renowned psychologist Abraham Maslow[1] described a clear hierarchy of human needs, and recognized that until basic needs are met, neither individuals nor groups are likely to address those needs that are further up the hierarchy. In Maslow's hierarchy of needs, physiological needs (food, water, shelter, clothing) will always take precedence over safety needs (see figure 10.1).

It is therefore reasonable to state that the first priority for the creation of any community is to provide its residents with access to assets; in other words, the

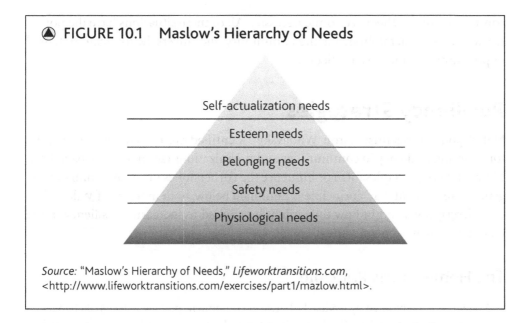

⬤ **FIGURE 10.1   Maslow's Hierarchy of Needs**

Self-actualization needs

Esteem needs

Belonging needs

Safety needs

Physiological needs

Source: "Maslow's Hierarchy of Needs," *Lifeworktransitions.com,*
<http://www.lifeworktransitions.com/exercises/part1/mazlow.html>.

ability to generate wealth. In the work of Piers Blaikie and colleagues,[2] a clear relationship is described between access to assets (wealth), vulnerability, and resiliency. Blaikie and colleagues' risk modelling (see chapter 7) indicates that a lack of assets is a root cause of social vulnerability and that the acquisition of assets is a path to increased resiliency to the effects of virtually any given hazard event. This can be seen in contemporary emergency management, when the usage of emergency shelters in communities is examined. In almost all cases, the people who require longer term use of emergency shelters during an emergency are those with the least assets.[3] In all cases, the presence or the absence of assets influences the community's relative resiliency to the effects of a hazard event. Indeed, sometimes the presence of a given type of risk within a community is created by the community's efforts to generate assets or wealth.

Communities also exist to share and manage risk. This has always been true, from the time humans first banded together to provide greater safety in numbers. A community forms not only to exploit economic opportunities, but also to help guarantee increased safety for its residents; it is, to some extent, a risk management device. It is when asset-generating activities, either by plan or by circumstance, go awry that vulnerabilities are created. Such situations may involve community placement to exploit a particular resource, such as water power; they may be economic, such as the reliance on a single major local employer; or they may involve risk acceptance, such as permitting a high-risk manufacturing facility to operate in the community out of sheer economic necessity. All of these situations have the potential to create vulnerabilities for the community and, inversely, to create potential opportunities to increase resiliency.

Resiliency Strategies

Noted political scientist Aaron Wildavsky[4] identified six fundamental principles for fostering resiliency in communities and organizations (see figure 7.3, page 109). Many of these principles form or influence the cornerstones of contemporary emergency management. Each principle is examined below, both in terms of Wildavsky's own descriptions and in how they might be applied to increasing resiliency in the emergency management context.

The Homeostasis Principle

> Systems are maintained by feedbacks between component parts which signal changes and can enable learning. Resilience is enhanced when feedbacks are transmitted effectively.[5]

The field of emergency management has historically tended to gather and transmit knowledge from each hazard event or emergency exercise in terms of "lessons learned." These lessons learned constituted feedback in the truest sense, and were intended to foster change in procedures and enhance individual learning. The key to Wildavsky's principle is "when feedbacks are transmitted effectively." Sadly, too often, lessons learned may be a misnomer. Lessons are frequently identified following events and exercises, but may not be acted on. This failure may be the result of organizational politics, resistance to change, or budgetary constraints, and far too often, after the problem has occurred once, the mantra "it can't happen here!" becomes "it can't happen again!" In any case, the follow-up action needed to close the feedback loop does not necessarily occur.

To illustrate, if one were to conduct a retrospective study of all the after action reports that followed emergency events or exercises, the results might be more predictable than imagined. Typically, the lessons learned included recurring phrases such as "inter-agency information exchange was inadequate," "emergency services radio systems should be interoperable," "inadequate control of the event perimeter was a problem," and "services must learn to work more closely together." An emergency management professional once advised me that she had performed a retrospective study in her own community, going back 50 years, and in the 50-year period the so-called lessons learned had not changed at all! If the same lessons learned keep arising several times a year after major incidents or emergency exercises without change, one must question whether there are really any lessons being learned at all.

This reality, while clearly a vulnerability in the community response system, also provides an opportunity for emergency managers to create and foster resiliency. In the past, too often such after action reports were completed simply because they were required; the belief was that it was unlikely that anyone would ever actually read or act on them. An emergency manager who could create a process for the systematic identification and resolution of all of the problems identified could help break this cycle. Doing so would not be easy ... there are vested interests and entrenched viewpoints to overcome, but with sufficient political authority (for example, from the mayor or city solicitor) on the emergency manager's side, inter-agency debriefing following events and exercises could become regular and systematic. Using project-management skills, the emergency manager could then ensure that the issues identified are finally resolved. The community would become more resilient because the problems that have been identified for years would at last be addressed.

The Omnivory Principle

> External shocks are mitigated by diversifying resource requirements and their means of delivery. Failures to source or distribute a resource can then be compensated for by alternatives.

In the emergency management context, this principle can be seen as addressing the community's or organization's potential vulnerabilities in the **supply chain** by not relying on a single source for any critical item. The availability of any critical item from more than one source helps ensure that even if the normal source of supply for the critical item is inaccessible due to the operation of the hazard event, it is ready for use from another source. Having multiple sources for a critical item reduces the vulnerability of the supply chain, thereby increasing resiliency.

Within either a community or an organization, the health of the supply chain can be a critical matter, and the supply chain itself may be viewed as critical infrastructure. This principle appears in the practice of emergency management in terms of the emphasis on multiple layers of **redundancy** for each critical system or resource. As such, it should be a fundamental part of an emergency manager's planning process, and one of the first areas in which opportunities for increased resiliency are sought.

To illustrate, a community or an organization normally relies on a single source for its electrical supply. Taking action to ensure that the community or organization is connected to more than one power grid increases community resiliency to an electrical failure on one grid, by having immediate access to another grid. When power delivery fails from one source, it can resume from another. This engineering solution is currently employed in many hospitals, which are frequently connected to more than one electrical source, water supply, sewer line, and telephone exchange.

As another example, this time in an industrial setting, a manufacturer may have a contract with one trucking company to deliver raw materials to its production facility. The same manufacturer may also have a formal contingency arrangement with another trucking company that comes into effect only in the event of failure of the first. In this manner, the flow of raw materials is uninterrupted, and the manufacturer's production process remains unaffected. Even if a crisis of some sort befalls the first trucking company, for the manufacturer with a contingency plan, it is business as usual.

The High Flux Principle

> The faster the movement of resources through a system, the more resources will be available at any given time to cope with perturbation.

This principle applies to both the supply chain and other major physical resources that may be present in a community. Resiliency is often about resources; those communities or organizations with greater resources will be more resilient to the effects of an emergency than those with fewer resources. What makes this principle interesting is that the community or organization does not necessarily have to own or even operate the resources in question; their very presence within the community increases a community's or organization's overall resilience.

When considering supply chains, it is helpful to understand the manner in which different ones normally operate. Many organizations, such as grocery-store chains, may have centralized purchasing to supply a large number of retail outlets. As a result, they require warehousing and a distribution network. Some elements of this network are often somewhat decentralized to provide better service. For example, a grocery-store chain might operate a number of regional warehouses or distribution centres to supply its retail outlets. While the local supermarket in the community might contain a one-week food supply for the community, a regional distribution centre might contain a one-week food supply for 20 to 30 supermarkets. If the regional distribution centre happens to be located in the emergency manager's community, then that community may have immediate access to far greater resources than the community that has a single supermarket. As a result, that community is likely to be more resilient to the effects of food distribution problems.

A similar supply chain exists for fuel distribution. A community might have a single gas station and a single heating-fuel supplier. Oil companies produce their products in refineries, and then distribute them, either by rail or by pipeline, to their various retail outlets. Often regional distribution centres are created, this time in the form of petroleum tank farms, to supply all of the gas stations in an area. If the petroleum tank farm happens to be located in the emergency manager's community, then that community may have immediate access to far greater resources than a community that simply has one gas station. As a result, the community is likely to be more resilient to the effects of fuel distribution problems.

The same principle holds true for some other types of facilities, such as hospitals. A community may have its own hospital, which is usually relatively small and accustomed to dealing with the throughput of a limited number of patients and the provision of a limited number of services. Its resources at any given time are limited by the nature of its normal level of service provision. More serious patients are usually referred to larger hospitals that provide greater levels of service, and this referral process may exist through several levels. The process typically culminates in the large, university-affiliated teaching hospitals that are accustomed to the throughput of a large number of patients and the provision of a full spectrum of medical services. Logically, it follows that the presence of one of these large hospitals provides a community with a greater level of resilience against the medical effects of an emergency than the presence of a small community hospital.

In most cases, more resources equals greater community resiliency. While this may be generally true, it may not always be the case; often, tradeoffs between resiliency and vulnerability must be considered. To illustrate, the presence of a petroleum tank farm in a community may create additional resiliency against fuel distribution problems and also economic resiliency because it adds to the diversity of employers. However, such a facility may generate additional vulnerability to major fires, explosions, or hazardous materials events. That said, mitigation measures may be possible, and the emergency manager and community planners must weigh both the benefits and the risks of tradeoffs.

The Flatness Principle

Overly hierarchical systems are less flexible and hence less able to cope with surprise and adjust behaviour. Top-heavy systems will be less resilient.

To respond effectively to emergencies, the command-and-control model used must be both fluid and adaptable to evolving situations. Information and events at an emergency scene can evolve rapidly, and the person in charge must be able to continually analyze the best information available and modify existing objectives to respond to situational changes. Part of the ability to do so relates directly to the effective flow of information. The more layers that exist in a command-and-control model, the longer it takes for critical information to reach key decision-makers, and for response instructions to reach those at the emergency scene. Moreover, each additional layer of authority and reporting structure increases the potential for each message to be distorted, and for critical information to be inadvertently filtered out of the message. As a result, an overly hierarchical command-and-control system loses its resiliency, and emergency operations are more vulnerable to failure.

To illustrate, a paramedic tasked with the triage of victims at a large train wreck notices a strange odour in the air. This fact is reported to the immediate supervisor, who passes the information up the chain of command to the operations chief, along with a comment that the paramedic is probably just smelling diesel fuel leaking from the overturned locomotive. In fact, the paramedic has just detected the first sign of a hazardous materials leak from one of the overturned rail cars. The operations chief, believing that this information is unimportant, based upon the interpretation of the supervisor, decides not to pass the information on to the Emergency Medical Services (EMS) incident manager to avoid overwhelming her with information.

The EMS incident manager, who is at a higher level of authority, never receives the information about the strange odour to relay to the fire service incident manager, who has the means at his disposal to react rapidly to a hazardous materials leak. As a direct result, the leak continues to develop and worsen, until the critical information is finally passed on to the fire service incident manager through another channel. The command-and-control model, by virtue of its multiple layers and complex reporting arrangements, was rendered too inflexible to respond rapidly to an evolving situation at the emergency scene.

Emergency managers are unlikely to ever exert direct authority over emergency response agencies and resources in the field. Emergency services are usually run by specialists who have a higher level of knowledge specific to their function than emergency managers. Moreover, emergency service command-level officers tend to be extremely territorial. That being said, with diplomacy, a careful approach, and good ideas, the procedures of such agencies can be influenced by emergency managers. In the context of emergency management, an examination of communications technology, and information and process flow among emergency services and elsewhere in the community may lead to opportunities for increasing resiliency.

The Buffering Principle

A system which has capacity in excess of its needs can draw on this capacity in times of need, and so is more resilient.

This principle can be applied in many ways. The most obvious is in sending more resources than are clearly indicated to a given emergency call. This approach is based on the belief that it is almost always better to over-respond than to under-respond and then discover that the emergency is worse than originally believed. For example, a fire service dispatcher sends a full first-alarm response (several vehicles) to a report of a kitchen fire in a private residence. All apparatus on the first-alarm assignment respond, but when the first officer arrives at the scene, he discovers that the situation is limited to a pot burning on a stove, and cancels all apparatus except a single fire truck, which will deal with the problem. However, if the call had turned out to be an actual kitchen fire and only one truck had been sent, precious minutes, and perhaps the entire house, would have been lost in waiting for additional fire apparatus to respond. In this manner, firefighting operations become more resilient to the evolving emergency situation.

Another application, which is more appropriate to emergency managers, is the deliberate stockpiling of resources that might be required for an emergency but aren't required on a daily basis. These resources could include such items as cots and food supplies that might be required for an emergency shelter operation. They could also include a program to enhance emergency response capacity within the community through the retention of "obsolete" resources. To illustrate, every year or two, a community replaces some of its fire apparatus, police cars, and ambulances to ensure that it always has access to the latest in response technology and that citizens receive state-of-the-art service. A prudent emergency manager promotes the adoption of a policy by the community that ensures that the community emergency equipment being replaced is retained instead of being sold. An effective rotation system is created, so that each time new equipment is acquired, the oldest of the retained equipment is sold or otherwise disposed of, and at any given time the community has two "generations" of each type of emergency equipment in its inventory. When a disaster strikes, the retained resources are turned over to the additional emergency service personnel who have been called in to help, and the community now has twice as many ambulances, fire trucks, etcetera, as it would have during normal operations. By virtue of the fact that it possesses additional resources, the community is more resilient to the hazard event.

The Redundancy Principle

> A degree of overlapping function in a system permits the system to change by allowing vital functions to continue while formerly redundant elements take on new functions.

Adaptability is pivotal to the successful response to any type of disaster or hazard event affecting a community or an organization. Key decision-makers can use staff and resources in ways that may not be part of normal and expected business operations.

Staff might be cross-trained to fill more than one emergency response role, as is the case in communities whose paramedics are also firefighters. Or, staff might receive additional training for roles that have some common characteristics with their daily functions; for instance, clerical staff could be trained to provide support services in the community's Emergency Operations Centre or answer calls in the public inquiry centre. Similarly, community and social services staff might be asked to provide assistance functions to the victims housed in an emergency reception centre during an emergency. Staff might also be trained for emergency response roles that are not closely related to their daily functions, but which may be required during an emergency, such as the training of public works staff in debris removal or light rescue.

With sufficient creativity and a solid understanding of their capabilities, community resources can also be used in different ways to great effect during an emergency. This is particularly true for those resources that are no longer required for their primary function, when non-essential services have been suspended. For example, municipal transit buses or school buses may no longer be required to service their routes during an emergency, but could potentially be used to great effect in assisting with either the evacuation of residents or the movement of additional emergency service workers. Similarly, a large water tanker normally used by public works might be adapted to support firefighting operations.

Facilities such as municipally owned buildings may also be adapted to new uses during a crisis. Most communities, apart from the truly large ones, do not have a dedicated **Emergency Operations Centre (EOC)**. The majority of EOCs are council chambers, boardrooms, and training facilities that are only converted to an EOC when a crisis actually occurs. Other facilities that could be used as either emergency reception centres or emergency shelters during an emergency include schools, recreation centres, and arenas.

Organizations that perform charitable works, such as service clubs and faith-based groups, may also be able to provide services during an emergency that are not normally a part of their functions. Service clubs may be able to assist with mass-feeding operations or shelter staffing during a disaster. Those such as the Red Cross have expertise in registration and inquiry and may be able to assist with those functions. Some faith-based groups, such as the Salvation Army, Seventh-Day Adventists, and Mennonites may already see themselves in specific roles in assisting the community during an emergency.

The first step in establishing this type of adaptability is understanding what resources are available as well as their capabilities. These resources include people (both staff and non-staff), facilities, and mobile resources. The next step is applying one's creativity to identifying new ways in which these resources might be used for disaster response and considering what is possible. The final step is securing authorization and/or agreements for the use of such resources (as well as instructions for accessing them), and including them in the community's emergency response plan. The presence of resources that are adaptable provides a community with a greater number of options to react and respond to an emergency. The greater the ability of a community or an organization to react and respond to new information or situations, the more resilient that community or organization will be to the adverse events generated by a disaster.

Community Resiliency Programs

Regardless of how well prepared they already are, all communities and organizations likely have opportunities to enhance their resiliency to various types of emergency events. To promote and foster resiliency, emergency managers must first understand exactly how the concept of resiliency might be applied in the emergency management context. Several of the steps required for a community or an organizational resiliency program have already been discussed, including the HIRA process and the assessment of vulnerabilities that are present in the community or organization. The next step is for emergency managers to identify and list all of the potential opportunities to enhance resiliency, and to secure approval and funding for the resiliency measures identified.

Identifying Opportunities for Resiliency

As a necessary and important first stage, emergency managers must become aware of those mitigation measures that have already been implemented in efforts to attempt to reduce the community's or organization's vulnerability and increase its resiliency. How effective have those measures been in achieving their intended goal, and what obstacles arose during their implementation? This information often provides emergency managers with useful insight into the awareness of hazards within the community, the political will to implement such measures, and the challenges associated with funding such measures in the face of a community's or organization's continually competing priorities. Armed with this information, emergency managers will be more able to anticipate resistance and arguments, and have counterarguments prepared.

In most communities or organizations, the opportunities for increased resiliency typically fall into a predictable set of areas, including communications, supply chain, community resources, interoperability of staff, critical infrastructure, people, and land use. Each of these areas is addressed below. Rather than provide a description, each section presents examples of the questions that emergency managers must answer. Those answers are likely to come from both an emergency manager's own knowledge and observations, and those of others in the community or organization. With answers to these questions, emergency managers will better understand what resiliency measures are feasible and how to go about achieving them.

Communications

1. Are the communications systems of the emergency services fully interoperable? If not, what are the deficiencies, and how might they be addressed?
2. Is the community served by more than one telephone exchange? If not, what are the vulnerabilities of that exchange, and how might they be addressed?
3. Does the community's Emergency Operations Centre have more than one means of external communications? Are these technologically independent of one another?
4. Do multiple redundancies exist in the ability of the community's other critical resources, such as emergency services, hospitals, reception centres, and shelters, to communicate? Are these technologically independent of one another?
5. What processes are currently in place to provide urgent information to the general public during an emergency?
6. What are mitigation measures likely to cost for each shortfall identified?

Supply Chain

For those resources within the influence of emergency managers, it may be possible to take steps such as establishing or negotiating dormant contracts or purchase orders to ensure their availability. However, many resources of the supply chain are beyond the control of emergency managers. As a result, discussions will need to occur with those who actually control these resources. Nonetheless, emergency managers may still be able to influence the use of resiliency strategies by others in the community.

1. Are multiple sources available for each of the following key items:
   a. food?
   b. fuel?
   c. heating fuel?
   d. water?
   e. sewer lines?
   f. electricity?
   g. medical supplies and pharmaceuticals?
   h. raw materials for key employers (for example, iron ore for a steel mill)?
2. For the applicable items above, what inventory levels are normally held in the community?

3. Are redundant delivery systems available for the following items:
   a. food?
   b. fuel?
   c. heating fuel?
   d. water?
   e. medical supplies and pharmaceuticals?
   f. raw materials for key employers?
4. What steps are feasible for improving the availability of and access to these supplies? How much are the steps likely to cost?

Community Resources

In most communities, emergency managers are advisers and facilitators, and do not exert direct control over a community's resources. As a result, they need to establish dialogue with the officials who do control community resources on a day-to-day basis. By doing so, emergency managers may be able to present new ideas and insights that could influence the decision-making process.

1. Does the community currently maintain a "reserve fleet" of older emergency vehicles for use during an emergency?
2. Are mutual-aid agreements in place among the various emergency services in the community and with those of surrounding communities?
3. Are there mobile resources, such as water tankers, that are not under the day-to-day control of emergency services that might be used to support emergency service operations? How would approval to use these resources be obtained?
4. Are there facilities within the community, such as schools, recreation centres, or arenas, that might fulfill a different function in response to an emergency? What resources do these facilities require to fulfill a new function? How would approval to use these facilities be obtained?

Interoperability of Staff

As with community resources, municipal staff are rarely under the direct control of emergency managers. As a result, emergency managers must establish dialogue with various officials to obtain approval for new staff roles and the required staff training.

1. Are there staff within the community or organization without clear roles and responsibilities regarding emergency operations?
2. Are there staff working in services that could reasonably be expected to suspend normal operations during an emergency?

3. What skills do these workers have?
4. How might those skills be applied to the community's emergency response? How would approval to engage staff during an emergency be obtained?
5. What additional staff training or resources would be required? How much is this likely to cost?

Critical Infrastructure

1. Are there elements of critical infrastructure, such as roads, rail lines, bridges, or distribution systems, without which the community would have difficulty operating?
2. Are those elements of critical infrastructure vulnerable? When? How? Why?
3. Are there feasible measures that might be taken to reduce the vulnerability of elements of critical infrastructure? How much are these measures likely to cost?
4. Is the community reliant on single sources for critical supply chain elements, or single major employers? Do these elements currently have business continuity plans?

People

1. Are there pre-existing public education and preparedness programs in the community?
2. Do those programs adequately address the vulnerabilities that have been identified?
3. Do community members see emergency preparedness as an important priority?
4. What additional public education or preparedness programs might be used to improve community resiliency?
5. How could such programs be developed?
6. How would such programs be delivered? By whom?
7. How much are such programs likely to cost?

Land Use

1. Are there areas in the community that are known to be subject to specific types of hazards, such as flooding?
2. Does the community currently pursue a policy of land use that precludes residential or industrial development, or the building of critical infrastructure elements in high-risk areas?
3. Do high-risk industrial activities occur in areas that are immediately adjacent to other elements of the community, such as residential housing?

4. How is the community situated with respect to transportation corridors such as major highways and rail lines on which hazardous materials are transported?

5. Are mitigation measures, such as relocation, either feasible or economically desirable?

Setting Priorities

By now, emergency managers should have developed a list of possible measures to enhance resiliency. It is likely that some ideas have been discarded for lack of feasibility. The measures that remain on the list are categorized by the type of action required for implementation. Once this categorization has been completed, the result is like a "blueprint" for leading the community or organization to ever-increasing resiliency (it is typically called a *community* [or *organizational*] *mitigation plan* or a *community* [or *organizational*] *resiliency plan*). Each resiliency measure is put into place once the required conditions have been met, and progress across the list of priorities should be tracked. The categories for resiliency measures follow.

Immediately Achievable

The proposed measure has no associated cost and requires no further approval. Such measures usually involve either simple procedural changes or immediate buy-in by senior officials or other key decision-makers.

Requiring Approval

The proposed measure may not have an associated cost, but requires various approvals because it either changes community organizational policy, affects the budget, or involves some other area of organizational operations.

Requiring Funding

The proposed measure has an associated cost that is beyond the spending authority of the emergency manager. As a result, it will have to be either included in the next annual budget process or dealt with separately by senior officials or other key decision-makers, like any other unbudgeted expenditure.

Significant Expenditure

The proposed measure, while achievable, is probably beyond the normal financial means of the community in question. This measure may only be achievable through grantsmanship, funding under a program from another level of government, or significant public pressure. It may very well be that the community or organization in question, and its key decision-makers, will simply choose to accept the level of risk as it exists, because the measure's cost is beyond its means.

Beyond Mandate/Control

The proposed measure involves property or resources held and controlled by either a private individual, a corporation, or another level of government. The measure may involve significant costs or changes in procedure or business operations, and may only be achieved through either the cooperation of the party or group involved or changes to legislation.

Obtaining Support and Approval

Whether working in a community or an organization, most emergency managers function in an environment that is fairly described as intensely political. Sometimes the politics involved are those that normally operate in any community, and relate to the approval of elected officials for changes to policy, operations, or budget. Other times, organizational politics will operate; bear in mind that emergency managers rarely have direct control over or responsibility for the resources, staff, or policies that they are attempting to affect. Moreover, the activities in question often have budgetary implications for departments or divisions for which other officials are responsible. Even when an idea is a good one, officials at senior levels of communities and organizations are typically very territorial, and will resist external attempts to affect their operations or budget.

It is under these conditions that the skills of a good emergency manager truly shine. Using their research and writing skills, emergency managers can develop a sound business case and make a submission that may obtain approval from elected officials or senior management. The mediation and facilitation skills of emergency managers will also prove helpful in persuading senior officials to support a program or a project, sometimes even when it creates problems within an official's area of responsibility. These skills may also be used to persuade individuals, corporations, and additional levels of government to support projects involving resources that are under their control, and in rallying the general public to support needed resiliency programs.

Conclusion

While all communities can and should have well-thought-out emergency response plans, it is incorrect to focus preparedness solely on this plan. The presence of high levels of resiliency can make a tremendous difference in the ability of a community or an organization to respond to and recover from the effects of a hazard event. Resilient communities and organizations respond more effectively to hazard events and typically experience lower response and recovery costs, and their emergency response plans achieve increased effectiveness. It is almost always less expensive to fix a problem before it occurs than to deal with the consequences after it happens. The resiliency of communities or organizations to the effects of hazard events does not occur automatically; resiliency must be conceived, grown, nurtured, and developed by an emergency manager. By not developing their resiliency, communities and organizations run the risk of becoming trapped in a cycle of simply reacting to each negative effect as it occurs. Communities and organizations conduct their other forms of planning to avoid reactive responses, so why should emergency management be any different?

KEY TERMS

Emergency Operations Centre (EOC)

redundancy

supply chain

LEARNING CHECK

Take a few minutes now to test your knowledge of fostering resiliency. Select the best answer in each case. Any score of less than 16 out of 20 (80 percent) indicates that you should re-read this chapter.

1. For emergency managers, the concepts of vulnerability and resiliency may be described as being
   a. occasionally interconnected
   b. paired
   c. unrelated
   d. both (a) and (c)

2. As a general principle, communities or organizations that are more resilient to the effects of a given hazard event may also be said to be
   a. immune
   b. more vulnerable
   c. less vulnerable
   d. reactive

3. In most cases, communities or organizations that are more resilient to the effects of a given hazard event may experience
   a. lower response/recovery costs
   b. increased impact
   c. a false sense of security
   d. more frequent occurrences

4. Place the following emergency management measures in the correct order:
   (1) create response plan
   (2) assess/evaluate risk
   (3) mitigate
   (4) assess vulnerability
   (5) identify hazards
   a. 1, 2, 3, 4, 5
   b. 2, 4, 3, 5, 1
   c. 5, 2, 4, 3, 1
   d. 4, 5, 3, 2, 1

5. In Maslow's hierarchy of needs, people are extremely unlikely to place much priority on safety needs until _____ needs have been met.
   a. physiological
   b. belonging
   c. esteem
   d. self-actualization

6. In the vulnerability modelling done by Blaikie and colleagues, the level of resiliency was directly tied to
   a. personal safety
   b. access to assets
   c. access to decision-makers
   d. political influence

7. A primary reason for human settlement in a given location is
   a. access to water
   b. access to assets/wealth
   c. access to housing
   d. access to schools

8. Emergency managers understand that community vulnerability, and therefore opportunities for resiliency, may result from activities that are intended to
   a. generate wealth
   b. control people
   c. educate the public
   d. inform decision-makers

9. A community that has capacity in excess of its needs that may be employed during a crisis is using the principle of
   a. flatness
   b. omnivory
   c. buffering
   d. redundancy

10. An organization that avoids the use of multi-layered, overly hierarchical command-and-control structures is using the principle of
    a. flatness
    b. omnivory
    c. buffering
    d. redundancy

11. An organization that has developed multiple sources for critical supplies and delivery systems is using the principle of
    a. flatness
    b. omnivory
    c. buffering
    d. redundancy

12. An organization that develops a degree of overlapping function to improve the flexibility of disaster response is using the principle of
    a. flatness
    b. omnivory
    c. buffering
    d. redundancy

13. An organization that relies on a large-scale flow of resources to ensure that
    sufficient resources will be available for an emergency is using the principle of
    a. high flux
    b. omnivory
    c. buffering
    d. homeostasis

14. An organization that relies on effective and consistent feedback among
    component parts is using the principle of
    a. high flux
    b. omnivory
    c. buffering
    d. homeostasis

15. Areas in which emergency managers may find opportunities to enhance
    resiliency include critical infrastructure, communications, and
    a. people
    b. legislation
    c. organizational politics
    d. both (b) and (c)

16. Emergency managers may find additional opportunities to enhance com-
    munity or organizational resiliency in the areas of community resources,
    supply chain, and
    a. land use
    b. interoperability of staff
    c. media support
    d. both (a) and (b)

17. The priorities for proposed resiliency projects may be categorized by means of
    a. immediate need
    b. requirements for implementation
    c. budgetary constraints
    d. legal mandates

18. The categories for proposed resiliency-enhancing projects include immediately achievable, requiring funding, and
    a. beyond mandate/control
    b. requiring approval
    c. short-term deferral
    d. both (a) and (b)

19. A resiliency-enhancing project that requires the approval and/or funding of a private individual, a corporation, or another level of government would be categorized as
    a. immediately achievable
    b. requiring approval
    c. beyond mandate/control
    d. requiring funding

20. A comprehensive program developed by an emergency manager to enhance the resiliency of a community or an organization is called a community/organizational resiliency plan or a
    a. community/organizational mitigation plan
    b. community risk response plan
    c. community succession plan
    d. continuity of governance plan

CASE STUDIES

A. As the emergency manager for your community, you have been asked to develop a community evacuation plan for use in the event of the derailment of one of the chemical trains that normally passes on the main rail line, located downwind of the community. This document will form an annex to the community's existing emergency response plan. In preparing to write the evacuation plan, consider each of the following:

   1. List all of the physical resources available in the community that might be used to provide reception, shelter, and feeding for the evacuees. Indicate how approval for their use would be obtained. List the resources that would be required for each intended function.
   2. List all of the mobile resources that might be required to assist with the evacuation process. Indicate how approval for their use would be obtained. List any advance steps that might be taken to secure their availability.

3. Describe the ways in which municipal staff might be engaged, in ways other than their normal functions, to assist with response to an emergency.
4. List all service clubs and faith-based organizations that might be able to assist in the emergency, and the roles that you would expect them to fill. List any advance steps that might be taken to secure their availability.

B. As the emergency manager in your community, you have been asked to develop a community resiliency program. Part of this process will involve the identification of opportunities for resiliency. As an initial step, consider each of the following categories, and identify areas that might be examined to identify those opportunities:

1. communications
2. critical infrastructure
3. supply chain
4. residents.

TO LEARN MORE

1. In your local community, select one element of infrastructure that you believe to be critical. This may be a built element, such as a building; a community service of some sort; a supply chain element, such as a road or railway line; or a business, such as a gas station or a bank. Identify its location and proximity to known hazards. What purpose does this element serve in the community? Why do you believe this element to be critical? What would be the immediate result if this element were lost to the community? How long could the community continue its normal function if this element were no longer available? Is the element a single resource, or are there multiple locations in the community that fulfill this function?

2. Using the same element that you have studied above, are there measures that might be put into place to reduce the vulnerability of the critical infrastructure element? What are they? Are there potential contingency arrangements that could be put into place to reduce the community's vulnerability to the loss of this critical infrastructure element? What are they? What are the potential barriers to implementation? Why do you think these measures are not already in place?

NOTES

1. Abraham H. Maslow, *A Theory of Human Motivation*, originally published in *Psychological Review* 50, 1943: 370–96, <http://psychclassics.yorku.ca/Maslow/motivation.htm>.

2. Piers Blaikie et al., *At Risk: Natural Hazards, People's Vulnerability, and Disasters* (London: Routledge, 1994).

3. Housing Recovery Working Group, FEMA and Central United States Earthquake Consortium, "A Housing Recovery Strategy for a New Madrid Earthquake," *Central United States Earthquake Consortium*, 1998, <http://www.cusec.org/PlansProgs/House/HRStrat.pdf>.

4. Aaron Wildavsky, *Searching for Safety* (London: Transaction Books, 1988).

5. The Wildavsky quotations presented in the discussion of the six principles can be found in Mark Pelling, *The Vulnerability of Cities: Natural Disasters and Social Resilience* (London: Earthscan, 2003), p. 8.

PART III
Preparedness

Source: www.CartoonStock.com.

CREATING AN EMERGENCY PLAN

Sooner or later, every emergency manager will need to write an emergency plan for a community or an organization. This type of document tends to have a variety of names, including *emergency plan*, *emergency response plan*, *disaster plan*, and *major incident plan*. For our purposes, the name of the document is not crucial, so we will use the generic term *emergency plan*. Emergency plans may take a variety of forms, including binders, flip charts, computer software, and even bound volumes. The creation of an emergency plan for a community or an organization is one of the most important tasks of an emergency manager and, yet, remains one of the most poorly understood.

Individuals and organizations tend to have differing ideas about precisely what an emergency plan is, but it is equally important to understand what it is *not*. An emergency plan is *not* step-by-step instructions for guiding a community or organization through all of the phases of every conceivable emergency incident. It would be daunting to attempt to use such a document, and it would be almost impossible to create it. Consider the broad range of emergencies that might occur in a community or an organization. Is it truly practical to try to address all of the contingencies that could arise from all of the possible emergencies within a single document, and what would such a document look like?

An effective emergency plan is a *framework* within which a community or an organization mounts its response to an emergency. It is also the framework within which a community or an organization formulates its recovery efforts. Finally, it is a comprehensive and exhaustive list of resources that might be required to manage an emergency effectively. It provides a starting point for emergency response and, it is hoped, demonstrates that due diligence obligations have been met should any public inquiry or legal challenge arise out of the emergency.

An effective emergency plan is based on a clear and well-understood set of objectives. It is risk based; it attempts to address the major issues arising from those types of emergencies most likely to arise within the community or organization. At the same time, it has a level of flexibility to be able to respond to those emergencies that were unforeseen.

Part III focuses on the development of an emergency plan. Chapter 11 describes the processes involved in creating and updating an emergency plan. Chapter 12 focuses on the key components included in an emergency plan. Chapter 13 discusses the centralized coordinating role of the Emergency Operations Centre as well as design considerations for its creation. Finally, chapter 14 considers the types of technologies required to support the functions of an Emergency Operations Centre.

CHAPTER 11

The Emergency Planning Process

Introduction

In the past, community emergency plans were often the result of one person's efforts. Ideally, they included input from consultation with some or all of the traditional emergency services, but beyond that, input from other stakeholders was uncommon. Such emergency plans tended to use a generic all-hazards approach, and were typically viewed by their authors as a project, with a defined beginning, middle, and end. Plans were rarely tested or reviewed, and, as a result, were seldom effective as anything other than bookshelf decorations. Although an emergency plan is central to community welfare in a disaster, it was typically considered as a "nice to have" rather than a "need to have" tool.

A variety of factors have combined to renew serious interest in emergency plans. In many communities and jurisdictions, they are no longer a suggestion, but a legally mandated requirement. Today, the creation of emergency plans is a collaborative process, and one that requires the **input** of a variety of community stakeholders. While emergency managers may be "experts" in emergency management, they are by no means the only people with valid contributions to make to the emergency planning process. Indeed, many others, while they may not fully understand emergency management, possess an intimate knowledge of how some aspect of a community functions and why. Emergency managers must tap into this knowledge to create an emergency plan that is both appropriate to and effective in the community.

The evolution of emergency management into a dynamic process is reflected in today's emergency plans and the way in which they are created and modified. It is no longer enough to simply write a generic plan, put it away, and hope that it is never needed; today's plans are living, breathing, "evergreen" documents. They exist in a state of constant review, input, testing, and refinement, hopefully growing more effective with the passage of time. The role of contemporary emergency managers is to facilitate the emergency planning process, and to ensure that the results remain within the guidelines of best practice.

Purpose

Effective emergency plans are essential for any community. Emergency plans are the foundation on which the response to all types of emergencies are based, and their success or failure is directly dependent on the quality of the planning process. The creation of emergency plans involves a dynamic process of planning, consultation, writing, testing, and refining. Emergency managers must be able to both understand and effectively manage the creation and refinement of emergency plans as a part of their duties.

Steps in the Emergency Planning Process
Understanding the Community and Its Resources

When emergency managers begin the emergency planning process, their first step is to gain a complete understanding of both the community and its resources.[1] This step includes learning about the topography and built environment of the community; for example, the location of roads, rail lines, lakes, rivers, and other surface features, and also the placement of key resources, such as the town hall, schools, police and fire stations. It also includes determining the location of critical infrastructure elements; for example, electrical lines, water mains, communication conduits (such as telephone trunk lines, fibre-optic cables, and cable-television systems), banks, hospitals, and retail areas. In short, emergency managers should know everything that might be essential for community welfare. See chapters 6 and 8 for a discussion of these elements.

Plotting all such features on a map of the community can be useful in terms of viewing and analyzing the relationships among various elements. This type of map provides a common reference point for all those assisting with the creation of the emergency plan. It is also an extremely helpful visual guide for those in charge during an actual disaster.

It is also necessary to consider another critical element of community composition: people. Demographic data for the community can help emergency managers identify vulnerable populations, their locations, and how those locations relate to both areas of risk and community resources (see chapter 4). Plotting this information on a map of the community can also be useful. An understanding of a community's people also helps emergency managers consider the relative needs of various subsets of the population and the levels of disaster services required to satisfy those needs effectively.

Hazard Identification and Risk Assessment

The next step in the emergency planning process is a Hazard Identification and Risk Assessment (HIRA) for the community. The HIRA clarifies the community's risk exposures and identifies their locations, which could also be plotted on a map of the community. This step helps emergency managers set priorities for planning and understand precisely what they are planning for. See chapter 8 for details on creating such a document.

Collecting Data on Community Resources

Emergency managers must develop a comprehensive list of all community resources in this step of the emergency planning process. How many fire trucks does the community own? Of what types? How many ambulances does it own? Does it own other vehicles, such as police cars, mobile command posts, public works vehicles, and transit buses? Are there schools, recreation centres, or other facilities that might be used to provide emergency services? Who is responsible for these resources on a day-to-day basis, and how can they be contacted during work hours and after hours? What service clubs and volunteer agencies operate in the community, what roles and services are they prepared to undertake, and how can decision-makers be contacted? Does the community have formal agreements in place for any or all of these resources?

Collecting data on community resources will probably require some type of formal research instrument, such as a questionnaire to the heads of all municipal departments and other relevant organizations. This type of survey represents substantial work, but it also provides emergency managers with a clear understanding of potential resource availability. A clear understanding of community resources, their capabilities, and what they are *not* capable of doing is essential to the planning process. Nothing in the emergency plan can be based on assumptions; if your local fire department does not have the capability of handling hazardous materials spills, the time to discover this fact is now. This step will prevent emergency managers and the emergency planning committee from wasting time on planning to use resources that may not have the expected capability, or which may not be available for use. The data-collection process also gives emergency managers the opportunity to solicit contacts for membership in the emergency planning committee.

Setting Objectives

When writing an emergency plan, it is absolutely necessary to understand what one is attempting to accomplish. It is important, before putting pen to paper, or fingers to keyboard, to have a clear idea of what the resulting document should be able to do. It is also important to state early on what the emergency plan is intended to accomplish, and also what it is *not* intended to accomplish. Such statements help define the scope of the document and provide terms of reference for the work involved in its creation.[2] Such statements may also help prevent those tasked with creating the document from "going off on tangents" and addressing issues that are not intended to be a part of the plan, thereby saving wasted effort.

To illustrate, one might include a statement such as, "This plan is intended to provide an organizational framework within which the Municipality of West River will mount its response to any major emergency occurring within municipal boundaries." One might also wish to include a limiting statement such as, "This plan is intended for use by the Municipality of West River, and is not intended for use in emergencies occurring outside of municipal boundaries." Both statements are equally clear; one defining what the emergency plan is intended for, and one defining what the emergency plan is not intended for.

An emergency plan is not meant to be a step-by-step guide to managing every conceivable emergency incident. Emergencies are complex events, and comprehensive planning is nearly impossible. To illustrate, two identical events, both chemical spills, although with different chemicals, generate completely different issues, decisions, and responses, despite the fact that both events fall into the same general category. The differences that occur are the result of the nature of the chemical, weather conditions, location, areas of threat, and resources available. These **variances** make cookie-cutter planning impossible.

An emergency plan is intended to provide a *framework* within which to mount and organize community response and recovery efforts to emergencies. The decisions and actions that occur in between activation and recovery must remain the responsibility of the people in charge, at each individual event. The community can provide support, tools, and resources to people in charge, but it cannot think for them!

Emergency managers should also provide a clear definition of the practices to be used in the creation of the emergency plan. Will the plan follow a risk-based approach or the older all-hazards approach? Is the plan intended to be used in conjunction with the Incident Management/Incident Command System? Will the plan provide for self-directed decision making by individuals in key roles, or will it employ specific "trigger points" at which certain events must occur? Addressing and defining these issues early on in the planning process will help create an emergency plan that has greater clarity and conciseness, and will provide better direction in almost formal terms to those creating the plan.

Soliciting Input

No emergency manager should ever attempt to write an emergency plan single-handedly. The input of stakeholders in the community is critical to the process; it provides differing perspectives and experiences, and also fills gaps in the knowledge of the emergency manager. It also gives stakeholders a chance to clarify their capabilities and understand what the community might expect of them during a crisis. Most important, an emergency plan that incorporates input and advice from a broad range of community resources and services is more likely to be practical and achievable, and also more likely to gain acceptance and buy-in from across the community.

An emergency planning committee is one of the most effective means for garnering community input. Committee members should be drawn from a wide range of municipal departments, emergency services, and community-service organizations to achieve a suitably broad information base and set of perspectives for the emergency plan. Political participation is also essential; having at least one elected official on the committee creates a link between the committee and the elected government, provides credibility, and may help open doors to resources that might otherwise be closed to committee requests. In addition, elected officials frequently act as "champions" for the emergency planning process.

Organizing Emergency Planning Committees

One of the challenges of the emergency planning committee is its sheer size. While it is essential to have the input and participation of every organization that would be involved in an emergency, it may be difficult to find a space large enough to accommodate the whole group. In addition, it may be difficult to keep such a large group focused, or even to arrange meeting times that meet the scheduling needs of all committee members.[3] The problems associated with a committee's size can be overcome by breaking the group into specialized subcommittees. Some useful subdivisions include an emergency services group, a public works and utilities group, and a social-services group. The emergency manager would act as a facilitator for all groups, a coordinator for the activities of the groups, and an information conduit among groups. Although the use of subcommittees involves more of an emergency manager's time, it allows committee work to proceed quickly and efficiently, while respecting the needs of members to perform their regular duties.

It may be necessary for emergency managers to conduct some preliminary training sessions for committee members. While committee members possess good knowledge of their own field, how many have any real knowledge of emergency management? Committee members who receive orientation have a better understanding of the process, the frame of reference within which they will work, the priorities of the process, and the reasons for those priorities. Such training will also give emergency managers the opportunity to clarify expectations, standards for work, lines of communication, and planning procedures for committee members, so that everyone can work harmoniously.

Once the subcommittees have formed, it is important to provide members with clear objectives and timelines. Emergency managers must never forget that each person on the committee has other duties and obligations, and these must be stringently respected. The project-management skills of emergency managers will play a central role in the success of the planning process, and the use of scheduling devices such as a **critical path**, **PERT charts**, and **Gantt charts** may prove useful. The identification of the critical steps and their sequence in the planning process will help move the process along, and will provide committee members with milestones that will help them see the progress they have made in their work. There are a number of highly effective project-management applications, such as Microsoft™ Office Project software, which can help with the coordination of such a large project. The subcommittees and their members must understand what they are expected to achieve, how long they have to accomplish their work, and how much of their time will be involved.

At this point, emergency managers should have a project plan in place: a body of information that provides a standard frame of reference and clear objectives for creating an emergency plan. Also, the resources required to perform the work have been assigned. Everyone understands what they are supposed to do and how to do it. The timelines for producing critical components have been developed. It is time to begin the process of writing the emergency plan.

Writing the Plan

The process of writing the emergency plan is, to some extent, a slow one. Each sub-committee completes its assignments and forwards the resulting documents to the emergency manager for editing to ensure format consistency. Emergency managers may wish to share documents with the other subcommittees to ensure that all groups are continually aware of what other groups are doing—which is important because the work of one group often has implications for another. For example, the work of one group may actually "feed" the work of another. To illustrate, the emergency service group might be aware that public works owns several water tanker trucks, and makes an assumption that these trucks might be used to support fire-fighting operations. Taking this plan back to the public works and utilities groups might reveal, however, that the hardware on the water tanker trucks is not compatible with the hardware on the fire trucks. The result might be a needed modification to the plan or the adaptation of the water tanker trucks so that they can be used.

It is also completely appropriate to share the work of individual subcommittees with the municipality's department heads, and to ask for feedback. This process will achieve several important results. First, it can be assumed that the department heads are subject-matter experts, at least within the operations of their own departments, and can offer feedback on the feasibility and practicality of the measures being proposed. It is also important to remember that department heads require a clear understanding of what is expected of them, because such expectations may have budgetary implications for their departments. In addition, the ability to see the contributions of their own departments is likely to lead to increased support for their participation in the planning process, and for the final emergency plan that will result from it.

Some elements of the emergency plan are likely to remain the sole responsibility of an emergency manager. He or she will craft these elements individually, and add them to the framework document. Such items include statements of principle, elements of law, and administrative and maintenance items for which the expertise of committee members is not required. These tend to be generic components (the components required in an emergency plan are discussed in detail in chapter 12).

Review and Approval

The process of writing, reviewing, soliciting input, and making modifications continues until a complete first draft of the emergency plan exists. The emergency manager edits the first draft of the plan to correct spelling and grammatical errors, and to ensure that the document, although created by many people, speaks to readers with a single "voice." The edited first draft should be shared with a variety of groups, and their comments invited. These groups might include the municipal department heads, the municipal legal department or the firm that handles the municipality's legal affairs, emergency managers of nearby communities, and the emergency management department at the regional level of government. Timelines should be included with the invitation for comment to prevent the consultation process from becoming "bogged down." Once comments have been received and the necessary amendments made, the emergency manager will have a final draft. It is time for the next steps in the plan-creation process.

The final draft of the emergency plan must be circulated once again. This time, the document is sent to those department and organization heads concerned for final approval. This step is necessary to obtain endorsement for the emergency plan, and to solicit formal agreements from each to both comply with the emergency plan and to provide the resources and services specified within it during an emergency. The final emergency plan should also be sent once more to the municipal legal department for final approval.

Once the endorsements of the key stakeholders and the municipal legal department have been obtained, it is time to take the emergency plan to the community's elected officials for final approval. The approval process varies somewhat from community to community. Typically, it consists of the presentation of the final emergency plan to the elected council and then ratification, usually in the form of official adoption of the emergency plan by means of a municipal bylaw. Once the plan has been approved by elected officials, it becomes an official document. It is now ready for publication in whatever form or forms are chosen, and for distribution to all stakeholders, neighbouring communities, and, in many cases, to the emergency management department at the regional level of government.

A Dynamic Document

Having an emergency plan does not, in and of itself, prepare the community to cope with emergencies; to guarantee effectiveness, the plan must be tested on a regular basis. Testing will provide insight into staff knowledge, communication problems, gaps in planning and knowledge, shortfalls in information flow, and procedures that, however well thought through, just don't work. There is a tremendous advantage to testing; the gaps, deficiencies, and problems found now, under controlled circumstances, can be corrected without the potential for human cost that occurs when they are discovered during an actual emergency. Emergency plans are generally tested by means of various types of emergency exercises, which are discussed in part IV.

After exercises or real emergencies take place, a process of information gathering begins. This process generally consists of debriefing those who participated in the event to identify what didn't work as intended, what unforeseen events occurred, and any suggestions for the improvement of the plan or its procedures. The information gathered may take the form of verbal debriefings, questionnaires, or after action reports. It may come from not only those who responded to the event but also elected officials, volunteer agencies, and possibly members of the general public. The information gathered is then taken and analyzed by the emergency manager and the emergency planning committee; changes to procedures may be called for and, where appropriate, recommended for inclusion in a revised emergency plan.

Emergency managers are not, in most cases, the final arbiter of which changes occur and which do not. Many proposed changes may involve the policies and procedures of another municipal department. Some, particularly those involving added expenditures, resource acquisition, or new bylaws may require the approval of the community's elected officials before they can be implemented. Once the proposed changes have been approved, they can be included in a new and improved emergency plan.

Changes in information or resources will require amendments to an emergency plan. They may require the rewriting of the entire plan, one section, or even just a page or two. Prudent emergency managers construct an emergency plan as an easily modifiable and dynamic manual so that relevant pages can be changed one at a time, as required. In a dynamic manual, each major topic or procedure is treated as a separate component with its own page(s), and each new major topic or procedure is added as its own discrete section. Thus, any amendment of the plan can be introduced by simply changing a page or two, rather than republishing and reissuing the entire document. Ideally, this process is ongoing, with the plan being continually tested and amended, either by exercises or real-life events, in a cycle of continuous improvement. It should continue right up to the moment when the next community emergency occurs, and then, armed with the lessons learned from the emergency itself, resume immediately following the restoration of normal or near-normal operations.

An essential part of this dynamic process is the need to record and track all amendments to the emergency plan. All amendments, along with their date of and reason for their occurrence, must be recorded and tracked as part of the community's ability to demonstrate due diligence. Legally, a party under review must be able to demonstrate that all "reasonable measures" necessary to respond to an emergency have occurred. It is not sufficient to do a "good job" of preparedness; one must also be able to *show* that one has done a good job.

The legal test is not best practice; it is what might be expected of the "average, reasonable" entity, under the circumstances described. In other words, the community and its officials must be able to demonstrate that they have done everything that might be expected of the "average, reasonable" community under the circumstances under review. Following an emergency, being able to demonstrate a continuous process of testing, refining, and improving the emergency plan in a coroner's inquest, civil action, or public inquiry will in great measure satisfy this legal test. Having detailed documentation may also be useful for civic officials required to testify as to how, why, and when any procedural changes evolved.

There are practical reasons for tracking amendments as well. Many communities have dozens, or even hundreds, of copies of their emergency plan in circulation. In some cases, they may even sit on every desktop in an organization. In these cases, the written tracking of amendments is the only practical method for being able to determine, at a glance, whether or not any given copy of the emergency plan is actually the latest version.

Conclusion

An effective, contemporary emergency plan is not a project; it is the result of an ongoing process. A good and effective emergency plan is an "evergreen" document that continues to grow and evolve, based on changes in community composition, the consultation process, and lessons learned. It draws on the knowledge and experiences of not only emergency services but also a broad spectrum of stakeholders in the community. The legal requirements for such a plan vary somewhat from one jurisdiction to another, and will change from time to time, but the most important factor driving the evolution of an emergency plan is the changes in the development and physical characteristics of the community, and also its growing and evolving needs. The process of creating an emergency plan never really ends, and the plan's evolution is a constant factor for consideration by emergency managers.

The consultation process is essential in the creation of an emergency plan. No emergency plan should ever be the work of a single person, no matter how knowledgeable or skilled that person might be. The consultation process broadens the content of the plan, adding the knowledge, thoughts, and perspective of a wide range of community stakeholders. Participation in that process also fosters a sense of ownership among community stakeholders and key decision-makers; they are much more likely to embrace an emergency plan when they feel that they had a role in its creation.

A good emergency plan must be, above all things, accessible. It does not provide step-by-step instructions for managing every conceivable emergency incident, but it does provide a framework and the critical information that the community needs to mount its response to any emergency. Finding the required critical information in the early stages of a crisis is a crucial step for those managing an emergency. During a crisis, key decision-makers will quickly discard an emergency plan that it is too difficult to use or whose information is too difficult to find. Always remember that for many users, the emergency plan is an unfamiliar document, even though it should not be. Good formatting of the emergency plan is essential: information must be provided in a manner that is logical, easy to find, and easy to understand.

By following these principles, and the essential steps of the planning process described in this chapter, emergency managers will create a plan that is relevant, accessible, and user-friendly. No two plans are identical, even when these steps are followed precisely. That is as it should be, because no two communities are identical. Each community has different needs, and emergency managers know that an effective emergency plan is intended to meet the needs of the community for which it is written, and to provide the framework of information, procedures, and resources with which the community will successfully rise to the challenge of effective response to whatever type of emergency confronts it.

KEY TERMS

critical path

Gantt charts

input

PERT charts

variance

LEARNING CHECK

Take a few minutes now to test your knowledge of the emergency planning process. Select the best answer in each case. Any score of less than 16 out of 20 (80 percent) indicates that you should re-read this chapter.

1. An effective emergency plan must attempt to define clearly achievable
   a. instructions
   b. operating principles
   c. standards
   d. objectives

2. An effective emergency plan must attempt to address those risks that
   a. are commonly believed to be present
   b. are covered in government guidelines
   c. are most likely to occur in the community
   d. have been the focus of media attention

3. An effective emergency plan must be flexible enough to also address those risks that are
   a. covered in government guidelines
   b. less common
   c. commonly believed to be priorities
   d. present in other parts of the world

4. Emergency plans should be subject to as broad a level of _____ as possible.
   a. stakeholder input
   b. media support
   c. funding support
   d. scientific input

5. Stakeholder-based emergency planning committees provide additional knowledge and expertise and facilitate
   a. community funding
   b. buy-in for the plan
   c. political approval
   d. standards compliance

6. Emergency managers recognize that the creation of an emergency plan is not a project, but
   a. an ongoing, dynamic process
   b. a legal requirement for the community
   c. an internationally recognized best practice
   d. a primary means of defence for elected officials

7. Clearly stated objectives at the start of the emergency planning process provide those working on the project with
   a. timelines for completion
   b. terms of reference
   c. comprehensive instructions
   d. the knowledge to complete the task

8. In addition to defining what an emergency plan is intended to accomplish, good objectives will help clarify
   a. what it is not intended to accomplish
   b. when the plan was created
   c. required changes to bylaws
   d. who has approved the plan

9. Clear objectives can also help specify
   a. the author of the plan
   b. the funding of the plan
   c. the practices to be used in the creation of the plan
   d. time to be spent on each area

10. Having an emergency plan is insufficient; to ensure that the plan will be effective when required, it should be regularly
    a. submitted for peer review
    b. submitted for third-party review
    c. presented to elected officials
    d. tested

11. The process used for the continued maintenance of an emergency plan should have, as its primary objective,
    a. continuous improvement
    b. meeting best practice
    c. meeting minimum standards
    d. interoperability with other communities

12. Ongoing consultation with community stakeholders provides the process with
    a. exemption from political criticism
    b. a wider range of expertise
    c. funding support
    d. compliance with standards

13. _____ will prove extremely useful to emergency managers in the planning process.
    a. Project-planning skills
    b. Understanding legal language
    c. Conflict resolution
    d. Changes in management

14. One advantage to drawing members of the emergency planning committee from as broad a base as possible is that this will provide the process with
    a. a large workforce
    b. additional funding
    c. a wide range of perspectives
    d. all of the required knowledge

15. One of the challenges of the emergency planning committee is its sheer size. Emergency managers may be able to overcome the problems associated with a committee's size by
    a. restricting committee membership
    b. holding longer, less frequent meetings
    c. creating specialized subcommittees
    d. both (a) and (b)

16. Many of the committee members, while knowledgeable in their own fields, might have little knowledge about emergency management. Emergency managers may be able to overcome this by
    a. conducting orientation and training
    b. including only those with prior knowledge
    c. assigning selected reading to committee members
    d. training all municipal staff to the same level

17. It is important for emergency managers to share the completed work of each subcommittee with other subcommittees because doing so
    a. fosters competition
    b. identifies planning implications for the other groups
    c. keeps the plan language consistent
    d. satisfies legal requirements

18. Emergency managers should share the work of individual subcommittees with the municipality's department heads to obtain feedback. Department heads require a clear understanding of what is expected of them, their staff, and their department, because such expectations
    a. may garner political support
    b. may not meet plan-creation standards
    c. may have associated budgetary implications
    d. are good to know

19. In the final stages of plan creation, emergency managers should circulate the final draft of the document to all stakeholders to solicit their agreement to comply with the plan and to
    a. avoid challenges during its presentation to council
    b. meet legal requirements
    c. identify spelling and grammatical errors
    d. provide the resources specified in the plan

20. A completed emergency plan should not be put into force until it has been
    a. approved by stakeholders
    b. approved by the legal department
    c. ratified by elected officials
    d. all of the above

CASE STUDIES

A. You are the emergency manager for a large, urban community with a population in excess of one million people. While the community does have an emergency plan, it has been many years since it has been completely rewritten. The community has grown substantially during this period, many issues addressed in the old plan have changed, and you have been tasked with the creation of a completely new emergency plan for the community.

   1. List the municipal departments who should contribute to the consultation process.
   2. List the voluntary and community agencies who should contribute to the consultation process.
   3. Set some basic objectives for the creation of the new emergency plan.
   4. List those community stakeholders who should be approached to sit on the emergency planning committee.

B. You are the new emergency manager for a community of approximately 100,000 people. As a first step in taking up your new position, you reviewed the existing emergency plan. When you reviewed the existing emergency plan, it appeared to be well-written, sensible, and easy to implement. However, it has never been tested. The last revision of the plan appears to have occurred two years ago, and the community's emergency planning committee was disbanded following the last revision.

   1. Describe the next steps that you would take to determine the effectiveness of the plan.
   2. Should the emergency planning committee be reconstituted? If yes, why? Who should be a member?
   3. Develop a work plan leading to the next formal revision of the community emergency plan.
   4. Should the existing emergency plan be completely rewritten as a priority? Why?

TO LEARN MORE

1. Visit your community's office of emergency management.
   a. Review the content of the existing community emergency plan critically. Does the plan contain all the components that you would anticipate finding? If not, which components are missing? Attempt to determine why they haven't been included.
   b. Look at the format of the plan critically. Does the existing format make the maintenance and amendment of the plan easy? If you could change the format of the plan, what changes would you make? Why?

2. A large number of emergency plans for communities and organizations are published on the Internet. These plans can be easily accessed using the keyword search "emergency plan" in any search engine. Find and read six to eight different emergency plans, ideally from different jurisdictions and different types of organizations, such as hospitals, universities, and private businesses.
   a. Does each plan contain all the components that you would anticipate finding? If not, which components are missing? Attempt to determine why they haven't been included. Are there components present that you have not seen before? Why do they appear to have been included? Are there any components that you feel might enhance the emergency plan for your local community?
   b. Look at the format of the plan critically. Does the existing format make the maintenance and amendment of the plan easy? If you could change the format of the plan, what changes would you make? Why?

NOTES

1. Emergency Management Institute, *Emergency Planning* (course materials) *Federal Emergency Management Agency*, <http://training.fema.gov/EMIWeb/IS/is235.asp>.
2. California Office of Emergency Management, *Emergency Planning Guidance for Local Government* (State of California, 1999).
3. T. Schreider, "The 10 Most Common Pitfalls in Contingency Planning," *Emergency Preparedness Digest* 21, no. 4 (1994): 22–25.

CHAPTER 12

The Components of an Emergency Plan

LEARNING OBJECTIVES

On completion of this chapter, you will

▶ Understand the key components that must be included in an emergency plan.

▶ Understand how each key component contributes to an emergency plan.

▶ Understand why each key component is necessary.

▶ Know where to find online examples of good emergency plans that are already in use.

▶ Be prepared to write an emergency plan for a community or organization.

KEY MESSAGES

1. The presence of a good, workable emergency plan is central to the ability of a community or organization to respond to any type of emergency that may occur.

2. Certain key components must be included in any effective emergency plan.

3. Some key components are necessary to make procedures operational in an emergency or to satisfy legal requirements.

4. Some key components are necessary to make an emergency plan accessible or to facilitate plan maintenance.

5. Even if it includes the best emergency procedures, an emergency plan is useless unless it is written in a manner that makes it accessible to infrequent users.

6. Some essential parts of a good emergency plan are not intended for general distribution or public release.

Introduction

As previously stated, an emergency plan is not intended to be a step-by-step guide to managing every conceivable emergency incident. An emergency plan is intended to provide a framework within which a community or organization can plan and mobilize its response and recovery efforts to emergencies. It identifies and describes general community emergency operations. It describes procedures to be used when additional resources are required. Finally, it provides a list of those resources that are available to the community during an emergency, and instructions on how each may be accessed when needed. Some emergency plans may also include components of information and procedures that are specific to various types of emergencies; in most cases, these components address events identified by the Hazard Identification and Risk Assessment (HIRA) as having the highest probability of occurrence and impact.

In chapter 11, we explored the information necessary for creating emergency plans, the objectives of such plans, and the process used to create and maintain such plans. This chapter focuses on how to produce an emergency plan. It identifies and describes the key components that must be included in the plan and the reasons they are necessary. Different from previous chapters, all references cited in this chapter direct readers to emergency plans for communities and organizations that are available online. These plans hail from a variety of different countries, and from large, medium, and small jurisdictions and organizations.

The intent of this chapter is not to provide readers with a single good example of an emergency plan or component. There is no one correct way of crafting an emergency plan; each community and organization will craft a plan that is specific to its own needs. There are strengths and weaknesses in each example used, and readers would benefit from examining in a critical manner each plan provided, identifying the strengths and weaknesses of each, as well as their commonalities and differences. Through this examination, readers will begin to understand what is possible, what has been accomplished elsewhere, and the pitfalls to avoid when crafting a plan of their own. In addition, a review of actual working emergency plans will help readers develop some sense of the format, writing style, and content appropriate to the document.

Purpose

While acquiring resources, training staff, and educating both elected officials and the general public for an emergency are all extremely important, the most important task of emergency managers is creating an effective emergency plan. The emergency plan is really what emergency management is all about, and all of the other elements of an emergency management program are intended to make that emergency plan effective and to support its use. Indeed, the competence of an emergency manager is judged according to his or her ability to create an emergency plan in which all information is accessible to infrequent users and enables the community to summon resources, organize itself, mount an effective response to an emergency, and restore normal (or at least near-normal) operations.

Emergency Plan Components

Organization and Accessibility

The key to organizing an effective emergency plan is ensuring easy access to the information contained within it. The best set of procedures in the world will fail if, during a crisis, the user cannot find those procedures or understand them. This section focuses on the design of an emergency plan for use in a community or organization and those components of the emergency plan that are intended to make critical information readily accessible.

Design

Most emergency plans are published in a simple, straightforward, three-ring binder format. A binder has a durable cover that protects the pages of the emergency plan, and it allows content to be updated easily when required.

From the start of the project, prudent emergency managers understand that the plan's components will need to be amended. Thus, they will probably elect to address items issue by issue, with a page or two allocated for each issue, and new pages for subsequent issues. While there may be a temptation to save paper and combine issues on the same page, the issue-by-issue approach is more effective over the long term: each time an amendment is made, emergency managers can simply change a few pages rather than have to republish the entire manual. Emergency managers must record and track amendments to demonstrate due diligence. For this reason, a record of amendments component should be included near the front of each copy of the manual. Also, it may be prudent to number individual copies of the manual, so that when an amendment occurs, no copy is inadvertently overlooked in the amendment process.

Publishing costs and the mandate of a growing number of governments to make emergency plans available for public review have led many emergency managers to post the manuals online at a publicly accessible website or via a corporate intranet. Having an online version of the emergency plan is useful; it makes the content widely accessible and easier to amend. It may be appropriate to direct staff to review the online version of the plan before it goes live, and to regard the online version as the most up-to-date copy of the plan. However, it is still necessary to have at least some paper copies of the emergency plan for use in the event of a computer network failure.

Record of Amendments

Any community or organization is expected, as a test of law, to do everything that could be reasonably expected of it to prepare for and respond to an emergency. This concept is known as *due diligence*. Having done everything reasonable is insufficient; one must also be able to demonstrate in a court of law or public inquiry that this has occurred. The record of amendments[1] component of an emergency plan is intended to help satisfy this requirement. Not only does it allow emergency managers to monitor the currency of each copy of the emergency plan, it also provides a "paper trail" that lists the changes that have occurred—when, why, and by whom. As well, this component demonstrates that the community or organization made a genuine effort to maintain the emergency plan in a state of continuous improvement.

Table of Contents

For any emergency plan to be used effectively, the information contained within it must be easy to find. Ideally, all intended users of an emergency plan will have read the plan thoroughly in advance and become familiar with its format. Too often, this is not the case. Most users typically scan the document when they first receive it, but may not touch it again until they actually need it during an exercise or a real emergency. To some extent, this reaction is human nature, and no emergency manager has ever successfully overcome it.

However, when a crisis occurs, the information contained in an emergency plan is required immediately. During a crisis, there is nothing more daunting than trying to search through a large, poorly organized binder or book for the one specific piece of information that is crucial at that particular moment. A simple page-numbering system and the inclusion of a formal table of contents[2] in the final document can ensure that information is quickly and easily accessible.

Statement of Scope

When commencing any type of project, a statement of scope[3] can be a useful tool, and this is particularly true for an emergency plan. A statement of scope provides users with a clear understanding of precisely where and when the emergency plan is intended to operate and where it is not. Such statements typically identify the geographic location covered: "This plan is intended to address response to emergencies occurring within the municipal boundaries of the Town of West Fork, Nebraska." They also tend to place any necessary constraints on the scope of the plan: "This emergency plan is intended to support and operate in conjunction with, but not to supersede, the emergency plan of the County of Newark. With the statement of scope, the community or organization provides a clear definition of what the plan addresses and what it does not. Such clarity can help eliminate confusion during actual emergency operations.

Statement of Objectives

The statement of objectives[4] provides a clear and concise understanding of what the emergency plan is intended to accomplish and what it is not intended to accomplish. Such statements are usually direct and to the point and specify intent: "This plan is intended to provide for the management of large-scale emergencies affecting more than one county, or crossing state lines." Similarly, boundaries for the plan may also be clearly identified: "This plan is not intended to replace the State Nuclear Emergency Plan, or any of its provisions." Once again, providing this level of clarity will help eliminate confusion during actual emergency operations.

Overview/Summary

The overview/summary[5] component is also called the *concept of operations* or *terms of reference* component in the plans of various jurisdictions, but the content of each is essentially the same. This component describes which individuals or agencies are responsible for the different aspects of emergency response, and how each aspect of emergency response will be overseen and coordinated. As well, it identifies general operating principles that are common to all agencies. To illustrate, if a community or organization has decided to use the Incident Command System or some other formal command-and-control model, it is in this component that this decision will be indicated. The key to this component is brevity. A statement that the Incident Command System is to be used will suffice; this is not the place in which to describe the system in detail. Consider this component as an "executive overview" of precisely how the provisions of the plan are to function during an emergency, with greater detail provided in other plan locations, such as an **annex**.

Major Planning Assumptions

The major planning assumptions[6] component is intended to provide background information on those areas that the authors of the plan assume will be operating at the time an emergency occurs. Essentially, it sets the stage for the rest of the content in the plan by describing in some detail the general circumstances in which the plan will operate. It may include a description of those areas assumed to be operational; for example, "It is anticipated that all normal staffing will be available, and that leaves of absence and vacations will be cancelled." It may also include a description of those areas that planners assume might not be working well during an emergency. There may be utility or transportation disruptions or anticipated casualty loads generated by the hazard event, which are indicated through statements such as, "It is assumed that the number of patients generated by the emergency will overwhelm the resources of our local hospital, and that some victims may need to be transported to distant locations for appropriate medical care." Much of this information will be based on the assessments of hazard, risk, and vulnerability, which should be performed prior to the creation of the plan.

Glossary of Terms

As has been previously stated, the information contained within an emergency plan must be accessible if it is to be of any practical use to users during an emergency. While one aspect of accessibility is plan organization, another key aspect is language. Many fields have their own jargon, and within their own familiar frame of reference, it provides a useful form of verbal "shorthand" for rapidly communicating information. However, for those who do not share that frame of reference, jargon can become an effective barrier to communication.

Wherever possible, the emergency plan should be written in plain language. That being said, however, the use of plain language may not always be possible. For example, the emergency plan, with input from the fire chief, may specify the use of the community's triple-combination pumper in one particular, and very necessary, role for which no other resource would be suitable. The mayor of the community, who is responsible for emergency response and reading the emergency plan, may have no idea what a "triple-combination pumper" is! Also, a vast array of jargon that is specific to emergency management is likely unfamiliar to the average reader. While it may be absolutely necessary and appropriate to include such elements of jargon in the emergency plan for reasons of specificity, emergency managers must always remember the average reader and ensure that clear definitions of unfamiliar terms and phrases are incorporated into the plan, if only as a glossary of terms.[7]

The Body of the Plan

Title Page

The title page[8] is, just as the name suggests, straightforward. There is, however, certain basic information that must be included on the page. The first item is the title itself; this may be "Emergency Plan," "Emergency Response Plan," or something similar, depending on the local preference for titles. The next item is the name of the jurisdiction or organization to which this plan applies. This information may be enhanced by the inclusion of a corporate seal, if required. It is also a good idea to include the name of the individual or group responsible for the creation of the plan, so that future users know who to contact with any questions that might arise regarding the plan content. If this information is not included on the title page itself, it should be included on the page that immediately follows. The final item for inclusion is the date on which the plan takes force. Including this date helps ensure that the plan remains current, and permits the reader to understand exactly how current the plan is. When an existing plan has been revised, it is also preferable to include the date of the last revision in addition to the date of creation of the plan.

Governing Authority

Most emergency plans, with the exception of those of some private businesses, are created and operate under a legal mandate from some level of government. These mandates may include legislation from federal or regional levels of government or bylaws enacted by the local authority. The type of governing authority[9] will be determined directly by the level of government or organization, and by the legal mandates that have been provided to them by senior levels of government, or by senior levels of the organization. It is important for all of those using the plan, and the general public, to understand that the provisions of the plan are not suggestions, but are backed by actual force of law. It is also important for emergency managers to ensure that the main body of any emergency plan is prefaced by a clear and concise statement that identifies the specific legislation that gives authority to the plan and its provisions. Such statements are the absolute minimum requirement for inclusion in the plan; many plans also summarize the relevant sections of applicable legislation for easy reference by users.

Levels of Incidents

It is important for the users of an emergency plan to clearly understand the scale of incident it addresses. Not all incidents are created equal and, as a result, it can be immensely helpful to provide clear levels of incidents[10] along with the anticipated responses for each. The system used to identify levels of incidents varies from one jurisdiction to another. The levels might be described as "small," "medium," and "large"; "normal incident," "crisis," and "disaster"; numerical levels; or some other system. It is not so much the system used to identify levels that is important; it is the definition of each level that is material to those using the plan.

That said, while the preceding statement is certainly true for purely local hazard events, emergency managers should also consider that many emergencies affect large areas. The use of different levels of incidents systems by adjacent communities may provide a jargon barrier, and may, as a result, hamper emergency information flow. It is highly desirable to have standardized emergency planning terminology within regions, and consultation with colleagues in neighbouring communities can help achieve such standardization. Everyone using the emergency plan requires a common frame of reference.

Plan Activation

The plan activation[11] component describes the who, when, and how of plan activation. It outlines the circumstances in which activation of the emergency plan is justified. It may include some form of **decision matrix** to enable inexperienced users to determine whether activation is required. Including a decision matrix is a good idea; whether a situation should lead to plan activation is not always immediately clear, and not every individual is comfortable with making this kind of decision.

This component identifies who has the authority to activate the emergency plan, since doing so frequently causes significant disruption in a community or organization and may have considerable financial implications. Even when an individual such as a junior supervisor does not have the authority to activate the plan, he or she will know who to contact to accomplish activation.

This component also indicates when the plan should be activated. This may include the description of a variety of circumstances in which plan activation should at least be considered. It may also include thresholds, or *trigger points*, at which plan activation becomes automatic, if this approach is endorsed by the community or organization. This information provides clear guidance to junior personnel and to those working outside of normal business hours.

The procedure for activation is also specified in this component. This procedure may vary considerably from one jurisdiction or organization to another. Usually, it consists of directions to contact a designated senior staff member or elected official who is "on call." The activation of a paging system or telephone "fan-out" list usually follows so that all required participants are summoned to a meeting point—usually the Emergency Operations Centre. The procedure should also include written instructions on the method of contact for the person who is on call and where his or her contact information (such as a pager number or home telephone number) can be found. As a general rule, the on-call person and participants should be identified by position rather than name because people often change positions. In addition, contact information (such as telephone numbers) should not be included in the main body of the plan but in an **appendix**. Having contact information in an appendix ensures that confidential information does not become incorporated into a public document and that changes in that contact information do not inadvertently "stale date" the plan or create inconsistencies in the plan's information.

This component should also include written instructions for all of the designated participants regarding exactly what steps are to be taken upon notification of plan activation. In some cases, participants will be instructed to report to a designated meeting point. In others, they will be instructed to call a particular telephone number or tune into a particular local radio station for additional emergency instructions. This component is meant to ensure that all of the key players in the community or organization are contacted and that they come together and get organized to analyze information and begin to mount a response to the crisis.

Emergency Operations Centre

Every community or organization requires some form of point of command from which to coordinate efforts in response to an emergency. This location is typically called an *Emergency Operations Centre*.[12] The centre may be a purpose-built or, more commonly, a designated and improvised space, where those responsible for the guidance of the community or organization gather throughout the emergency. (Emergency Operations Centres are discussed in detail in chapters 13 and 14.)

This component should indicate the primary and backup locations for such a centre. It should state who is expected to work there, their roles, and their responsibilities. It should also describe in broad, general terms the resources available in the Emergency Operations Centre and the manner in which the centre's emergency business will be conducted. This component should not include floor plans, staff lists, or equipment lists. These items belong in a separate annex.

Roles and Responsibilities

The roles and responsibilities[13] component clarifies which organization or agency is responsible for a given role during a crisis. There are a number of approaches to addressing roles and responsibilities. In the United States, the most commonly accepted approach is the Emergency Support Function model;[14] in Canada, the Emergency Site Management Doctrine[15] tends to dominate. Other jurisdictions use other approaches; in the United Kingdom, for example, the London Resilience Group has drafted a complete command-and-control protocol as part of their emergency planning arrangements.

The purpose of this component is to state who will have primary responsibility for which activities, as well as designate other agencies likely to provide a support function to the agency with primary responsibility. While there will almost always be some degree of overlap of responsibilities, designating them in advance will help eliminate confusion or arguments during a crisis. The inclusion of this information in the body of the plan provides clear direction to all and places the legal weight of the plan firmly on the division of responsibilities.

Details of Operations

It is important for all users of the plan to have details of operations[16] to clearly understand exactly how the emergency response, including the Emergency Operations Centre, will be conducted. In many cases, the response to an emergency follows a progressive set of stages—for example, "normal," "monitoring," "partial activation," and "full activation"—with each stage being activated when it is necessary to do so. The US Department of Homeland Security uses a similar scale[17] for advising staff and the public about terrorist threat levels. Such scales are useful; however, it is important to ensure that the plan clearly describes the meaning of each stage, as well as the various actions and responses associated with it.

This component also typically identifies functions that are expected to be carried out by various agencies. The roles and responsibilities component assigns specific roles, but the details of operations identify specific initial tasks and operating strategies for each of those roles. This guidance should be considered to be a "starting point," because tasks and operating strategies can readily change as the circumstances of an emergency change.

Declaration of Emergency

The declaration of emergency[18] component outlines the process by which the community can signal its need for outside assistance. In many circumstances, it may also state which key individuals will have emergency powers for a designated time period to ensure that the response to the emergency remains effective. The legal standards for such declarations may vary by regional government, but they do have some commonalities.

This component should specify who has the authority to issue an official declaration. In most cases, this authority rests with the elected head of the local authority council or the council itself. In some jurisdictions this authority rests with a very senior staff member; but this situation is quite rare due to the potential political and financial implications arising out of a declaration. This component should also specify the format of the declaration and the information to be included in it (for example, the emergency's location, the nature of the emergency, its expected impact, and the resources required to respond to it). It should also indicate the steps to be taken in the declaration process. This process usually involves an official written notification to senior officials of the next level of government.

It is also important to clarify what a declaration of emergency actually means. If the declaration means that an individual will be given special powers, special spending authority, or the right to suspend operations of the local elected council, this information should be specified. If the declaration means that the manner in which the community or organization responds to an emergency will change substantially, then this information should also be specified. The advantages and disadvantages of issuing a declaration of emergency should also be stated.

Stand-Down Procedures

All emergencies will eventually come to an end, and the business of the community or organization will return to normal or near-normal operations. Just as there is a plan for activating emergency response mechanisms, there must be a plan for "turning everything off." The stand-down procedures[19] component should describe those factors that must be considered with respect to the cessation of emergency operations. It must also identify the specific procedures necessary for the withdrawal of emergency resources, as well as the staging of that withdrawal. Such decisions are likely to be the result of a set of complex factors, and any advance planning and information that can be provided will prove to be helpful.

Some of the stand-down procedures may begin even while response to the emergency is ongoing. These procedures will be set in motion based on the hazard event's characteristics and on simple common sense. To illustrate, a major fire is occurring, and firefighting operations are ongoing. Evacuation orders may need to remain in place, but once all of those with injuries have been removed from the scene, is it really necessary for a large contingent of ambulances to remain on standby for the fire? Determining a logical sequence for the withdrawal of services requires some careful thought, but, executed properly, will help the community recover and begin to restore some sense of normalcy.

Recovery

The recovery[20] component describes considerations related to the return of the community to normal or near-normal operations. The focus shifts from responding to the actual hazard event, to restoring services and assisting community residents with their personal recovery efforts. The issues are complex, but include **repatriation** of evacuees, interaction with insurance companies, restoration of utility services, and the resumption of business within the community. As well, residents may need personal support that includes psychological services, such as counselling for victims.

Emergency services and government staff will also require some degree of recovery as well. Staff will need to be rested and rescheduled, expendable supplies will need to be replaced, and major equipment will need to be cleaned, reconditioned, and restocked so that it is available for the next emergency. Staff will also need to be debriefed to determine what can be learned from the response to the event and what might be done better next time.

Community recovery from a disaster can be a complicated process that can take months or even years to fully accomplish. The considerations included in this component will represent a partial list only. There is clearly too much recovery information for it all to be included in the main body of the plan. Recovery should be considered in an abbreviated fashion in the main body of the plan; a detailed recovery checklist can form a separate annex.

Termination of the Declaration of Emergency

The time will come when outside assistance is no longer required. When that time comes, it is appropriate to undertake the termination of the declaration of emergency[21] that was previously issued. The specific procedures for terminating a declaration vary by jurisdiction. This component should describe exactly who has the authority to terminate a declaration of emergency, and when that step should occur. The exact procedure for termination should be described in detail, including any external notifications that are required, such as those to senior levels of government.

Optional Inclusions

There are a number of other components that could be potentially included in an emergency plan that, while not widely used, are worthy of consideration. These components are new and evolving processes in the field of emergency management, and are, in some cases, just good ideas. These components should be at least considered and presented to senior decision-makers. Ultimately, the call to include these components should not rest solely with the authors of the plan, but with senior decision-makers. An example of an optional component is the Emergency Support Functions model. Ten years ago, this method of identifying responsibility for key aspects of plan response was an innovation, but it is increasingly becoming regarded as a key plan component, particularly in the United States.

Emergency Powers

In some jurisdictions, recent changes to legislation have given key officials the right to exercise emergency powers and issue emergency orders. In Ontario, for example, the commissioner of emergency management may issue an emergency order, directing one community to provide resources to another during a declared emergency, whether or not mutual-aid agreements between the two communities exist.

In other jurisdictions, the elected head of council may have the authority, under the terms of the emergency plan bylaw, to suspend the operations of council (but not its reporting obligations!) for a designated period during an emergency. This issue can be politically sensitive, and should be approached cautiously. Any proposed inclusion of emergency powers should be discussed with senior decision-makers to determine the community's comfort level with this type of authority, along with what powers would be appropriate and how long they should last, prior to their addition to the plan.

Spending Authority

Most governments and organizations exercise strict controls on spending, and on a day-to-day basis, this is appropriate. However, the nature of an emergency is such that situations may arise where immediate expenditures for the response to the emergency are required, but where those who would normally approve such spending may not be readily available. As a result, it may be prudent to specify a pre-authorized emergency spending level for at least one senior official (perhaps the mayor) for use during an emergency, and to incorporate that authority into the body of the plan.

Supporting Documents

Plan Ratification Signature Sheet

For an emergency plan to have any force, it must be ratified and approved by the government or organization for which it was written.[22] In local authority settings, ratification occurs most often by means of a bylaw; at regional and federal levels of government, ratification occurs by means of appropriate legislative measures, such as state or provincial emergency planning laws. Many governments and organizations take ratification a step further: they have the final document reviewed and signed off by a senior elected official, such as the mayor, or by the entire elected council, or, in the case of organizations, by the chief executive officer or the board of directors. At other levels of government, this duty of formal ratification may fall to a cabinet minister, the governor, or some other senior elected official. Emergency managers will also have the document signed off by the heads of all applicable municipal departments, voluntary agencies, and key stakeholders. This measure gathers support for the plan, and indicates that those responsible for key stakeholder organizations are aware of their obligations under the plan. In some cases, the signature sheet will be reproduced either at the front of the plan, prior to the table of contents, or as an annex (this is largely a stylistic choice).

Annexes

A basic emergency plan is a generic document. It is intended to provide the means by which a community or organization can organize itself and mount a response to any type of emergency. It is not intended to address the specifics of each individual type of emergency; it is intended merely to organize response and recovery efforts, and identify available resources. Emergency response will be adapted based on the specific circumstances of the emergency. It is this generic approach that provides an emergency plan with the flexibility required to achieve these objectives.

From time to time, however, communities and organizations may wish to expand the emergency plan to make provisions for specific types of hazard events that have been previously identified as high risk or high probability. Such sub-plans are typically referred to as *annexes*,[23] and appear after the main body of the plan. Information such as detailed instructions for specific emergency procedures, maps, charts, and diagrams may also be incorporated as annexes to the main body of the plan. Annexes typically fall into two categories: functional and case specific.

Functional annexes may be used to describe specific procedures, such as how to assemble the Emergency Operations Centre or produce a declaration of emergency. They may also include organizational charts, responsibility matrices, or mutual-aid plans. They provide critical information that may be used as either a reference source or a "how-to" manual for activating and establishing specific functions during an emergency.

Case-specific annexes are used to provide contingency plans for specific high-risk or high-probability hazard events, and are often determined by the HIRA process. Such annexes describe specific procedures and may provide risk-exposure maps or other useful information dealing with particular types of events. These sub-plans are subordinate to the main emergency plan and may address specific events, such as floods, tornadoes, or hazardous materials spills. The case-specific annexes required by each community or organization are different because their risk exposures are different.

Appendices

The final component of any emergency plan is perhaps one of its most important. A large amount of information is required to make the plan operational. Unfortunately, most of this information should not be made generally available and, in particular, should not be available to the general public. The inclusion of confidential information is particularly problematic when there is a legal mandate to make the final emergency plan available for public inspection, as is the case in many jurisdictions. Typically, confidential information includes telephone contact lists for key stakeholders (often including home telephone numbers), detailed resource lists, lists of suppliers, purchase order numbers, and "back channel" telephone numbers (numbers that are unpublished and not routed through the main telephone system) for all of the agencies, adjacent communities, and levels of government with whom planners commonly work.

Appendices should include 24-hour contact instructions for the mayor or head of council and all applicable elected officials. It should also include 24-hour contact information for all relevant municipal department heads and their designated alternates. If an on-call shift rotation has been established, this should also be stated. At a minimum, particularly where telephone fan-out lists are used for plan activation, appendices should include the contact information for the top individual on each telephone "tree," as well as their designated alternate. In some communities, particularly smaller ones, this information is often expanded to include home telephone numbers for all staff.

It is important to also be able to access all suppliers of critical resources or services at any time. Emergencies rarely seem to happen during normal business hours, so it is important to maintain a list of 24-hour contact information for all critical suppliers, including, where necessary, purchase order numbers for the resources required. If 24-hour access arrangements are not in place, it is prudent to specify them as a requirement in any future purchase negotiations.

When emergencies occur, the main switchboards and telephone numbers of all sorts of agencies tend to be overwhelmed by individuals seeking information or assistance. This can create a serious problem for emergency communications between agencies and levels of government. Most emergency managers will develop a list of "back channel" telephone numbers for all applicable agencies, adjacent communities, and levels of government, and ensure that the same "back channel" arrangement is made for their own operation. While the creation of such a system may involve considerable work, the availability of such a list can be invaluable during a crisis. Since the intent is to not make the telephone numbers generally available, their inclusion as an appendix to the main body of the plan is entirely appropriate.

Incorporating these items as appendices is an effective strategy for ensuring that confidential information remains confidential. It also permits the main body of the plan to be made available to lower-level staff and to the general public without the confidential appendices. In this way, the requirement to make the plan available for public inspection can be satisfied, while ensuring the confidentiality of sensitive information.

Conclusion

The creation of an emergency plan is the most important task that any emergency manager will ever perform. An effective plan can make the difference between the success and failure of the community's or organization's response to the crisis in question. For a plan to be effective, the information contained within it must be easy to access and easy to understand. Information must be organized in a user-friendly manner, and the plan itself should be formatted in a manner that makes it easy to maintain. Above all, the plan must contain the information required to turn it from words on paper into an operational response. The task is not an easy one, nor should it be; if anyone could write an emergency plan, emergency managers would be unnecessary.

This chapter has provided readers with an overview of the required contents of an effective emergency plan. It has also provided the rationale for the inclusion of each of the plan components. In the notes at the end of this chapter, readers are provided with website addresses for more than 20 emergency plans, including those from various levels of government, communities large and small, and other types of organizations, and are encouraged to examine each in terms of style, format, and content. In doing so, readers will gain a better appreciation of exactly what is required in an effective emergency plan, and also how to go about creating one.

KEY TERMS

annex

appendix

decision matrix

repatriation

LEARNING CHECK

Take a few minutes now to test your knowledge of the components of an emergency plan. Select the best answer in each case. Any score of less than 16 out of 20 (80 percent) indicates that you should re-read this chapter.

1. A community's ability to respond effectively to an emergency is in large measure determined by
   a. the resources available
   b. the training of staff
   c. a good emergency plan
   d. legal mandates

2. Certain information must be included in any effective emergency plan. This information could be described as
   a. legal requirements
   b. policy statements
   c. the mayor's message
   d. key components

3. Some of the information in an emergency plan is necessary to make procedures operational or to
   a. satisfy legal requirements
   b. keep the plan organized
   c. meet the requirements of emergency services
   d. guarantee community safety

4. Some of the information in an emergency plan is necessary to make the
   plan accessible or
   a. reduce printing costs
   b. clarify the roles of subordinate staff
   c. facilitate plan maintenance
   d. satisfy governmental requirements

5. The best emergency procedures in the world are useless unless
   a. the information is accessible
   b. they meet strict legal requirements
   c. they are approved by emergency services
   d. they are supported by the business community

6. Some essential parts of a good emergency plan are not
   a. available to decision-makers
   b. intended for general distribution
   c. open to interpretation
   d. both (a) and (c)

7. An effective emergency plan is intended to provide a framework within
   which a community or organization can plan and mobilize its response to
   emergencies, and
   a. restore normal or near-normal operations
   b. address the issues of every type of emergency
   c. provide political guidance
   d. direct the work of volunteers

8. The effectiveness of an emergency plan is generally the standard by which
   the _____ of an emergency manager will be judged.
   a. political skills
   b. negotiating skills
   c. knowledge
   d. competence

9. Activities that are part of an emergency program, such as staff training, public education, educating elected officials, and the acquisition of resources are intended to support
   a. legal mandates
   b. the effectiveness of the emergency plan
   c. dealing with the media
   d. emergency service operations

10. The purpose of the record of amendments is to permit emergency managers to ensure the currency of all copies of the emergency plan and to
    a. provide an overview of operations
    b. demonstrate that the emergency manager is working
    c. satisfy due diligence requirements
    d. ensure that each amendment is approved by those in authority

11. The annexes to the emergency plan may be described as either functional or
    a. case specific
    b. person specific
    c. department specific
    d. general

12. The component of the emergency plan that provides a brief and concise overview of how the plan will operate is sometimes referred to as
    a. the executive summary
    b. the concept of operations
    c. the terms of reference
    d. both (b) and (c)

13. The use of a three-ring binder for publishing the emergency plan allows emergency managers to
    a. make amendments without republishing the whole document
    b. distribute the plan as widely as possible
    c. ensure that no plan component is lost
    d. track any changes to the plan

14. The statement of scope is intended to describe where the emergency plan is intended to operate and to
    a. describe the responsibilities of key players
    b. describe the legal authority for the plan
    c. place boundaries on where the plan will operate
    d. place boundaries on the circumstances of use

15. The plan component that is used to provide readers with an understanding of jargon and acronyms incorporated into the plan is called the
    a. terms of reference
    b. index
    c. table of contents
    d. glossary of terms

16. The plan component that is used to describe the legal basis on which the plan operates is called the
    a. glossary of terms
    b. governing authority
    c. mission statement
    d. appendix

17. Information that must be included in the main body of the plan is the procedure required to
    a. declare an emergency
    b. terminate a declaration
    c. exercise emergency spending authority
    d. both (a) and (b)

18. The manner in which the business of the Emergency Operations Centre should be conducted would be described in
    a. the optional inclusions
    b. the details of operations
    c. the executive summary
    d. an appendix

19. The duties of those working in the Emergency Operations Centre would be described in
    a. the roles and responsibilities
    b. the spending authority
    c. the executive summary
    d. an annex

20. Sensitive information not intended for public consumption should always be placed in
    a. the introduction
    b. the governing authority
    c. an appendix
    d. an annex

CASE STUDIES

A. You are the new emergency manager for a community of approximately 100,000 people. When you were given the job, one of the mayor's major complaints was that, during a recent community emergency, he pulled out this "massive binder" and spent most of his time trying to find the information he needed. As a result, you have decided that the emergency plan will ultimately need to be completely rewritten, but as an interim measure, you must reformat the existing emergency plan to make the information contained in it more accessible.

1. What will you need to do before the proposed reformatting can occur?
2. What steps can you quickly take to make critical information more accessible?
3. Will these steps require any other approvals? If yes, why?
4. Develop a work plan for the project.

B. You are the new emergency manager for a community of 500,000 people. The community has an emergency plan that is three years old. In that time, the plan has not been tested by either an exercise or a real hazard event. You understand that the plan should probably be completely rewritten, but competing demands for your time mean that only a revision can occur right now.

1. Describe the key components of the plan that will need to be revised immediately.
2. Why do these particular components require immediate attention?
3. Describe the process required to revise these key components.
4. Develop a work plan for the revision of the emergency plan.

TO LEARN MORE

1. Select one of the key components of an emergency plan described in this chapter. Find several examples of this component in the online emergency plans that are presented in the notes at the end of this chapter, then consider the following questions for each example: Why is this component included in the emergency plan? What purpose is it meant to serve? Is this component written differently from the other examples? Does this component achieve its objectives in the emergency plan? Why?

   Can you see any ways in which this component might better achieve its objectives?

2. Based on the information that you have gathered in the activity above, create the same component for your school's or organization's existing

emergency plan. Once you have completed your draft, examine it critically. Are there any obvious weaknesses? Make any necessary revisions. Now, ask your colleagues to review the draft and provide any observations, criticisms, or ideas for making the component stronger. Rewrite the component, addressing your colleagues' feedback. Does the final product meet the needs of your emergency plan?

NOTES

1. Governor's Office of Homeland Security and Emergency Preparedness, *State of Louisiana Emergency Operations Plan*, 2007, <http://www.ohsep.louisiana .gov/plans/EOP.pdf>.
2. Corporation of the City of Stratford, *Emergency Response Plan*, 2007, <http://www.city.stratford.on.ca/documents/EmergencyPlan/ Emergency%20Plan.pdf>.
3. London Borough of Sutton, *Emergency Plan*, 2003, <http://www.sutton.gov .uk/NR/rdonlyres/E8649911-2309-4337-8432-2C683AD63F65/0/ Borough_plan.pdf>.
4. West Virginia Division of Homeland Security and Emergency Management, *West Virginia Emergency Operations Plan*, 2004, <http://www.wvdhsem.gov/ EOP/WVEOP_basic_plan.pdf>.
5. Government of Saint Lucia, *National Emergency Management Plan*, 1996, <http://www.geocities.com/CapitolHill/Lobby/6075/Natpln-1.htm>.
6. Virginia Department of Health, *Emergency Operations Plan: Pandemic Influenza*, 2007, <http://www.vdh.virginia.gov/PandemicFlu/pdf/ DRAFT_Virginia_Pandemic_Influenza_Plan.pdf>.
7. Nova Scotia Agricultural College, *Emergency Response Plan*, 2006, <http://www.nsac.ns.ca/admin/policies/emergresplanjune06.pdf>.
8. Northamptonshire County Council, *Northamptonshire County Emergency Plan*, 2007, <http://www.northamptonshire.gov.uk/ncc/Templates/ PrintFriendly.aspx?guid={2586783A-8580-4059-B977-0F3694F37B79}>.
9. Emergency Management Unit, Ontario Ministry of Health and Long-Term Care, *Ministry Emergency Response Plan*, 2007, <http://www.health.gov.on.ca/ english/providers/program/emu/emerg_prep/emerg/emerg_resp_plan.pdf>.
10. Brock University, *Emergency Management Plan: Response and Recovery*, 2006, <http://www.brocku.ca/oehs/emp.pdf>.
11. Canterbury City Council, *Canterbury City Council Major Emergency Plan*, 2006, <http://www.canterbury.gov.uk/assets/emergencyplan/sect2.pdf>.

12. County of Grey, *County of Grey Emergency Management Plan*, 2006, <http://www.greycounty.ca/files/pagecontent/Emergency%20Management%20Plan,%20Schedule%20A.pdf>.

13. London Resilience, *Command and Control Protocol*, 2006, <http://www.londonprepared.gov.uk/downloads/c&cprotocol_may2006.pdf>.

14. US Department of Homeland Security, *National Response Base Plan*, 2007, <http://www.dhs.gov/xprepresp/committees/editorial_0566.shtm>.

15. Ron Kuban, *The Emergency Site Management System: A Doctrine Paper* (Ottawa: Emergency Preparedness Canada, 1998) <http://ww3.ps-sp.gc.ca/research/resactivites/emerMan/PDFs/1997-D002_e.pdf>.

16. Office of Emergency Management, *City of Toronto Emergency Plan*, 2005, <http://www.toronto.ca/wes/techservices/oem/pdf/emergency_plan.pdf>.

17. US Department of Homeland Security, *Homeland Security Advisory System*, 2008, <http://www.dhs.gov/xinfoshare/programs/Copy_of_press_release_0046.shtm>.

18. City of Victoria, *Victoria Emergency Plan*, 2006, <http://www.victoria.ca/common/pdfs/emergency_plan_0107.pdf>.

19. London Borough of Southwark, *Strategic Services*, 2006, <http://www.southwark.gov.uk/Uploads/FILE_22609.pdf>.

20. Supra note 12.

21. Township of Pelee, *Emergency Response Plan for the Township of Pelee*, 2007, <http://www.townofessex.on.ca/pdf/fire/Emergency%20Response%20Plan-091007.pdf>.

22. Disaster Services, *Alberta Emergency Plan*, 2007, <http://www.aema.alberta.ca/documents/ema/aep2000.pdf>.

23. City of Newport Beach, *Emergency Management Plan*, 2004, ss. 2, 3, <http://www.city.newport-beach.ca.us/EmergManagementPlan/EmerManagementplan.htm>.

CHAPTER 13

Emergency Operations Centres

<table>
<tr><td>

LEARNING OBJECTIVES

On completion of this chapter, you will

▶ Be able to describe the role of the Emergency Operations Centre (EOC) in community emergency response.

▶ Understand the manner in which the EOC is organized and operates.

▶ Understand the type of interaction that takes place between the EOC and emergency responders in the field during an emergency.

▶ Understand design considerations for both improvised and purpose-built EOCs.

</td><td>

KEY MESSAGES

1. The presence of an effective EOC is central to the community's ability to provide the necessary coordination of information, logistics, and services during an emergency.

2. The success or failure of the community's emergency response may be determined, to some extent, by the presence of an effective EOC.

3. An EOC may be purpose-built, but more often uses an improvised space.

4. The design of the EOC plays a major role in its effectiveness as a working environment.

5. Poor EOC design actually creates problems for those tasked with coordinating response to the emergency.

6. In an EOC, the most important concerns are information and how well that information flows both in the EOC and other locations focusing on the emergency response.

</td></tr>
</table>

Introduction

In any major emergency situation, there are two key components to the community's or organization's ability to respond to an emergency. The first is the command-and-control structure adopted by emergency responders in the field. The second is the central point from which information and resources that would otherwise be unavailable to emergency responders are managed and provided. This central point is meant to reduce the workload of emergency responders by assuming functions that, while essential, would overwhelm field operations. It also serves as a location from which the community as a whole can continue to be managed during an emergency, in terms of both governance and the provision of essential services to all residents. In most communities, this central point is called the *Emergency Operations Centre (EOC)*.

This chapter describes the EOC in terms of both structure and function. It also explores the roles and responsibilities of those within the EOC. The business process used within the EOC is described, as well as the interaction between those in the EOC and emergency responders in the field. Finally, the critical role of design in both EOC creation and operations will be examined, as well as different approaches to EOC assembly.

Purpose

Strong central coordination is required for emergency responders at the scene of an emergency and those responsible for guiding the community throughout the emergency. Emergency responders require information and logistical support to handle the victims. Meanwhile, wherever possible, the life of the community or organization must go on during the emergency, with essential services continuing to be provided elsewhere in the community. In an emergency, the EOC becomes the community focal point, providing and coordinating all of the above services, and ensuring that key decision-makers have an environment in which they can be as effective as possible. Detailed knowledge of EOCs and their operations is essential knowledge for emergency managers.

The Role of the EOC

When it functions as it should, the EOC becomes the "nerve centre" of the community's emergency response efforts. The key decision-makers in the community are brought together in one place to receive and process information, analyze issues, set objectives, and expedite access to resources for on-site emergency responders and the overall community. The EOC is where those with the highest levels of authority and decision-making powers gather to guide the entire community throughout the emergency.

While those in command positions within the traditional emergency services exercise authority and decision-making powers on a day-to-day basis, a large-scale emergency is not "business as usual." As a result, often issues arise or resources are required that are considerably beyond the scope of authority of emergency service commanders. To manage an emergency effectively, information may be required that is not ordinarily immediately available. Similarly, the management of an emergency may require resources that are not usually available within the community, and, as a result, must be imported or even purchased from elsewhere, placing them beyond the normal reach of a commander in the field.

In many cases, the hazard event generates issues that are beyond the normal expertise of emergency services. These issues include sheltering and caring for victims who may have been displaced by the event or integrating the services provided by other municipal departments, public utilities, or voluntary agencies. Often, traditional emergency services are stretched to their limits managing the issues of the disaster scene itself and dealing with the immediate effects of the hazards generated by the event. Managing the scene of the event is not managing the emergency, and other efforts are required if the emergency is to be brought under control and the community is to be returned to a state of normalcy.

Coordination and support that go well beyond traditional mutual-aid agreements are often required between adjacent communities. Cooperative efforts involve not only sharing emergency response resources such as fire trucks but also providing the emergency services of one community to another. Truly large emergencies may also require the intervention and assistance of senior levels of government that may be located far from the community. Coordination and support require ongoing dialogue and negotiation; something that the emergency service commander at the emergency scene lacks both the time and the expertise to accomplish.

Information can be critical to the successful response to an emergency, and much of this information may only be available in forms that are not immediately accessible by emergency service commanders at the scene. To illustrate, a fire service commander may find weather information useful while managing a hazardous materials incident, but how can he or she reliably obtain good information while out in the field? Similarly, an emergency medical service commander may need information regarding the availability of hospital beds within the region, but will have difficulty in obtaining it, or possibly negotiating for it, from the field. In either case, even if direct access to such information could be provided, there is a strong possibility that attempting to manipulate or analyze it would distract emergency service commanders from the task at hand: managing the emergency scene.

At the same time, away from the emergency scene, the activities of the community must carry on (as much as this is possible). Critical services must continue to be delivered, although sometimes in altered forms. Normal business operations need to continue where it is practical to do so. In some large communities, life may continue unaltered in neighbourhoods located at some distance from the emergency scene. Planning will need to begin early during the event for the recovery of the community and the restoration of a state of normal or "near-normal" operations. The governance of the community must continue, and, as much as is possible, life must go on.

The management of all of these issues and more are the responsibility of the EOC. Its role is to provide much-needed information and other forms of support to those tasked with managing the emergency scene, to ensure the continued function of the balance of the community where possible, and to plan and create the recovery operation that will return the community to daily life. Performing these tasks requires a special group of people; access to exceptional resources; and an environment that is conducive to information sharing, complex interaction, and high levels of decision making and authority.

The Occupants of the EOC

Those who work at the EOC typically fall into three basic groups: the Municipal Control Group, the Municipal Support Group, and the EOC support staff.[1]

Municipal Control Group

The first group is responsible for guiding the community throughout the emergency. This group has primary and, often, legislated responsibility for the management of the emergency. In many jurisdictions, it is called the **Municipal** (or Organizational) **Control Group (MCG)**.

The MCG is headed by the mayor or elected head of council, or in the case of another type of organization, by an individual with absolute authority for decision making. In the municipal setting, this group typically consists of the heads of the traditional emergency services, such as police, fire, and Emergency Medical Services (EMS), or their delegates. It also includes those from other agencies considered to have a major role in emergency response. These agencies may include public works and transportation departments, and community services such as welfare and housing. In jurisdictions where such positions exist, it will also include the CEO or municipal manager and, in some cases, a representative from the legal department of the private firm used by the community to provide legal advice and services.

The MCG assumes a variety of roles. At the emergency scene, the MCG supports the **incident manager** by analyzing and providing him or her information, as well as providing requested resources. Away from the primary location of the emergency, this group is tasked with providing facilities, resources, and other necessities to victims of the hazard event, such as emergency shelter and mass-feeding operations. It is also tasked with the ongoing provision of essential services elsewhere in the community. The MCG is responsible for making the decision to declare or terminate a local emergency, managing the media and public information, and coordinating information with adjacent communities and other levels of government.

In most communities, often the division of responsibilities between those at the scene and those in the EOC is determined by the event perimeter.[2] Once a clear perimeter has been defined for the actual location of the emergency, issues arising within the perimeter are typically the responsibility of the incident manager at the scene. The support required within the perimeter and those issues arising outside of the perimeter will be the responsibility of the EOC. In all cases, however, the incident manager is wholly accountable to the EOC, and the staff of the EOC provides the policy framework and the authority with which the incident manager will actually operate in the management of the emergency.

Municipal Support Group

The second group is responsible for providing support and resources to key decision-makers during an emergency. People in this group are usually not in the business of emergency response, but are nonetheless stakeholders, such as those from non-critical government services, public utilities, and voluntary agencies. This group is called the **Municipal** (or Organizational) **Support Group (MSG)**.

The MSG comprises stakeholders from municipal services, transit, public utilities (such as electricity, water, and sewage systems), and telephone service providers, among others. It also includes key representatives from those voluntary agencies that have agreed to participate in disaster response, such as the Red Cross, faith-based groups, and others. These individuals support the MCG, and are generally placed under the authority of the deputy mayor or some other senior civic official. Their task is to conduct research and information gathering, and to provide resources such as work crews, vehicles, and specialty resources. In some jurisdictions, the MSG may also comprise individuals in subordinate positions within the agencies participating in the MCG, and may act as an information filter, assessing all incoming information and determining which items actually need to be brought to the attention of the MCG.

EOC Support Staff

The third group is responsible for keeping the EOC functioning and available to those in the decision-making role. People in this group, while not key decision-makers, are nevertheless critical to successful operations, because they are the individuals who possess an intimate understanding of exactly how the tools and resources located within the EOC work. This group is called the **EOC support staff**.

This group typically operates under the authority of the emergency manager. It comprises both support staff and specialists, such as those with the knowledge and skills to provide technical support for information and telecommunications technology. Also assigned to this group are clerical support staff, housekeeping staff, dietary and hospitality staff, and EOC security staff. These people ensure that all the resources available to the MCG and MSG continue to function, and that a safe, comfortable, and effective work environment is provided for both groups. While this group's role is supportive, the EOC cannot function effectively for a protracted period without it.

The Business Cycle

The key role of the EOC is to manage both information and resources. To do so effectively, the MCG requires a management process that meets its needs in a consistent and effective manner. The occupants of an EOC are not meant to sequester themselves and handle the emergency by remote control. The process involved in responding to an emergency is dynamic and requires a certain level of management. This process is generally referred to as the *business cycle*.

Members of the MCG will meet on a regular basis, at a level of frequency to be determined by either the person in charge or group consensus. The level of frequency will vary, according to the amount of information to be processed, the nature of the emergency, and the needs of the community. In many communities, the MSG may operate with a business process that is similar and parallel, but separate. The business process itself is typically very high-level management, focusing on issues rather than on direct management of resources: the group meets, shares information, identifies and analyzes issues and resource requests, proposes solutions, sets both objectives and timelines for their completion, and assigns tasks to specific individuals or agencies within the group. When information or resources are not readily available, the MCG may assign the MSG with the task of finding and proposing solutions. In some cases, it may be necessary for members of the MCG to meet on a continual basis; in other cases, the MCG may disband periodically, with its members regathering at designated times to measure progress. In each case, the approach used will be determined by both the nature and the scale of the emergency. The MCG and its supporting staff will continue to meet—assessing and using information, and identifying and resolving issues—until such time as no new issues arise and the emergency is over.

The communication of information and progress is critical to the effective management of an emergency. As a result, following each business-cycle meeting, or at designated intervals when the meeting process is continuous, the EOC will issue a document called a **situation report**, often abbreviated as "**sitrep**." The intent of the sitrep is to summarize the activities that have occurred up to that point, the issues that have been generated and how they are being managed, and any outstanding issues requiring resolution. Information in this standard format may be circulated internally, among the community's senior staff, or shared with adjacent communities or other levels of government. Sitreps are generally regarded as working briefing documents, and are not usually intended for distribution to the media or the general public. Copies of all sitreps are retained over the long term to support the chronological record of events and also for the creation of an after action report, once the emergency is over.

EOC Design

All EOCs must provide an environment that is supportive, comfortable, and conducive to the business activities being conducted within it.[3] A variety of basic design models are in common use and available for review and consideration.[4] While some EOCs, particularly in large communities or organizations and at senior levels of government, may be purpose-built, others are much more likely to be improvised spaces that are put to other uses between emergencies. These improvised spaces may include boardrooms, classrooms, or even local authority council chambers.

EOCs, whether improvised or purpose-built, require certain common features. These features are driven by the need to provide an environment that is conducive to working. They include a requirement for emergency power and multiple layers of redundancy for the technologies employed in support of the EOC (EOC technologies will be discussed in detail in chapter 14). For now, suffice it to say that in a well-designed EOC, as many items as possible are supported by at least one layer of redundancy, ideally technologically independent from the primary layer, and with support system requirements (such as cabling) discreetly installed well in advance of activation and use. The interfaces between such systems should be as simple and user-friendly as possible, because the users of such systems tend to have little knowledge of how they are created and assembled, or what makes them work.

Environment

The environment of the EOC should always be the top priority when deciding on location or design. The primary factors that must be considered are lighting, ventilation, workspace, and noise. Among these, noise is paramount. (See "Lighting, Ventilation, and Noise Reduction" on page 245.) The EOC is, by its very nature, a high-stress environment. When an EOC is operating, a great deal is typically at stake for the community, and this fact alone will create significant stress for participants. Any design features intended to reduce environmental stressors will contribute to creating a more effective working environment. While no EOC design seems to fully address all of the above-mentioned environmental issues, it should at least try to minimize them.

Many EOCs function as a multi-purpose meeting space. A meeting area with a large table for the group is required, with clear lines of sight to projection screens, flip charts, and other forms of information display. A separate meeting area may be required for both the MCG and the MSG. In many EOCs, workstations are provided for individual members of the groups. These are typically arranged along outside walls, facing away from the primary meeting table, and include telephones, whiteboards, and computers. Workstations permit the members of the team to remain within the EOC, working on key issues or assignments, between business-cycle meetings. When a business-cycle meeting is about to occur, individuals simply conclude what they are working on and move their seats a short distance to join the main table. In other designs, workstations are located at one end of the meeting area or immediately adjacent to the meeting area. Space can be an issue; ideally, when selecting an EOC space, it is wise to attempt to allocate at least 80 square feet (7 square metres) of working space per occupant, with 100 square feet (9 square metres) being optimal. The work at hand is trying enough, without having a truly confined space contributing to stress levels.

Furnishings

The furnishings of the EOC are also an important consideration. While the furnishings may not be elaborate or expensive, they must, at a minimum, be conducive to a comfortable working environment. Furnishings should be in reasonable repair, with appropriate work surfaces and seating arrangements. Standard office chairs and desks are appropriate; folding chairs and tables are not. When selecting furnishings for an EOC, your own personal preferences will probably be a valid indicator. Ask yourself how comfortable *you* would be working on folding furniture for a week or more.

Access Control and Security of Information

EOCs require strict access control. The only people who should be inside an EOC are those actually assigned to work there. There is a well understood and potentially troublesome process known as "convergence," in which anyone who feels that they might have something to contribute tends to congregate in the EOC. The presence of anyone else, however well intentioned, has the potential to disrupt EOC operations. A well-placed receptionist or security guard, controlling access to the facility, can substantially reduce such disruptions and, therefore, provisions should be made for a workspace for such an individual (ideally just outside of a secured entrance).

The security of information is another important aspect that should be considered when selecting or designing an EOC location. EOCs typically process a great deal of potentially sensitive information, and providing the general public with access to that information may not necessarily be desirable. Having access to large windows contributes directly to a positive working environment, but when an EOC is located on the ground floor of a building, such windows may provide portals through which the media, armed with long-lens cameras or sensitive listening devices, may be able to pick up sensitive information. Design arrangements should be made to protect the security of information.

Lighting, Ventilation, and Noise Reduction

The lighting used in an EOC can either minimize or directly contribute to the stress of the occupants. Certain types of lighting, such as standard blue-range fluorescent lighting, have been demonstrated to contribute significantly to stress, particularly with prolonged exposure. Where fluorescent lighting is to be used, it is preferable to consider the use of full-spectrum fluorescent tubes, because these do not have the same stress-generating effect. Ideally, lighting should be variable, so that the occupants of the EOC are not working under a harsh glare, regardless of the hour of the day or night. Individual lighting in workstations should also be considered. This variable-lighting option can be adjusted to meet the needs of a single occupant, without unnecessarily disturbing others nearby. This lighting arrangement is particularly important during nighttime operations, and when variable lighting is used as the primary lighting system for the EOC.

Adequate ventilation of the space, along with heating and cooling, is also an important consideration. A significantly large group of people will be doing high-stress work within an enclosed environment. Reasonable temperature control and adequate air flow can make a big difference in how the occupants function. A large group of people, a confined space, and stuffy air are a recipe for high stress and conflict among EOC occupants—a situation to be avoided wherever possible. That being said, some tradeoffs may be necessary; large fans, for example, provide improved ventilation of the space, but also contribute significantly to noise levels.

When considering EOC design, noise is a major enemy of emergency managers. Unnecessary noise not only disrupts the business process of the EOC and makes it difficult for occupants to hear what is being said, it can also contribute directly to occupant stress levels. A great deal of the noise that must be addressed is ambient noise, such as fans, footfalls, telephones, and media devices.

As a first step in addressing this issue, emergency managers should strictly eliminate noise-generating devices from the main meeting area of the EOC. This includes a strict ban on two-way radios (emergency service chiefs love them), media devices such as televisions and radios, loud fans, and telephones that ring. It is often necessary to have a television within the EOC meeting area, but the sound should remain turned off, and the model used should include a closed-captioning option so that information is accessible without contributing to noise. Telephones selected for use in the EOC and its workstations should be equipped with flashers to identify incoming calls, and should have the ringer function turned completely off. There can be as many as 20 individual telephones in an EOC; try to envision the noise level generated when they are all constantly ringing, and the necessity of this measure becomes evident.

If a designated EOC is to be built, features to control noise should be incorporated in the design. Such features might include the installation of sound-absorbing materials on all of the interior walls to eliminate sound reflection and echo. At a minimum, flooring such as a good-quality industrial carpet should be used to deaden the sound of footfalls and the movement of furniture, such as chairs.

The Challenges of Improvised Space

Using an improvised space for the EOC presents some additional challenges. Emergency managers must not only address all of the above issues, but also those related to the assembly of the EOC. If a space has been designated, some advance steps, such as wiring and telecommunications cabling, can and should occur. However, there are other elements of assembly that cannot even be considered until the facility is actually required to operate. Not the least of these is where and how all of the required resources will be stored, and how they will be mobilized when required. There are two general approaches to dealing with these resource storage and use issues: the *push system* and the *pull system*. The nature of the space to be used will determine which system will work best in each case.

In an improvised space that uses the push system, all of the equipment required for EOC assembly is stored in a secure location somewhere near the space that is intended for use. The equipment is usually secured in large bins or plastic containers, and may even include a cart of some sort to facilitate its movement. When the EOC is required, the designated person will obtain the equipment and "push" it into the intended EOC site, where it will be assembled and tested prior to activation. The cart and storage containers are then removed, and what remains is a functional EOC. After the hazard event has ended, all items are disassembled, catalogued, and returned to storage, until they are required again.

The pull system operates somewhat differently. The required equipment is stored in locked cabinets within the intended EOC site. When the EOC is required, the cabinets are unlocked and the equipment is "pulled" out, assembled, and tested.

When testing is complete, the EOC is functional. After the hazard event has ended, the equipment is disassembled and returned to its assigned storage cabinet until the next time it is required.

The pull system is a little more costly to implement than the push system (cabinets cost more than carts and bins). However, it provides an advantage in that the equipment does not need to be moved any significant distance, and this means that assembly time may be reduced.

While economic necessity leads a community or organization to one of these two approaches, they both present some significant problems for emergency managers. The majority of staff lack the expertise to install and test computer networks or telephones, and, even when trained, typically do not practise these skills often enough to retain them indefinitely. The result is that the EOC will be reliant on support staff with specific skill sets. If these individuals become difficult to contact for any reason, the establishment of a fully functional EOC may be considerably delayed, and participants will need to perform their roles in a less-than-optimal environment. These issues can be overcome somewhat by selecting systems with easy installation, and by creating manuals that provide easily accessible and understandable step-by-step instructions for EOC assembly and testing.

Support Facilities

Apart from the primary meeting area, there are a number of facilities that are likely to be required to support EOC activities. These include both operational-support components and also "creature comforts" for occupants of the EOC. Such facilities may be incorporated into the EOC design or made available in locations adjacent to the EOC, but it is important that in all cases that they are nearby to ensure that they remain useful.

Operational-support components include separate rooms for monitoring on-scene radio communications, operations by radio amateurs when they are used, and the mass media's reporting of the event. All such facilities tend to generate large amounts of noise, which can be both disruptive to the business operation of the EOC and stressful for its occupants, but each has an important role and is therefore necessary. Such facilities should be placed in sequestered areas that are adjacent to the main EOC, but where the noise generated will not interfere with EOC operations. Where soundproofing such facilities is possible, it should be undertaken.

It is highly desirable to have "breakout" rooms located immediately adjacent to the main EOC. These rooms will allow any necessary "sidebar" meetings to occur between EOC members and their support staff, without interfering in the business process of the EOC. Such facilities do not typically need to be large; they merely need to be private. The types of resources normally found in a boardroom or classroom are required in such locations.

It is also useful to have a facility for the representatives of the mass media. This facility should provide basic amenities and work environments for the press corps, and will be the location in which media conferences and interviews are conducted. For reasons of security, this facility should be located somewhere near the EOC, but with clearly defined boundaries beyond which the media will not be permitted. This area should remain under the authority of the individual tasked with the public information function and that person's support staff.

The type and level of creature comforts required for EOC members and staff will be determined, to some extent, by the nature of the hazard event. At a minimum, dining and rest areas should be provided, along with washroom facilities. Such facilities should be quiet and away from any meeting areas, but immediately accessible. In large or protracted emergencies, it may be necessary to expand these facilities to include a kitchen, sleeping accommodations, and shower and sanitary facilities for those who are unable to leave the EOC for extended periods of time.

Conclusion

An EOC that is well equipped and well organized can fulfill a critical support function for those responding to a community emergency, and play a vital role in both response and recovery activities. It is a high-stress environment, filled with "high-stakes" players who must be able to work together effectively, regardless of what is happening around them. This challenge is further complicated by the fact that most communities and organizations do not possess the space or the resources for a purpose-built facility; an improvised facility will always have variables that may be difficult to control.

EOCs need to be planned in advance of an emergency; improvised facilities developed during an emergency almost never work as well as preplanned facilities. With good design, a great deal of thought, and some regular testing, the majority of design and environmental issues can be overcome. An effective EOC is a "nerve centre" that meets the needs of those who work in it as well as those of the emergency responders in the field and the overall community or organization, regardless of the type of emergency that occurs.

KEY TERMS

EOC support staff

incident manager

Municipal Control Group (MCG)

Municipal Support Group (MSG)

situation report (sitrep)

LEARNING CHECK

Take a few minutes now to test your knowledge of Emergency Operations Centres. Select the best answer in each case. Any score of less than 16 out of 20 (80 percent) indicates that you should re-read this chapter.

1. The presence of an effective EOC is central to the community's ability to provide meaningful coordination of information, logistics, and
   a. work direction
   b. services
   c. legal support
   d. both (a) and (c)

2. The success or failure of the community's emergency response may be determined, to some extent, by the presence of
   a. community involvement
   b. senior levels of government
   c. an effective EOC
   d. all elected officials

3. A community EOC may be purpose-built, or may occupy
   a. an improvised space
   b. the town hall
   c. the emergency services dispatch center
   d. a space at the scene of the incident

4. The effectiveness of the working environment in an EOC will be largely determined by
   a. funding
   b. political support
   c. cooperation
   d. design

5. Those tasked with the coordination of emergency activities may actually experience problems that are the direct result of
   a. funding
   b. poor EOC design
   c. lack of political support
   d. interference by senior levels of government

6. In an EOC, the most important concern is
   a. information
   b. cooperation
   c. how well information flows
   d. both (a) and (c)

7. An EOC generally assumes responsibility for support functions, such as victim management, to allow emergency responders to
   a. have rest periods
   b. focus on scene-related issues
   c. minimize resources at the scene
   d. both (a) and (c)

8. In a community EOC, the group headed by the mayor or elected head of council and tasked with primary EOC operations is generally referred to as the
   a. Municipal Control Group
   b. Municipal Support Group
   c. EOC support staff
   d. mayor's emergency committee

9. In a community EOC, the group consisting of voluntary agencies, non-critical municipal services, and public utilities, gathered to advise key decision-makers, is generally referred to as the
   a. Municipal Control Group
   b. Municipal Support Group
   c. EOC support staff
   d. mayor's emergency committee

10. In a community EOC, the group providing security, telecommunications support, information technology support, and housekeeping services under the direction of the emergency manager is generally referred to as the
    a. Municipal Control Group
    b. Municipal Support Group
    c. EOC support staff
    d. mayor's emergency committee

11. The stress levels of the EOC environment can be adversely affected by a variety of factors, including noise, confined spaces, poor furniture choices, and
    a. poor lighting
    b. computers
    c. telephones with flashers instead of ringers
    d. carpeting

12. The single largest factor with the potential to create disruptions and stress for EOC occupants is
    a. poor lighting
    b. furniture design
    c. computers
    d. noise levels

13. The security of the EOC site is important, because unauthorized people tend to gather there and disrupt EOC business operations due to a process called
    a. curiosity
    b. convergence
    c. confluence
    d. power seeking

14. When fluorescent lighting must be used in an EOC area, the type that causes the least stress for occupants is
    a. standard fluorescent lighting
    b. compact fluorescent lighting
    c. incandescent lighting
    d. full-spectrum fluorescent lighting

15. Apart from isolating radio equipment and using telephones with flashers instead of ringers, the most effective way to reduce unnecessary noise in an EOC involves
    a. choice of flooring materials
    b. directing "sidebar"conversations outside
    c. eliminating socializing
    d. having a designated dining area

16. The storage of required EOC equipment in locked cabinets within the designated site where they can be removed and assembled when required is known as a
    a. push system
    b. pull system
    c. integrated system
    d. compact system

17. The storage of required EOC equipment in another secure location, to be moved into the designated EOC site for assembly when required, is known as a
    a. push system
    b. pull system
    c. integrated system
    d. compact system

18. In the EOC, the business cycle is a series of regularly timed meetings of the MCG conducted to provide information, identify and analyze resource requests, assign tasks, and
    a. set objectives
    b. brief the mayor
    c. develop media releases
    d. brief emergency responders

19. In the EOC, all information and resource requests should be time limited and tracked to
    a. control expenditures
    b. satisfy legal requirements
    c. ensure completion
    d. avoid duplication

20. The MCG should periodically provide current information to all key stake-holders, adjacent communities, and other levels of government by means of
   a. an event log
   b. telephone calls
   c. a situation report
   d. media releases

CASE STUDIES

A. You are the emergency manager for a medium-sized community. The elected council has decided that a purpose-built EOC is beyond the financial means of the community, and has decided that the council chamber should be used to provide an improvised EOC for the community. You have been assigned to develop a plan to convert that location into an EOC quickly and easily, when required.

   1. When viewing the facility from an ergonomic perspective, what are the environmental factors that you must consider in the creation of a working environment that will be as stress-free as possible during emergency operations? Why?
   2. In addition to the council chambers, what other types of facilities will be required to support Municipal Control Group operations?
   3. What are the security considerations involved in the use of the council chambers as an improvised EOC?
   4. What are the basic technological considerations involved in the use of the council chambers as an improvised EOC?

B. In your community, a decision has been made to build a dedicated EOC. As the emergency manager, you have been asked to provide the architect responsible for the project with a list of specifications as a part of the design process.

   1. What are the space requirements to make the new EOC an effective working environment?
   2. What are the ergonomic requirements for the use of the space in this role?
   3. What types of creature comforts will be required for those working in the EOC?
   4. What types of support function spaces will be required for the EOC?

TO LEARN MORE

1. Contact your community's emergency manager and ask for a tour of the EOC. How are the various groups (MCG, MSG, EOC support staff) composed in your community? What types of facilities have been included in the EOC plan, and what is the purpose of each? Do the facilities allocated appear to meet the needs of those who will be using them? How? Are there any features that have not been included? Why? If you had the opportunity to redesign the existing EOC and support facilities, what changes would you make? Why do you feel that these changes are necessary?

2. If possible, speak to your local emergency manager and obtain an invitation to observe an exercise involving the EOC. What types of issues did the MCG deal with? What types of functions did the MSG perform? What types of functions were performed by EOC support staff? Did the roles in these groups differ from what has been described in this chapter? Why? Did the respective groups appear to function effectively? Why? If you had the opportunity to make changes to the community's emergency response structure, what would they be? Why?

NOTES

1. Ron Kuban, *The Emergency Site Management System: A Doctrine Paper* (Ottawa: Emergency Preparedness Canada, 1998), <http://ww3.ps-sp.gc.ca/research/resactivites/emerMan/PDFs/1997-D002_e.pdf>.
2. San Antonio Post Society of American Military Engineers, *Emergency Operations Center: The Critical Tool for Incident Management* (San Antonio, TX: author, 2005), <http://www.same-satx.org/briefs/070313-mitchell.pdf>.
3. Emergency Management Institute, *IS-275: EOC's Management and Operations Course* (course manual for independent study program), (Washington, DC: Federal Emergency Management Agency, 1995), <http://training.fema.gov/EMIWeb/downloads/IS275complete.pdf>.
4. Art Botterell, *A Design Language for EOC Facilities*, 2002, <http://www.incident.com/eoc_design.html>.

CHAPTER 14

Emergency Operations Centre Technologies

LEARNING OBJECTIVES

On completion of this chapter, you will

▶ Understand the types of technologies used to support Emergency Operations Centre (EOC) operations.

▶ Understand the basics of how each type of technology functions.

▶ Understand how each type of technology is used in the EOC.

▶ Understand the support requirements for each type of technology.

▶ Understand the strengths and weaknesses of each type of technology.

▶ Understand the princples of redundancy and technological independence.

▶ Understand the need for low-technology alternatives.

KEY MESSAGES

1. The EOC is the information and communications hub of a community or an organization during an emergency.

2. Information is the currency of emergency management.

3. Without access to good information and a smooth flow of delivery of information, the emergency response will eventually degrade.

4. An EOC that relies exclusively on any one type of technology for any function has created its own level of vulnerability.

5. Given the varying nature of emergencies, any high-technology function should be backed up by a low-technology alternative.

6. While the support of specialists in information technology and telecommunications systems may be available, emergency managers must have at least a preliminary understanding of how these systems function.

Introduction

Information processing is perhaps the most important function of an Emergency Operations Centre (EOC). Information is the currency of disaster management; the more information you have, the more you can do, and the better you will be able to respond to the emergency. Those in the EOC must be able to gather information effectively, analyze it, and then share it effectively, both among themselves and also with those at the scene of the emergency, and, in many cases, with the general public, nearby communities, and other levels of government. In emergencies where the flow of information fails or ceases entirely, the response to the emergency most commonly degrades and critical components of the community response may fail outright.

Technology has always played a role in EOCs, but with the advent of the computer age and new telecommunications technologies, this role has expanded dramatically. As but one simple example, when a community is faced with a serious chemical spill, those in the EOC may be able to determine the nature of the chemical, risks, and emergency procedures at the push of a button. The incorporation of weather data and special software permit the plotting of the likely path of a dangerous chemical plume. The addition of more layers of data permits the identification of high-risk locations with respect to the path of the plume, such as residential areas, schools, hospitals, and nursing homes. Decisions can then be made with respect to evacuation versus **sheltering-in-place**, and this information can be quickly communicated to potentially vulnerable residents. Issues and interrelations among data that once took hours to understand can now be identified and acted upon in minutes, or even seconds.

However, there is a price associated with an increased use of technology. Too often, communities and organizations become reliant on one form of technology and may actually increase their own vulnerability, should that technology fail. This chapter focuses on the technologies that are available for use in an EOC, their strengths and weaknesses, and how to select the appropriate technologies for use. EOC technology generally falls into one of two categories: telecommunications and information management. Both categories are examined in some detail. Finally, the chapter addresses the need for alternative low-technology systems for use when primary high-technology systems fail.

Purpose

In any community or organizational emergency, the ability for those in the EOC to rapidly access and disseminate information is critical. Quick access to information is crucial for both the key decision-makers in the EOC and emergency responders in the field. An effective EOC must maintain communication links among those in the field, key decision-makers, and, in many cases, other communities, organizations, and levels of government. Without the ability to access good information and ensure a smooth flow of information delivery, the EOC is essentially useless.

Technologies exist to support these functions. As the community or organizational "expert" on emergency management, the primary emergency planner, and, in many cases, the primary lead for EOC design and creation, an emergency manager has a central role to play in selecting technologies for inclusion in the EOC, and for the maintenance of those technologies. To ensure that these technologies remain effective, an emergency manager must understand how they work, what is possible, and what is not possible.

General Considerations

The development of advanced technologies has represented a boon for emergency managers. Many of the information and communications functions that were once performed manually and as long, slow processes can now be achieved in minutes and, in some cases, seconds, rather than hours. While such systems are extremely useful in the management of a community emergency response, there are also a number of problems associated with many of them. Emergency managers must make wise choices; choosing technologies that are both useful and sustainable, and ensuring that backup systems for each type of technology exist wherever possible.

It is important for emergency managers to have a reasonable understanding of each technology under consideration for inclusion in the EOC. It is not necessary to be a technology expert. However, it *is* necessary to have at least a preliminary understanding of how a technology functions, and how to troubleshoot any basic problems with it until an expert is available. There is a very real danger that once a type of technology has been embraced, those in the EOC may become solely reliant on it, and this creates a level of inherent vulnerability. What will happen if, for any reason, that technology is unable to function?

A fundamental principle of emergency management is having multiple layers of redundancy; each process and technology used in the EOC requires some reasonable alternative in case that process or technology becomes unavailable. Always have a "plan B" in case "plan A" doesn't work! Such backups can be similar high-tech systems, but it is always wise to have a low-tech alternative available in case it is required. To illustrate, the EOC may be equipped with a state-of-the-art telephone system for primary communications, but in the event of a telephone system failure, it is prudent to have a backup plan involving the use of runners to physically carry messages to where they must go.

Another fundamental principle of emergency management is that of **technological independence** for backup systems. This principle is often poorly understood. In a survey of Canadian hospitals,[1] respondents were asked how they would recall staff, a critical function, in the event of a telephone failure, and over 70 percent of respondents indicated that they would use pagers as a backup system. This would result in a complete failure of the ability to recall staff, since the backup system is technologically dependent on the primary system; if telephones don't work, it is unlikely that pagers, which use the telephone network, would continue to function. This poor level of understanding of technologies is not uncommon, and emergency managers must carefully consider how each type of technology selected may be dependent on other potentially vulnerable technologies.

There are challenges associated with the acquisition of technologies, not the least of which is cost. Most emergency managers have a limited budget with which to develop a fully functional EOC. While there may be a great many technologies available, emergency managers must make prudent choices; they must obtain those technologies that will actually be useful, can be sustained, and will be fiscally responsible. The price of high-tech and high-cost "toys" that provide only limited information or would be used infrequently may place other needed resources and services beyond the reach of the EOC.

When selecting technologies, emergency managers begin with the Hazard Identification and Risk Assessment (HIRA). What types of events are most likely to affect the community, and which are likely to have the greatest impact? What types of information and communications resources will the community require to manage these events? Which technologies (products and services) are likely to provide the required functionality? Are these technologies easy to maintain locally, or do they require a level of expertise or technical support that is not normally readily available in the community? What types of repair services and technical support are provided with the technologies, and will these meet your immediate needs during a crisis? Above all, what is each of these options likely to cost, both for immediate purchase and for long-term maintenance?

Once these questions are answered, emergency managers will have a much better understanding of what is actually needed and what can be afforded. Typically, any technology that is selected should be very user-friendly, to the point of being intuitive, where possible. New technologies should, at a minimum, appear to be similar to those technologies used on a day-to-day basis. Indeed, many organizations use standard software for daily functions, without fully understanding the product's potential. It is not unlikely that existing software, used correctly and to its full potential, might even eliminate the need to purchase other software. When a community uses an improvised space for an EOC, any technology selected must be easy to assemble and operationalize by local staff with minimal or even no training. Also, such technologies should be easy to maintain, ideally with problem-solving and repair assistance immediately available at the local level.

In addition, when a designated EOC exists, one must consider how new technology will interact with the older technologies already present. Will the older technologies be replaced entirely, or will they become the backups for the new technology? Will new computer software work effectively with existing computer software? Do they share a common operating platform? When information is compiled in one type of database software, the choice of new software based on an incompatible platform will create serious problems for users. New software that cannot use years' worth of data already on hand, is incompatible with existing software, or has backward incompatibility with older versions of the same software is of limited value. In all cases, the technology should serve the user, and not the reverse.

Technologies that meet multiple needs may be helpful and cost effective, but they too represent challenges. To illustrate, an all-in-one printer can eliminate the need to purchase separate printer, photocopier, scanner, and fax machines, but it is important to be mindful that when such a device malfunctions, *all* of those functions will be lost at once. The same is true for many of the emergency management software products that are available; they may perform and integrate a vast array of functions within the EOC, but what happens when the computer network, on which such software products are totally reliant, is disabled by the events surrounding the emergency? These examples are not intended to preclude the use of such technologies, but they do caution emergency managers about the pitfalls of making the entire operation solely reliant on any one system.

Ultimately, the process for purchasing technologies is the same as the process for making any other major purchase. Carefully consider what you need and what is possible. Consider how the new technologies will interact with those already present. Consider their strengths and weaknesses. Consider their vulnerabilities and what types of backups are possible. Once all of the facts have been considered, emergency managers will be in the best position to select those technologies that meet the community's or organization's needs, and its budget.

Telecommunications Technologies

Telephone Systems

In virtually every EOC, the telephone system typically forms the backbone of communications activities. The system itself is extremely user-friendly. By simply keying a few numbers, information can be rapidly transmitted locally, regionally, and even internationally by a user with only a preliminary understanding of how the technology functions. The system can support the transmission of voice, data, and even images. The technology involved is well tested, and normal usage procedures are easily understood at least at the user level, although very few users have any real understanding of exactly how the technology works. Telephone technology is an essential tool in most EOCs. However, the system is not without limitations, and emergency managers must clearly understand what these limitations are. The emergency manager's understanding of such limitations and also the options that are available on the telephone system will each play a role in the selection of communications technologies and strategies, and in the design and selection of equipment for the EOC itself. To illustrate, potential design restrictions caused by the telephone system's wiring needs may influence the selection or placement of furniture within the EOC.

Telephone systems are usually provided not by a government entity such as a public utility, but by a private business that exists to make a profit. Understanding this fact is essential, because it helps explain why some elements of the telephone network operate in the way that they do. For example, although it may seem like an unlimited resource to the end-user, the truth is very different. There are practical limitations on the simultaneous use of telephone sets within a given local network or exchange. In North America, typically this limit is simultaneous use by about 20 percent of the telephone sets on the exchange; elsewhere in the world this limit may be even lower. When a local network is overloaded or malfunctioning, users may get no dial tone or a rapid busy signal.

Long-distance telephone services may have a similar limitation. The ability to complete a call between two distant points may be restricted by the carrying capacity of the main telephone line between the two points. In modern telephone systems, this capacity may be expanded somewhat by routing calls to their destination through less-direct lines, where carrying capacity is available. This limitation appears in larger centres but may also appear, although less often, in smaller, more isolated communities that are served by a single trunk line from a central point. This limitation may also operate on international calls, based on the constraints of the carrying capacity of either undersea telephone cables or satellites. Typically, telephone companies design their systems to accommodate a level of use that is representative of their busier days plus a limited size "buffer" of additional availability; when the system's capacity limit is reached, no further calls are possible.

During a community emergency, situations where the finite limits of the telephone network are reached can occur frequently. The telephone network, its lines, and its exchanges may be susceptible to damage from the hazard event itself. The network is also immediately at risk of becoming overwhelmed either by those affected by the disaster, calling their friends and families to advise them that they are unharmed, or by worried loved ones, attempting to call into the affected area to check on the welfare of others. System overload is a common consequence of hazard events.

In many locations, telephone-service providers have attempted to address the issue of system overload for communities and emergency responders through the provision of priority service. Some providers call this service *line load control,* while others call it *priority access for dialing.* This service allows emergency agencies to pre-designate high-priority telephone lines, typically about 10 percent of available numbers. In most cases, the organization or community can determine which lines will be registered and which will not. When the system becomes overloaded, registered lines will receive priority for available telephone lines. This service also typically gives registered lines priority for restoration of service, should telephone networks fail. Priority service is not offered by all telephone-service providers, and emergency managers should discuss this with their local provider in advance, rather than simply assume that it is available.

There are other practical considerations regarding the availability of telephone service. As previously stated, most telephone services are provided by private businesses that seek to make a profit. The profits for telephone systems are generated in two forms: fixed monthly service rates and fee-generating services. In most cases, the telephone company's income from monthly service rates is fixed, and is unaffected by interruptions. Fee-generating services, such as pay telephones and long-distance calling, on the other hand, cease to generate revenue every time they are disrupted. As a result, many telephone-service providers place a priority on the restoration of fee-generating services. The practical result for emergency managers is this: even when one cannot make a local call (lines may be busy or there is no dial tone), it may be possible to make a long-distance call; and when no other telephone in the building functions, the pay telephones in the lobby may continue to function.

When emergency managers select telephone sets for use in the EOC, there are several important considerations. Older-style analog telephone sets (those with rotary dialing, for example) draw their operating power directly from the telephone line itself, while newer digital telephone sets require an external power source. While there are clear advantages (such as caller ID) to using digital telephone sets (and these will probably be the preferred choice), each set *must* be connected to the emergency power supply of the EOC, or it will not operate during an electrical failure. Even when they select digital telephones, prudent emergency managers will retain a cache of analog telephones as a backup arrangement (if the local telephone system will support them).

Telephones are a useful communications tool as long as they remain available. Others outside of the EOC also understand this fact, which can pose communication problems in the EOC. The telephone lines within the EOC can become overloaded unless certain precautions are taken. When it is possible to do so, every position within the EOC should be served by two telephone lines, and even separate handsets. The first line at each position should be allocated for incoming calls, with a published and/or distributed number for that position. This line provides those needing to speak with EOC members with the means to do so. The second line, equipped with an unpublished number and the caller-ID function blocked, is for outgoing calls *only*.

Such numbers should be jealously guarded, perhaps even from the users themselves. Failure to take this measure often results in someone calling the outgoing line the first time the incoming line is busy. In a worst-case scenario, the EOC may end up with all lines acting as incoming lines, and no EOC occupants able to place critical outgoing calls!

All telephone calls must be answered at all times. During an emergency, telephone calls may provide time-sensitive, perhaps even critical, information. If telephone lines are allowed to be answered by voice mail, even during a business-cycle meeting, the potential exists for information that should be dealt with in five minutes to languish in an answering system for 20 to 30 minutes or even be entirely overlooked. For this reason, no EOC telephone line should ever be assigned to voice mail or some other answering system. As an alternative, it is preferable for the EOC to assign someone in a clerical function to answer all unattended lines at all times, so that no item of critical information is ever delayed or overlooked.

While telephones are certainly necessary in the EOC, they can pose a significant distraction from EOC business. The constant ringing from incoming calls will disrupt conversations and meetings, and also contribute substantially to the ambient noise level (and consequently the stress level) in the facility. Try to visualize ten telephones ringing constantly within the confined space of an EOC. For this reason, telephone handsets should be equipped with flashers that identify incoming calls, and should have the ringer function turned off completely.

Teleconferencing Systems and Fax Machines

Teleconferencing systems can be useful in the EOC. They permit the Municipal Control Group (MCG) to incorporate the incident manager at the scene into the business-cycle meeting, when required. They also permit conference calling with other nearby communities, other emergency responders (such as hospitals), or other levels of government. While they are a useful form of information exchange, they are subject to the same types of concerns and restrictions as conventional telephones, and should be treated accordingly.

Fax machines are telephone system–based tools that can also be highly useful for the EOC. Fax machines permit the rapid transfer of hard copies of critical documents, such as emergency declarations, and also the provision of key information from those located at a distance. They also pose a number of problems, some related to telephones, and others that are unique to that particular technology. Just as with the telephone, it is wise to have two fax machines where possible—one for incoming and the other for outgoing transmissions.

Another issue related to fax machines involves maintenance. There should be a supply of spare paper and toner cartridges for each machine available at all times, as well as someone who understands the procedures for adding paper, clearing paper jams, and changing cartridges. The person in charge and the person who knows how to change a toner cartridge are rarely one and the same! It is also prudent to have at least one spare machine available as a backup. In many communities and organizations, when technology such as a fax machine is replaced, the old one is serviced and stored. This retention of technology from one generation back can be a useful and cost-effective way in which to generate the multiple layers of redundancy required.

Cellphones, Satellite Phones, and VoIP

Cellphones are not a suitable substitute for conventional telephone lines. A number of problems accompany cellphone use during an emergency; one of these relates to how the system operates and the other to how people tend to use their phones. A cellphone is essentially a two-way radio operating between the point where the user is located and the nearest "cell" or "node." At this point the service is transferred to the conventional land-line telephone system. It follows that the failure of the main telephone system in an area will generally result in the failure of the cellular system almost immediately. Some cellphones, depending on location, may still be able to access a cell or node in an unaffected area, but service will generally be greatly degraded.

The other problem with cellphones is the sharp upswing in their use once an emergency has occurred. This electronic convergence arises as those in the affected area begin to call emergency services, the news media, and their loved ones. Additional load is created by incoming calls from concerned family and friends. Another problem is that members of the media will arrive at a disaster scene and call their offices, leaving the line open to ensure rapid contact. All of these uses combined will quickly overwhelm the local area cell or node. This problem was noted both in Manhattan during 9/11 (2001), and at the Oklahoma City bombing (1995).

In some jurisdictions, technology is used to overcome this problem. For example, the United Kingdom uses a system known as *Access Overload Control (ACCOLC)* to restrict mobile telephone usage in the event of emergencies. In this system, the SIM card in each cellphone is assigned a priority number ranging from 1 to 15. Numbers from 1 to 9 are used by the general public, and numbers from 10 to 15 are reserved for the police, emergency services, the military, and senior levels of government. When an emergency occurs, if required, a senior police official may invoke this system. When this system is in use, the local cell or node is switched off, and then reset to permit access only to telephones with SIM cards in the 10 to 15 range. The decision to invoke the system involves a great deal of disruption and financial loss for telephone-system operators and, as a result, it is never made lightly, and only in serious emergencies. This technology is currently unavailable in North America, which uses a different type of cellphone system.

Satellite telephones are an alternative, but only as a last resort. The current technology requires users to have a sightline to the horizon while using a satellite phone; as a result, these phones can rarely be used inside buildings (such as an EOC). The other problem with satellite telephones, as anyone who has ever made a ship-to-shore call can attest, is that the per-minute usage fee is prohibitively expensive; therefore, they are inappropriate for the long-term usage usually necessary for managing an emergency. That being said, the presence of one or two satellite telephones in the inventory of an isolated community can often make the difference between getting help and not being able to communicate the need for help at all.

The final issue to be considered with respect to telephony is the use of Voice over Internet Protocol, or VoIP. This system allows telephone calls to be placed using the Internet instead of conventional telephone lines. While at the time of writing VoIP is still relatively new and experiencing some "growing pains," it is now sufficiently developed to suggest it as a potential backup resource for conventional telephone systems. When some VoIP telephones are included within the EOC, telephone calls remain possible even when the conventional telephone system has failed. Such calls can only be made to telephones outside of the affected areas, and are only possible when the EOC's Internet service is not provided through a conventional telephone line but uses an alternative provider, such as a cable operator.

Emergency Service Radio

Almost all local authorities use some form of radio system to control their resources on a daily basis. Such systems can be extremely valuable in coordinating the response to an emergency. Most emergency services broadcast over their own radio frequency, so that one could expect to find a radio network for police, one for fire services, another for emergency medical services (EMS), and so on. In some cases, the dispatch function can be quite elaborate, and supported by enhancements such as computer-aided dispatch, automatic vehicle location (a "first cousin" of global positioning systems), and the ability to patch from the radio network to the telephone system, as is often the case with emergency medical services. The dispatch function may even incorporate the use of direct land-line telephony with points of frequent contact, such as hospitals.

In many jurisdictions, emergency services may also be coordinated on a regional level, for the purpose of mutual aid among communities. In Ontario, for example, all ambulances are required by law to be equipped with a common radio frequency for use across the province in addition to their own assigned operating frequencies. In this manner, ambulances from one community can communicate with those from another during a crisis, and ambulances from a distant community responding to a request for mutual aid can speak with and receive call assignments from a local dispatcher. Similar arrangements are in place for both fire apparatus and police vehicles.

In many jurisdictions over the past 20 years, particularly in North America, public service radio frequencies have migrated from the Very High Frequency (VHF) band to the Ultra High Frequency (UHF) band to provide better radio coverage and improved broadcast quality. This change, along with the advent of trunked radio technology, has provided such systems with other technological improvements as well. When all public services use a similar radio system, inter-agency communication becomes possible. In many communities, an ambulance may be able to communicate directly with a police car or a fire engine, and vice versa. Trunking allows the creation of distinct "talk groups," which permit emergency services to have separate, on-scene inter-agency communications without adversely affecting each service's ability to dispatch its own resources. Trunking also provides the ability to communicate with additional resources, such as hospitals or public works vehicles, which are not typically participants in an emergency service radio network.

The use of an emergency service radio system can be extremely useful to the EOC, if emergency managers are able to incorporate it. The presence of such a radio system allows for the immediate updating of the MCG and the continuous monitoring of events. In some cases, particularly in isolated communities, it may also be possible for such a system to be used by the EOC to communicate with the "outside world" in the event of a telephone network failure.

Even in those cases where a community does not yet have such technology, it is useful to maintain a base station radio for each of the emergency services and any other municipal radio networks. Having direct access to all resources, whether at the emergency scene or elsewhere in the community, can help provide an important level of coordination during an emergency. However, just as with telephones, these radios will generate substantial levels of noise. As a result, all radio functions should be installed in a room adjacent to the EOC, where the noise generated will not disrupt EOC operations.

Several considerations must be addressed before incorporating this type of radio technology into EOC design. The first, noise, has already been discussed. In addition, all such radios will require priority placement on the EOC's emergency power system to ensure continued and reliable functioning. In addition, each radio will require the installation of an antenna on the rooftop of the EOC, and the associated cabling to the point of installation. Some systems may be able to share a single antenna, but this will need to be determined locally, based on radio type and the frequencies assigned. Even when these systems are to be used in an improvised EOC space, the advance installation of emergency power and antennae for each radio will be required so that during an emergency, the radio sets themselves can simply be brought into the workspace and easily installed.

Using radio technology requires a certain level of knowledge and expertise. For example, it is important to know that many radio frequencies have user restrictions, and many jurisdictions require radio operators to be licensed. Moreover, emergency services are likely to be extremely reluctant to have anyone other than a member of their own service operate their radios. As a result, advance arrangements must be made for the scheduling of approved radio operators. A significant advantage of using radio technology is that its presence allows emergency managers to ban portable emergency service radios, which senior officers are notoriously reluctant to part with, within the EOC environment.

Amateur Radio

Radio amateurs are active in many parts of the world and can provide a significant potential communications backup system for the EOC. Active since the infancy of radio technology, radio amateurs are avid hobbyists, many of whom possess a level of knowledge with respect to telecommunications technology that can approach that of an engineer. Most people tend to have misconceptions of what amateur radio is really all about. Radio amateurs are no longer limited to Morse code (indeed most jurisdictions no longer have a Morse code licensing requirement) and voice transmission; these days amateur radio includes data transmission and, in some cases, even television signals. Amateurs are capable of sending information from point to point locally, and many are capable of international transmission.

In many jurisdictions, there is a separate subset of amateurs who focus on the provision of communications in communities during emergencies. In North America, these groups are part of the Amateur Radio Emergency Service (ARES) and, in the United Kingdom, they are part of the Radio Society of Great Britain— Emergency Communications. Such groups have a specific interest in participation in emergencies by means of providing emergency communications, and, for them, this is a hobby! They can provide critical backup resources for a community EOC; however, like any worthwhile resource, arrangements to incorporate them into your EOC should be negotiated in advance. Emergency managers must attempt to find such individuals in the community and determine their interest in participation in any future community emergency response. These individuals or groups will also be able to provide emergency managers with reliable advice on the installation of amateur radio equipment within the EOC.

The requirements for installing amateur radio equipment in the EOC are straightforward, and will closely resemble those for installing emergency service radios.

Noise, emergency power, and antenna installation will all need to be considered. Depending on discussions with local radio amateurs, the community may wish to purchase its own radio set, or have one provided by the amateurs themselves. At a minimum, the radio amateurs in the community will be able to provide knowledge-able guidance on the selection of an appropriate radio set. Individual radio sets must be licensed as radio stations in most jurisdictions, and may only be operated by individuals with the appropriate amateur radio licence. While some effort and advance work are required to locate and recruit local radio amateurs, the effort is worthwhile, and emergency managers may be able to provide the EOC with a valu-able resource for use when all other forms of communication fail.

Broadcasting

Emergency managers must also consider the role that commercial broadcasting can play in the EOC's emergency communications strategy. It must be remembered, however, that the incorporation of commercial broadcasting is a double-edged sword. Commercial broadcasters can be extremely effective at the provision of emergency information to the general public. However, this cooperation carries a price: the broadcaster who assists with emergency information will invariably also have a news division that requires information on the emergency for their own telecast. As a result, any emergency communications strategy should be developed in tandem with an EOC media plan, which is a formal process for providing the public with emergency information by means of the broadcast and print media.

Television

In most cases, with the exception of public broadcasters, television and radio are generally commercial in nature, and may be divided into several general categories: broadcast television, radio, distant signal television, and local cable television. Dis-tant signal television services are broadcast services that originate in distant cities, and which may be made available through local cable television or satellite provid-ers, although in some cases, these are special interest television channels that may not be broadcast at all. Distant signal television only rarely provides any solutions or resources to emergency managers, and, as a result, will not be considered here. Television is typically a regional service, and, while it may be interested in news coverage of a local hazard event, it is typically reluctant to broadcast emergency messages, since its audience is often quite large and widespread, and the actual emer-gency may only affect an isolated subset of its viewers. The real value of television is in its ability to report the event, thereby providing information and images to the EOC from the emergency scene itself.

Local Radio

Local radio has been the traditional mainstay of emergency messaging. For many years, local residents have often been educated to tune in to a particular local radio station for information and instructions during an emergency. That being said, the industry itself has changed and a number of local radio stations have disappeared. Stations that used to be operated within the community by local residents have become automated in many cases. Music and news may be bought from a national service, and the local presence largely disappears. Typically, the last elements of the local radio station to vanish are the news department and the marketing department. The marketing department generates local advertising revenue and is of little interest to emergency managers. However, the local news department may continue to function in some fashion to maintain the impression that the station is a local operation. If this is the case, emergency managers may be able to cultivate relationships to support the emergency communications strategy. All the same, recall that most radio stations are entirely or at least partially automated. There may be very few people actually at the radio station, particularly after business hours. As a result, emergency managers will need to develop 24-hour contact information for local radio station personnel.

Local Cable Television

Local cable television services can provide an extremely useful resource for emergency messaging. They are already being used during emergencies in some areas, such as the State of Florida, and may become an important resource elsewhere in the future. Increasingly, almost all homes, at least in North America, use either a cable television service or a satellite dish service for their home television reception. The cable television company does not provide just some of the signals to the home; in fact it controls *all* of the signals to the home. The technology exists to permit an EOC, with prior discussion with and agreement from the cable television service provider, to pre-empt all television signals entering the home and replace them with emergency messaging. This arrangement would permit text messages or even broadcasts from the EOC to homes, and could be limited to the affected area. Incorporating this technology in the EOC will require the advance approval of the cable television service provider, and will also require the purchase and installation of special equipment. While this technology is useful, it must be remembered that it cannot reach *every* home. Only those homes with the television on and connected to the cable television service will receive the emergency messaging.

EOC Technologies

The primary use of broadcast technologies within the EOC is to permit its occupants to monitor the events at the scene and elsewhere in the community, and also to monitor what is being said in the media about the emergency response. Some monitoring is also required to ensure that any emergency messaging is factual and accurate. These functions can occur with relatively simple to use, widely available technologies.

The creation of a media-monitoring facility, similar to the room used to monitor emergency radio transmissions, can be an asset for an EOC. A media-monitoring facility should incorporate one or two radios capable of monitoring commercial broadcasts (as opposed to emergency services broadcasts), and one or more televisions. This facility should be under the control of the individual tasked with public information, and should monitor the media continuously and provide regular information updates to others in the EOC. It may be desirable to incorporate recording technologies so that individual reports may be shared with others in the EOC. However, including this monitoring function in the EOC itself will add to ambient noise levels and distract participants from the business-cycle process.

When selecting recording technologies, it is important to remember that virtually none of the available technologies are interoperable. Whatever technology is chosen for the media centre will need to be reproduced in the EOC itself; you can't mix VCRs with Digital Video Recorders (DVRs), and so on. Video-recording technology is evolving, and older recording formats are rapidly becoming obsolete. It is anticipated that videocassette recorder technology will be removed from the marketplace, in North America at least, within the next two years. There is little point to maintaining any type of technology inventory that will be difficult to repair, and so, even where such technology is already in place, emergency managers should make its replacement a priority. The preferred mode of video recording should be the DVR.

Older style tube televisions are also a thing of the past, and are no longer in production. Within about two years, broadcasting in the current analog format will end, and broadcasting in digital format only will be the norm in most jurisdictions; as such, older televisions will have very limited value. The television of the future is the flat-screen, high-definition type. As a result, this is the only type of television selected for new EOCs or to replace aging equipment in older EOCs. There are several advantages to this type of technology, the most important of which is that they are not just used for television reception.

The latest televisions essentially resemble a very large, flat-panel computer monitor. With the appropriate connections, they can be used to display not only television coverage but also maps, charts, diagrams, PowerPoint presentations, and documents. In fact, anything that can be displayed on a computer monitor can also be displayed on the latest televisions. Their larger size also makes them extremely useful as a presentation tool. These factors combine to make such a television (one or even several) a valuable addition to the EOC. All of the information under consideration can be visually available to all of those participating in the decision-making process. As with all other aspects of EOC operations, the elimination of noise is highly desirable whenever possible. As a result, any television added to the EOC itself should be equipped with closed captioning, so that story content can be provided without the associated disruptive noise.

If the above-mentioned equipment is regarded as essential, it must be connected to the emergency power supply. In addition, in keeping with the concept of multiple layers of redundancy, at least two forms of signal provision should be selected. Having two forms of signal provision will ensure that even if the primary provider's service is affected by the emergency, access to the required information will not be lost entirely. Signals are typically received by broadcast (poor quality), cable television, telephone service provider, and satellite. Whichever forms of signal provision are selected, they must include local or at least regional television stations (sometimes a problem with satellite service), since these will be the primary sources of information. There is no point in trying to locate meaningful coverage of a local emergency on a national or international service.

Information-Management Technologies

The use of computer technology has revolutionized the community EOC. Information that used to take hours to gather and collate can now be gathered and assembled in a matter of minutes. This increased speed greatly enhances the analysis of information and the decision-making process. In addition to the gathering and interpreting of information, the computer is increasingly becoming a powerful communications tool. Computer technology is also typically divided in terms of *hardware* (the actual machines) and *software* (the information or instructions that tell the machine how to perform the required functions). The types of computer technology that are useful can be summarized as software that resides on the local computer, proprietary applications that are only available within the community, and web-based applications. Hardware may be defined as the computers and peripherals, such as printers, that are necessary to operate the required software applications.

Hardware

Computer hardware can be defined as the computer itself and the various types of equipment attached to the computer, such as a printer, a scanner, or a mouse (usually called *peripherals*), to perform specific functions. Computers are generally divided into two groups: the large, non-portable variety, called *desktops*, and the portable variety, called *laptops* or *notebooks*. There are advantages and disadvantages to each. A desktop computer is usually more powerful than a laptop (although this is changing), and has a larger screen. However, it is difficult to move from one place to another and requires a constant connection to a power supply. A laptop, by contrast, although it has a smaller screen size and is usually more expensive than a desktop, is extremely portable and can even operate on an internal battery for a limited period of time.

When selecting computers for use in the EOC, emergency managers must consider a number of factors: computing power, length of life, versatility of use, and cost. Most users assess computing power according to the size and operating speed of the central processor or chip, the amount of memory available (required to run software), and the amount of storage available for both software and data. All of these aspects are variable, and each will help to determine, to some degree, the cost of the computer.

Length of life is also an important factor, and one that means that the least expensive computer may not ultimately represent the best value. Computer technology evolves rapidly, and the price of a given computer generally decreases the further from the cutting edge one goes. Is a low-cost computer that is going to be obsolete in six months really good value? There is a valid argument that says that to obtain the best value, one should purchase the most current model, regardless of the price difference, because it will remain current for a much longer period.

Versatility is another important factor. Few communities or organizations, with the possible exception of senior levels of government, have the resources available to dedicate a large number of computers and peripherals, regardless of type, for the exclusive use of an EOC. As a result, the computers selected are likely to be used elsewhere within the organization, and moved to the EOC when they are required there. This means that these devices must also meet the day-to-day needs of other users. It also means that the portability of such devices is an important factor in their selection. When computers are used for day-to-day operations and then moved into the EOC during emergencies, they can be equipped with more than one "software configuration." Each software configuration will have its own password access and will provide the user with different software access (one set of software for day-to-day use and another for emergencies). This permits emergency managers to deny access to potentially sensitive information or services to anyone who doesn't legitimately require them. Any information technology professional can install additional software configurations.

There are two potential approaches to addressing the issue of versatility. Essentially, one may select desktop models and make provision for their reassignment and movement to the EOC when required. This approach, while resulting in a somewhat lower cost, adds to the degree of complexity in the assembly of the EOC. One may also select laptops for the EOC, and assign them for the daily use of individuals expected to play a role within the EOC. This approach, while resulting in a somewhat higher cost, leads to an ease of EOC assembly. With each approach, some form of tradeoff is required.

Peripherals, like computer technology, evolve rapidly; a model that is current today may be obsolete six months from now. Peripherals too are likely to be used elsewhere, between assignments to the EOC. The good news is that the price of most types of peripherals is considerably lower than that of a computer. The trend within the industry has been to combine certain types of related technologies as well. Therefore, it is possible to obtain a single unit that performs the functions of a printer, a scanner, a photocopier, and a fax machine at a much lower cost than the separate purchase of each of these types of technology. While such peripherals are highly useful, they also create a level of vulnerability for the EOC. The loss of a single device means that all of its functions are lost, whereas the loss of a separate device means that only one function is lost. The point is not that such devices should be excluded, only that the potential for vulnerability should be considered and weighed against potential benefits.

For all of the EOC hardware to work together effectively, it must be connected to a network. In the case of a large network, hardware will be coordinated by a single, large computer called a *server*, but in the case of a smaller network, a smaller device called a *router* will probably suffice. The EOC network can be a part of the larger corporate network or may be independent. In either case, provisions will be required for the interconnection of all of the devices on the network. This may take the form of pre-wiring the intended EOC site with network (Ethernet) cabling (and this is the only really practical option for desktops). Laptops may also be connected in this manner, using a peripheral called a *docking station* in which the laptop is locked into a desktop device, connecting it to both power and network cabling.

Establishing a network may also include establishing a "wireless" network, using the appropriate router technology. This solution is much more practical for laptops, which often come with the required technology installed. It must be remembered that networks are not particularly secure and may be prone to "eavesdropping" unless suitable firewalls are installed. It is important for emergency managers to consult with the appropriate information technology specialists who can assist with both equipment selection and network design.

Software

There is no shortage of potentially useful software applications that are available to the EOC. Indeed, commercial software applications have an added advantage in that they are often already familiar to the EOC occupants, since people in the community probably use many of them in their day-to-day business operations. For example, the word-processing software that is used daily can also be used to create situation reports, resource requests, and after action reports. The spreadsheet data that are used daily for accounting purposes can also be used to track response costs and to collect data for other applications. The email program that staff use to communicate on a daily basis can also be used for both communication and data sharing with neighbouring communities or other levels of government.

Proprietary software is often also in place in various communities. This type of software is typically developed at a local level to meet local needs, and may not be exactly like any other system anywhere else. Communities use proprietary software to dispatch emergency vehicles, to manage traffic, to monitor and control their utilities, and for a variety of other functions. While none of these functions is likely to be specific to emergency management or EOC operations, they can provide valuable information regarding the day-to-day functions of the community listed above, and should be considered.

There are several advantages to using both types of software in the EOC. They are already familiar to staff, the required software licences are already in place, and there is usually no additional cost associated with them. With respect to commercial software, communities frequently purchase such products for their staff in "suites" of programs that typically include a relatively high degree of inter-program compatibility. This compatibility greatly simplifies the movement of information from one program to another. The compatibility of proprietary software with other EOC applications should be assessed. It is also wise to ensure that all systems use the same version of any software, because backward incompatibility issues sometimes arise when older versions of software are unable to fully recognize work done with newer versions of the same software.

A variety of specialty software that is useful to emergency managers is available in the marketplace. This software includes applications that can generate maps, plot data, and layer data to understand relationships among variables. Such software can be used to plot data such as an estimate of the size, height, and configuration of a chemical plume from a hazardous materials spill or map the locations of vulnerable population or facilities. When using mapping software, it is important to ensure that the same scale is used for all plots so that the resulting information is accurate. Some versions of this software use latitude and longitude plotting, while others use postal codes. In either case, software that translates from one plotting format to the other is also available. Such software typically requires expert users, which may be somewhat of a disadvantage. However, the majority of data entry requires no particular expertise; Microsoft® Excel® software or some other commercial spreadsheet software can be used for data entry, so the number of expert users required is minimal.

Web-Based Applications

The Internet can also provide valuable resources for use in the EOC. While many of these resources are free, some are not. Web-based resources include specialty sites for emergency management, information sites that are useful during a crisis, and also communications sites. Each of these resources has its strengths and weaknesses, but perhaps the greatest weakness is the need for users to be connected to the Internet to access them. It would be unwise to become reliant on any information source that could potentially be disrupted by the events of an emergency. As a result, while web-based resources provide "nice to have" information, wherever possible, "need to have" information should be available without web access.

Emergency management websites are often fee-for-service operations. Once the computer operating system is understood, they can provide virtual "one-stop shopping" for most of the resources required to manage an emergency. The use of such sites, while extremely useful, is not inexpensive, and the expense involved may be acceptable in some circumstances, such as in a community without the resources to provide such services on its own. For a community with limited resources facing an infrequent level of emergencies, "renting" such services may actually prove less expensive than "buying" whole software packages. That being said, unless the community's Internet service provider is functional during an emergency, such websites may not be accessible.

Other types of websites can also provide useful information at little or no cost. Useful information may comprise safety information on hazardous materials spills,[2] current weather information (including colour weather radar images[3]), or reference sources for local, regional or federal laws.[4] In some communities, local television stations broadcast on the web and, in some cases, even traffic-monitoring cameras are made available to web users.[5] Such information, where it is available, can provide potentially useful background information that is not critical to the emergency response.

Search engines are also useful types of websites. A variety of search engines are in common usage, one of the most popular being Google.[6] Such websites are free to use, and the entry of a single carefully selected keyword can lead to page after page of potentially useful information. The searches can be refined by modifying keywords, and, as the user becomes more adept at the search language and the search becomes more specific, vast amounts of truly useful information can be generated. A word of caution: the typical search engine rarely differentiates between reliable information from factual sites and information from less reliable sources.

With the appropriate software, it is possible to have real-time conversations with anyone in the world, regardless of location, using Internet Relay Chat (IRC). Two excellent examples of this type of software are Windows Live™ Messenger[7] and Yahoo!® Messenger,[8] both of which are available free of charge for download. IRC conversations are typically conducted using text, although voice and video conferencing and file transfer are also typically supported. Even in text-messaging format, these systems accommodate the instantaneous transfer of documents, photographs, maps, charts, diagrams, and other useful tools between users who may be thousands of kilometres apart. This feature alone can provide the EOC with instant access to critical information resources that would normally be beyond reach. Such conversations can occur between EOC workstations, locally, regionally, or even around the world.

The addition of an inexpensive web-based camera (webcam), microphone, and speakers or a headset can be used to provide video-conferencing capability to any computer. This makes it possible to conduct face-to-face conversations, supported by document transfer that allows instantaneous transfer of maps, diagrams, documents, and other electronic files to anyone, anywhere in the world, as long as they are using a similarly equipped computer. Such applications use a variation of the same technology that is used to provide the VoIP telephone service previously discussed. Since there is no fee associated with the use of this application, it can dramatically reduce the costs incurred by long-distance telephone calls and provide support features not available on a conventional telephone system.

Web-based applications are not without their issues. For example, voice transmission over the Internet may have some degree of "garbling," an echo effect, or a noticeable delay—problems that do not appear in conventional telephony. However, these quality issues have been significantly improved in recent years, and will probably continue to improve. Another potential problem with web-based applications is the security risks inherent in them. Conversations and data shared over the Internet are not necessarily private, although the knowledge of how to intercept them is not widespread. The Internet can also be a portal for computer viruses, but this problem is not insurmountable. For example, the adjustment of corporate firewalls to accommodate instant messaging should be complemented by good antivirus software that is capable of monitoring instant-messaging traffic; this software must be updated regularly because viruses emerge almost daily.

Commercial applications that will permit the creation of a "chat room" function on a purely local network are also available. The cost associated with these applications is minimal, and such a system, while not providing international communication, may provide a useful tool for communication between workstations within the EOC. Emergency managers will need to determine the correct software solution for an EOC after a careful consideration of both the risks and benefits associated with each option.

Low-Tech Alternatives

Computers are wonderful tools … when they work! A variety of issues, such as electrical and Internet service provider failure and computer viruses, have the potential to deny an EOC the use of its computers. Given the principles of multiple layers of redundancy and technological independence, prudent emergency managers will ensure that suitable low-tech backup systems exist for every critical function that normally resides on a computer. Essentially, this is a matter of going back to the old-fashioned methods of performing these functions. A number of low-tech alternatives are discussed below.

Maps

The management of any emergency involves a careful examination of physical space, including both the emergency scene and the balance of the community. It also requires a consideration of how such physical spaces are used, population distribution, and critical facilities, along with their physical interrelationships. For these reasons, maps are an essential component of the EOC "toolkit." Every emergency manager should strive to ensure that the best and most current maps of the community are available in the EOC at all times.

In most cases, large-format maps are preferable. Such maps may be mounted on the wall or simply laid out on the main meeting table as a reference point for those involved in information analysis and the decision-making process. These maps are frequently produced by the planning office of a community. Other sources for these maps are the departments of regional governments tasked with managing natural resources, or local conservation authorities. If such maps are not readily available, commercially produced roadmaps that include streets, key facilities, and major surface features can be used instead.

Once the initial plotting is complete, the resulting maps may be produced at a relatively low cost by anyone with a large-format printer called a *plotter*. Most commercial printing companies possess such a device, as do most municipal planning departments. It should be remembered that all maps that are used should be of identical, or at least similar, scale, so that the interrelationships between information are not distorted. Ideally, such maps will be laminated as well. This step will permit the addition of developing information, such as resource deployment, chemical plumes, or flooded areas, using a simple dry-erase marker, and will greatly enhance the durability and prolong the life of the maps. Taking an idea from mapping software, emergency managers may elect to have a few sheets of durable clear plastic available that can be overlaid on the map (and on each other) to create "layers" of data. When the emergency is concluded, these tools can be simply wiped clean, making them available for re-use in the next emergency. When not in use, such tools can be simply rolled up and stored in a durable container, such as a shipping tube, until they are needed.

Written Material

There is no item of critical information available by computer that cannot also be provided in a hard-copy format. Word-processing documents can be stockpiled as paper copies, resource databases can be replaced by the resource annex from the emergency plan, and so on. Critical reference resources available online are also frequently available in hard-copy format. To illustrate, the online reference material on hazardous materials described earlier is also available, free of charge, in the form of a book called the *Emergency Response Guidebook*.[9] Emergency managers should continuously build a library of hard-copy reference materials for the EOC, for use when computers are unavailable.

Bulletin Boards and Whiteboards

While an electronic database is a wonderful tool for managing requests for information and resources, a paper-and-pen approach can also be effective. A simple bulletin board or whiteboard with dry-erase markers can be used to track such items. The absence of a permanent record when using a whiteboard has been addressed by the development of the electronic whiteboard. With such a device, information is treated in much the same manner as a conventional whiteboard, with one important difference: once all of the entries on the board have been made and are no longer required, the push of a button will advance the movable surface to a completely clean section of whiteboard, erasing the old information in the process—but not before the device provides a paper copy of all the information currently on the board. The conventional and electronic versions of these devices are within the means of most communities, and can often be justified by their daily use in other activities, such as staff training.

The inclusion of low-tech alternatives in EOC design fulfills important considerations. They allow emergency managers to constantly attempt to provide high-quality information in the EOC while keeping costs under control. They also provide the EOC with a level of resiliency that will ensure that it continues to function, even when high-tech alternatives are unavailable.

Evaluating Technologies

When considering technologies for use in the EOC, emergency managers must balance a range of considerations. There are advantages and disadvantages to every option. A good analogy for this is a homeowner who must choose a new lawn mower to mow a large lawn. The first option is a manual push lawnmower. It will do the job, the maintenance required is low, and the cost is low, but the effort required is substantial. The second option is an electric or gas lawn mower. It too will do the job, but the cost is somewhat higher and the maintenance required is increased, but the effort required is reduced somewhat. The third option is the riding mower. It too will do the job, and with far greater ease, but both the cost and the maintenance are significantly higher than the first two options. The homeowner will ultimately make a choice based on the ability of each device, the effort that they are prepared to provide for its use, and the resources that they have available for both purchase and maintenance. The acquisition of technology for the EOC follows a very similar process.

The considerations for EOC technology acquisition include the benefits of each particular technology to the EOC, the limitations of each particular technology, the inadvertent creation of vulnerabilities within the EOC (generally through the creation of technological dependence), the opportunities for enhanced EOC operations and capabilities, and the cost associated with its acquisition. All of these factors need to be carefully weighed and balanced against each other to arrive at the most workable and useful decision. This process can be performed by emergency managers using a simple assessment technique called *SWOT*, which is borrowed from mainstream management studies. SWOT is an acronym for *Strengths, Weaknesses, Opportunities, and Threats.*

Strengths

What are the potential services provided by this technology? What services will be provided that are not available in the current model? Will this technology provide significant improvements in operations?

Weaknesses

What does this technology cost? Is the technology difficult for the average user to understand or use? Are there limitations on what the technology can accomplish? Is the technology vulnerable to the disruption of other services, such as electricity, telephone, or Internet services?

Opportunities

Can the technology provide substantial improvements in EOC operations, information management, or communications? Will the technology provide information that was not previously available?

Threats

Will the introduction of this technology substantially change or disrupt EOC operations? Does it create the potential for new vulnerabilities? What causes these vulnerabilities? Are mitigation measures available?

By listing the answers to all of these questions on a single page or chart, emergency managers gain a single, coordinated view of all of these issues. SWOT can provide a consistent process by which informed decisions can be made, priorities set, and technologies either acquired or deferred. Emergency managers can then make the best choices from a varied selection of options, based on the capability of the technology, its ease of use, and the resources that are available for its acquisition.

Conclusion

Technology can greatly enhance the capabilities of a community or organizational EOC. Used correctly, it can actually make it easier to manage an emergency through improved information flow and communications. But without careful consideration, the introduction of new technology may actually have the unintended result of creating new vulnerabilities for the EOC operation through the development of dependency. All use of technologies within an EOC must be based on the fundamental principles of having multiple layers of redundancy and using backup systems that are technologically independent of the primary systems.

Not everything that is new is necessarily better. Emergency managers must consider each new technology carefully, balancing strengths, weaknesses, opportunities, and threats. In every case, new technologies must also be considered in the light of resource availability. By pursuing this balanced approach, emergency managers can create an EOC with appropriate technologies—some high-tech, others low-tech, each with its own layers of redundancy—that will remain functional regardless of the circumstances, and that is within the financial means of the community or organization.

KEY TERMS

sheltering-in-place
technological independence

LEARNING CHECK

Take a few minutes now to test your knowledge of EOC technologies. Select the best answer in each case. Any score of less than 16 out of 20 (80 percent) indicates that you should re-read this chapter.

1. The EOC is the information and communications _____ of the community or organization during an emergency.
   a. backup
   b. hub
   c. source
   d. both (a) and (c)

2. During an emergency, one of the most important functions of an EOC is the management of
   a. information
   b. legal issues
   c. on-scene activities
   d. media

3. Without access to good information and a smooth flow of delivery, the emergency response will eventually _____.
   a. be effective
   b. resolve itself
   c. degrade
   d. escalate

4. An EOC that relies exclusively on any one type of technology for any function will
   a. generally be successful
   b. possess inherent vulnerability
   c. manage information well
   d. support the decision-making process

5. Given the varying nature of emergencies, any high-technology function should be backed up by
   a. a low-technology alternative
   b. another high-technology function
   c. parallel identical technology
   d. repair resources available within one day

6. With respect to information technology and telecommunications systems installed in the EOC, emergency managers should, in the first instance, rely on
   a. books and manuals
   b. advice from experts
   c. manufacturers' repair services
   d. their own knowledge

7. As a general principle in EOC design, any technology incorporated should be supported by
   a. local repair services
   b. multiple layers of redundancy
   c. manufacturers' warranties
   d. duplicate backup devices

8. As a general principle of EOC design, any backup system installed in the EOC should be
   a. identical to the primary system
   b. able to interact with the primary system
   c. technologically independent of the primary system
   d. both (a) and (b)

9. As general categories, EOC technologies may be classified as either information management systems or
   a. scheduling systems
   b. email systems
   c. recording systems
   d. telecommunications systems

10. In North America, the capacity of the local telephone network for simultaneous usage is normally about
    a. 10 percent
    b. 20 percent
    c. 30 percent
    d. 50 percent

11. In the United Kingdom, the system used to prevent local cellphone "cells" or "nodes" from becoming overwhelmed during an emergency is called
    a. line load control
    b. load regulation
    c. Access Overload Control
    d. priority access for dialing

12. Local telephone service providers typically obtain revenue by means of monthly billings and
    a. government funding
    b. fee-generating services
    c. property taxes
    d. both (a) and (c)

13. When selecting recording technologies for the EOC, it is important to remember that most different types of recording technologies
    a. are incompatible
    b. have limited compatibility
    c. are fully compatible
    d. are interoperable

14. One advantage to the use of the newer flat-panel, high-definition televisions is that they can be used
    a. to reduce stress
    b. to view television broadcasts
    c. to display different types of information
    d. both (b) and (c)

15. One problem with the use of local radio stations for emergency messaging to the general public is that they
    a. are rarely interested
    b. have policies that preclude this use
    c. are increasingly automated
    d. are only interested in news stories

16. The connection of a series of computers into a network will require the use of either a large computer called a *server* or a smaller device called a
    a. director
    b. switchboard
    c. router
    d. controller

17. When selecting computers for an EOC, it may be appropriate to select newer, higher-priced models because, over the long term, they represent
    a. the state-of-the-art
    b. better value
    c. adherence to purchasing guidelines
    d. a better image for the EOC

18. When selecting basic software for the EOC, it is preferable to use software that is already in use in the corporation, because
    a. staff are already familiar with it
    b. licences are already in place
    c. there may be no additional cost
    d. all of the above

19. When using web-based applications, it is important not to rely on them for essential functions because they
    a. can be confusing
    b. are often unproven
    c. can be difficult to use
    d. will not work when Internet access fails

20. When using instant-messaging technology for conversations, file transfers, or video conferencing, it is important to remember that
    a. such services are expensive
    b. such services require special training
    c. such services are not particularly secure
    d. such services are difficult to understand

CASE STUDIES

A. You are the new emergency manager for a medium-sized community. In reviewing the existing EOC operation, you discover that the EOC is solely reliant on a functioning telephone system for emergency communications outside of the community.

1. Prepare a list of easily affordable backup communications systems that might be incorporated into the existing EOC design.
2. What are the strengths and weaknesses of each system?
3. Identify those technologies that cannot be used in a backup capacity, and explain why each cannot be used.
4. Prepare a long-term plan to make EOC telecommunications functions more robust.

B. You are the emergency manager for a large community. The existing EOC was designed some 15 years ago, and you have been tasked with creating a plan to return the EOC to its original state-of-the-art information-management technology.

1. Consider the types of information-management technology that would be useful in the rejuvenated EOC.
2. Are there any barriers to the incorporation of those technologies? What are they? How might they be addressed?
3. What steps would you take to ensure that older technologies already present could interoperate with new technologies? What would you do with older technologies?
4. Develop a work plan for your technology updating program.

TO LEARN MORE

1. From the long list of potential EOC technologies described in this chapter, select the technology about which you know the *least*, and conduct some research. How does this type of technology work? What is its history? Is it currently in widespread use in EOCs? What are the advantages of this type of technology? What are its limitations? Are there any vulnerabilities that would be generated through the use of this technology? How and when might these vulnerabilities occur? What technologically independent backup systems might be selected to support the use of this technology?

2. Visit your local EOC. Learn how and where the EOC equipment is stored when not in use. If permitted to do so, assist with the routine assembly of the EOC. With permission, learn how to perform both assembly and basic maintenance functions for each type of technology in use. This would include assembly and "logging on" of computers and their networks, changing paper and toner cartridges in both printers and fax machines, and assembly of the telephone network. By the time you leave, you will not be an expert, but you should be able to perform these functions if necessary.

NOTES

1. Norm Ferrier, *A National Assessment of Emergency Planning in Canada's General Hospitals* (Ottawa: Public Safety Canada, 2000), <http://ww3.ps-sp.gc.ca/research/resactivites/planPrep/Ferrier/2000-D012_e.pdf>.
2. CANUTEC website, <http://www.tc.gc/canutec/en/guide/guide.htm>.
3. Intellicast website, <http://www.intellicast.com>.
4. Government of Ontario website, <http://www.e-laws.gov.on.ca/index.html>.
5. City of Toronto website, <http://www.toronto.ca/rescu/index.htm>.
6. Google website, <http://www.google.ca>.
7. Windows Live Messenger website, <http://get.live.com/messenger/overview>.
8. Yahoo! Messenger website, <http://messenger.yahoo.com/>.
9. Transport Canada, *Emergency Response Guidebook* (Ottawa: Government of Canada, 2004).

PART IV

Emergency Management Education and Funding

FOSTERING A CULTURE OF PREPAREDNESS

One of the primary roles of an emergency manager is to foster a culture of preparedness within a community or an organization. A chain is as strong as its weakest link. If a community or organization is not fully prepared to deal with the crisis at hand, its response will fail. Emergency managers must take the necessary steps toward preparedness: understanding and evaluating the nature of risk exposures, formulating plans to address the risk exposures, and providing the means to coordinate plans and response activities when an emergency occurs. Although these steps are essential, they are, by themselves, insufficient. A community or organization is the sum of its parts; unless its individual components and individual members are well trained to respond to an emergency, their response may prove deficient.

In previous parts, we discussed the evolution and role of emergency management, the nature of hazard, risk, and vulnerability along with how to determine them, and the steps required to prepare the community or organization for the eventual occurrence of an emergency. This part focuses on the creation of preparedness among those who will respond to emergencies (including departments and staff, organizations, and other stakeholders), primarily by education but also by the acquisition of resources and the funding of special programs.

Chapter 15 focuses on the educational theory upon which emergency exercises are based as well as the process of exercise creation. Chapter 16 explores the major types of emergency exercises available, as well as the purposes, strengths, and weaknesses of each. This chapter identifies the considerations associated with creating and staging emergency exercises, and also the use of such exercises to drive and refine the development of the emergency plan. Chapter 17 addresses the creation and use of public education programs to foster community preparedness. Chapter 18 focuses on the process of educating key decision-makers to gain their support for the goals of emergency management. Finally, Chapter 19 examines the different types of funding, including grantsmanship, used to acquire resources and develop emergency management programs.

CHAPTER 15

Emergency Exercise Planning

LEARNING OBJECTIVES

On completion of this chapter, you will

▶ Understand the basic educational theories that apply to the use of emergency exercises by emergency managers.

▶ Understand how and why participants learn through participation in exercises.

▶ Understand how to predetermine and generate learning outcomes as a part of the exercise-planning process.

▶ Understand the potential barriers to learning in an emergency exercise and how to overcome them.

▶ Understand how to turn individual learning into collective learning through the exercise-debriefing process.

▶ Understand how to use the data gathered from an emergency exercise to identify gaps, errors, and omissions within a community's or an organization's emergency response capabilities, as well as opportunities for mitigation.

KEY MESSAGES

1. In most educational contexts, adults learn best by doing and feeling.

2. Learning situations that are directly relevant to learners are more likely to be absorbed and retained.

3. A competitive environment is conducive to learning; a threatening environment is not.

4. The credibility of the learning environment plays a direct role in a learner's acceptance and retention of content.

5. It is important to test the plan and train the staff (rather than test the staff!).

6. Effective exercises can drive the development and refinement of an emergency plan, and provide opportunities for educating key decision-makers, staff, and the general public.

Introduction

The emergency exercise is perhaps the most powerful preparedness tool available to emergency managers. Well-crafted exercises play a critical role in education efforts. They can also be used to demonstrate the need to acquire resources as well as drive the refinement of the emergency plan. Very few elements of emergency management will not be affected, either directly or indirectly, by a well-designed emergency exercise.

To be effective, emergency exercises must be well written and credible. If an exercise is "unreal" or "artificial," participants will rarely achieve the desired learning outcomes. The exercise process is based on principles of adult education, which emergency managers should understand. With a clear understanding of those principles and the learning objectives that are based on them, an emergency manager becomes not only an educator but also a force for change within the community or organization.

This chapter focuses on emergency exercises, starting with the basic educational theory on how they work. It explores the need to create a subjective learning environment in which participants can meet the required learning objectives. The potential problems and pitfalls in the planning process are examined as well. Finally, the use of emergency exercises to gather meaningful data, perform gap analysis, and drive the evolution of the emergency plan are considered.

Purpose

Emergency managers are much more than planners; they are also educators and team leaders. Emergency exercises are perhaps the most powerful tool in an emergency manager's arsenal. With effective emergency exercises an emergency manager can provide powerful educational experiences for key decision-makers, staff, and the general public, and can foster the development of the emergency response team. Emergency exercises can also be a tool for change, and a powerful force to refine and enhance an emergency plan. Detailed knowledge of this process is essential for emergency managers, regardless of the environment in which they work.

The Process of Planning Emergency Exercises

Educational Theory

An emergency exercise is far more than a simple review of procedures or previously conducted training. It is a process for the education of all of those who are likely to play some role in a community or organizational emergency. An emergency exercise goes far beyond simple role play and imaginary situations; it creates an environment in which processes and interactions can be analyzed and new information imparted to participants. It represents education in its purest sense, and is a critical function for emergency managers. To understand exactly why and how participants will be affected by an exercise, emergency managers require at least a preliminary understanding of exactly how the process of learning works.

To a large degree, emergency management education is about teaching and learning specific skills. Skills may be related to particular roles or to providing a better understanding of the entire emergency management process. Emergency management education is the process by which a person (or people) shares their knowledge of emergency management with others who require it. This knowledge may be theoretical, but it also may encompass the transfer of experience, judgment skills, and wisdom from experienced staff to junior or inexperienced staff. Education occurs throughout a person's life, and it includes not only academic learning, but also lessons learned as a result of facing life's challenges. Ideally, the transmission of knowledge is not unidirectional. Each learner should exchange knowledge with the instructor and other learners. Therefore, both storytelling and metaphor can play a major role in the educational process.

Types and Modes of Learning

There are three types of education: formal, informal, and nonformal. *Formal education* refers to learning that takes place in institutionalized, structured academic programs or trades/technical training schools. Formal education is the system most commonly recognized as "education." *Informal education* encompasses the unstructured, personal, lifelong learning that people achieve through their own experiences and the experiences of others (such as family, friends, co-workers, and the media). For example, those who work in emergency services commonly share "war stories" with one another. These stories are shared not only for their entertainment value but also for the knowledge they impart about specific topics. Listeners learn from others' experiences and incorporate what they learn into their own body of knowledge. *Nonformal education* is organized learning outside the formal education system that is designed to improve the skills and knowledge of particular subgroups in a population.

A sizable body of work exists on how we learn, but one of the most popular views is that we learn through three modes of sensory perception:[1]

▶ *Kinesthetic mode:* Learning takes place by engaging in activities and performing specific physical tasks.
▶ *Visual mode:* Learning takes place by seeing and observing.
▶ *Auditory mode:* Learning takes place by listening to instructions and information.

Educational processes often use a mix of these learning modes, since it is believed that all participants have a preferred mode of learning. In medical education, for example (although many lay people would be horrified to hear this), the primary approach for imparting new skills to students can be summed up as "See one … Do one … Teach one …" While this sounds like a simplistic approach, it is theoretically sound. Student physicians, nurses, and paramedics watch a skill being performed, using both the visual and auditory modes. They then perform the skill themselves, using the kinesthetic mode to reinforce visual and auditory learning. Finally, they teach the skill to someone else, consolidating the process by performing the skill again (kinesthetic) while describing it to someone else (visual and auditory). Such approaches are of use, and in use, in other areas as well.

The Learning Environment

The environment in which learning takes place plays a major role in successful educational outcomes. As a result, emergency managers must give careful consideration to all environmental elements, both physical and psychological. At a minimum, the learning environment should be as real and as credible as possible. Participants who find a learning environment or situation to be incredible are much less likely to achieve the desired learning outcomes. This factor may play a role in the selection of venue, and will definitely play a role in the selection of a scenario and the development of some of the exercise inputs.

Emergency managers may find that selecting an appropriate learning environment is a complex task. Given the type of learning required, the typical learning environment—one that is warm, dry, comfortable, and low stress—may be unsuitable, particularly when participants know perfectly well that such an environment is not one in which an event would actually occur. According to the experience of many emergency managers, a high-stress environment may actually reinforce learning more effectively, given the type of learning and the participants doing the learning. Suffice to say that in most circumstances, the credibility of the environment will play a greater role in learning than will environmental comfort.

Emergency managers must also consider the psychological effects of the learning environment. On the one hand, a learning environment that is competitive is fine; most participants are likely to be quite competitive by the nature of the work that they do. On the other hand, a learning environment that is seen as threatening (either in terms of being judgmental or in relation to internal politics) is problematic. It may be useful to establish some ground rules at the outset of an exercise, such as "what happens in the exercise, stays in the exercise," and "in this setting, finding problems actually constitutes a successful exercise."

Bloom's Taxonomy

Bloom's taxonomy is one of the most widely accepted models of learning in the educational field, and is certainly the most relevant to the field of emergency management.

Created in 1956 at the University of Chicago by psychologist Benjamin Bloom and colleagues,[2] this model classifies forms of learning (called *domains*) by which individuals learn most effectively. The three parts of Bloom's taxonomy are the *affective, psychomotor*, and *cognitive domains*.

Affective Domain

The educational objectives of the affective domain focus on emotional reactions and the ability to feel another being's pain or joy. Affective learning objectives typically target the awareness of and growth in attitudes, emotion, and feelings. This domain has five levels of learning objectives,[3] organized progressively from the simplest to the most complex:

1. *Receiving:* The person is aware of a phenomenon and is prepared and willing to learn.
2. *Responding:* The person not only acknowledges a phenomenon, but actively reacts to it in some way.
3. *Valuing:* The person places some value on a phenomenon (from acceptance to commitment).
4. *Organizing:* The person has the ability to put together different values, information, or ideas, and is able to compare, relate, and elaborate what has been learned.
5. *Characterizing:* The person incorporates the new knowledge, and it begins to produce an effect on his or her behaviour.

Psychomotor Domain

The educational objectives of the psychomotor domain focus on the ability to perform specific physical tasks, such as the use of a particular type of skill or the operation of a piece of equipment.[4]

Cognitive Domain

The educational objectives of the cognitive domain focus on the acquisition and understanding of knowledge, and the ability to apply and evaluate it. This domain has six levels of learning objectives, organized progressively from the simplest to the most complex:

1. *Knowledge:* The person is able to remember and recall previously learned skills, facts, and information.
2. *Comprehension:* The person is able to understand facts through organizing, comparing, and translating them, among other skills.

3. *Application:* The person is able to solve problems by using the new knowledge, or by using it in a different way from that originally described.
4. *Analysis:* The person uses the information by breaking it down into components, and by identifying relationships, motives, and causes.
5. *Synthesis:* The person reorganizes the elements of a piece of knowledge in a new way and can propose alternatives.
6. *Evaluation:* The person is able to make judgments with respect to the quality or validity of information, based on criteria.

One can see how many of these learning objectives would play a role in the educational efforts of emergency managers. However, it is helpful to understand that the majority of adults tend to learn most effectively in the psychomotor and affective domains; adults learn best by doing and feeling. Learners then use the cognitive domain to synthesize the information and experiences gathered in affective and psychomotor activities into new knowledge. The recognition of this fact—by providing a learning environment that is high stress and has a high emotional content—is essential for emergency exercises. The effects of exercises that incorporate these domains are extremely powerful. When the scenario and setting created by emergency managers are highly credible, and when participants can be persuaded to suspend disbelief and participate in the event (even to the point of becoming stressed), the result is often learning outcomes and retention that are almost as good as if participants had been involved in the actual type of event being simulated.

Establishing Learning Objectives

The first stage in the development of any exercise is establishing specific learning objectives.[5] Remembering that the primary goal of any exercise is to test the plan and train the staff (and not to test the staff!), there are two general categories under which an exercise's learning objectives should fall: (1) those intended to test elements of the emergency plan, and (2) those intended to provide preparedness learning outcomes for participants. Emergency managers must consider a number of important questions before they begin developing an emergency exercise.

Questions related to the goal of testing the emergency plan can be quite straightforward. What specific elements of emergency preparedness or response should be tested? How should they be tested? To what extent should they be tested? In what manner should they be tested? The answers should be similarly straightforward: the learning objectives should validate the emergency planning process or identify gaps in it or in the resources available.

Questions related to providing preparedness learning outcomes can also be straightforward. What types of situations will test the elements or impart the required knowledge most effectively? What specific knowledge or messages must be imparted to participants? What are the intended learning outcomes? How will these learning outcomes be accomplished? How will an emergency manager know whether the exercise has been successful? As this last question indicates, the achievement of these learning objectives may be less obvious, and may require that emergency managers devise a methodology for the measurement of success or failure.

Virtually every exercise has three clear and distinct objectives that relate to the objective of testing the emergency plan and its components. *Primary objectives* are the publicly stated reasons for creating and conducting the exercise. These objectives may be described by statements like "The objective is to test the ability of staff to quickly assemble the improvised Emergency Operations Centre in the designated location." *Secondary objectives* may be created to quietly test some specific subsection of the emergency plan or meet the exercise and learning needs of another stakeholder agency. These objectives may be described by statements like "While the main body of the emergency plan is being tested by the town, the volunteer fire department will test the effectiveness of their firefighter alerting system." *Tertiary objectives*, which exist in almost every exercise, are the exercise's unstated objectives, and while they may not provide learning outcomes for participants, they can potentially provide required learning outcomes for key decision-makers. These objectives speak to issues that are in the back of an emergency manager's mind, but which, for political or other reasons, cannot be publicly stated. For example, senior staff may believe that the system for recalling staff during an emergency is foolproof (although the emergency manager has reason to believe otherwise) and are unwilling to invest in a better system. In this case, the emergency manager may decide to create a situation in which senior staff is forced to address the failure and consequences of the "foolproof" system. To state this objective would be counter to the emergency manager's purpose, and so it is not included in the publicly stated objectives (but it remains very real, nonetheless).

The implementation of learning objectives requires a certain degree of both skill and political astuteness. Once emergency managers have a clear and achievable set of learning objectives, they can begin the process of exercise creation.

Selecting a Scenario

The next stage in the creation of any exercise is the selection of a scenario. This stage can be critical to the success of the exercise, since it "sets the stage" for participants. There is a natural tendency, and one which is often succumbed to, to select a scenario that, while unlikely, is easy and/or inexpensive to stage. Emergency managers must always remember that a learning environment should be created with participants in mind. One of the key features of an exercise is an environment in which participants can suspend disbelief and immerse themselves in the experience. An exercise with a scenario that is not credible will alienate participants, making it difficult for them to suspend disbelief and maximize potential learning outcomes.

For these reasons, it is often prudent for emergency managers to revisit the Hazard Identification and Risk Assessment (HIRA) before they begin to craft an exercise. The HIRA can provide emergency managers with an entire menu of potential scenarios that either have a high probability of happening or will have a significant impact on the community or organization. Participants are often fully aware of what is possible and what is not; the selection of one of the events from the upper-scoring range of the HIRA will provide the exercise with significant credibility, right from the start. If participants do not feel that their valuable time is being wasted by performing role play in silly circumstances, they are much more likely to fully participate. That being said, it is perfectly acceptable to select a scenario that is not the most highly scored, when that scenario has already been used recently, or when another scenario would better satisfy the learning outcomes and other learning objectives of the exercise.

Creating an Exercise

Once the exercise's learning objectives and scenario have been determined, it is time to create the actual exercise. This can be a complex process, and often requires a great deal of work. Therefore, whenever possible, emergency managers will want to develop an exercise development committee. It is true that exercises can be, and frequently are, created by a single person, but unless that person does a great deal of this specific type of work, he or she will find exercise creation to be a huge task. Many hands make light work! Including others in the design process brings different experiences, expertise, and perspectives to exercise creation and can actually help facilitate buy-in for the exercise from a variety of stakeholders within the community or organization.

Designing Inputs

An exercise is created from a series of elements of discrete information, generally referred to as *inputs*. An input, or a series of inputs, is designed to elicit a particular type of response from one or more of the participants. Inputs may include information, or, in more elaborate exercises, may include people. To illustrate, let's say that an exercise is meant to test a community's ability to set up and operate an emergency reception centre. If one of the learning objectives is to determine the ability of staff to deal with disruptive elements, one might consider including an individual "victim" with some type of psychiatric condition or form of aggressive behaviour in the exercise.

Inputs may be divided into five basic categories: primary, secondary, improvised, filler, and "Murphy" types. A **primary input** is intended to meet one of the stated learning objectives of the exercise. To illustrate, if a learning objective is to test evacuation using a train-derailment scenario, it might include information that a particularly toxic substance is leaking from one of the rail cars.

A **secondary input** is intended to meet one of the emergency manager's unstated objectives or meet the objective of some other stakeholder who is participating in the exercise. To illustrate, if an emergency manager has been trying unsuccessfully to obtain funding for a backup communications system for the Emergency Operations Centre (EOC), he or she might add an input that disables the primary communications system, so that participants can better understand the need for a backup system.

An **improvised input** is a reality of exercise play. No matter how well the exercise designers have anticipated the possible responses and information requests from participants, there will invariably be something that is requested by participants, but was overlooked in planning. The response to such a request will have to be improvised on the spot to continue exercise play, and will need to be immediately shared with the entire exercise control team to guarantee consistency. Such inputs cannot, by their nature, be developed in advance. To illustrate, exercise participants may decide that they require the use of military helicopters based at some distance from the site, but which they are aware of. If the intent of the exercise is to compel participants to use the resources that they have at hand, the exercise controller may choose to advise them that "weather conditions near the helicopter base are below the required minimum, and, as a result, the helicopter will not be available for several hours" or that "the requested helicopter is already working on another mission, and will not be available for several hours." In this manner, the exercise controller denies participants the use of the helicopter in a credible manner, and refocuses the participants on the existing exercise content and resources.

A **filler input** is often background information from outside sources or information that is intended to "move the exercise along." To illustrate, a filler input might include a weather or local traffic report.

Finally, there is **"Murphy" input**, based on the old adage, Murphy's Law, that whatever can go wrong, will go wrong and usually at the worst possible time! Such inputs describe events that are unrelated to the objectives of the exercise, but which are intended to introduce new problems to slow participants down when they are proceeding with the exercise information too quickly to fully obtain all of the learning outcomes. To illustrate, a "Murphy" input might involve an unrelated situation of someone trapped in an elevator. A wise emergency manager will always have five or six such inputs tucked away for use, but only when required.

Primary inputs are created to meet the learning objectives of the exercise. They provide participants with the opportunity to problem solve and, in doing so, discover new information and achieve learning outcomes. As a result, when creating a new exercise, it is completely appropriate to craft these inputs first to ensure that the learning objectives of the exercise will be met. The credibility of primary inputs is critical; each input must be carefully researched to ensure that the information provided is as factual and as credible as possible. Failure to do so will often result in the immediate disconnect of participants from the learning process and from the exercise itself. To illustrate, if one creates a scenario in which an element of public works infrastructure fails in a manner that is simply impossible, participants from public works are likely to immediately recognize that fact and think to themselves "that just *isn't* possible!"—for them, the exercise is over. They are no longer able to suspend disbelief, and are unlikely to remain sufficiently engaged to achieve the learning outcomes.

The same issue holds true for the creation of secondary inputs. Like primary inputs, they require a high degree of factuality. These inputs may be addressed to particular subsets of participants, but will also serve to provide information to the larger group of participants about exactly how that particular group functions. Lack of appropriate research has the potential to not only misinform members of the group but also alienate the participants for whom the input was intended. Primary and secondary inputs are always created first, and then laid out in a rough chronological order of events that makes sense to the flow of the exercise. If event "X" always precedes event "Y" in a real event, it should do so during the simulation of events during an exercise.

Once the primary and secondary inputs have been created, it is time to create the filler inputs. Filler inputs are intended to create a level of continuity in the exercise itself. They may foreshadow certain primary or secondary inputs, or may be intended simply to occupy the participants in order to achieve realistic time frames for the primary and secondary input events. When developing these inputs, it is often useful to look at the primary and secondary inputs in chronological order and ask, "What precursor events are required for this event to happen?" and "Understanding the way in which our organization or community operates, what secondary events are likely to occur between these two primary inputs?" Once both questions have been answered, the filler inputs can be created. Their presence creates a sequence of events that is both logical and recognizable to participants, and contributes directly to the realism of the simulated event.

Delivery of Information to Participants

When all of the preceding inputs have been created and placed in a rough chronological order, it is time to consider the delivery of information to participants. This area includes exercise timing (at what point in the exercise is this information to be delivered?), and also the more abstract concept of elapsed time within the simulated event. Who, among the exercise control group, will be responsible for the provision of each input to participants? Given the limited time available to run an exercise, it may be necessary to employ time compression to squeeze events that would normally occur over three days into a two-hour exercise. Both types of timing are important: one keeps participants occupied and stressed, and the exercise running; the other provides a realistic chronology of the real event.

At this point in the design process, the focus turns to the delivery of the actual information. Is there a logical and/or normal source from which such information flows? Would information on rising river levels in a flood scenario be provided by the fire department, the local conservation authority, or a similar group? Choosing an appropriate source of the information adds to the credibility of the information and to the realism of participants' exercise experience. Similarly, what mechanism or system would be used to provide such information on a daily basis? Would it arrive by telephone, two-way radio, email, or television news broadcast? Answering these questions will ensure that the inputs used and the exercise experience as a whole remain as realistic as possible.

Once all of the inputs have been determined, as a final step, they are assembled into a coherent exercise script. The exercise is essentially complete, at least as a first draft, and could be run by simply using the inputs. An overarching exercise script will allow the **chief controller** to coordinate the conduct of the exercise. By referring to the script, the chief controller can prompt individual controllers to provide information, and can mark the progress of the exercise until its completion.

Armed with a first draft of the exercise, emergency managers should stage a run-through for the entire group charged with exercise design. Each input is read aloud, in chronological sequence, and then discussed by the group. The group considers whether the input is fully factual, occurs in a logical sequence, occurs at the correct time in the exercise, and, perhaps most important, whether any key element is missing. The group should also consider whether the information provided is understandable or potentially confusing to participants.

The inputs should be discussed openly and critically, without any proprietary interest by their creators. If problems are identified, they should be fixed, and if one member of the group finds an input confusing, it is highly likely that participants will experience that same confusion. The group has been chosen for their knowledge and expertise; allowing them to use it will contribute greatly to the credibility and effectiveness of the exercise itself. Once all of these items have been considered and addressed, the exercise itself is, for all practical purposes, complete and ready to use.

Exercise Logistics

After the exercise is created, emergency managers must consider all of the variables associated with staging it. Even a well-written exercise can be effective only if it is staged properly and in the appropriate environment. Creating an effective environment and acquiring the required support resources can pose a challenge for emergency managers, but this challenge is not insurmountable. Being well-organized and having good project management skills will help ensure that all of the required background logistics to support the staging of the exercise are in place.

The amount and type of logistical support required for an exercise can vary considerably. Factors that influence logistics are the type of exercise, its anticipated duration, and the expected number of participants. Typically, the logistics required increase in complexity along with the exercise itself. A case study or tabletop exercise may not require much more than meeting space to run the exercise, review of the script and any associated maps or floor plans, use of a computer and projector, a debriefing of the exercise, and some light refreshments. A more complex exercise, such as a functional or **full-scale exercise**, typically has greater space requirements and may also require the use of resources that are not normally under the control of emergency managers. The precise logistical requirements will be determined by the exercise itself.

A sound approach to determining the appropriate logistical support is to treat the staging of an exercise as a project. As such, many emergency managers use a critical path type of approach. The first step is to create an exhaustive list of the resources needed for the exercise, along with the identification of who the resource in question belongs to, their contact information, and any costs associated with the use of the resource. It is prudent to obtain advance permission for the use of any space or resource prior to its inclusion in the exercise plan; there is little point to wasting time or energy in planning to incorporate a resource that might turn out to be unavailable for any reason. Many emergency managers find it helpful to develop a comprehensive checklist of all exercise logistical requirements.

Human Resources

The first resource emergency managers should consider is the people who will be tasked with conducting and evaluating the exercise. These people are often referred to as the *exercise control group* or **exercise controllers**. This group is responsible for running an exercise, usually under the supervision of an emergency manager who takes on the role of chief controller. In most circumstances, exercise controllers are drawn from the group that helped the emergency manager write and develop the exercise. The emergency manager will need to solicit their agreement (and that of their managers) to act in this role and participate on the day of the exercise itself.

The exercise control group may be supplemented, at the discretion of the emergency manager, by the use of official **observers**. Such individuals have no direct role to play in the exercise itself; during the exercise they are, for all practical purposes, invisible. They can, however, make valuable observations, offer insight, and critique the performance of specific tasks. Observers may be drawn from virtually anywhere, but they typically include representation from nearby communities or partner organizations, or from emergency management specialists from other levels of government. The names and contact information for individuals in both the controller and observer groups should be listed for future reference.

Physical Resources

Emergency managers must identify the space required to conduct the exercise and seek permission for its use. Once a general site has been determined, specific locations at the site can be identified. In the military, this is often accomplished by means of a **Tactical Exercise Without Troops (TEWOT)**. In a military context, TEWOT involves the inspection of the mock battle site by officers to predetermine the initial placement of resources. In the context of an emergency management exercise, TEWOT involves a simple walkthrough of the entire site by those charged with planning the exercise. They identify the spaces to be used for specific purposes, along with their "ownership." As well, they identify the resources required to support the uses planned for each space. Finally, they determine, analyze, and resolve any potential site safety issues.

In the case of simpler exercises, such as a case study or tabletop exercise, all that may be required is the use of a simple meeting room. For more complex exercises, such as functional or full-scale exercises, it may also be necessary to secure the use of the actual exercise area, a staging area for resources responding to the exercise event, a **control cell**, dressing and makeup areas for simulated victims, and debriefing, feeding, and rest areas for participants. These spaces are normally under the day-to-day control of an individual or department, and their use must be secured with written permission in advance.

Obtaining permission to use spaces may involve a considerable amount of advance discussion; it is likely that those responsible for the site selected may need to be satisfied with respect to issues such as liability, insurance coverage, and disruption of normal service operations. Time frames will also need to be established for the use of a particular space; granting permission to use a site for six to eight hours for an exercise is one thing; it does not cover the storage of props well in advance of the exercise, or leaving props in place for an extended period. Emergency managers must be prepared to define all of these needs and satisfy the concerns of those responsible for the location if permission for its use is to be secured.

Emergency managers must know how many people will be involved in the exercise, and where they will come from. How many controllers, observers, participants, and simulated victims will be present during the exercise? This information will help determine the need for support facilities, such as dressing rooms, feeding areas, and rest areas. It will also help determine the size of the physical area required for the debriefing process. In addition, it will be useful for determining the amount of food and other "creature comfort" needs.

Are any exercise props required? With a case study or tabletop exercise, props may involve maps, floor plans, or a simple collection of photographs, in either paper or electronic format. More complex exercises may involve the use of actual response resources, such as a portable decontamination facility, or even the EOC itself. In major full-scale exercises, props can become truly complex, involving the use of vehicles, "wrecked" buildings, or even simulated aircraft wreckage. In either case, emergency managers need to know where the resources required are available, how they can be obtained, and what is involved in securing permission for their use.

In full-scale exercises, the participation of actual physical response resources and staff, or the use of a community space, such as a school, recreation centre, or arena, may also be required. Will participation in the exercise be during or after normal working hours? Will the use of emergency response resources such as police vehicles, fire trucks, and ambulances be dedicated or drawn from fleet "spares," or will the resources need to remain available for emergency calls? Where does the emergency manager need to go to secure the participation of such resources? What commitments will be required for their use? As with other potential work spaces, emergency managers must consider the needs and concerns of the "owners" of such resources, as well as issues of liability and insurance coverage.

An exercise may require the use of other tools, by either participants or controllers. These items may include two-way radios, patient-care equipment, "turnout" gear (such as the protective clothing worn by firefighters), or similar materials.

Such items are not normally under the direct control of emergency managers, and permission may be required for their use. For each item, it is important to know exactly when the equipment can be made available and when it is expected to be returned.

Communications Resources

Virtually all exercises involve some type of communications equipment, and emergency managers must identify the means for accomplishing communications during the exercise. Communications equipment can be divided into two groups: (1) that required to conduct the exercise and (2) that required by exercise participants. It is almost always a good idea to have some separate form of communication for exercise controllers; they should remain out of earshot of exercise participants because they will share information and transmit directions aimed at facilitating the flow of the exercise. The communications equipment used by participants should be realistic to ensure that participants function in as authentic an environment as possible. If a firefighter's work direction would normally come by radio, this is the way that it should arrive during the exercise. Emergency managers will need to make arrangements to secure the use of communications equipment.

Emergency managers must also ensure that exercise communications and real-world communications do not mix. In an ideal situation, separate radio frequencies should be used to ensure that no inadvertent exercise radio messages take place on real emergency channels. At a minimum, a means must be devised to ensure that every exercise-related message is clearly identified. If no other option is available, this may be as simple as prefacing *every* radio transmission with the phrase "This is an exercise message …"

Real emergencies also occur at exercise sites and during exercises. As a result, emergency managers must have a clear procedure for identifying emergency messages that are *not* a part of the exercise. The most common approach to this is to preface a legitimate mid-exercise emergency radio transmission with the phrase "No Duff!" While the origins of this phrase are unknown, it is widely used in emergency management circles. The procedures for dealing with actual emergencies during an exercise must be clearly understood, and should be included in the pre-exercise briefing of all participants.

Other Considerations

Emergency managers must also consider creature-comfort measures for exercise participants, and these too will vary, according to the type and duration of the exercise. For a small, simple exercise, light refreshments will usually suffice, but for an exercise that is large, long, or complex, an actual feeding plan may need to be developed. In addition, washroom and changing facilities may need to be provided, and, in some cases, even showers may be required. Participants may also require areas in which they can rest and relax prior to and between periods of exercise involvement.

Some of these items, most notably the feeding of participants, may have a financial cost associated with them. Costs may also be associated with the use of certain resources or exercise props in some locations. Emergency managers must carefully consider any costs and list these for each item of exercise logistics. They must also seek advance approval for the required expenditures.

It is important to realize that very little of the equipment required for conducting an emergency exercise is under the direct control of an emergency manager. Many items will be borrowed; typically from other municipal departments, outside agencies, or even from private enterprise. It is essential that such items be returned to their owners promptly once they are no longer required. They should also be returned in a condition that is clean and ready for use, and also in a condition that is as good as or better than when they were obtained. Generally, it is a good idea to write a formal thank-you note to the owners of borrowed equipment, and to acknowledge their cooperation publicly. Such measures will greatly increase the likelihood that other equipment can be borrowed from the same source in the future.

Chronology, Timelines, and Performance Measurement

Once all of the resources have been identified, the next step in the process is to identify all of the critical events that must occur before the exercise can be staged, and to place them in a rough chronological order. Any measures that must occur prior to a critical event should also be placed in that chronology, in advance of the related critical event. Critical events can be mapped out, and, in doing so, emergency managers frequently discover that the critical events have a logical sequence. Some critical events may be dependent on the completion of other critical events, while others may be independent of other critical events and able to operate in a parallel process. What is essential is that all the prerequisites for the exercise, whether dependent on one another or not, must be completed in time for use during the exercise. A large whiteboard or project-management applications, such as Microsoft® Office Project software, can greatly aid in both organizing this process and making it understandable.

Once the critical events have been organized, timelines can be established. The first important date to establish is when the exercise will be staged. Once this date is determined, emergency managers can go back to each critical event and determine a reasonable date for completion. A similar approach can be used for the prerequisite for each critical event. Emergency managers then have a list of project milestones, and a means for measuring progress toward their completion. By monitoring progress, emergency managers can intervene any time an objective is delayed or a problem is encountered. The tasks needed are now ready for assignment to members of the exercise development team, and progress on the development of the project can be monitored.

Once an exercise is complete, emergency managers must measure performance in relation to the list of learning objectives associated with that exercise. Emergency managers develop checklists for members of the exercise control group and any observers, as well as debriefing questionnaires for participants to measure performance. Such information plays a major role in determining the effectiveness of the exercise, and therefore the development of data-gathering tools requires careful thought and planning. The performance-monitoring and work-management skills required by any competent manager apply to the tasks outlined in this section.

Creating a Learning Environment

A critical stage in the creation of any emergency exercise is the selection of the environment to be used. This will vary according to the type of exercise chosen and, to some extent, the scenario and learning objectives. As in any type of educational planning, the environment often plays a critical role in the effectiveness of the learning of participants. For the purposes of emergency managers, the exercise environment should be considered within two separate and distinct categories: physical and psychological. Each category has a role to play in the exercise process, and, executed correctly and with careful forethought, each will contribute in its own way to learning outcomes.

Physical Environment

The physical environment in which an exercise is conducted will be determined largely by the exercise. For case studies, tabletop exercises, or some types of **functional exercises** (such as those related to telecommunications), the environment is often a classroom, a boardroom, a meeting area, or perhaps an EOC. Usually, such environments do not include environmental stressors. The environment should be comfortable for participants, with adequate seating, ventilation, lighting, and noise control. Access to the exercise environment should be controlled to ensure that exercise play can be conducted with a minimum of distractions. There should be adequate work space for all participants, as well as seating for observers, if they are a part of the exercise. Seating for observers should be arranged in a way that makes their presence inconspicuous to participants and unintrusive in exercise play. Similarly low-profile work spaces should be provided for exercise controllers.

The choice of environment will be different for full-scale exercises and many types of functional exercises. As an important distinction, while primary learning is accomplished in the affective domain, practical exercises such as the functional and full-scale types often seek to either provide or reinforce learning that is best accomplished in the psychomotor domain. Such learning would include specific procedures, or the reinforcement or practising of specific mechanical skills.

In full-scale exercises and many types of functional exercises, the objective of emergency managers is to provide participants with an environment that is as realistic as possible to persuade them to suspend disbelief during an exercise. Often, such exercises are conducted outdoors and may involve a simulated disaster scene, such as a wrecked bus or aircraft. They may also, in the case of functional exercises, require a space in which specific types of equipment and operations, such as a decontamination facility, may be set up and run by participants.

The outside environment is, of course, less controlled and subject to issues such as heat, cold, and adverse weather conditions. It is appropriate, in most circumstances, to include these factors, as environmental stressors will directly contribute to the realism of the experience for participants. The degree to which environmental stressors will operate should be decided in advance by the emergency manager, based upon the degree of realism or extent to which a particular process or function is to be tested.

If the intent is to conduct a review of procedures, as with a drill, the nature of the environment may not play a key role, and a decision may be made to only conduct the exercise when fair weather is present. On the other hand, if the intent is to identify the failure point in a procedure or process, it might be necessary to conduct the exercise in adverse conditions. Weather can be unpredictable to some extent, particularly over the long term. Conditions cannot be entirely foreseen, particularly when planning an exercise over the long term. Unanticipated weather conditions will require careful consideration on the day of the exercise; the emergency manager must decide either to postpone the exercise or to exploit an unexpected situation to enhance the educational experience.

During an exercise, safety is always a primary consideration. The site should be carefully chosen and any props included should be examined carefully to ensure that there is nothing present that might harm a participant. Access to the exercise site should be strictly controlled, so that observers and bystanders are not inadvertently placed in harm's way. A final site safety check should always be conducted just prior to the start of the exercise. A site safety officer should be appointed, as would be the case in a real event, and that person should be given the mandate and authority to continually inspect operations during an exercise and stop exercise play at any time if a potential safety hazard is identified. The emergency exercise, regardless of type or scale, is an educational process, and there is never a valid reason for a participant to become injured during exercise play.

Psychological Environment

Equally important to emergency managers is the psychological environment in which an exercise will be conducted. The intent is not to create a low-stress environment for all exercises; many exercises are best carried out in a high-stress environment. Learning in the affective domain has a strong emotional component, which makes it particularly effective for adult learners. A high-stress environment can help participants to both absorb and retain the experiences provided over the long term. As a result, in most types of exercises, stress is actually desirable. Some useful types of exercise stressors include time-sensitive components or information that creates a sense of urgency for participants. They also include physical factors calculated to increase stress, such as the presence of the media or large numbers of deceased victims in public view.

While exercise stress is desirable, it should also be calculated and controlled by emergency managers. The stressors provided to participants should be carefully monitored. This process is not a game; the intent is to test the plan and procedures, not the participants. While stress will aid in learning and retention, pushing it to extremes may very well result in a participant "shutting down" psychologically, with all desired learning outcomes lost. Everyone who will assist with conducting the exercise must be briefed in advance regarding exercise stress, and should be sure to monitor high-stress situations carefully throughout the exercise.

The exercise environment must be psychologically safe, and, to some extent, this also means politically safe. Many organizations have their own unique political environments, and many are highly competitive on a day-to-day basis. Participants who fear repercussions, such as the ridicule of colleagues, are unlikely to fully participate in the exercise and may respond to information only in ways that they judge to be "politically safe." This type of highly conventional "safe" thinking will effectively circumvent any attempts to generate experimental problem solving, if this is an exercise objective. One approach to this problem is to set ground rules for exercise play, including the solicitation from the participants of an agreement that "what happens during the exercise and debriefing process, remains there." Participants who experience an exercise environment that is nonjudgmental and politically safe are much more likely to participate in future educational efforts. Exercise environments, both physical and psychological, which are carefully monitored and controlled, are much more likely to contribute to the desired positive learning outcomes. The responsibility for monitoring the exercise environment and ensuring that it remains safe rests with the emergency manager and all members of the exercise control team.

Measuring Effectiveness

Before an exercise begins, it is a good idea to develop some standard for how its effectiveness will be measured.[6] In all cases, the first measure of effectiveness will be how well the exercise met its learning objectives. Thus, the learning objectives identified at the outset of the design process become the starting point for measuring success. The success of an exercise can be measured subjectively or objectively.

Subjective Measurement

Subjective measurement is the easiest approach, because anything that is subjective can generally be quantified by the reported responses of the participants. This measurement may take place through the occurrence of events or responses to inputs that were specifically identified during the development of the exercise. An example of this measurement might include an expectation that within a given time frame of a certain triggering event, each department head would activate staff telephone fan-out procedures; measurement would entail how many met the performance standard. Over multiple exercises, performance standards can be benchmarked to measure progress with compliance. It is also possible to quantify, at least to some degree, the responses of participants to specific questions in exercise debriefing questionnaires. A word of caution: any researcher knows that the size of the group responding has a direct bearing on the validity of the response. For example, let's say that a questionnaire that has a 20 percent response rate and 50 percent of respondents make a given recommendation. The weight of that recommendation is different from what it would be if the questionnaire had a 70 percent response rate. Emergency managers must ask themselves whether the response is the voice of a vocal but interested minority or the majority opinion of the larger group. Responses to questionnaires must always be qualified by the context of the overall response rate.

Objective Measurement

Most of the assessment of the success of an exercise will take another form: unquantifiable opinion. Did the exercise meet its objectives? Were the desired learning outcomes achieved? Did the exercise identify any problems/gaps within the emergency plan? This last question is critical; while we are conducting an educational experience for participants, we are also attempting to validate the emergency plan and its associated procedures. The first measure of success for an exercise is always its ability to identify gaps and shortcomings in the emergency plan—now, while there is no associated human cost. It might even be argued that an emergency exercise that does not accomplish this is indicative of a fundamental failure of the exercise process itself, and a waste of time and resources. The identification of problems should never be viewed in a negative light; it is a major indicator of exercise success. Together, subjective and objective measurements will guide emergency managers to a conclusion about the effectiveness of an exercise as well as areas for its improvement.

Debriefing Participants

The data generated by the exercise as well as the experiences of participants and the comments of observers are essential parts of an exercise process. This information helps emergency managers judge the effectiveness of the learning experience for participants. Similar to a real emergency, debriefing after an exercise allows emergency managers to "harvest" the information that will lead to improvements in plans and procedures, and possibly even to the acquisition of new resources for a real emergency.

Exercise participants may be debriefed in a variety of ways, including collective and individual verbal debriefings, and also through the use of questionnaires. Each approach has its strengths and weaknesses. Each will yield different types of information. As a result, most emergency managers employ some mix of these debriefing types.

One commonly used debriefing approach is **"hot-wash" debriefing**. In a hot-wash, the debriefing is conducted collectively, immediately following the completion of the exercise. The advantage of this approach is that participants often reveal information while still under exercise stress that might not be forthcoming if a "cooling off" period were permitted. This approach should be used cautiously; as stated earlier, an exercise environment can be politically charged. It is necessary for the hot-wash facilitator to establish some basic ground rules, such as prohibiting personal comments and finger pointing, accepting statements of fact rather than assignment of blame, and establishing agreement that what is said in the debriefing remains in the debriefing. Given the political cultures of some types of organizations and communities, it may also be necessary to consider separate debriefings for senior staff and lower-level workers.

Individual debriefings are also a useful tool, if somewhat time-consuming. The advantage of this approach is that some individuals may be more likely to candidly share their experiences and observations when the debriefing is conducted in private as opposed to the potentially politically charged environment of the hot-wash. Given the scale of most exercises, and the time required for individual debriefing, emergency managers may wish to select only key participants for inclusion in this process.

Individual-debriefing questionnaires can provide useful information as well. While the emotional content of hot-wash debriefing is likely to be lost, the anonymity of this approach will likely lead to greater candour from respondents. Questionnaires provide participants with the luxury of time to consider their responses; while responses tend to be more measured, they are also more likely to incorporate individual ideas and potential solutions to the problems identified. Questionnaire responses can also be quantified by emergency managers to some extent. The major problem with the use of debriefing questionnaires is that often they have a dismally low return rate. According to accepted wisdom, if participants are allowed to leave the debriefing area with their questionnaires, it is unlikely that the majority of those questionnaires will ever be seen again. That being said, while the return rate may be low, the quality of information provided by such a process can be extremely high. As a result, emergency managers should always consider including this approach in the debriefing process.

Applying the Data

The emergency exercise has been completed, and data has been gathered through the debriefing process. The task now falls to emergency managers to apply this information to affect meaningful change within the community or the organization. The information gathered is likely to fall into one or more of three general categories.

The first category is the identification of gaps, errors, and omissions within the existing emergency plan. Emergency managers must note, prioritize, and then address these findings, with the highest priority problems given immediate attention for revision in the emergency plan.

The second category is the identification of gaps, errors, and omissions within the response processes of specific groups within the community or organization. These may involve individual departments or voluntary service organizations. Emergency managers must also note and prioritize these findings, but their resolution is likely to be dealt with differently. Most organizations accept that errors occur and that changes may be required; they may even have identified the need for these changes independently as a part of their review of the exercise results. That said, both communities and organizations are typically politically sensitive environments, and they may react badly to public disclosure of their shortcomings. For emergency managers to be a force for change, they must understand how to navigate within politically sensitive environments. They should share the information gathered (at least in the first instance) with the person in charge of the department or organization in question, giving that person the opportunity to affect the required changes in an atmosphere that is free of embarrassment. When people in charge are resistant to making any changes, it may become necessary to create political pressure to affect change. However, the first approach is much more likely not only to achieve change but also to build alliances for future emergency management activities.

The data gathered during an exercise may also identify both new ideas related to emergency management and the need to acquire new resources for response to emergencies. Perhaps such resources are not already present because of an oversight by key decision-makers, a lack of understanding of the issues by key decision-makers, or a lack of funds with which to acquire those resources. In any case, it is unlikely that the issues identified by the exercise process will be resolved quickly; continued gentle pressure may be required to resolve issues identified by the exercise process. The data gathered is a tremendous resource that can help build the business case and support for the acquisition of new resources, as well as the implementation of new ideas.

The final category is the identification of fundamental deficiencies in the emergency management education process. It may well be that key decision-makers, staff, or the general public simply did not understand what was expected of them during an exercise. This information should lead to better emergency management education, either through more comprehensive educational programs, the targeting of groups not previously considered for educational efforts, or the provision of more frequent educational opportunities. Emergency managers will need to consider these results on an item-by-item basis.

Conclusion

Given careful forethought and planning, a well-crafted and well-executed emergency exercise can achieve many goals for emergency managers. The exercise can provide critical information on community or organizational vulnerability, and gaps and weaknesses in both the emergency plan and its associated procedures. It can become a force for change—educating key decision-makers, altering opinion, and resulting in the acquisition of new emergency response resources. Emergency exercises, when planned and executed properly, provide data that forms the basis by which the emergency plan can become an "evergreen" document—engaged in a cycle of continual improvement.

The emergency exercise is the centrepiece of the ongoing educational process in emergency management. It is a powerful preparedness tool. It is also one of the most powerful tools emergency managers possess for educating key decision-makers, staff at all levels, and the general public. With a solid understanding of the educational theory behind exercises, emergency managers can create learning environments and opportunities in which knowledge not only will be absorbed but also retained by participants for an extended period of time. With the essential skill of emergency exercise creation, emergency managers can help communities or organizations become both better prepared for emergencies and safer.

The process involved in creating and conducting exercises can be extremely time consuming, but the necessary time will vary by type of exercise. It may be possible to generate a useful case study or tabletop exercise with just a few hours of work, while truly large, full-scale exercises may require six months to a full year of effort to take them from concept to actual execution. In virtually all cases, this time is well spent; the results will yield valuable information about community or organizational preparedness, and will provide opportunities to resolve problems before they occur in a real emergency. Even when the benefits are not immediately obvious, it is rare that any efforts aimed at improving emergency preparedness within a community or an organization are ever completely wasted over the long term.

KEY TERMS

Bloom's taxonomy

chief controller

control cell

exercise controller

filler input

full-scale exercise

functional exercise

"hot-wash" debriefing

improvised input

"Murphy" input

observer

primary input

secondary input

Tactical Exercise Without Troops (TEWOT)

LEARNING CHECK

Take a few minutes now to test your knowledge of emergency planning exercises. Select the best answer in each case. Any score of less than 16 out of 20 (80 percent) indicates that you should re-read this chapter.

1. In most educational circumstances, adult learners will learn best by
   a. didactic teaching
   b. directed self-study
   c. doing or feeling
   d. independent self-study

2. A learner is more likely to absorb and retain information when it is
   a. directly relevant
   b. critical to the organization
   c. from recognized sources
   d. presented in a high-stress environment

3. Learning is much more likely to be effective when it occurs in a competitive environment than when the environment is
   a. non-competitive
   b. threatening
   c. stress free
   d. both (a) and (c)

4. The material being presented is most likely to be absorbed and retained when the learner finds the learning situation to be
   a. amusing
   b. credible
   c. formal
   d. supportive

5. The primary purposes of an emergency exercise are to test the emergency plan and to _____ staff.
   a. test
   b. motivate
   c. train
   d. frighten

6. In addition to providing educational opportunities, emergency exercises can be used to drive the _____ of the emergency plan.
   a. development
   b. creation
   c. refinement
   d. both (a) and (c)

7. The process of education may involve the transfer of theoretical knowledge, experience, and also
   a. judgment skills
   b. procedures
   c. the creation of new knowledge
   d. both (b) and (c)

8. The process of education may use models that are formal, informal, or
   a. theoretical
   b. representational
   c. nonformal
   d. dependent

9. The generally accepted modes of learning may be described as the kinesthetic, visual, and _____ modes.
   a. esthetic
   b. theoretical
   c. auditory
   d. experiential

10. In Bloom's taxonomy of learning, the domains of learning are described as affective, psychomotor, and
    a. transitory
    b. cognitive
    c. experiential
    d. self-directed

11. For the purposes of emergency managers, the goals involved in creating an emergency exercise may be described as those that provide learning opportunities, and those that
    a. generate revenue
    b. satisfy political requirements
    c. satisfy legal requirements
    d. test the emergency plan

12. When creating an emergency exercise, the first step an emergency manager takes is to
    a. select a scenario
    b. create the most important inputs
    c. set objectives
    d. determine methods of measuring success

13. The inputs used to create an exercise may be described as primary, secondary, improvised, "Murphy," and
    a. problematic
    b. definitive
    c. filler
    d. coordinated

14. When crafting an emergency exercise, the primary and secondary inputs are usually determined by
    a. budget considerations
    b. exercise objectives
    c. the emergency manager
    d. the exercise committee

15. When crafting exercise inputs, it is absolutely essential that they be
    a. factual
    b. brief
    c. credible
    d. both (a) and (c)

16. When conducting an emergency exercise, the presence of the right type of stressful environment may actually
    a. aid the participants in recalling the plan
    b. enhance the learning process
    c. identify failures in participants
    d. make the process enjoyable

17. One of the functions of the emergency exercise is to identify
    a. those best able to function in an emergency
    b. best practices
    c. gaps, errors, and omissions in the emergency plan
    d. existing knowledge of participants

18. When debriefing participants using the "hot-wash" method, the emergency manager may obtain responses that might not otherwise be given, because the participants
    a. are eager to share their experiences
    b. feel that the environment is less threatening
    c. will elaborate on each other's points
    d. are still subject to exercise stress

19. One major problem with the use of questionnaires for exercise debriefing is
    a. the low return rate
    b. reluctance to put information in writing
    c. fear of identification
    d. both (b) and (c)

20. The data generated by emergency exercises may be used by emergency managers to
    a. affect changes to the emergency plan
    b. acquire new resources
    c. resolve response shortfalls in individual groups
    d. all of the above

CASE STUDIES

A. You are the emergency manager for a medium-sized community. It has been two years since the last community exercise took place. That exercise identified a number of problems, resulting in the complete revision of the community emergency plan. Your emergency plan has just been completely revised and distributed, and it is time for that plan to be tested.

1. Describe the basis upon which your scenario for the emergency exercise will be selected.
2. Identify four to five clear learning objectives/outcomes that should arise from the exercise.
3. Describe your method for creating an exercise setting that will maximize the learning potential for all of the participants.
4. Explain the methodology used in question 3 in detail.

B. You are the emergency manager for a large community. For several years, the community has conducted an annual emergency exercise. This exercise is slated for next month. The scenario has been selected, the learning objectives have been identified, and the script has received final approval.

1. Describe two potential processes for data collection following the exercise.
2. Describe the strengths and weaknesses of each process.
3. Select a process or processes to be used for data collection. State the rationale for your choice.
4. Describe the manner in which the data collected will be employed upon completion of the exercise.

TO LEARN MORE

1. Volunteer to participate in an exercise being run by a local community or organization, ideally in one of the controller positions, and observe what occurs. Looking at the inputs used, identify all inputs by type. What do you believe was the intent of each input provided to participants? How did participants react to each input? What element of the input content do you believe caused that reaction? Did each input meet its objectives? How? Are there inputs that might have been added, or other ways in which the exercise might have been strengthened? What did the post-exercise debriefing reveal?

2. Create and stage a case study or tabletop exercise for your classmates. Ensure that you have identified the desired objectives for each input in advance.

How did the participants react to each input? What element of the input content do you believe caused that reaction? Did the input meet the pre-identified objectives? Did the input fail to meet the desired objectives? Why? Are there other inputs that might have been added, or other ways in which the exercise might have been strengthened? What learnings did the participants achieve through participation in your exercise?

NOTES

1. Raymond H. Swassing, Walter B. Barbe, and Michael N. Milone, *The Swassing-Barbe Modality Index: Zaner-Bloser Modality Kit* (Columbus, OH: Zaner-Bloser, 1979).

2. Benjamin S. Bloom, David R. Krathwohl, and Bertram B. Masia, *Taxonomy of Educational Objectives: The Classification of Educational Goals* (New York: David McKay, 1956).

3. "Bloom's Taxonomy: An Overview," *Teacher Vision*, 2007, <http://www.teachervision.fen.com/teaching-methods/curriculum-planning/2171.html> and Don Clark, "Learning Domains or Bloom's Taxonomy," *Performance, Learning, Leadership, and Knowledge*, http://www.nwlink.com/~donclark/hrd/bloom.html>.

4. Bloom and colleagues provided only a broad view of this taxonomy, which is why no learning levels are presented here.

5. Emergency Management Institute, *IS-120.A: An Introduction to Exercises: Student Manual* (Washington, DC: Federal Emergency Management Agency, 2007).

6. Emergency Management Institute, *IS-130: Exercise Evaluation and Improvement Planning* (Washington, DC: Federal Emergency Management Agency, 2008).

CHAPTER 16

Types of Emergency Exercises

LEARNING OBJECTIVES

On completion of this chapter, you will

▶ Know the major types of exercises used in emergency management.

▶ Understand the purposes of each type of exercise.

▶ Be able to describe the strengths and weaknesses of each type of exercise.

▶ Understand the essential components of each type of exercise.

▶ Be able to provide examples of the application of each type of exercise.

▶ Understand the physical requirements for conducting each type of exercise.

KEY MESSAGES

1. Emergency exercises can be used to accomplish a variety of goals within the context of an emergency management program.

2. Full-scale exercises are not the only valid, or most effective, type of exercise.

3. The type of learning objectives sought often dictate the type of exercise to be used.

4. Exercises do not necessarily need to be complex or expensive.

5. The most effective exercises bring learning to as many people in the organization or the community as possible, and not just to a small group of participants.

6. Exercises are most effective when they are part of an ongoing process of continual improvement of emergency management arrangements.

Introduction

While all aspects of a community's or an organization's emergency management program are important, no other program has as much power to train staff and create change as the emergency exercise. Each type of exercise has its own applications and purposes, and, when selected carefully, can be used to effect desired changes in any element of a community or organization.[1] While scenario selection is important when planning an exercise, so too is the type of exercise chosen. In an emergency management education program, the use of different types of exercises provides not only variety but also an element of cost control. The type of exercise chosen can also lead to very different types of learning outcomes for participants. Given that generating learning outcomes is one of the main purposes of using emergency exercises, selecting the right type of exercise is essential.

In chapter 15, the educational theory behind the use of emergency exercises, the process of exercise creation, and the logistical considerations for staging exercises were explored. This chapter presents the major types of exercises that are available to emergency managers. Each major type of exercise is explored in detail, along with its strengths and weaknesses (all types possess both). The specific purposes of each type of exercise are discussed as well. Finally, the requirements for conducting each type of exercise are described.

By selecting the most appropriate scenario and type of exercise, emergency managers can not only move the emergency management program and emergency plan forward, but can also achieve a variety of objectives[2] that raise general awareness of emergency management issues and justify the acquisition of new response resources and methods at a local community level. The emergency exercise process is also a tool for educating staff, key decision-makers and others, as well as the general public. The ability to select the right exercise for the right purpose is an essential skill.

Purpose

Every type of exercise has its strengths and weaknesses, and each type can be used to generate specific information regarding response procedures, capabilities, and learning outcomes. Within the context of a comprehensive community or organizational emergency management program, each type of exercise plays a specific role.[3] Emergency managers must be familiar with all types of exercises and how they can be used as part of an effective emergency preparedness program.

Major Types of Emergency Exercises

Every type of exercise has a specific purpose or purposes; each is devised to generate specific results that include the identification of issues, experimental problem-solving, and the practice of specific physical procedures within an emergency preparedness program.[4] Similarly, each has its own requirements, strengths, and weaknesses. With a solid understanding of the various exercise options available, emergency managers will be able to use a mix of exercise types that can help drive the emergency preparedness process forward. There are five major types of emergency exercises, as well as computer-simulated options that are not yet widely used. Each of these types is described below.

Case Study Exercises

The **case study exercise** is the simplest form of exercise to stage, and it often yields valuable results for emergency management programs. This type of exercise is extremely helpful in identifying potential issues within a community or an organization that require resolution. It is relatively simple to conduct a case study exercise; it involves the ability to gather and assess information from past practices in the emergency response of some other community or organization. While simulated scenarios can certainly be used in this process, the more common approach is to learn from actual events that have occurred. The point is to learn from the mistakes and successes of others without having to experience the effects first-hand.

Establishing Learning Objectives and Analyzing Facts

As with any type of emergency exercise, the first step is to establish a clear set of learning objectives. Then, it is possible to select a real event that best meets those objectives. What follows next is a process of meticulous research—gathering as much information and as many facts as possible about the event itself. Such information may come from after action reports, discussions with those involved, research studies on the event, or coverage of the event by the mass media. The goal is to obtain as much information as possible about the event in question, and to arrange the information into a rough chronology. The next step is to analyze the facts surrounding the event in a logical manner; root cause analysis (described in chapter 9) may help with this step. Once this process is complete, emergency managers are in a good position to make value judgments about the event and the information surrounding it; they will have a sound understanding of what went well, and, possibly, any gaps, errors, and omissions.

The point of this process is to generate a targeted message for participants; all education involves conveying specific information (or messages), and the emergency exercise process should be no different. Emergency managers need to bear in mind the set of learning objectives they developed at the outset, because a significant part of the case study exercise will be geared to guiding participants to conclusions that meet those objectives. A case study is not merely a reiteration of events; it is a form of guided learning.

Editing Information

Once they have a clearer picture of the event, emergency managers can then begin editing the available information. Which items of information are relevant to the learning objectives and should be included? Which are irrelevant? Which are likely to mislead or confuse participants? Information may be accepted, relegated to the status of background information, or discarded. A word of caution: editing is intended to guide participants to logical conclusions based on real and full information; it is not intended to manipulate participants to particular conclusions based on selective information. Emergency managers should always be aware that some information may be situation-specific; what holds true for the exercise scenario under development may not be true in every single circumstance. When information is potentially contradictory, the emergency manager should focus on the specific scenario and objectives under development, making note of the potential contradiction, developing contingency inputs for use in refocusing participants should that information conflict arise during the exercise, and noting the need to address the potential conflict with the participants during the exercise debriefing process. The material retained at the end of the editing process represents the exercise inputs.

Creating Questions

The next step in developing a case study exercise is the creation of the questions to be considered by participants. The selection of questions to be considered is critical; it is these questions that will potentially yield useful information and issues, and guide participants to the desired learning objectives. The questions selected should not only identify issues but also make both the issues and any conclusions locally relevant within the emergency manager's community or organization. Participants might be asked to consider whether the event in question is possible in a local context, and what some of the more likely results would be. Participants might also be asked to consider such issues as whether the resources required to deal with the event in question are present in the community or organization, whether these resources should be acquired in advance, or where such resources might be drawn from if a local emergency were to occur. As with exercise inputs, the questions should be intended to expose the participants to new information related to the type of scenario being encountered, reinforce old information, and identify issues, but should not manipulate participants to any particular result.

Presenting Information

With the required advance research completed, and the questions developed, it is necessary for emergency managers to consider the manner in which the information will be presented to participants. The research leading to the development of the case study exercise has probably yielded a rich array of potential exercise props. These may include photographs of the event, newspaper clippings, and even video news coverage. All of these items can be displayed quite effectively, using computer technology. Emergency managers must select those items that best illustrate the event and provide visual support for the exercise inputs that have been generated.

An emergency manager is now ready to select the venue and conduct the case study exercise.

Selecting the Venue and Conducting the Exercise

A variety of venue options are suitable for a case study exercise. Often, a small number of participants take part in this type of exercise. As a result, the venue is likely to be a simple meeting room, a classroom, or the Emergency Operations Centre (EOC). The availability of physical spaces and the anticipated number of participants will determine the actual size of space required. Any space that is comfortable, well lit, and appropriate for a presentation and facilitated discussion will suffice. If a multimedia approach will be used, the space must have the resources required to support the presentation of information, such as a computer and projector. Since such exercises are normally of a relatively short duration, a limited number of "creature comforts," such as light refreshments and access to washrooms, are required.

The case study exercise is run in much the same manner as any other exercise, although it is somewhat smaller in scale. An emergency manager will probably take on the role of the exercise controller, although in an exercise of this type, that term may not even be officially used. Participants are assembled in the designated location and briefed on how the exercise will be conducted and are given any ground rules of the exercise. After the background information is presented at the outset, the individual exercise inputs are presented. Participants are then given time to consider each new item of information in the context of the exercise questions. Emergency managers may elect to facilitate discussion after each input or series of inputs, or may elect to simply debrief the group as a whole, using a facilitated discussion at the conclusion of the exercise. The group's findings and conclusions are recorded throughout the exercise for future use. When the discussion has been completed, the exercise is over.

Strengths and Weaknesses

One of the strengths of the case study exercise is its ability to identify issues that are potentially relevant locally. It is possible to learn effectively from the mistakes and successes of others. Another strength is its minimal cost. Given that the development of such an exercise involves little more than an emergency manager's time, it can be repeated (and the learning opportunity reproduced) for as many target audiences as necessary. Emergency managers can provide an educational opportunity for a large group of people in a relatively short period of time, at minimal cost and, in the process of doing so, incorporate a wide range of experiences and perspectives into the refinement of the emergency plan.

The weakness of this type of exercise lies primarily in the potential for bias. There is a very real danger that emergency managers will inadvertently inject their own biases into the exercise during its design. Emergency managers must be conscious of this danger at all times. At every point in the exercise design process, emergency managers must attempt to take an objective view of the information being considered for presentation. If participants recognize a deliberate bias in the exercise, the educational opportunity will be damaged and so too will the credibility of the emergency manager who developed the exercise. The point of this exercise is to allow participants to analyze information and arrive at conclusions, and not to manipulate participants to any particular result. Meticulous research will help deal with this issue, by ensuring that the exercise inputs represent the actual facts of the event and not the thinly disguised objectives of an emergency manager.

Tabletop Exercises

The **tabletop exercise**, like the case study exercise, is typically presented to relatively small groups in a controlled environment. The primary purpose of this type of exercise is to give participants the opportunity to engage in experimental problem-solving and interaction within a safe environment. The tabletop exercise, just as its name suggests, is conducted around a relatively large table containing props that

Figure 16.1

Source: Atomic Energy Council, Taiwan (2006), <http://www.aec.gov.tw/english/emergency/images/exercise_2006-4.jpg>.

serve as the focal point for participants. These props may include a floor plan of a building, an area map, a large-scale aerial photograph of the area, or perhaps a three-dimensional scale model of a real or simulated community.

This exercise originates from the military; readers may have seen old newsreel footage from the Second World War, with generals and others gathered around a large table containing a map or, in some cases, surface features sculpted out of sand, movable simulated military resources, and battle plans. The concept is essentially a simulated advance staging of a battle (or, in our case, an emergency) to anticipate, problem solve, and work through the issues related to response. Over many years, this approach has been applied to emergency management education and the refinement of emergency plans.

Establishing Learning Objectives and Selecting a Scenario

As with any type of exercise, the first steps in developing a tabletop exercise involve creating a clear set of learning objectives and selecting a scenario. The next consideration must be the types of props required. To some extent, emergency managers may be limited by the types of props available or by the budget with which to create them. The nature of the props to be used may place certain constraints on the scenarios that are possible during the exercise. Therefore, props must be considered prior to any further exercise development.

Using Props and Models

As previously stated, props can take a variety of forms. When one is creating a tabletop exercise for an organization (such as a school or a hospital), it might be logical to simply use the floor plans for that facility as the focal point for the exercise. In the case of a community, a large-scale map (often available from the planning department) or a large-scale, high-resolution aerial photograph of the community, or even a given area, might be used for the same purpose with great effect. If such maps are not readily available, emergency managers who possess minimal artistic skills can usually create a map (although perhaps not to precise scale) using any computer with the simplest of software. This map can then be reproduced at minimal cost by virtually any commercial printer possessing a large-format plotter. It is useful to have the map laminated, at little extra cost, by the same printer. Lamination provides durability and allows participants to write or draw on the map surface with dry-erase markers during an exercise. A map is a tool that is useful not only as a prop during an exercise, but also as a reference point in the EOC during a real emergency.

Some communities are fortunate enough to possess three-dimensional (3-D) scale tabletop models of their community for use during training. 3-D models may

▲ **Figure 16.2**

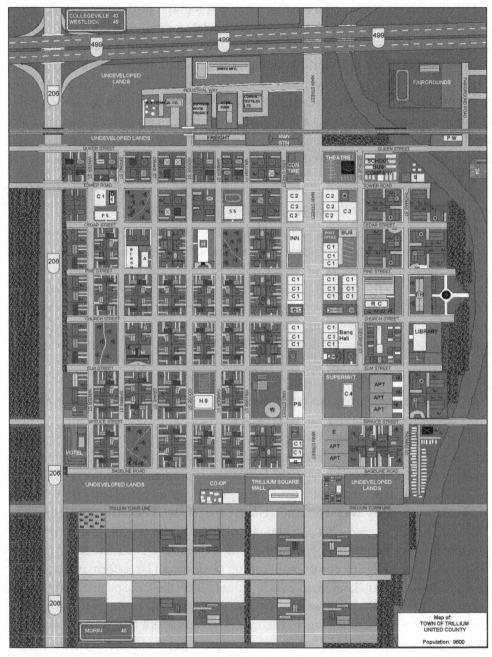

This Canadian model, "Trillium," is printed on large format laminated paper to make it easily portable between training locations.

Source: Courtesy of Norman Ferrier.

represent an actual community or a simulated community that is used for exercise and training purposes. These models can include not only surface features such as rivers, roads, and rail lines, but also detailed scale models of buildings within the community. The most elaborate model kits include response resources such as police cars, fire trucks, ambulances, and public works vehicles. The point of using a 3-D model is to simulate emergencies, to consider problems, and to deploy response resources based on the information provided within an environment that is physically simulated and affords participants the objectivity that can only be obtained by a bird's-eye view.

Three-dimensional tabletop models are available commercially, although at a considerable cost. These commercial models also have the disadvantage of limiting emergency managers to a simulated community instead of their actual community. It is possible to build a 3-D model of one's own community from scratch, if one possesses the expertise and skills to do so. A valuable community resource for such a project may be local model railroaders, who have considerable expertise drawn

▲ **Figure 16.3**

Tabletop exercises may also feature complex 3-D models of communities.

Source: Courtesy of City of Toronto Office of Emergency Management.

from the creation of their own model railroad layouts. Either way, the costs associated with tabletop models are considerable. At a minimum, building a 3-D model will involve hundreds of hours of work time and several thousand dollars worth of material. By contrast, buying a 3-D model can cost $50,000 or more. The more time and money spent, the greater the degree of accuracy.

One disadvantage of 3-D tabletop models is that, once assembled, they are extremely difficult to move. Consequently, a permanent space in which the model will reside must be allocated and participants must come to the model for training. While some models can be dismantled and reassembled, experienced emergency managers know that doing so is rarely worth the effort involved. As a result, unless an emergency manager is considering doing a great deal of ongoing training in a single location, it may be difficult for the community to justify the expenditure. By contrast, laminated maps, floor plans, and aerial photographs may be simply rolled up for storage when they are not required, or easily transported to where they are needed.

Creating Exercise Inputs, Conducting the Exercise, and Debriefing

Once emergency managers know what props are available for use, it will quickly become evident what types of situations and responses will and will not be possible during a tabletop exercise scenario. They can now begin to create exercise inputs aimed at achieving specific learning objectives, placing them within the appropriate physical locations on the map or in the model. Issues such as train derailments, plane crashes, fires, or even chemical plumes may be either physically simulated in the model or drawn in line form on the map. The inputs are arranged in chronological order, the timing considered, and the exercise script created.

An emergency manager usually takes on the role of exercise controller and assembles participants. A pre-exercise briefing may occur around the focal point, or even in an adjoining room. The participants are introduced and oriented to the model or other props, and the basic orientation to the exercise setting and resources is provided. Once this has occurred, participants are then provided with regularly timed, pre-scripted exercise inputs, prompting them to take certain actions or to draw certain conclusions about the event. At the conclusion of the exercise, a post-exercise debriefing generally occurs, either around the table itself, or in another room. An emergency manager may facilitate this debriefing and record all findings, problems, and recommendations identified by the group.

Strengths and Weaknesses

The tabletop exercise has several strengths. It gives participants the opportunity to consider their own approaches to incident management, including such issues as the requirements for and deployment of specific types of resources such as hazardous materials management equipment that may or may not be currently present in the community. The tabletop exercise also gives participants the opportunity to rehearse and review inter-agency interactions in advance of any real emergency. Participants are provided with a safe environment in which to consider and attempt experimental problem-solving; while they may discover that some proposed solutions do not work, they will at least possess this information in advance of any real emergency. In an ideal situation, participants may actually develop new or more effective procedures.

This type of exercise also has several weaknesses. The first of these is the credibility factor. As has been stated previously, a major issue in the effectiveness of an exercise is the ability to persuade participants to suspend disbelief. This process can be substantially disrupted if the exercise is not carried out carefully, and can be particularly problematic when a generic model is used instead of a model of the actual community. There may be a tendency to believe that since the model itself is simulated, the resources are simulated as well, and so all things are possible. The failure of participants to buy into the exercise process often means that the exercise may not be taken seriously by participants and that the desired learning outcomes will not occur.

An additional weakness, particularly in relation to 3-D tabletop models, is the cost involved. It is rare to find any worthwhile 3-D model with a price tag of less than several thousand dollars. While the expenditure may be a one-time event, the costs associated with the initial development of the 3-D model may well substantially exceed those of a full-scale exercise. The use of a 3-D model also sharply limits the types of scenarios that can be used. To illustrate, it might be very difficult to stage a severe flooding scenario in a model that incorporates only a section of the community in which flooding may not normally occur. The lack of portability of such models also places constraints upon their use.

Tactical Exercise Without Troops (TEWOT)

The Tactical Exercise Without Troops (TEWOT) is the first practical exercise that focuses on the physical space of the actual community or organization. The TEWOT has its origins, like many other exercise types, in the military. In the military, generally prior to a simulated battle, the officers involved will physically walk across the simulated battle environment together, predetermining the placement of the physical operating areas required, along with the logistics required to support them. A similar exercise can be used for emergency management purposes in a community or organization.

An emergency manager, generally accompanied by emergency planning committee members, will assume that a simulated scenario is taking place and will travel across the community or organization, identifying potential locations for all of the resources and services that may be required. This step includes the identification of the physical placement of resources, the logistical support for their intended use, and any advance work that might be required to secure the use of the resource in question during a real emergency.

In most cases, the location of the community's or organization's EOC has already been established, but there are many other physical work spaces that might be required. For example, the EOC might need a space for a media centre, telecommunications support facilities, or a rest area. Emergency services might need physical spaces for the staging of response resources until they are required at the scene, refuelling locations, areas that might be used for decontamination, and staff rest areas, among others.

The support of disaster victims may require an emergency reception centre for registration and inquiry, emergency shelters, mass-feeding locations, and spaces for the management of donated goods, among others. Specialty facilities, such as hospitals, will have their own requirements to predetermine, such as spaces for the triaging of victims, spaces for the family members of victims, and temporary treatment areas. A TEWOT is also useful for determining traffic flow to specific facilities, such as access and egress routes, parking, and traffic management plans. It is possible to pre-identify all of these resources. It is also possible, using a TEWOT, to determine back-up locations for use when the emergency denies the use of the primary site.

Once all such sites have been predetermined, it is possible for emergency managers to develop a work plan for their use. First, emergency managers must obtain permission for the use of each proposed site, and identify the location of the resources required for its use and how they will be activated during an emergency. Once these actions are completed, emergency managers can enhance the emergency plan by identifying the operating sites, predetermined and preauthorized, that can be used during any emergency. These operating sites represent community resources in much the same way that ambulances, fire trucks, and transit buses do, and they should be listed in the emergency plan in the appropriate section.

Strengths and Weaknesses

The primary strength of this approach to exercise planning or, indeed, the emergency plan itself, is that it helps predetermine all major areas for specialty operations. Ownership of the space in question can be identified and permission sought and secured for its use. This approach also creates an opportunity to predetermine the types of resources required to support operations in a particular area, and to determine where they will come from. The only real weakness in the TEWOT arises when the operation in question does not receive sufficient assessment. As has been previously stated, the concept of multiple layers of redundancy is fundamental to the practice of emergency management. The same is true for emergency exercise design. Emergency managers should always attempt to identify multiple sites that can be used for the same exercise function, in case circumstances on the day of the exercise deny the use of the original site. To illustrate, if one were to pre-select an outside location for the command post, and weather on the day of the exercise made its use impractical, it is wise to have an alternative operating site in an indoor location. The same approach should be used for all predetermined operating sites.

Functional Exercises

The functional exercise is useful, in that it permits the testing of a defined and discrete set of procedures within the emergency plan, either by the community or a specific group within the community. This exercise is typically a smaller version of the full-scale exercise, directed at testing one or two specific elements of the emergency plan. Some communities or organizations may not even think of a functional exercise as an exercise, choosing to call it a *drill* or giving it some other name. It is an exercise nonetheless.

This type of exercise might be used to test the assembly of the EOC, the assembly and operation of a decontamination facility, the emergency notification procedures of a community or an organization, or any other individual element of the emergency plan. In specialty facilities, such as a school, it may be used to test a single process, such as a lockdown or evacuation procedure. In the case of organizations or groups with specific functions, this type of exercise may be used to test that specific function in isolation, rather than along with the operations of the whole community or organization. Functional exercises are intended to ensure that both staff and others remain familiar with a set of procedures that they may not use on a regular basis.

The requirements of a functional exercise are relatively straightforward. They include the physical space and the actual equipment required for the function to be tested. These requirements will vary according to the nature and scale of the function and the degree to which the function is to be tested. A functional exercise may involve a few participants or a larger group. To illustrate, an exercise in which local firefighters assemble and operate a portable decontamination facility for an hour is considered small scale, while the fire and evacuation drill regularly conducted in a public school is considered larger scale. Although each of these exercises has different space, staffing, and resource requirements, they are both functional exercises.

A functional exercise may or may not incorporate the use of scenarios. Given that the point of the exercise is to test and review specific processes and procedures, a scenario may not be required. As with all other exercises, emergency managers must have specific learning objectives, performance standards, and a method for measuring performance for functional exercises. Given the lack of necessity to develop a full exercise script for a functional exercise, this type of exercise is often an attractive part of a community's emergency management education program.

Strengths and Weaknesses

A functional exercise has several strengths. It provides potentially comprehensive testing of specific procedures and ensures that staff remain fully conversant with those procedures and processes, even when they are performed infrequently. This type of exercise tends to be relatively simple, and does not require a great deal of time or resources for its development. The low cost typically associated with this exercise means that it can be reproduced to reach a broad range of people. Its low cost also means that it can be conducted regularly to maintain skill levels in the required personnel.

The weaknesses associated with this type of exercise mirror its strengths to some degree. While a functional exercise provides regular testing of and orientation to specific procedures and processes, typically it does not go beyond those procedures

▲ **Figure 16.4**

Functional exercises may be used to test a specific function or operation in isolation; in this case, decontamination.

Source: Werkfeuerwehrverbrand Hessen (Hesse Fire Brigade), Germany (2002), <http://www.wfv-hessen.de/bilder/2812.jpg>.

and processes. It tends to be used to test one defined element of an emergency plan, but not the emergency plan itself. As a result, while functional exercises are extremely useful, they do not guarantee community or organizational preparedness, and so cannot stand on their own. They must be part of a broader emergency management education process, and must be supplemented periodically by full-scale exercises intended to provide comprehensive testing of the entire emergency plan.

Full-Scale Exercises

The full-scale exercise is perhaps the most widely practised and best-known form of emergency exercise. It is the full-scale "dress rehearsal" for a real emergency event. Like so many other types of exercises, it has its origins in the full-scale simulated "war games" used by the military for training purposes. All of the community's or organization's emergency response arrangements and equipment are brought out and tested in an environment that is as realistic as possible. The entire emergency plan is tested, along with the operation and interaction of all of the community's response resources to identify gaps, errors, and omissions within both the emergency plan and the response arrangements and procedures of specific groups.

Exercise Development

The development process for a full-scale exercise incorporates virtually all of the elements of the various exercise types described thus far, and, as a result, will generally occupy a great deal of an emergency manager's time. Emergency managers will need to develop learning objectives for the exercise; for this type of exercise, it is likely that the list of learning objectives will be fairly long and comprehensive. The learning objectives will likely include not only the overall objectives of the community or organization but also the objectives that are specific to groups, departments, or other stakeholders. Emergency managers need to consider, explore, and develop exercise inputs to ensure that the learning objectives are met.

The exercise inputs for a full-scale exercise may also vary considerably. In a case study or tabletop exercise, inputs could be simple pieces of paper. In a full-scale exercise, inputs may take the form of radio or telephone calls, simulated newscasts, preprogrammed individual "victims" acting as inputs, or related events (such as a fire or explosion) that occur during the exercise itself. This type of exercise may often include the need to develop a physical exercise environment through the use of large props (such as simulated aircraft wreckage), turning the environment itself into an input of sorts for participants. Such an exercise may also involve the incorporation of a large number of simulated casualties who require processing and services, and these individuals too may be thought of as inputs. Each exercise input, whether information, physical space, or human, is present in the exercise scenario to either elicit or test a specific type of response.

Coordination

In a large and complex full-scale exercise, coordination plays a major role. It is entirely possible that during a full-scale emergency exercise any number of events may be occurring simultaneously at different locations within the community, just as they would in a real emergency. The timing and coordination of such events is a critical part of the exercise design process. Emergency managers will need to ensure that events flow in a logical sequence, with the correct timing and in an integrated manner. Achieving these goals requires complex advance planning and scripting, and often the efforts of a large team of exercise controllers. The exercise script will also need to include filler inputs, used to facilitate exercise flow, and also "Murphy" inputs to slow exercise play, in much the same manner as other types of exercises. These inputs will need to be developed in advance. Once the inputs have been created and placed in chronological order, exercise timing will need to be planned. The resulting exercise script, for use by the chief controller, is likely to be many pages in length.

Logistics

Emergency managers also need to consider the logistical requirements for an exercise of this scale. Logistics will be determined to some extent by the scale and scope of the exercise, but given that the intent is to test overall community or organization response, the size of the group is likely to be substantial. Sites will need to be secured for each major element of exercise play, such as an EOC or a simulated crash or derailment site. Sites will be required for community response functions, such as emergency shelters, if these are a part of the exercise. They will also be required to provide support and creature-comforts, such as dressing rooms, makeup areas, dining areas, rest areas, and washrooms, to participants, controllers, observers, and simulated victims. If the exercise is large enough, it may also require a media facility. A designated area in which the post-exercise debriefing(s) will occur is also necessary.

Emergency managers and others developing a full-scale exercise need to consider not only the allocation of space for each of the exercise's functions, but also the resources required to support those functions. Support equipment for each space, perhaps a feeding plan for all involved, transportation of simulated victims, and related logistical considerations will also need to be addressed. Without the resolution of all logistical issues related to the exercise, it will not run effectively and learning outcomes may be lost.

As previously stated, the conduct of such an exercise may require a large team of exercise controllers. It is likely that each of these individuals will be operating in a different physical location (at the EOC, at the incident site, perhaps at an emergency shelter, in a resource-staging area), but the activities of all will require coordination by the chief controller. As a result, it is highly desirable that such a group possess its own communications system for the purposes of coordinating input delivery, identifying problems and solutions, and achieving consistency. The system can be either a telephone or two-way radio system, but it must be out of earshot of participants.

Emergency managers must remain mindful of real emergencies; both those occurring as a part of the community's normal life, and those occurring at the exercise site. Every conceivable measure must be put into place to ensure that the conduct of the exercise in no way interferes with the response to real emergencies occurring while the exercise is running. These measures include, where possible, the assignment of separate radio frequencies for exercise play, and a procedure for ensuring that exercise transmissions are never confused with real emergency radio traffic. Similarly, the exercise plan must contain procedures to address any real emergency that arises at the exercise site, in the event that any participant becomes ill or injured during exercise play.

Emergency managers will need to arrange for and secure the use of physical spaces, response resources, and even people or groups, well in advance of the exercise. This will often involve detailed discussion and negotiation with other stakeholders within the community. The use of physical spaces has an obvious requirement: they are all owned by someone, and their use may disrupt normal business processes. The same is true for emergency response resources. The use of staff for the purposes of the exercise requires advance approval from their managers. Finally, groups of volunteers, whether from service organizations or local schools, will need to be negotiated in advance.

There is very little associated with a full-scale exercise that does not carry a cost. This cost will need to be considered in detail. Some groups may require simple feeding, while others will be faced with the costs associated with the replacement or reconditioning of the equipment used following the exercise. There are also likely to be costs associated with cleaning and restoring those sites used as a part of exercise play. A clear understanding of who will pay for what should be a part of the advance negotiation process. Once all of the costs associated with a full-scale exercise have been identified and clarified, an emergency manager will likely need to develop a full budget for the exercise and submit that budget for the required approvals, prior to the staging of the exercise.

Once the exercise has been staged, participants will need to be debriefed. While the process of debriefing a large number of participants (there can be hundreds) can be daunting, the data obtained is absolutely critical to the emergency plan. A "hot-wash" debriefing may need to take place in groups, each with its own facilitator. The use of debriefing questionnaires, while not ideal, may be a necessity to capture as much of the data as possible. The process of collecting, interpreting, and applying the data obtained can, in some cases, take nearly as long as the exercise creation process.

Strengths and Weaknesses

The strength of the full-scale exercise is its ability to thoroughly and comprehensively test all or most aspects of a community's or an organization's ability to respond to an emergency. It should identify any gaps, errors, or omissions that, when resolved, will result in a stronger and more effective emergency plan. It should also provide much-needed experiential learning opportunities for a range of individuals, including the opportunity to practise coordination activities between agencies that have little day-to-day contact.[5] Many people within the community or organization will learn a great deal about one another's roles as a direct result of well-crafted and well-conducted exercise play.

This type of exercise has several weaknesses. In the first place, such exercises tend to be extremely complex and difficult to both write and arrange. A full-scale exercise can take anywhere from several months to a year to organize. It will occupy an emergency manager often on a nearly full-time basis and will require a sizable team of people that needs to be organized, each of whom will also experience significant demands on their time and normal workload.

▲ **Figure 16.5**

Full-scale exercises can require complex staging and resources to contribute to overall realism. For this reason, they can be a potentially expensive venture.

Source: British Broadcasting Corporation, United Kingdom (n.d.), <http://newsimg.bbc.co.uk/media/images/42941000/jpg/_42941443_emergency.203.jpg>.

A full-scale exercise is also typically a fairly expensive step for emergency managers, often costing in the tens to hundreds of thousands of dollars to stage. This type of exercise also has an impact on the daily business of organizations. Full-scale exercises represent a significant investment of time, effort, and money for a community or organization. As a result, they can generally only be staged once, and learning outcomes will be limited to some degree to those staff who were fortunate enough to actually be able to participate. For these reasons, and others, full-scale exercises usually occur infrequently, and should only be run once a combination of other exercise types have moved the emergency preparedness program to a stage where the comprehensive confirmation of emergency arrangements is required.

The Future: Computer-Simulated Emergency Exercises

As with all aspects of emergency management, the technology available to support emergency exercises is changing and evolving and, in some cases, the emergency exercise process may evolve with them. There are already fairly sophisticated computer simulations of various types of disasters that are commercially available. At this writing, many of these simulations are actually marketed as computer games, but there are many that will go considerably beyond simple gaming. Many versions of electronic "one-stop shopping" emergency management software products also contain the capability of staging emergency exercises.

The strengths of such products lie primarily in their cost; once the software has been purchased, it can be used over and over to reach a broad audience. They can be used by any employee in any location with a computer. They also tend to support time-shift training, so that employees are not taken away from their regular work for training purposes, but can manage to complete training over a period of time by participating in small segments, whenever there is a "lull" in their normal workload or during off-peak hours. Many software products break the total exercise experience into manageable segments, and both track the staff member's progress through the exercise experience and provide written progress reports for individual staff members to emergency managers. Such programs are also extremely good for staff review of procedures.

While such products are extremely good at reviewing procedures, they do not provide much support for the acquisition of physical skills by staff members. They also fail to provide training in how to perform the same functions when the computer network is unavailable for any reason. Mechanical items such as the rapid assembly of an EOC still require staff training in the physical realm. In addition, most of these programs operate in a simulated environment, which may or may not closely resemble the actual community where the program is being conducted. It is possible to make some of these products location-specific, but this step usually requires fairly costly reprogramming, or computer skills that are beyond those of the average emergency manager. They typically also contain a fairly limited number of scenarios, and the expansion of these to address all of the potential problems within a community or organization presents the same types of programming challenges described in making the software location-specific.

Such products are rapidly becoming more sophisticated; many products that permitted only a single user in the past can now support multiple users and player interaction as the exercise evolves. As computers and their software become more powerful and more elaborate, they will become increasingly useful in emergency management training. The future for the use of such products by emergency managers is bright, particularly if progress in the development of these products continues at the current pace.

▲ Figure 16.6

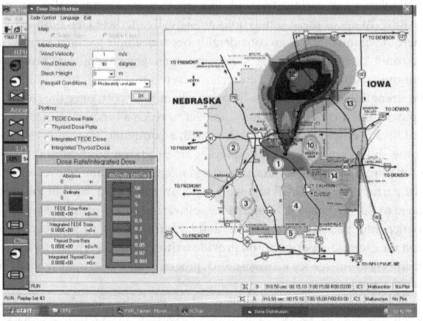

Electronic exercises may use complex computer modelling to provide information in a format that is as realistic as possible.

Source: Micro-simulation Technology, USA (n.d.), <http://www.microsimtech.com/images/puff_oppd.gif>.

Conclusion

Whether through policy or legislative mandate, most communities and many organizations conduct regular emergency exercises. The emergency exercise process is not just a tool for raising awareness or meeting legislated mandates. Emergency exercises provide emergency managers, and the community or organization, with a potentially important and valuable tool for education, acquisition of resources, and the refinement of the emergency plan—but only if used correctly. For an emergency exercise to be effective, emergency managers must combine the right set of learning objectives, the right scenario, and the right type of exercise with effective performance measurement and data collection.

Emergency managers must understand the educational theory behind emergency exercises and possess a detailed knowledge of exactly how the exercises work to be able to use them to their full potential. The correct use of emergency exercises provides the fuel with which to transform a community's or organization's emergency plan from a simple periodic project into an "evergreen" document. It also helps foster an organizational culture of constant preparedness for any type of untoward event. Ultimately, emergency managers must consider the emergency exercise in much the same manner as they do the emergency plan itself—as a process, not a project.

KEY TERMS

case study exercise

tabletop exercise

LEARNING CHECK

Take a few minutes now to test your knowledge of the types of emergency exercises. Select the best answer in each case. Any score of less than 16 out of 20 (80 percent) indicates that you should re-read this chapter.

1. Within the context of an emergency management program, emergency exercises can be used to accomplish
   a. a variety of goals
   b. staff training on the emergency plan
   c. achievement of regulatory requirements
   d. political influence

2. When selecting an exercise type, it is important for the emergency manager to remember that full-scale exercises are
   a. usually the only type recognized by others
   b. not necessarily the most effective type
   c. difficult to obtain approval for
   d. a means of training large numbers of staff

3. The type of exercise chosen for use by emergency managers will frequently be dictated by
   a. political mandate
   b. legislative requirements
   c. exercise objectives
   d. budget

4. When seeking approval to conduct an exercise, it is important to inform key decision-makers that emergency exercises
   a. are the only way to train staff
   b. need not be complex or expensive
   c. will solve all emergency planning problems
   d. are a legislative requirement

5. The most effective types of exercises are capable of bringing learning to
   a. as much of the organization or community as possible
   b. only key decision-makers
   c. only emergency service personnel
   d. the general public

6. Emergency exercises operate most effectively when
   a. they have been approved by all stakeholders
   b. they receive comprehensive funding support
   c. they are part of a comprehensive program
   d. they force change by resistant stakeholders

7. The primary purpose of the case study exercise is to identify
   a. resource deficiencies
   b. natural leaders
   c. budgetary requirements
   d. issues requiring resolution

8. One of the most important considerations when designing a case study exercise is to ensure that participants will be
   a. familiar with the actual event
   b. guided, not manipulated
   c. aware of all issues related to the event
   d. familiar with the environment in which the event takes place

9. One of the greatest strengths of the case study exercise is that it can be staged
   a. inexpensively
   b. for a broad audience
   c. repeatedly
   d. all of the above

10. When conducting a tabletop exercise, the focal point used for the group may be
    a. floor plans
    b. maps or aerial photographs
    c. a 3-D model
    d. all of the above

11. One of the primary strengths of the tabletop exercise is the ability of the participants to engage in
    a. competition
    b. experimental problem-solving
    c. inter-agency dialogue
    d. identification of issues

12. Often, a TEWOT is used by emergency managers to
    a. identify potential work locations
    b. identify resource requirements
    c. identify potential emergency types
    d. both (a) and (b)

13. The real value of the TEWOT is that it will assist emergency managers in
    a. enhancing the emergency plan
    b. determining budget requirements
    c. experimental problem-solving
    d. identifying disaster-related issues

14. The assembly and use of an EOC or an emergency reception centre in isolation are examples of a
    a. case study exercise
    b. full-scale exercise
    c. functional exercise
    d. tabletop exercise

15. The functional exercise is intended for the discrete testing of
    a. total emergency response
    b. functions or procedures
    c. patient triage
    d. telecommunications systems

16. The functional exercise is limited, in that it will not
    a. refine the emergency plan
    b. test overall emergency response
    c. amend existing procedures
    d. identify gaps, errors, or omissions

17. The generally intended use for the full-scale exercise is
    a. comprehensive testing of the emergency plan
    b. experimental problem-solving
    c. public education
    d. staff training in plan details

18. The challenge of the full-scale exercise is that it is often
    a. extremely expensive
    b. logistically complex
    c. extremely time-consuming
    d. all of the above

19. The nature of the full-scale exercise is such that in many jurisdictions it is typically used
    a. only for confirmation
    b. at six-month intervals
    c. for small numbers of staff
    d. to train the general public

20. An emergency exercise can only be fully effective when emergency managers use good performance measurement practices and
    a. the right learning objectives
    b. the right scenario
    c. the right type of exercise
    d. all of the above

CASE STUDIES

A. You are the emergency manager for a medium-sized community. You have identified a need to improve emergency plan knowledge and emergency response procedures for approximately 150 junior and mid-level management staff from the various departments that make up your community's municipal structure.

   1. Select a type of emergency exercise for use in this scenario.
   2. Explain your rationale for the type of exercise selected.
   3. List the types of resources that will be needed to stage this exercise.
   4. Describe the strengths and weaknesses of the type of exercise selected.

B. You are the emergency manager for a medium-sized community. Over the past several years you have been active in providing emergency management education to various groups within your community. These efforts have included an entire series of relatively small and simple exercises that have led to considerable improvements in both your emergency plan and the community's emergency response resources. You believe that the community is currently in reasonably good shape with respect to emergency preparedness, and that a more comprehensive test is in order.

   1. Select a type of emergency exercise for use in this scenario.
   2. Explain your rationale for the type of exercise selected.
   3. List the types of resources that will be needed to stage this exercise.
   4. Describe the strengths and weaknesses of the type of exercise selected.

TO LEARN MORE

1. Examine the advance plan for an exercise that has already been conducted, and, if possible, discuss it with the author. What were the objectives of the exercise? What types of physical spaces were required for exercise play? How did the author go about securing their use? What types of logistical support were required to stage the exercise? Where did these come from? What types

of permissions did the author of the exercise have to obtain, and how were these obtained? Did the author devise a method of measuring achievement of the objectives? How did this work? Was the measurement methodology effective? Why?

2. Examine the final report following an exercise that has already occurred. What types of useful information was the author able to obtain by staging? How did this occur? How did the author go about transforming raw exercise data into useful information? Were there methods that were not used that might have led to better information? What were these? Why would they have worked better? Were any problems identified with respect to the actual staging of the exercise? Was a method for eliminating these problems from future exercises identified? Do you have any ideas that might have eliminated problems that were identified, or might otherwise be used to strengthen future exercises?

NOTES

1. Homeland Security Emergency Exercise Program, *Training and Exercise Plan Workshop: User's Handbook* (Washington, DC: Federal Emergency Management Agency, 2007).
2. Canadian Nuclear Safety Commission, *G-353: Guidelines for Testing Emergency Measures* (Ottawa: Government of Canada, 2007).
3. Sarah Renner, "Emergency Exercise and Training Techniques," *The Australian Journal of Emergency Management,* Winter 2001: 26–32.
4. Kevin O'Kane, *Writing Operational Exercises for Emergency Management* (Wellington, New Zealand: Ministry of Civil Defence and Emergency Management, 2002).
5. Emergency Management Institute, *IS-139: Exercise Design—Student Manual* (Washington, DC: Federal Emergency Management Agency, 2007).

CHAPTER 17

Public Education

LEARNING OBJECTIVES

On completion of this chapter, you will

▶ Understand why public education is an essential component of a comprehensive emergency management program.

▶ Understand the issues that are most likely to motivate the general public toward emergency preparedness.

▶ Be able to describe the strategies used to teach the general public about emergency preparedness.

▶ Understand how various types of public education strategies can be designed.

▶ Understand how to identify potential allies in the community during the process of public education.

▶ Be able to design a preliminary emergency preparedness public education program for a community.

KEY MESSAGES

1. In emergency preparedness, any community or organization is only as strong as its weakest members.

2. Preparedness for emergencies translates directly into increased resiliency to the effects of emergencies.

3. Members of the general public tend to be motivated by self-interest; they care foremost about themselves, their homes, and their families.

4. For the average person, physiological needs such as food, clothing, and shelter take precedence over matters of personal safety.

5. In emergency management, effective public education is not just about disseminating information; it is about providing people with the motivation to change.

6. Community partnerships, such as those with service organizations, are a highly effective method of enhancing both preparedness and resiliency.

Introduction

One of the greatest challenges faced by emergency managers is "getting the word out" to the general public with respect to emergency preparedness. Even when elected officials and other stakeholders are convinced of the need for preparedness, the general public might not be. There is a strong and direct relationship between the preparedness and resiliency of individual members of a community or an organization and the overall resiliency of a community or an organization as a whole.

Many communities invest in attractive emergency preparedness brochures or websites in their public education efforts, but such items really only scratch the surface of the problem of public education. The best-designed brochure or website is only useful if the information contained within it is acted on. The most interesting public presentation on emergency preparedness is effective only if the information in it leads to increased interest and the desired actions by those listening to it. For public education in the field of emergency management to be effective, it must motivate changes in behaviour in members of the community.

This chapter examines the strategies used to teach the general public about emergency preparedness. It briefly revisits motivation and educational theory as they apply to public education programs. The various options for information delivery are examined, along with their strengths and weaknesses. Non-traditional approaches to public education are also explored, including public–private partnerships, the creation of new support resources such as interested and motivated volunteer groups, and the creation of emergency preparedness "focal points" within a community. The benefits of an effective public education program for emergency management are also discussed.

Purpose

Effective emergency preparedness education cannot simply involve distributing relevant information; it must also involve motivating people to adopt behaviours that will enhance both preparedness and resiliency. Individuals can be difficult to motivate to this end. They will rarely take some action merely for the greater good; they must be shown why the required action is important to them and to their families. Understanding how to motivate people is as essential as understanding how to design a brochure or teach a course. As a result, being able to provide public education programs that are capable of motivating change is essential for emergency managers.

"Getting the Message Out"

The personal preparedness message is a key feature of any comprehensive emergency management education program. Getting this message out to the general public is not without its challenges. The entire point of the effort is to motivate individuals to take actions that will lead to better individual preparedness and resiliency. However, the simple distribution of preparedness information is seldom effective for the reasons that will be discussed in this chapter.

Emergency managers should produce a clear personal preparedness message (or series of messages) for the general public. This message, combined with an understanding of what motivates human behaviour and a sound multi-modal communications strategy, will help emergency managers communicate with members of the community in a meaningful way that will motivate them to enhanced preparedness.

Principles of Adult Education

The principles of adult education are central to the process of public education. (See chapter 15 for more on how adults learn.) For most people, simply being provided with information that asks them to take certain actions is rarely sufficient to motivate them to do so. People are bombarded with information every day, and, in an effort to avoid being overwhelmed by it, they have become adept at discarding information that is not immediately relevant or is uninteresting. New information that is read may provoke a moment or two of thought, but generally it does not lead most adults to process that new information in a meaningful way. As a result, such information is often discarded, and readers move on to other stimuli and priorities that are competing for their attention.

The way in which we treat information is hardly surprising when we consider Abraham Maslow's hierarchy of needs[1] (see chapter 10). According to this theory, people tend to deal with their needs, including the need to process and act on information, within a clear hierarchy of priority. For example, few people give much thought to information on safety, including emergency preparedness information, unless a situation arises that is immediate and pressing, and only after they have satisfactorily addressed the physiological needs of day-to-day life. Even when people do decide that safety information is worthy of further consideration, they are unlikely to act on it immediately, unless it contains information that they believe is relevant to the safety of either their families or themselves. Self-interest is perhaps the most powerful motivator of all when it comes to taking an interest in emergency preparedness information.

If we consider the perspective of Bloom's taxonomy[2] (see chapter 15), it becomes clear that the format in which information is provided plays a role in its acceptance. The processing of written material, such as a brochure or a website, is a cognitive-domain skill, and we have already established that adult learners typically learn best in the affective psychomotor domains. The affective domain is learning with an emotional content. Thus, the issue of the safety of home and family carries increased weight. Unless people are able to accept, respond to, and value the information they receive, and place it into a relevant context, they are extremely unlikely to produce the desired behavioural response.

All modes of learning and domains are part of the public education process to some degree. For example, each individual has his or her own preferred mode of learning, which suggests a need to consider a variety of delivery approaches, and to attempt to address as broad a range of potential learning modes as possible. There is a place for written content within the mix of public education materials, but that content should be affective. Information that is written or spoken will be absorbed by those who receive it to some degree. However, for information to be internalized, some form of interaction is required. As a result, it is preferable to accompany information with a demonstration followed by some form of physical participation on the part of subjects. Adult learners learn best by feeling and doing.

Print Materials and the Accessibility of Information

The use of print materials has always played a role in emergency preparedness education, and for good reason. These materials represent a relatively inexpensive method of reaching a mass audience with important information. The air raid precautions information cards inserted in cigarette packages[3] that were described in chapter 1 are an excellent example of an early print campaign on critical safety information geared to the general public. If you rummage around in the back room of any emergency management office that has been around for a long time, you might even find a copy of printed instructions for the creation of a backyard fallout shelter intended for mass distribution. Good design and eye-catching colours and photographs can enhance printed materials. An attractive brochure may catch the eye of a passerby and entice him or her to pick it up. However, the likelihood is slim that that individual will read the brochure, and then act upon the information contained in it simply because the information is in hand.

Information must be accessible, and it must be relevant. Each of these requirements presents particular challenges. One of the key issues in the accessibility of information is language. Newspapers understand this; virtually all are written for readers with a particular education level to make the information accessible. For information to be accessible, it must be crafted in a language that is easily understood by readers and not full of highly technical language or unfamiliar jargon.

The same is true for the language used to communicate emergency preparedness information. The world is an increasingly cosmopolitan place, and, particularly in larger cities, people may originate from different countries and speak different languages. Even when people have developed some comfort level with the spoken version of the majority language in a community, there is little guarantee that they can read or write that language with any degree of fluency. For this reason, emergency managers may have to consider the translation of written materials into other languages spoken in the community in order to make their information accessible to the greatest number of people.

In all cases, for all of the reasons described, print materials are unlikely to achieve the desired behavioural outcomes on their own. Ultimately, a more comprehensive approach to public education is required by emergency managers to motivate people to change. This approach is likely to include a broad range of educational efforts, including public speaking, public displays and demonstrations, and public events such as an Emergency Awareness Day. Print materials have their place, but often they are most useful as a method of introducing the general public to other types of emergency management education.

When emergency managers possess good writing skills, they might consider pursuing other forms of print-based information-sharing with the general public. Most communities have a local newspaper; in large communities these are published daily, while in smaller communities they may be published weekly. If emergency managers are up to the challenge, they might seek to create a weekly or monthly newspaper column on the subject of emergency preparedness, addressing a different aspect of preparedness in each writing. They might write about the emergency management process, the history of emergency management, real disaster events, or information related to the traditional emergency services. Through a newspaper column, emergency managers can also introduce readers to different aspects of personal preparedness. The column can even become interactive, by simply including the answers to one or two reader questions at the end of the column.

Many local newspapers are open to this type of column. They are in the business of providing information of interest to as many readers as possible to sell advertising space, and their agreement to such a column would also speak to their commitment to the community. It should be noted, though, that an emergency manager's writing must be of high quality—at least as high as the quality of the writing that appears in the newspaper—or such a column can damage his or her credibility (or it simply won't be published). Another factor to consider is reliability. This is important to newspaper editors; once readers become accustomed to seeing a particular column, it must appear regularly and reliably. As a result, it is often best to have the columns for the first two to three months in hand when approaching an editor with the idea. The good news is that this reliability tends to create readership, and a well-written column on personal preparedness, appearing regularly, will begin to develop a following in the community, and may even lead to both increased public support for emergency management and the creation of focal points of preparedness within the community.

Websites

A relatively new development is the use of web-based communications in emergency preparedness public education. Some websites are small and simple, while others are elaborate and highly effective communications tools for emergency managers. There are clear advantages to using websites in an emergency preparedness public education program: usually their costs are comparable to the costs of producing and distributing one high-profile brochure in the community; they can be updated easily; and, if well done, they can provide a level of interaction that greatly enhances the learning process for visitors. More effort and a greater initial investment are required to achieve a fully interactive website, but over the long term the results are considerably better than for print materials.

Consider the learning modes used by visitors at a website. A well-crafted website provides the bright colours, photographs, and content of a brochure, as well as current weather reports, games, quizzes, and downloadable material to help build visitor interest. The ease with which content can be changed also means that the website can be a dynamic device, constantly growing and evolving, providing new and valuable information to visitors. A website that is kept current and has a range of useful content keeps visitors interested so that they are much more likely to make repeat visits.

A community's emergency management website should encourage visitors to accept, respond to, and place a value on the content of the website. By including information, such as current weather reports or information on local emergencies, an emergency manager makes content on the website relevant to visitors, both in their daily lives and during an emergency. It follows that once visitors judge certain information at the website to be relevant and of value, they are much more likely to view other website content, such as the personal preparedness message (or messages) as equally valuable.

Website content must be personally relevant to visitors (such as weather and traffic reports), but it should also include content that supports the personal preparedness message. This message is, after all, the primary reason for the website's existence. Remember that content which reflects the self-interests of visitors will almost always be given greater importance. Consider making such items as home safety checklists[4] or even a personal family emergency plan[5] available for downloading by visitors. Once again, consider exploiting the potential for interaction to accomplish learning outcomes. Emergency managers could make a neat, tidy, and complete generic family emergency plan available. However, providing visitors with a template that requires them to consider questions and fill in answers to create their own emergency plan makes it personal, applicable to their home and family, and therefore completely relevant and valuable. The interaction required to complete the emergency plan has moved the learning process from simple cognitive-domain learning to the affective domain. Visitors are much more likely to absorb, value, and retain the content, and that content is much more likely to motivate further personal preparedness activities.

There is another advantage to using a well-crafted website. With the right software, a website can actually track usage, providing emergency managers with valuable information regarding the effectiveness of messaging. Elements that can be tracked include the number of website "hits" and the locations both within the community and beyond it from which they originate; the number of times that key materials, such as the emergency plan document, have been downloaded; and the usage of the features incorporated in the website. A good website can even allow dynamic interaction between an emergency manager and the members of the community, either through email exchanges or through the use of facilitated discussion boards.

A wealth of information on and examples of emergency preparedness websites are readily available on the Internet. Emergency managers should take the time to browse these sites. At the time of writing, a simple keyword search for "emergency preparedness" in a commonly used search engine yielded nearly 5.5 *million* websites. Some websites will provide good ideas for content that emergency managers might consider incorporating into their community's emergency management website. Ultimately, the review process will provide emergency managers with a clear idea of what works and what doesn't for their purposes. It then becomes a matter of taking those ideas that are useful, and incorporating them into the local website. The advice of a good webmaster can be invaluable in the creation of the website, and the review process will enable emergency managers to know what to ask for.

Public Displays, Public-Speaking Engagements, and Public Events

Public displays and presentations are also useful tools in the public education arsenal of emergency managers. These may involve displays or booths set up in schools (for example, on parent night) or shopping malls. Such displays can be bright, colourful, and dynamic, and can do much to spark the interest of individual members of the community, particularly if displays can be made interactive through the use of question-and-answer sessions or the opportunity to practise a particular skill. It is useful to make such displays locally relevant; while the stark photographs of 9/11 may be eye catching, it is generally more effective to display photographs of local disaster events. This takes the display to another level, silently reminding the general public that disasters can and will happen in their own community.

To illustrate, it is one thing to advise the general public to develop 72-hour personal evacuation kits (even to provide them with a list of kit contents) and quite another to actually allow them to physically examine a completed kit and have their questions about the kit answered by an expert. Such a display can also be used to address other aspects of emergency preparedness, such as home safety audits or personal family emergency plans. A display is typically far more effective than simply passing out brochures, because it embraces the principles of adult education previously discussed.

For public displays to be effective, they must be planned strategically. The target audience must be understood in advance, and the messaging tailored to meet specific objectives. There should be a clear reason for staging the display—an opportunity to hand out brochures is insufficient. Ideally, the display should lead interested viewers to other, more detailed sources of information created by an emergency manager. For example, an emergency manager could set up a display at a mall during a local festival or holiday to publicize the existence of a comprehensive website or individual training programs. The display not only provides members of the general public with initial information but also directs them to other more elaborate, ongoing public education efforts.

Public-speaking engagements can also represent an important educational tool to emergency managers, particularly when they are conducted as a part of an overall emergency preparedness strategy. Local service organizations such as the Lions or Kiwanis clubs, local legions, voluntary organizations (such as the Red Cross), faith-based groups (such as the Salvation Army), and local women's groups, among others, are almost always in the market for good-quality speakers. Speaking to these groups provides emergency managers with an opportunity to convey important public information interactively, but, with the right strategy, can accomplish far more.

Typically, these groups are composed of individuals who see beyond their self-interests and have a personal philosophy of community service. Often, such groups seek methods by which to make additional contributions to the quality of life of the community, and an emergency manager may be able to provide such opportunities. By speaking to such groups on a regular basis, an emergency manager not only increases public awareness of the issues surrounding emergency preparedness, but also begins to develop a relationship with them. In time, and with discussion, these groups may be persuaded to accept specific roles within the community's emergency plan or even to fundraise for emergency response equipment that might not be available to the community through other channels. This process can help an emergency manager develop a political constituency of sorts; the people in these groups are courted by local politicians at election time, and if emergency preparedness is important to them, it is likely to be seen as more important to elected officials.

When it comes to emergency preparedness, emergency managers should not overlook the educational opportunities presented by local schools. Schools often welcome visits from the community's emergency manager to speak to students, most typically as a part of the social studies or civics curriculum. The approach used with schoolchildren is somewhat different from that used for older students; most will be fascinated by disasters and emergencies of various types and will be easy to motivate, but care must be taken not to overwhelm or frighten them.

By making presentations to school groups, emergency managers may be able to foster an interest in personal preparedness that will last a lifetime, and may even influence career selection for some students. When speaking to students, one is actually addressing two groups: the children themselves and their parents. Anyone with school-age children is aware that when a school project is brought home, it often requires parental involvement, and may even evolve into a family project. The use of interactive projects surrounding home safety audits or personal family emergency plans lends itself well to the type of interactive learning that emergency managers should be seeking to provide. Moreover, the display of such projects in the school will ensure that the personal preparedness message continues to be present and generate interest long after the emergency manager has departed.

The use of public events can also provide substantial opportunities for an emergency preparedness public education program. Many communities stage an annual Emergency Preparedness Day, targeted at raising public awareness of preparedness issues. Some countries (such as Japan) stage such events on a national basis. In Canada, the first week in May is Emergency Preparedness Week, with emergency managers at the federal, regional, and local levels of government all staging media events, public demonstrations, mall displays, speaking engagements, and even community exercises in a coordinated effort to raise public awareness and encourage personal preparedness activities. Such events play a valuable role in making the public aware of both the role of emergency manager and the genuine necessity for personal preparedness.

These activities need not be limited to such events, however. Emergency management is about people, and any place people gather can provide a venue for emergency preparedness education efforts. Even when a given community does not have an Emergency Preparedness Day, there are still county fairs, local festivals, and other types of celebrations where it is appropriate for emergency managers to participate for the purpose of public education. Where a community does not currently stage an Emergency Preparedness Day event, this may be a simple oversight at the local level. Once elected officials begin to understand that this event is important to the well-being of the community (or that the community considers it to be important), it may be possible for an emergency manager to persuade the mayor or local council to issue a proclamation naming a specific day or week for the purpose of emergency preparedness education, thus beginning a new community tradition.

As with all other forms of emergency preparedness education, emergency managers should approach public events strategically. It is completely appropriate to have a set of specific objectives for an event, even if they are unstated. Efforts to produce an event should be coordinated and always focused upon a larger goal: community preparedness. While events will provide opportunities for public presentations, displays, and demonstrations, prudent emergency managers will always be alert for opportunities to use these to direct the general public to more comprehensive educational efforts, and to build community support for emergency preparedness process. The keys to a successful event are to enter into it with specific objectives and a work plan, and to ensure that all activities reflect an understanding of the principles of adult education.

Public–Private Partnerships

One often overlooked aspect of the emergency preparedness education program is public–private partnerships. Most communities have one or more major employers, and many of these employers possess a desire to be seen as good corporate citizens. In addition, most businesses will have concerns similar to communities regarding the effects of an emergency; a given emergency may substantially affect a community, but it will also affect the ability of employers in that community to conduct their business. Local citizens affected by a disaster may not be able to report for work, communications and supply chains may be disrupted, or the production facility denied a critical resource (such as electricity) that it requires to function. In some respects, many businesses may have a better understanding of such issues than the communities that they call home, and many, at least the most prudent, already have the private-sector version of an emergency plan, called a *business continuity plan.*

Once these common interests are understood by emergency managers and business people, it may be possible to create partnerships in emergency preparedness at the local level. In a particularly supportive arrangement, businesses might provide the use of meeting spaces for educational activities, sponsor the creation of public education materials, or donate prizes for community emergency management competitions. The purchase and donation of large emergency response resources such as fire trucks or ambulances by local major employers is not unheard of. Businesses should certainly be interested in the subject of personal preparedness; after all, an employee who is better prepared is less likely to be sitting in a shelter or dealing with family support issues, and better able to report for work.

As with all other aspects of public education, emergency managers should consider the potential for public–private partnerships from a strategic perspective. Emergency managers should possess an understanding of what the community needs and what the business might be able to provide. It is also necessary to have a clear understanding of exactly how both the community and the business would benefit from such an arrangement. For example, it may be appropriate to provide basic preparedness training for the company's workforce or assist with the development of a business continuity plan without charge, in exchange for other services to the community. All such issues should be considered carefully by emergency managers in advance of an initial approach to a local business. While public–private partnerships may not always be successful, when they are, they have the potential to provide substantial and real benefits to both groups.

Local Volunteers

In many communities, the potential exists to include local volunteers in a strategy for emergency preparedness education. In the past, many communities, particularly those in North America, had a roster of volunteer firefighters and paramedics (although this is less the case today since these roles tend to be filled by paid staff). Thus, the potential may exist to use the same type of community-minded individuals as emergency management volunteers. These types of programs have a long and honoured tradition in places such as Europe and Australia,[6] and began following the Second World War. This evolution of the use of volunteers is more recent in North America, but continues to grow and develop. Readers may recall that a great deal of modern emergency management can trace its roots back to similar community volunteerism, such as the air raid wardens of the Second World War (see chapter 1).

In Australia, volunteer emergency management groups are called **State Emergency Services (SES)**, while elsewhere in the world they may be referred to as civil defence or civil protection volunteers. In North America, the most common description for this group is the **Community Emergency Response Team (CERT)**.[7] Such groups consist of specially trained and vetted volunteers, typically working under the direction of professional staff. While those providing work direction or oversight to such groups varies by jurisdiction, they are usually either professional emergency managers or senior staff from the traditional emergency services.

The training for volunteer emergency management groups varies, depending upon their agreed-upon roles during an emergency. Training typically includes first aid and CPR, light firefighting and rescue, and crowd and traffic management. Other specific training may be added at the local level, as need and opportunities arise. They typically have their own policies, procedures, and equipment, and train together on a regular basis until they are needed. Each member must meet minimum training standards, determined by the local jurisdiction, before they become eligible for deployment during an emergency.

In North America, the idea behind creating such groups is to have a team of volunteers who can start operating quickly at the local neighbourhood level during a disaster, usually under some form of professional direction (such as the local fire chief). They are intended to attempt to address low-priority emergency events while full-time emergency responders cope with more serious events, or provide some level of response when the community's normal emergency response apparatus is overwhelmed. They are seen as a valuable resource by emergency responders in their local communities.

In Australia and elsewhere, emergency management volunteers are not limited to emergency deployment. As well, they may be used to supplement and provide support and assistance to the community's normal emergency response resources during emergency events both large and small. In some cases, they have assumed specialist functions as well, including such roles as cliff rescue and volunteer marine rescue.[8] In many jurisdictions, they also perform functions at planned events such as parades, fairs, and festivals. Their functions might include traffic or crowd management, or the provision of first-aid services. The intent in planned events is to maximize the potential of traditional emergency response resources through the delegation of low-priority functions to individuals other than fully trained police officers and paramedics.

All of these groups provide a tremendous resource to their local communities through volunteerism. They may also be capable of providing emergency managers with a valuable resource for public preparedness education efforts. The members of such groups are typically highly regarded individuals and, potentially, credible spokespersons on the subject of emergency preparedness. Their high visibility, training, and knowledge is such that they already understand the issues surrounding personal preparedness and may be effective at communicating those issues to others in the community, with the same type of credibility given to police officers, firefighters, or paramedics within their own field of expertise.

The presence of such groups within communities can provide a "focal point" or a framework around which additional preparedness efforts can be built. When these groups are present within the community, emergency managers might ask for their support in literature distribution, public education displays, and other types of public awareness activities. The expansion of their role to include such activities provides the group with added value, by providing them with a role not only during emergencies, but also in preparing the community for an emergency before it happens. As a result, even when such groups do not exist within a given community, emergency managers may wish to consider the potential for their creation, in cooperation with the traditional emergency services and local elected officials.

Conclusion

An effective public education program can result in substantial increases in both personal preparedness and resiliency, and the preparedness and resiliency of the community as a whole. Such a program can result in increased public support for emergency management activities and perhaps access to previously unavailable resources for dealing with emergencies. Accomplishing these goals requires good communication skills and an understanding of how to motivate people to effect change. These processes can be further enhanced through the use of both community partnerships and public–private partnerships in emergency preparedness, and through volunteerism.

It is not enough merely to "get the message out." One of the primary functions of any emergency manager is to make information that is complex, confusing, or frightening accessible and to do so in a manner that motivates behavioural change. For any emergency preparedness message to be effective, it must be listened to, understood, and acted on. Delivery of the message using methods and channels that enhance the information will directly affect the resulting preparedness activities of the general public. With the appropriate communications strategies, both the community or organization, and the individuals within it, will be better prepared for emergencies and, therefore, safer than they were in the past.

KEY TERMS

Community Emergency Response Team (CERT)

State Emergency Services (SES)

LEARNING CHECK

Take a few minutes now to test your knowledge of the public education process. Select the best answer in each case. Any score of less than 16 out of 20 (80 percent) indicates that you should re-read this chapter.

1. In most communities and organizations, the actual degree of resiliency will be determined by the level of preparedness of
    a. individual members
    b. emergency services
    c. the community as a whole
    d. senior levels of government

2. In most circumstances, whether at a community or individual level, preparedness will translate directly into
    a. risk awareness
    b. resiliency
    c. acquisition of resources
    d. increased budget

3. In almost all cases, the primary motivator of individuals is
    a. cost
    b. training
    c. self-interest
    d. the greater good

4. For the average person, physiological needs such as food, clothing, and shelter, will take precedence over
    a. self-actualization
    b. safety concerns
    c. available resources
    d. self-esteem

5. In emergency management, effective public education is not just about disseminating information, it is about providing
    a. an increased budget
    b. individual resources
    c. motivation to change
    d. access to leadership

6. One highly effective method of both promoting and enhancing preparedness and resiliency is through the use of
   a. community partnerships
   b. military resources
   c. municipal bylaws
   d. direct mailings

7. One substantial disadvantage to the development and distribution of print material as a preparedness education strategy is that such materials lack
   a. sufficient information
   b. the ability to motivate change in all cases
   c. sufficient grounding in the principles of adult education
   d. interest

8. Unless print materials are able to appeal to the motivated self-interest of the individual, they are unlikely to be
   a. approved for funding
   b. retained, valued, and acted on
   c. approved for distribution
   d. read by the individual

9. As a consideration in the design of preparedness materials, emergency managers should be aware that the information presented is more likely to be remembered and acted on if it includes
   a. some degree of interaction
   b. precise instructions
   c. humour
   d. an endorsement from the mayor

10. As a general rule, emergency managers should regard printed preparedness education materials as being most effective when they
    a. provide only basic information
    b. provide detailed information
    c. lead to more comprehensive educational sources
    d. provide contact telephone numbers

11. When considering and designing public education programs, emergency managers will benefit from the presence of
   a. a local champion
   b. a communications strategy
   c. a skilled, professional designer
   d. good photographic skills

12. When considering the use of a website for preparedness education, emergency managers should remember that the effectiveness of the information on the website will be directly affected by
   a. a visitor's ability to interact with it
   b. the design and colours used
   c. the presence of colour photos
   d. the number of visitors

13. The use of websites provides an additional benefit to emergency managers in that with the right software, its usage can be
   a. monitored in real time
   b. limited or restricted
   c. tracked and reported
   d. made mandatory

14. A well-designed website can provide an emergency manager with dynamic interaction with members of the community, either through email exchanges or through the use of
   a. Voice over Internet Protocol
   b. video conferencing
   c. providing telephone contact information
   d. facilitated discussion boards

15. A major value in the use of public displays is that they provide emergency managers with the ability to
   a. conduct detailed lectures
   b. interact and demonstrate
   c. raise their public image
   d. listen to complaints and concerns

16. Public-speaking engagements are a useful tool for emergency managers because they not only convey public education information but also lead to
    a. additional response resources
    b. increased community support
    c. additional funding
    d. both (a) and (b)

17. When speaking to school groups, it is important for emergency managers to remember that they are communicating not only with the students, but also indirectly with
    a. elected officials
    b. their parents
    c. school staff
    d. the media

18. A significant advantage to public–private partnerships is that the company and the community often share common interests and concerns with respect to disasters, and that
    a. the community has an obligation to support employers
    b. both groups may potentially benefit from the arrangement
    c. such activities stimulate media interest
    d. such activities result in political approval and support

19. In addition to providing additional funding and sponsorship sources, public–private partnerships may result in
    a. increased local employment
    b. disclosure of sensitive information
    c. voluntary exchange of services
    d. additional emergency management staff

20. One significant advantage to the presence of volunteer emergency management groups, such as CERT teams, is that they can often provide
    a. fundraising activities
    b. a "focal point" for preparedness education efforts
    c. low-cost alternatives for emergency services
    d. leadership for the emergency manager

CASE STUDIES

A. You are the emergency manager for a medium-sized community. Your emergency response resources appear to be adequate, and are tested regularly. To the best of your knowledge, no efforts at educating the general public regarding individual preparedness have ever occurred.

1. Describe your first priorities with respect to the development of personal emergency preparedness. Why are these necessary?
2. Identify the target groups within your community. Are there some groups that are potentially more vulnerable than others? Why?
3. Describe a strategy for distributing emergency preparedness information within the community. What are the potential problems with such a strategy?
4. Describe different methods for delivering emergency preparedness education.

B. You are the emergency manager for a medium-sized community with admittedly limited resources. Your Hazard Identification and Risk Assessment has revealed that, should an emergency occur within the community, local emergency responders would be severely taxed in dealing with the emergency event itself, without any consideration for the ongoing needs of residents.

1. Describe a potential strategy for meeting the ongoing needs of community residents while the traditional emergency services are occupied with the emergency.
2. How would such service delivery be organized? How would it receive work direction and assignments?
3. From where might these supplemental resources be recruited? What training or equipment would be required?
4. What approvals would be required to implement such a process?

TO LEARN MORE

1. Analyze the emergency preparedness public education program in your own community. What types of public education efforts are currently being conducted? Is the public education program targeting specific information? How is it being presented? Why? Are there other ideas for public education that might work? What are they? What is the single largest barrier to public education efforts in your community? Name three strategies that might be used to overcome that barrier.

2. Visit your community's planning office and look at the information revealed by the last census. What special groups (language, socio-economic status, age, gender) are present in your community, and in what numbers? Does the existing public education program specifically target these groups? Are any obvious groups overlooked? Why? What strategies could be used to bring the existing public education program to those groups that are not currently receiving it? How would you go about doing this?

NOTES

1. "Maslow's Hierarchy of Needs," *Lifeworktransitions.com*, <http://www.lifeworktransitions.com/exercises/part1/mazlow.html>.
2. Benjamin S. Bloom, David R. Krathwohl, and Bertram B. Masia, *Taxonomy of Educational Objectives: The Classification of Educational Goals* (New York: David McKay, 1956).
3. Peter Hibbs, "Air Raid Precautions Cigarette Cards," *NBCD*, <http://www.nbcd.org.uk/arp/cigarette_cards/index.asp>.
4. "Be Ready Home Survival Plan," New South Wales, State Emergency Services, <http://www.wellington.govt.nz/services/emergencymgmt/pdfs/bereadyhome.pdf>.
5. Toronto EMS website, <http://www.toronto.ca/ems/pdf_files/ferrier_002.pdf>.
6. Victoria State Emergency Service website, <http://www.ses.vic.gov.au/CA256AEA002F0EC7/HomePage?OpenForm&1=Home~&2=~&3=~>.
7. Community Emergency Response Team website, <https://www.citizencorps.gov/cert/about.shtm>.
8. Queensland State Emergency Service website, <http://www.emergency.qld.gov.au/ses/about>.

CHAPTER 18

Educating Key Decision-Makers

LEARNING OBJECTIVES

On completion of this chapter, you will

- ▶ Be able to describe the hierarchical structure by which most governments are organized.
- ▶ Be able to describe the roles of elected officials and paid senior staff in government.
- ▶ Understand the common barriers to obtaining approval for emergency management programs.
- ▶ Be able to describe the process for educating key decision-makers, whether elected officials or senior staff, about emergency management.
- ▶ Be able to describe the steps that emergency managers may take to raise the profile of both themselves and their programs with key decision-makers.
- ▶ Be able to describe a strategy to increase the influence of emergency managers on key decision-makers with respect to community planning, emergency preparedness, and emergency management program approval.

KEY MESSAGES

1. Emergency managers must understand that the manner in which a community or an organization is organized for day-to-day business frequently determines the framework within which emergency management activities are conducted.

2. Emergency managers must understand the political environment of a community or an organization, because this environment provides the context within which emergency management activities occur.

3. Emergency managers must have detailed knowledge of the legislation and regulations associated with emergency management, as they affect a community or an organization.

4. Emergency managers must have detailed knowledge of the standards associated with emergency management, as these provide the basis on which the community's or organization's emergency preparedness and response activities will be judged.

5. The approval and effectiveness of emergency management programs depend somewhat on an emergency manager's degree of influence.

6. A key strategy to increase an emergency manager's influence on key decision-makers is to place and ally the emergency management office at or near a point of significant power within the community or organization.

Introduction

This chapter has been titled "Educating Key Decision-Makers," but this title may be something of a misnomer. While the education of key decision-makers is a critical function of emergency managers, the chapter is also about how emergency managers develop their position of leadership and influence within a community or an organization. All three of these factors are absolutely necessary when attempting to achieve objectives such as resource acquisition and program approval.

Both communities and organizations are political entities, operating within a complex environment. The environmental factors that affect communities and organizations include legislative mandates, public pressure, competing political influences, competing demands for limited resources, and competing priorities. It is within this matrix of factors that larger decisions regarding emergency management programs are made, and, as a result, emergency managers must be adept at both recognizing all of these factors and being able to influence decisions when they are operating.

This chapter discusses the political environment of a typical community and how it functions. The need for a solid understanding of relevant legislation, regulations, and standards, as well as their meaning and intent, is explored. The methods used for educating key decision-makers are examined. Finally, the strategies emergency managers can use to develop both leadership and influence within a community's or an organization's politically charged environment to achieve emergency preparedness objectives are discussed.

Purpose

Emergency managers are never the final authority on emergency management programs. Emergency managers are not in the position to make certain larger decisions independently; they must pursue the support of key decision-makers for such decisions. Usually, key decision-makers are elected officials or paid staff in senior positions in government. Emergency managers must be able to educate and influence key decision-makers to achieve their objectives. They must have thorough knowledge of legislation, regulations, and standards, along with a detailed understanding of the political and power processes that operate within communities or organizations.

Influencing Key Decision-Makers

Government and Politics

In virtually all situations, emergency managers must function within an environment that is, by its very nature, intensely political. Although all levels of government are political, local governments can be one of the most politically charged environments of all. Emergency managers must understand how the government that employs them works, and, perhaps more important, precisely how the politics of the environment in which they work operates, on both the stated and unstated levels.

Government Hierarchy

In most countries, governments tend to be organized at the federal, regional, and local levels. Regional governments tend to be either provinces or states, while local governments tend to be counties, cities, towns, or villages. In most jurisdictions, governments exist within an established hierarchy, from the federal to local levels. The duties, roles, and responsibilities of each level are defined to some extent by mutual agreement, and formalized as **laws** and **regulations**. Senior levels of government may provide legislated mandates to subordinate levels, and these mandates may or may not be funded by the level of government providing them. In some cases, the development of programs and their funding may be the result of intergovernmental negotiations or agreements. There is a role for emergency managers at each level of government.

In most jurisdictions, each level of government comprises two groups of people: elected officials and paid staff. These groups include senior elected decision-makers and the senior levels of the civil service. Those in the former group change from time to time (based on election results), while those in the latter group generally change jobs much less frequently. In almost any introductory political science course, students learn that senior decision-makers provide the force for change within the community, while the senior (indeed all!) levels of the civil service represent the "bureaucratic inertia" that slows change and prevents it from becoming a runaway process.

Elected officials create change within a community, while paid staff are generally limited to influencing that change. That influence can be significant; the heads of municipal departments are often subject-matter experts within their own fields and for their community, and elected officials usually rely on their advice and guidance. However, municipal department heads do not have the power to unilaterally change anything. They are fully accountable to the community, by way of the elected council. For example, a municipal department head may want to create a new program of service delivery, but without the approval and funding of elected officials, that program is unlikely to occur. The real power within a community lies with elected officials, and, in all cases, while the influence of paid staff may be significant and important, the decisions made by elected officials are the ones that truly matter.

Elected officials receive their mandate to run the community and its associated services from members of the community. They are intensely political by nature; after all, each was the winner in a competitive political process to reach office. Most found their way into the political arena through a desire to perform community service and to resolve some issue or set of issues that they judged to be important. Their term of office is generally defined by legislation, with most jurisdictions allowing elected officials to run for more than one term. Their powers and authority are clearly defined, and founded in legislation created by senior levels of government.

Political Motivation

A constant source of motivation for elected officials is public opinion, because it will determine whether or not they are re-elected to subsequent terms of office. While they are constantly attempting to assess, balance, and provide the needs and resources of the community, the next election is rarely very far from their thoughts. This reality can be problematic for senior civil servants, but is especially so for emergency managers. Emergency preparedness efforts and emergency management programs generally require considerable vision and a long-term view, but elected officials often find it difficult to see any part of the future that lies much beyond the next election.

Public image is important to elected officials; ultimately, it is what will lead to their success or failure in the next election. Politicians generally wish to be seen by the public doing positive things and fixing problems. They often engage in short-term "fixes" to problems, even when those "fixes" result in longer-term problems. When the longer-term problem finally arises, they will cheerfully and busily engage in "fixing" that problem too. Politicians understand that in most cases the public has a short collective memory and is less likely to recall exactly what caused the new problem in the first place. While this approach to problem solving can be frustrating for emergency managers, it is important to keep it in mind when dealing with elected officials.

It is also important to keep in mind that politicians must constantly balance both limited resources and competing priorities. For example, at a given time, a community might require a new school or hospital, a major reconstruction of infrastructure, and an increase in the provision of essential services for residents. All of these demands must be prioritized and balanced against both legislated mandates and a limited budget. Emergency managers who attempt to gain approval for a proposed emergency preparedness program that is based simply on their belief in its necessity will likely be unsuccessful. They are highly likely to receive a response asking why, in the face of competing immediate priorities for resources and budgetary demands, the council should consider funding or approving a program to address something that might never happen. Politicians rarely take the long-term view, unless they can be motivated in some manner to do so.

Senior staff operate differently, but within an environment that is often just as intensely political. For example, municipal department heads are not subject to re-election, although increasingly in communities they are subject to employment contract renewal. As a result, they are better able to look further ahead than elected officials. The problem is that they are constantly aware that they are directly competing against one another for access to a limited pool of resources. They tend to be extremely competitive, and also somewhat parochial. All of them have their own agenda and set of priorities for their own department or division, and they actively work to ensure that their department's needs are met first, even when they can see the importance of some competing priority.

Senior staff generally understand their own field of expertise extremely well, and to have risen to senior management are probably quite adept at functioning within a political environment. However, they may have only a minimal understanding of the issues surrounding other aspects of the community. Some will have a better understanding of certain issues than others. For example, those responsible for the traditional emergency services are much more likely to possess a good understanding of the needs and issues of emergency managers, but this will not prevent them from competing against those needs and issues to achieve their own department's goals.

Obtaining Support

Emergency managers must strive to achieve their own objectives for the community in the midst of the workings and machinations of these two groups. Elected officials rarely support or fund a program simply because it seems like a good idea; their world is full of good ideas competing for their time and attention. However, their support can be obtained through the use of influence. Part of this influence takes place during the education process—when emergency managers provide elected officials with good, well-researched information that supports their proposal. Another part of this influence takes place less directly—when emergency managers work to obtain public support for a project from the majority of members of senior staff or, in some cases, key individuals such as an emergency service chief (or chiefs).

Obtaining support for a program is often a slow process. At a minimum, emergency managers will need to convince an individual of the necessity of the proposal, often by providing that individual with detailed information and by giving him or her an opportunity to ask questions and raise issues. This process can take a considerable amount of discussion, and will take time. Prudent emergency managers will explore methods of developing the proposal so that it benefits more than one department to achieve the needed support. To illustrate, a community preparedness proposal that also results in the acquisition of new hazardous materials management equipment or the purchase of additional training for the fire department is much more likely to obtain the fire chief's support than such a proposal would simply on its own merit.

Obtaining support for a program can also be the result of tradeoffs between the key players as well. In some cases, this tradeoff will be quite straightforward. For example, the police chief may advise that he or she is about to table his or her own proposal, and that public support for that proposal will result in the police chief's public support for the emergency manager's emergency preparedness proposal. In emergency management, particularly at the local level, such tradeoffs and compromises are not uncommon, and emergency managers must understand that they are a reality and be prepared to use them. There is an old saying that in local government it seems that the majority of council decisions are made in the council chamber, but they are actually made in the corridor outside. Wise emergency managers will always remember this point.

Laws, Regulations, and Standards

In most cases, the conduct of emergency management is governed by laws, regulations, and **standards**. These legal documents provide general guidance to communities and organizations for the creation and operation of all types of emergency preparedness activities, and each is distinct and has its own role to play. Emergency managers must be thoroughly conversant with all laws, regulations, and standards relevant to emergency management. Since an emergency manager is likely the only person within the community with a full-time (or in some cases, part-time) mandate for emergency preparedness, it is both reasonable and logical to assume that the emergency manager would possess the most detailed and comprehensive knowledge of related laws, regulations, and standards within the community. Emergency managers should possess a level of knowledge that allows them to educate others in the community regarding these legal documents and to consult with and advise key decision-makers on both compliance with the provisions and the intent of these documents.

Laws

Laws are the rules of conduct by which a given society agrees to operate. The creation of formal written laws dates back to Egypt in approximately 3000 BC. Laws typically tend to reflect the customs and common practices of a society, and create ideal standards by which the members of a society are expected to behave. Individual laws may obligate a certain type of behaviour, such as agreeing not to steal or kill, or provide penalties for non-compliance. Laws are created by governments to regulate all types of activities, including emergency management.

Laws are created by all levels of government for purposes specific to the mandate and authority of that level of government. In most countries, the creation of laws is guided by a national constitution: a fundamental document that provides the authority to governments for the creation of new laws, and which specifies what types of laws are, or are not, permissible. It is on the basis of the constitution that the country's judiciary may rule on laws, either validating them or striking them down.

Laws created by the federal level of government address issues that are important to the entire country, or issues related to international relations. Laws created by the regional level of government address issues within that region, and within the responsibility of that government, as defined by agreements on responsibility-sharing among the different levels of government. At the local authority level, at least within North America, such laws are generally called *bylaws*. Laws created within a given jurisdiction will only apply within the jurisdiction in question: local bylaws apply only within the community where they were created, the laws of regional governments apply only within the region where they were created, and only the laws created by a federal government have force within the entire country.

Legislation is a law or a series of laws that have been enacted by a legislative body; the term is also used to describe the process of creating new laws. The language in which legislation is written is important and often determines the effect of the legislation. The language of legislation may be permissive: it provides a group with the ability to take a certain action or to spend public funds to achieve a certain goal, but the language used does not make the course of action mandatory. Or, the language of legislation may be directive: it provides a clear legislative mandate for some form of compulsory action. Whether a particular course of action is suggested or compulsory is determined largely by the language of the legislation in question. In emergency management, laws with directive language tend to be more effective at achieving the desired results.

A common belief is that laws are created by the elected officials within a community, but this belief is mistaken. Laws may be proposed and championed by elected officials or groups within the community's legislative body, but the content of such laws is drafted more often by those in the community's civil service sector. This group has the greatest body of knowledge surrounding the issue for which the law in question is being created. Individuals or groups within the civil service often spend a great deal of time preparing a first draft of legislation, explaining the intent, and developing supporting materials, such as a business case.

The draft of the proposed law is presented to a legislative body for acceptance (which is called a "reading"), and may or may not be voted on, depending on the jurisdiction. The draft is then subjected to a process of review, either by elected officials, special interest groups, or the public at large. The draft may then be modified and re-read in the legislative body. Once again, it may or may not be voted on. Following second reading, the draft is typically sent to a committee of elected members for final revisions and any final adjustments to language. It will then receive a third and final reading, and will be voted on. If the vote passes, the new law will be publicly proclaimed, and will go into effect on a specified date.

It is important for emergency managers to understand the process of law creation. Like other civil servants, emergency managers are expected to possess a body of knowledge regarding their own field of expertise. As a result, it is likely that emergency managers, regardless of which level of government they work in, will be consulted with respect to legislation that has an impact on emergency management, and may even be asked to assist with the development of draft legislation. When emergency managers have a specific legislative objective that they want to achieve, they may even initiate this legislative process, supported by a champion or champions from among the elected officials.

Regulations

While individual laws provide guidance to the community, they are generally crafted in language that may be broad and subject to interpretation. Regulations, on the other hand, are created to provide specific instruction regarding what constitutes compliance with a particular law. To illustrate, a regional law may state that communities within the region are required to create an effective emergency plan, and to review that plan on a regular basis. The associated regulations will describe exactly what constitutes an effective emergency plan, may specify that the review must be annual, and may require annual submission of a copy of the reviewed and amended emergency plan to some branch of the regional government. The regulations associated with a particular law may generally be amended when required, without the full participation of the legislative body, as would be necessary to amend the actual law.

There is an important role for emergency managers in this process. The creation of regulations is generally performed by the civil service, through public and stakeholder consultation. It is entirely likely that emergency managers may be asked to draft such regulations within their own level of government, or to participate in and review the creation of regulations by senior levels of government. In some cases, it may be possible for emergency managers to achieve a particular preparedness goal through the creation of a regulation, or the amendment of an existing regulation. One good example of this would be the amendment of local community development and planning regulations to support local disaster mitigation efforts.

Standards

Standards are not usually created by governments, but by stakeholder groups. Such groups may be industry associations, or may be national bodies tasked with the creation of a broad range of standards for use by a variety of groups. In Canada, the Canadian Standards Association provides national emergency management standards; in the United States, the National Fire Protection Association provides these standards. Standards can describe best practices or expected minimum performance, and provide the basis on which a product, a service, or, in the case of emergency management, a disaster response, may be judged.

Unlike laws and regulations, standards have no legal force. Compliance with standards is a voluntary matter in most jurisdictions. There are, however, several strong incentives for compliance with standards. From the perspective of a manufacturer or the provider of a given service, compliance with standards is often a marketing tool. People are much more likely to purchase a product or service that has been found to be compliant with and approved by a standards organization, such as Underwriters Laboratories, than one that has not. Another important incentive for compliance lies in the fact that the standard simply exists. In the wake of some form of emergency, the presence of a standard for some element of emergency response often provides the basis on which the response to the emergency will be judged. Laws and regulations provide the basis for any criminal action resulting from the emergency. Similarly, compliance or non-compliance with a published standard may form a large part of the case for any civil action arising from the emergency response. At a minimum, the demonstration of non-compliance with a published standard will place the community or organization in a bad light. At a maximum, the demonstration of non-compliance may result in an expensive civil compensation settlement.

There is an important role for emergency managers in the creation of standards. As previously stated, standards tend to be developed by stakeholder groups. This process usually consists of striking a committee of "experts" within the industry or field in question, drafting a standard, and then circulating that draft standard within the industry or field for review. The draft standard is then amended, based on the feedback received, into a final draft form, and then finally published. When a committee is struck to create standards that relate to emergency management generally or to any of its elements in particular, it is quite possible that an emergency manager will be asked to take part as a committee member. At the very least, an emergency manager is likely to be given the opportunity to review and comment on these types of standards during the creation process.

The conduct of emergency management and emergency preparedness activities is determined by laws, regulations, and standards created by various levels of government and other organizations. Ensuring that the community or organization is in continual compliance with all of the associated laws, regulations, and standards is one of the tasks of emergency managers. Emergency managers are likely to possess the best and most comprehensive knowledge of laws, regulations, and standards associated with emergency management; their intent; and what precisely constitutes compliance. As such, emergency managers are often seen by elected officials within a jurisdiction as "experts" in these matters, and a source of both advice and guidance.

The potential influence of emergency managers is substantial. Emergency managers provide much-needed, and often poorly understood, information to both elected officials and senior staff members. In many jurisdictions, emergency managers operate training sessions for newly elected officials to ensure that they understand relevant laws, regulations, and standards and how to comply with them, as well as their roles as elected officials during a community emergency. This training ensures that emergency managers begin to be recognized as the local "experts" on emergency management matters and enhances the degree of influence they might have on the new group of key decision-makers. Emergency managers may be able to influence the process of creating laws, regulations, and standards, as well as provide a substantial degree of influence on compliance at the local level.

Educating Key Decision-Makers

Elected officials and senior staff members are ordinary citizens who have risen to the challenge of serving their community. Typically, they possess no more understanding of emergency preparedness or its associated issues than other members of the community. This point is particularly true for newly elected officials, but also may be true for elected officials in communities that do not have an active emergency management program. Emergency managers are called on to provide elected officials with the same type of information that is given to the average citizen in the community, but in much more detail. Elected officials need greater information by virtue of their office: they participate directly in the emergency preparedness process and often will have a specific role to play during an actual emergency. Through the education process, emergency managers gain the opportunity to present emergency preparedness issues and program requirements to an important audience, to develop relationships, and to become recognized by elected officials as having expertise in their field. The education process creates a channel for future alliances with and, potentially, influence on key decision-makers.

Key decision-makers require two distinct forms of education: (1) an orientation to emergency management laws, regulations, and standards, and (2) guidance on how to put the information provided into practice. These forms of education are discussed below.

Orientation to Emergency Management
Laws, Regulations, and Standards

Elected officials require an orientation to the laws, regulations, and standards within the field of emergency management, as well as their legal obligations to these elements as elected officials. They need to understand how and why emergency management operates the way it does, both within the community and elsewhere, and how community emergency preparedness efforts are created. Also, they need to understand why such information is important, and how it affects them specifically. While the information required by elected officials may be similar to that required by ordinary citizens, its effect and application vary considerably.

The political context in which elected officials operate must never be overlooked; examples provided during education can and should include relevant political content, as well as the appropriate background information, such as the findings of the community's Hazard Identification and Risk Assessment (HIRA). At the end of the education program, the elected official must be able to speak knowledgeably, although not at the level of an expert, on the subject of emergency management. To illustrate, a local citizen may require information on a home safety mitigation program. An elected official must be able to explain to that average citizen why such a program is necessary, and why public funds are being spent on such a project. As a result, whenever possible, emergency managers should attempt to include another, more experienced elected official, perhaps even the mayor, in the teaching process. Ideally, this person is already a champion of the emergency preparedness process within the community.

Senior staff within a community or organization also require much the same type of information as elected officials. Remember that while senior staff members may be experts in their own fields, it is likely that they know little more about emergency management than the average citizen or the newly elected official. As a result, the curriculum for elected officials and senior staff may be similar. There will, however, be differences in how such information is applied by each group to the operation of individual departments or to the community as a whole, during response to an emergency. Therefore, placing the two groups in the same classroom can create potential problems. Remember that department heads tend to be competitive; placing them in the same group as elected officials may result in an attempt by them to expand their own influence rather than focus on the information and materials being presented. Although this behaviour may occur discreetly, it will detract from the process of educating both groups. As with most aspects of emergency management, some strategic thinking is required.

The educational information provided during a class must be as complete and concise as possible, as well as credible and valuable. The facts should be stated clearly and be supported by detailed handouts. In this context, the presentation of additional handouts is likely to be effective, since the education process should already have created interest and an understanding of the information's relevance and value. Always allow time for questions and facilitated discussions, but never force the process or drag it out. Usually, the community's elected officials and senior staff are extremely busy people. In some communities, elected officials' positions are part-time arrangements that coincide with full-time employment elsewhere, not to mention that these people will have family obligations. In any case, time is important, and emergency managers will find that showing respect for the time of elected officials and senior staff will be reciprocated.

Such education efforts play a valuable role in the community's emergency preparedness process. They provide new key decision-makers with insights into issues with which they were previously unfamiliar or to which they had given little thought in the past. Well-informed elected officials are better able to see the value of emergency preparedness efforts to the community. In addition, this initial interaction can lay the groundwork for the continued influence of emergency managers on key decision-makers—influence that will be beneficial when emergency managers attempt to gain approval for future preparedness efforts. As a result, any emergency manager should actively consider providing an educational opportunity with each change of elected officials.

Putting Information into Practice

The second form of education required by both elected officials and senior staff is the opportunity to put the information that they have been given into actual practice. This form of education takes place through case study exercises, tabletop exercises, and other types of emergency exercises. Such educational opportunities, conducted on a regular basis, provide both groups with needed insight into the community's actual emergency response apparatus, and a better understanding of the issues surrounding emergency preparedness. This type of affective-domain learning allows participants to take the theory that they obtained in the classroom and apply it in a practical sense, ensuring their understanding and retention of the information.

The participation of members of both groups in an emergency exercise should be directly relevant to their actual role within an emergency. They need to do what they would be expected to do in an emergency to make the educational experience valid and real. The incorporation of a mock press conference for an elected official, or the creation of exercise inputs in which an elected official might be required to interact with other elected officials from a nearby community are two examples of realistic exercises. Including such opportunities generally requires some simple adjustments to a pre-planned exercise or the inclusion of a handful of additional exercise inputs.

The regular use of emergency exercises helps emergency managers achieve a number of objectives. Regular participation by key decision-makers in such exercises maintains a level of awareness in emergency preparedness among elected officials, and may even generate some additional enthusiasm for the process. The intent is for elected officials to begin to see the evolution of a culture of preparedness within the community, and to see emergency preparedness as an issue of value. If elected officials desire, their participation in such exercises could be given media attention. This decision needs to be considered carefully; while most elected officials are in favour of positive media exposure, they may be reluctant if their comfort level with the exercise process is not substantial. No politician wants to be seen making a mistake in public.

An effective and dynamic process of educating both elected officials and senior staff provides substantial benefits to any community's emergency preparedness program. Well-informed elected officials understand issues and make good decisions. The community's key decision-makers are provided with the opportunity to see community emergency preparedness in a positive light. Emergency managers' influence on elected officials for future preparedness efforts is enhanced, and the community becomes a little more prepared with each step in the process. The key to success in such efforts is to ensure that all of the participants are able to achieve a learning outcome, and to derive benefits that they see as tangible and important.

Developing Influence

The development of influence is a key leadership skill.[1] Influence may be divided into three general categories: *position*, *interpersonal*, and *domineering*. At some point, all three types of influence operate in emergency management, generally determined by the situation. Some work better than others, but emergency managers must be constantly aware of them, not just with respect to their own style of developing influence, but because other key stakeholders, including both elected officials and senior staff with whom emergency managers are required to interact, typically incorporate one or more of these types into their own management style.

Position Influence

Position influence is derived, as the name suggests, from a person's position or rank. With this type of influence, a person achieves an objective by using his or her level of authority within the organization. To illustrate, employees will generally do what their boss tells them to do because the boss has a position of authority over them. This type of influence is common among elected officials. It is used as well with a substantial degree of comfort by those in senior positions in the emergency services. The organizational culture of emergency services is often paramilitary in nature, and such influence is a normal part of operations; staff have learned to exercise this type of authority as they have risen through the ranks.

This type of influence can be highly effective for emergency managers. It is achieved when emergency managers are seen as the local "experts," and when the emergency management process is seen as an important community priority. An emergency manager can stand before an elected official and influence his or her choices in a significant way, simply because of the credibility that the emergency manager has when speaking. Many municipal department heads rely on this type of authority, or attempt to develop it, when they make presentations to elected officials or to the community at large.

Interpersonal Influence

Interpersonal influence does not come with a position or title; it must be earned. This is truly the best type of influence, and one that every emergency manager should aspire to. This type of influence is not the result of fear or coercion, or an appeal to authority; rather, it is a consistent application of personal skills to build an atmosphere of respect and trust with another person. People want to work with an emergency manager to achieve objectives, because past experiences have been positive and enjoyable. They know from past experiences that the work process will be collaborative and based on mutual respect. It is this type of influence that can be used to facilitate team building and change management within a community or an organization.

Domineering Influence

Domineering influence is a method of last resort. Attempting to achieve one's objectives by this means amounts to bullying. It is usually based on frustration, and is likely to involve loud voices and/or harsh words. In its more subtle forms, it can often involve backroom pressure tactics, or even thinly veiled threats. Some people are surprisingly good at this technique, but it is not without its pitfalls. The consistent use of this type of influence will often achieve objectives, but at a cost of permanently damaged business relationships, and damage to the reputation of the person doing the influencing. As a result, it should only be attempted when the issue is truly important, and when all other methods of exerting influence have failed.

The whole point of exerting influence is to persuade those in charge to make decisions that meet the objectives of an emergency manager,[2] whether for program funding, the acquisition of new resources, or the approval of procedures. The use of the term *decision-makers* is not accidental; the final decision on any program or process is rarely within the authority of an emergency manager. Communities elect officials to make critical decisions about how the community will operate on their behalf. It is these individuals who will have the final authority on any program being proposed. Understanding how the decision-making process operates is essential knowledge, if an emergency manager intends to influence its outcome.

Positioning Emergency Managers

Approaches to Decision Making

People tend to make decisions based on their own personal biases and style. The nature of an individual's past experiences will often affect the style of decision making they most often employ. Physicians, for example, typically base decisions on empirical data, facts, and best practices. Others may use a more intuitive approach to the decision-making process: what "feels right." Some decion-makers employ careful thought, exploration, and consideration. Others, emergency service commanders in particular, are accustomed to making major decisions very quickly, particularly during a crisis. Some forms of decision making, consensus decision making for example, carry a high degree of conventionality. Others pursue a more radical course, attempting the immediate resolution of an issue, monitoring it, and making additional decisions if required. The specifics of decision making often involve some combination of personal bias, style, and circumstances.

Understanding Self-Interest

It is arguable that the most important factor that can be influenced in the decision-making process is self-interest. This factor is continually operating, and may do so even when the decision required is not personal but involves the whole community or organization. Indeed, many individuals, perhaps without even realizing that they are doing so, often see themselves as so central to the community or organization that their own interests and those of the community or organization are one. While this is not always the case, it occurs often enough that it provides a good strategy for influencing the decision-making process.

Emergency managers must attempt to understand who all of the "players" in key roles are, and what their self-interest is likely to be. In some cases, the self-interest may be obvious; for example, a police chief or some other senior staff member who attempts to protect the turf of his or her own department. Another example is an elected official who wants to be able to win a subsequent election. In other cases, the self-interest may be more subtle. Some people may belong to factions, cliques, and allegiances, and their self-interest is to support the objectives of their group. Other people tend to be highly conventional; they attempt to achieve consensus in all decisions and never really go "out on a limb."

All decision making is political, and to understand the politics of decision making, emergency managers would do well to put themselves, however briefly, in the position of each decision maker that they are attempting to influence.[3] In all cases, the individual involved in the decision-making process is often searching for a solution that is "safe" (according to their own definition of what "safe" actually means). In many cases, past practice is viewed as success,[4] with success equalling safety; the danger in this approach is that any proposed change by emergency managers will be viewed as a potential threat to that safety.

Wise emergency managers attempt to identify self-interest issues in advance, then they attempt to build consensus for their program by finding a way to make it as safe and as beneficial as possible for each of the individual "players." Building consensus involves making a program a "win–win" situation for as many of those concerned as possible. Those without clear self-interests will often be the consensus group, and will often fall into line as they see the evolution of support by the majority. By making projects a win–win situation, emergency managers not only achieve their specific objectives, but also position themselves in an increasingly favourable light for the presentation of future projects and proposals. People are much more likely to cooperate when doing so meets their own needs, and when they expect that the experience will be positive. Prudent emergency managers who wish to develop real influence will attempt to move the community or organization from a state of mere consensus to one of collaboration.[5]

Expertise and Education

Emergency managers must be seen by key decision-makers as a valuable resource to the community with respect to both emergency preparedness programs and emergency management as a whole. Wise leaders, whether elected or otherwise, will quickly learn that one of the best approaches to providing effective leadership is to surround themselves with smart people and good information. Leaders need not be experts on every single aspect of the community's operations, but they do need to know where they can find such experts immediately when they require them. This approach, in fact, is the basis on which most senior staff members in a community operate: the fire chief is understood to be the local expert on fire and rescue;

the manager of public works is understood to be the local expert on roads, water, and sewers; and so on.

Emergency managers should attempt to position themselves as local "experts" on emergency management, community preparedness, and any topic related to disasters. They should possess a detailed knowledge of local, regional, and federal laws and regulations, and how emergency procedures are intended to operate. An emergency manager is the person within the community (and often the only person) with pre-established contacts in other communities and other levels of government. If an emergency manager does not have the information required instantly available, he or she knows where to access it immediately. When a crisis strikes, an emergency manager should be the person the mayor and elected officials want to have close at hand.

Achieving this expert status will require a certain amount of strategy on the part of emergency managers. The elected officials and senior staff within a community must possess confidence in the emergency management process. Expert status is affected to some degree by the visibility of emergency managers within the corporate structure, and this is a key part of the strategy in educating elected officials and senior staff. Gaining and having the confidence of key decision-makers is one substantial outcome of the well-organized process of providing education to them. In educating key decision-makers, emergency managers are presented with an opportunity to demonstrate their knowledge and competence, and also their ability to function in a team environment, since most education tends to be interactive. Having participated with emergency managers in a teacher–student relationship should contribute directly to a participant's degree of confidence in the practitioner. That said, such a relationship alone will only rarely accomplish all of the objectives of emergency managers. The arena in which emergency management is conducted in most communities is one of power politics, and emergency managers must understand and be able to function effectively in such an environment.

Navigating Corporate Structure

In addition to educational efforts, another measure will help position emergency management within the municipality's corporate structure. To have influence, one must be heard. More often than not, the influence of emergency managers is not direct, but is an extension of some other power base or process. An office of emergency management that is attached to the mayor's office or that of the city solicitor will have a much more effective voice than one that has been added as an afterthought to some other department. Similarly, the ability to position an emergency manager at some central point within the community's development process can also be highly effective in creating safer communities, with the added benefit of pursuing mitigation strategies.

Emergency managers must constantly be on the alert for opportunities to develop influence among key decision-makers, and to position themselves as community leaders in their area of expertise. It should be remembered that the correct process will involve the facilitation of win–win situations with key decision-makers, and not self-aggrandizement. Prudent emergency managers find ways to develop good programs, and even to allow those programs to be introduced or publicly championed by some elected official or senior staff member. In this way, the elected official promotes his or her public profile, and the emergency manager gets the desired program, a public champion for it, and a potential ally for future initiatives. While emergency managers are rarely at centre stage, needed programs do get approval, and their influence within the circle of key decision-makers is effectively expanded.

Conclusion

Emergency managers are not responsible simply for the creation of an emergency plan or even an emergency management program. They must guide emergency management efforts through the complex process of community approval, funding, and adoption; otherwise, such efforts, however well written, would be nothing more than plans on paper. Emergency managers must act as a force for change within the community, changing attitudes and priorities, and, in the best circumstances, fostering a culture of preparedness.

These objectives will not be achieved overnight; the process is often long and slow. Emergency managers must persuade key decision-makers that changes are needed, but before this can occur, those same decision-makers must recognize that a problem exists, and that an emergency manager represents a credible and valuable source of potential solutions. The education of such individuals is a part of this process, but will not be effective alone. Information, and its source, must be accepted and valued before it will be acted upon. The process required is not merely one of education, but rather a strategic application of subject-matter leadership, political influence, and effective education. Only when all three of these processes occur in the correct balance will emergency management and preparedness programs successfully move from paper plans to real programs.

KEY TERMS

Incident Management System (IMS)
laws
regulations
standards

LEARNING CHECK

Take a few minutes now to test your knowledge of the process of educating and influencing key decision-makers. Select the best answer in each case. Any score of less than 16 out of 20 (80 percent) indicates that you should re-read this chapter.

1. The manner in which a community or organization is organized for day-to-day business will frequently determine the _____ within which emergency management activities are conducted.
   a. context
   b. framework
   c. political environment
   d. both (a) and (c)

2. The political environment of a community or an organization provides the _____ within which emergency management activities occur.
   a. context
   b. framework
   c. political environment
   d. both (b) an (c)

3. For an emergency management program to be effective, emergency managers must possess detailed knowledge and understanding of
   a. pertinent legislation
   b. associated regulations
   c. municipal budget
   d. both (a) and (b)

4. In emergency management, a clear understanding of any relevant standards is important, because such standards provide the basis on which
   a. resources will be acquired
   b. programs will be funded
   c. emergency management activities will be judged
   d. political approval will occur

5. The approval of programs and their effectiveness will be dependent to some degree on an emergency manager's
   a. degree of influence
   b. knowledge of legislation
   c. ability to raise funds externally
   d. ability to generate public pressure

6. A key strategy to increase the influence of an emergency manager is to place and ally the emergency management office at or near
   a. the fire department
   b. a point of significant power
   c. the council chambers
   d. likely locations for disasters

7. In the face of conflicting demands and competing priorities, elected officials may not place a priority on the approval of emergency preparedness programs because
   a. they can be difficult to understand
   b. the need may not be immediately evident
   c. they fall outside of normal spending guidelines
   d. both (a) and (c)

8. While senior staff cannot unilaterally create new programs or services, they may be able to cause their adoption by the community by means of
   a. public pressure
   b. media campaigns
   c. exerting influence
   d. presentations to council

9. It may be difficult to persuade a member of senior staff to support an emergency management proposal when that proposal
   a. could displace a proposal produced by his or her department
   b. is difficult to understand
   c. is likely to result in public approval
   d. results in new resources for other departments

10. One approach to obtaining the support of department heads for emergency preparedness programs is to ensure that they
    a. result in new resources for those departments
    b. raise the public profile of elected officials
    c. have no significant budget impact
    d. will create the need for change in another department

11. The three key legal elements that influence a community's emergency preparedness activities are laws, regulations, and
    a. guidelines
    b. best practices
    c. standards
    d. legal rulings

12. When laws are created, the language used in legislation may be permissive or
    a. directive
    b. demanding
    c. coercive
    d. both (b) and (c)

13. Laws that are created within a given jurisdiction are applicable
    a. internationally
    b. in adjoining regions
    c. only when compliance is appropriate
    d. only within that jurisdiction

14. While compliance with published standards is considered important, in most jurisdictions it is typically
    a. compulsory
    b. legally mandated
    c. voluntary
    d. strongly suggested

15. When providing educational opportunities for newly elected officials, it is important for emergency managers to remember that these individuals typically possess
    a. a good understanding of the issues
    b. knowledge similar to that of the average citizen
    c. substantial interest in the subject
    d. both (a) and (c)

16. When conducting emergency preparedness education for elected officials, it is important for emergency managers to provide information regarding
    a. statutory obligations
    b. the elected officials' role in emergency response
    c. principles of adult education
    d. both (a) and (b)

17. It is important to provide elected officials with learning opportunities such as emergency exercises because
    a. theoretical learning is important
    b. it provides an opportunity to apply and retain information
    c. they will have to fund future exercises
    d. both (a) and (c)

18. Emergency management education efforts for elected officials can be effective if participants find the information provided to be
    a. credible
    b. valuable
    c. cost-effective
    d. both (a) and (b)

19. The degree to which emergency preparedness programs are accepted and funded may be determined in large measure by the _____ of the emergency manager.
    a. education
    b. influence
    c. rhetoric
    d. both (a) and (c)

20. One extremely effective method of obtaining support for emergency preparedness programs from elected officials and senior staff is to find ways to make their support
    a. a legislated mandate
    b. an economic necessity
    c. a win–win situation
    d. more important than competing priorities

CASE STUDIES

A. You are the emergency manager for a large community. The federal level of government has recently introduced a new standard for community response to emergencies. Within that standard the use of the **Incident Management System** has been mandated, but no funding for its implementation at the local level has been provided. Your local fire department already uses a variation of this system, the Incident Command System, but no other municipal department, including both the police and Emergency Medical Services (EMS), has adopted the new system. Given the lack of funding, the heads of all municipal departments are resisting your encouragement to adopt the new command-and-control model.

1. Create a position paper aimed at persuading the heads of other municipal departments, and especially the police and EMS chiefs, that the system should be adopted, despite the lack of funding. Explain your reasons in detail, and also the benefits to each department.
2. Describe a legislative approach to mandating the use of the Incident Management System by all municipal departments.
3. Draft a proposed bylaw for consideration at a future council meeting.
4. Describe other means by which you may be able to influence either the voluntary adoption of the model or the passing of the bylaw by council.

B. You are the emergency manager for a medium-sized community with limited resources. The community is due for a full-scale exercise. The cost to conduct the exercise is relatively small, but there is no funding available within the current budget for such a project. It is nearing the end of the community's fiscal year, and the mayor has publicly promised no new tax increases in the coming fiscal year. You are aware of a relatively small budget surplus in both the police department and EMS, but these department budgets are beyond your control.

1. Describe a means of persuading the chiefs of police and EMS to commit some portion of their budget surpluses to conducting a community emergency exercise.
2. Describe the factors that are likely to influence whether they decide to support this project.
3. Describe approaches that might be used to make the project a win–win situation for all of the parties involved.
4. Describe other approaches to the funding of the project that may have to occur if you are unsuccessful in obtaining this support.

TO LEARN MORE

1. With your local emergency manager's consent, attend a meeting of the community's emergency planning committee. Sit quietly in a corner and observe the interaction among members. Which members tend to take a more active role in the planning process? Why? Based on the information in the chapter, what types of influence are being used, and by whom? Does one method of attempting to influence the group seem to be more effective than others? Are there "leaders" other than the emergency manager operating within the group? Why? Are there examples of "dealing" or "bargaining" occurring on issues? Which issues? Why do you think this is occurring? Are there disruptive elements within the group, and how does the emergency manager deal with them?

2. Attend a meeting of your community's elected council. While the ideal time would be when an issue related to emergency planning is being considered (check with your local emergency manager), this is not absolutely necessary. Observe the interaction of the various members of council while each proposal is being considered. Do groups or factions appear to be operating in the council? Why? While the mayor may be actually running the meeting, are there other elected members who seem to be leading groups? What types of influence are operating? How do the senior staff of the community interact with the elected council? Are there members of senior staff who appear to be attempting to influence council? How is this occurring? If you had to get this body to approve a proposal, how would you go about doing this? Why?

NOTES

1. Emergency Management Institute, *IS-240: Leadership and Influence Independent Study Course Manual* (Washington, DC: Federal Emergency Management Agency, 2005).
2. Emergency Management Institute, *IS-241: Decision Making and Problem Solving Independent Study Course Manual* (Washington, DC: Federal Emergency Management Agency, 2005).
3. John R. Schermerhorn, James G. Hunt, and Richard N. Osborn, *Managing Organizational Behavior* (New York: John Wiley and Sons, 1982).
4. James A. Autry and Stephen Mitchell, *Real Power: Business Lessons from the Tao Te Ching* (New York: Riverhead Books, 1998).
5. John E. Rehfeld, *Alchemy of a Leader: Combining Western and Japanese Management Skills to Transform Your Company* (New York: John Wiley and Sons, 1994).

CHAPTER 19

Emergency Management Funding

LEARNING OBJECTIVES

On completion of this chapter, you will

▶ Understand how the budget process typically works within communities.

▶ Understand the differences between capital and operating funds.

▶ Understand the approval requirements of a community budget process.

▶ Understand the requirements of grants for funding emergency management programs and projects.

▶ Understand where to search for grant funding.

▶ Understand the value of service organizations and public–private partnerships in funding emergency management programs and projects.

KEY MESSAGES

1. While emergency management programs are important, they are subject to the same budgetary and funding processes as other community services.

2. Emergency management program approval is reviewed by key decision-makers in the light of competing priorities from a range of other municipal services.

3. Even in the presence of a legal mandate for emergency management from a senior level of government, communities are often challenged to find sufficient funding for emergency management programs.

4. Programs that enhance the emergency management and emergency preparedness processes do not necessarily have to be operated under the banner of emergency management.

5. Emergency managers who can successfully exploit alternative sources of funding for programs give their position added value within the community.

6. Funding through grants, service organizations, and public–private partnerships can enhance a community's emergency preparedness and keep the related costs to the community under control.

Introduction

The one consistent fact about emergencies, whether in a community or an organization, is that they cost money. The most obvious cost relates to responding to an emergency, but this is by no means the only type of cost associated with emergency management. Activities aimed at generating community or organizational preparedness, and therefore resiliency, also have associated costs. Response costs are easier to deal with in most cases; the adverse event has happened, and there is little room for debate with respect to whether or not the situation should be addressed. In most jurisdictions, processes exist to supplement the monetary resources required for the community's response to an emergency. Typically, supplemental funding is triggered by a formal declaration of emergency and through application to disaster financial assistance programs.

However, paying for the costs associated with emergency preparedness is another matter. Most communities and organizations have a budget for some sort of emergency plan and an individual responsible for that plan, but funding for activities beyond the basic plan are subject to the same competing priorities and limited pool of community resources as any other community activities. Key decision-makers must balance the immediate and pressing needs of the community against the need to prepare for what is, it is hoped, an infrequent event. Many key decision-makers within communities either adopt that old nemesis, the attitude that "it can't happen here," or question the need to direct limited resources away from clearly needed public programs to preparations for an event that "might never happen." When it comes to funding preparedness activities, emergency managers often must be creative: they may need to seek funding not only from the "public purse" but also from other non-traditional sources.

This chapter focuses on the funding of emergency management programs, with a particular emphasis on the funding of emergency preparedness activities that are outside the emergency management budget. It describes the municipal funding process generally, given that the process varies from one jurisdiction to another. The chapter explores the non-traditional use of municipal resources, such as volunteer groups and municipal organizations, to provide added value and keep costs under control. It also explores alternative approaches to funding community preparedness activities, including grants, service organizations, the exchange of resources and services, and public–private partnerships. Such approaches enhance an emergency manager's preparedness "war chest" and provide added value to the position of emergency manager within the community. They also provide the added benefit, in many cases, of increasing community involvement and interest in preparedness activities.

Purpose

Emergency management, and emergency preparedness in particular, is only rarely fully funded by communities and organizations. Such groups typically fund only those activities for which they have received a specific mandate. Even when the community will to fund additional activities is present, key decision-makers in the community face competing demands for limited resources, and they must make difficult choices. Emergency preparedness public education programs, the acquisition of resources, staff training, and the conduct of exercises often rely on funding from a variety of sources other than the public purse. Effective emergency managers must be able not only to manage the funds provided by the community, but also to exploit other resources, such as **grant** funding and donations, in order to create a truly effective preparedness program.

Funding at the Municipal Level

All communities require emergency management, but, unfortunately, many do not see this function as a priority. Communities are essentially economic entities, involved in the delivery of services to residents. All must operate within the limits of their ability to raise operating capital—either through taxation and service fees or through funding provided by other levels of government in the form of transfer payments. In many cases, local governments are specifically precluded from deficit spending; they are required by law to "live within their means."

A community's limited pool of resources must be used to operate schools; community services such as shelters, housing, and social assistance; recreation and leisure activities; emergency services such as Emergency Medical Services (EMS), fire protection, and policing; roads and other public works; public utility services; economic development; and, in some cases, hospitals. The actual services may vary somewhat by jurisdiction and arrangements with senior levels of government, but the demand for services is continuous and sometimes pressing. When faced with so many competing demands for limited resources, it is easy to understand how key decision-makers might be reluctant to spend limited funds that are immediately needed elsewhere on contingencies such as emergency management.

In many communities, smaller communities in particular, compromises such as multiple job functions are often necessary. For example, emergency management may be an extra responsibility added to some other community job such as that of the local fire chief or EMS chief, a senior member of the police, or a mid-level manager from a municipal department.

In many communities, compromises regarding funding are often necessary. There is no specific emergency management budget; it exists as a budget line in the **operating budget** of the appropriate municipal department. It is also not uncommon, unless a specific legal mandate or funding from a senior level of government exists, for a community to expect emergency management activities to be performed entirely within the existing budget of a department, using budget surpluses when and if they can be found. Such situations, while not ideal, are part of the day-to-day reality of many emergency managers. With funding typically in such short supply, it is critical for emergency managers to understand how the funding process works and to be creative and innovative in identifying alternative sources for needed funding.

The Budget Process

Every community has an operating budget. An *operating budget* is the plan used to provide funding for the delivery of a broad range of municipal services to community residents. The funds for these services are generated in a variety of ways, including property taxes, business taxes, service charges, and licensing fees. These funds may, in some cases, be supplemented by money from other levels of government (usually referred to as *transfer payments*) to fund specific programs. It is from this limited pool of revenue that communities must pay their employees and fund all of the day-to-day services that we take for granted. In most cases, there is some flexibility in how programs are funded, although those funds received as part of transfer payments must be spent on the specific programs for which they have been allotted.

When it comes to providing services, most communities must make choices. Those choices are driven by the availability of resources, public demand, and legal requirements—and they may not be easy choices to make. The budget process is a balancing act, with key decision-makers trying to please as many constituents as possible without overspending. In many jurisdictions, overspending (called *deficit budgeting*) is not permitted. Where it is permitted, it must be used cautiously, because it creates both debts and interest payments for residents in the future. It is in this complex environment that the funding of emergency management and preparedness programs occurs, and emergency managers must understand this complex process in some detail. Specific budgeting systems and legal requirements may vary substantially between communities, and emergency managers must know how the local budget process operates.

In most communities, the budget process is an annual event. The budget for emergency management activities may represent a separate component of the municipal budget, or it may be incorporated into the budget of another department, such as the police, the fire department, or, in the best circumstances, either the municipal solicitor or the office of the city manager. In all cases, there are specific requirements regarding the inclusion of specific information regarding the details of proposed projects and spending. These requirements, and the budget process itself, vary from one community to another, and it is important to know how the local process works.

Capital Funds and Operating Funds

Budget information is normally divided into two separate and distinct categories: capital funds and operating funds.

Capital funds are used for the acquisition of durable resources, such as vehicles and equipment, or for the construction of permanent facilities.[1] An example of a **capital budget** item would be the construction and equipping of an Emergency Operations Centre (EOC) for the community. Capital budget items are those that provide lasting value to the community, as well as big-ticket items, such as vehicles, which depreciate in value over time.

Operating funds are used for salaries, benefits, and more transient issues, such as individual programs. The salary of an emergency manager is an example of an operating budget item, as are office supplies, and vehicle fuel and repairs. Community preparedness activities, such as public education, are also normally funded through an operating budget. The costs associated with these items are not as significant economically to the community, and funding for them is subject to change. A community may decide not to fund a public education program from one year to the next, whereas the funding to pay for a vehicle or a permanent facility is fixed and does not change.

The lack of flexibility in spending due to contractual obligations and the amount of money involved in capital budget items means that key decision-makers are typically far more cautious about them than they are about operating budget items. A capital budget item is a commitment of significant community funds for a considerable period of time, and one that cannot be reversed easily. The same is normally true for the recruitment and hiring of new staff. Such decisions are not made lightly.

Global and Zero-Based Budgeting

The two most common approaches to municipal budgeting are *global* and *zero-based budgeting*. In a global budget, once a budget submission is approved, a block of funds is allocated to the particular department or operation that made the submission. Usually, this type of budget is based on what was spent in the previous fiscal year, and may be supplemented by additional funds to cover inflation. It may also be adjusted downward, if the department or program happened to generate a surplus at the end of the previous fiscal year. This approach assumes that programs and operations will remain largely the same for the department or program. It provides some flexibility in the use of funds: the individual budget items describe how it is anticipated that the money will be spent, but some discretion normally exists with respect to the actual use of funds within the budget, as long as the total global budget is not exceeded. The money in this budget can be spent on the approved items and on any other project for which the department or operation is able, through various economies, to make funds available. This approach, although it has long existed in most communities, is not the most efficient way of allocating funds. Indeed, there is normally an incentive to spend every dollar of the allocation to ensure that the following year's budget allocation is not reduced, based on any surplus that might be present.

Increasingly, communities are using zero-based[2] budgeting. With this approach, each department or operation starts with zero funding, and must detail and justify how every single dollar will be spent. Each item is added, resulting in a cumulative total that becomes the department's or program's operating budget for the year. In a zero-based budget, not only is there little surplus, but there is also less flexibility to use funds for other activities not indicated in the budget. Depending on the community's guidelines, expenditures may need to be entered into a calendar and tracked closely. The argument in favour of this approach is that each department or operation receives funding only for those programs for which they can demonstrate actual need, and the result may be more funding available for other programs that might not normally be achievable. The argument against this approach is that all discretion is removed, and any program not cited in the budget submission will require separate approval from council.

Stages in the Budget Process

For most departments or programs, the budget process begins with an internal consultation process. Various managers within departments are asked to propose their operations for the coming year and to estimate the associated costs. These budget items will be reviewed by a committee of senior staff and will be either accepted or rejected, based on their practicality and the likelihood that they will survive the rest of the budget process. Some operating budget items, such as staff salaries, have fixed values, and are incorporated into the final submission as such. A draft budget for individual departments or operations is then prepared by senior staff members, and made ready for the submission process.

In most communities, the next stage in the budget process is review of the proposed budget by one or more committees of the elected council. These committees are normally composed of elected officials, supported by staff from the community's executive staff. They review the individual details of the proposed budget in what is normally a public process, and may have the authority to accept or reject individual items outright, to modify individual items, or to direct the department or operation to completely redraft their budget proposal to meet certain priorities. To illustrate, a committee might direct a department to redraft and resubmit a new budget proposal that includes a fixed percentage decrease in overall spending. Such committees may normally oversee the day-to-day activities of individual departments or oversee the entire budget process for the community. In many cases, the approval of the budget by more than one committee will be required. In all cases, those who present the draft budget will be expected to address concerns regarding every single line within the budget, including proposed programs and significant changes to past operations. Thus, good presentation skills are a definite asset.

Once the required committee approvals have been obtained, the final budget will be submitted to the entire elected council for approval, generally during a public meeting. Department heads or their designates may be required to answer questions from elected members of council who did not participate in the committee process, and the council may even receive public deputations from individuals or groups with a specific interest in either the budget or in some program funded by it. Finally, the elected council votes to approve or reject the budget, and, if approved, the department or operation receives its operating funds and a mandate for capital program spending for the coming year.

This process continues until the proposed budget items for all departments and operations have been approved. It results in an overall budget for the community for one fiscal year. The start and end of a fiscal year varies from one community to the next. Individual choice or, in some cases, governing legislation determines whether the community uses either the standard calendar year, with a January 1 start, or some other arbitrary date within the year. Most communities strive to balance their budget, so that outgoing spending matches incoming revenue relatively closely, although many attempt to maintain a reserve fund of additional money that is intended to cover unforeseen contingencies such as community emergencies.

Even after a budget's approval is obtained, the process of budgetary oversight continues. Department and operation heads and program managers are frequently required to calendar their proposed expenditures and to track spending in detail. Many communities require quarterly or even monthly reporting on how budget dollars are being spent. Significant cost overruns or underspending on projects, called *variances*, must be tracked and reported in writing, usually through the city manager or some other senior-level executive. In this way, the community's funding of programs is transparent, and members of the community are assured that their tax dollars are being spent responsibly.

Beyond the Budget: Funding for Special Programs and Projects

The community may also elect to fund special programs and projects outside of the normal budgetary process. Such funding is typically referred to as **special appropriations**.[3] Such appropriations occur during the fiscal year and cover events, programs, or opportunities that may not have been known when the official budget was prepared. Funds for special programs and projects are normally drawn from either the community's reserve fund or from funds that were made available in the budget for projects that did not proceed for various reasons. In some cases, special programs and projects occur to take advantage of unforeseen program funding that becomes available from senior levels of government to help communities meet regional or federal priorities.

Unplanned funding opportunities are of particular interest to emergency managers. Special programs and projects that were not approved due to a lack of funds in the normal budget process may be possible when additional funds become available. The process for securing such funds is much the same as the process for obtaining grants (see the next section), although the terminology may differ somewhat. Emergency managers must prepare a well-researched and documented business case for the project (or program) in question. The proposal will need to be added to the council's official meeting agenda, and it is likely that a presentation by the emergency manager or other municipal staff will be required. The council will vote on the project proposal and may approve it, assuming that sufficient funding is available. This process applies to the acquisition of specific resources, such as a vehicle or equipment, or to the start-up costs for the project in question. Once approved, ongoing funding, beyond that fiscal year, will need to be included in the regular municipal budget process. Prudent emergency managers are constantly aware of the budget process and alert for unplanned funding opportunities.

Alternative Sources of Funding

The use by emergency managers of alternative sources of funding for emergency preparedness programs has several positive outcomes. The first, and most obvious, is that it gives the community access to programs and services that might not otherwise be economically feasible. As a direct result, the reputation of the emergency manager is likely to be greatly enhanced in the eyes of key decision-makers as an individual who, rather than constantly attempting to access the public purse, is prepared to go out and source other types of funding for community programs. This ability provides added value and influence for the position of emergency manager in the eyes of key decision-makers. Success in this process will also raise the profile of emergency management and preparedness programs in the minds of key decision-makers; programs important enough to attract outside funding are probably more important than previously thought. Finally, the process involves a range of other groups in the emergency preparedness process, making the community's emergency plan and associated programs a community effort, instead of the work of an individual. Alternative sources of funding include grants, service organizations, and public–private partnerships.

Grants

A variety of agencies, some governmental and others privately owned, may be able to provide emergency managers with grant funding for specific programs or projects. Some governments provide grant funding for special programs or projects through senior levels of government. Private foundations disburse funds to programs or projects that fall within their specific mandate. As well, colleges and universities provide funding in support of research that might provide emergency managers with access to resources. Each of these sources provides different opportunities for funding that emergency managers should explore and understand.

Government

Government grant programs represent the only source of grant funding with a specific mandate for improving community preparedness and resiliency to disasters. Grant programs typically provide shared funding to the community for the acquisition of new emergency response resources, the operation of public education programs, the conduct of exercises, and other preparedness activities. They typically do not provide full funding, placing an onus on the community to accept some of the financial responsibility for preparedness, but they can be extremely useful in helping communities acquire resources and programs that might be just beyond their normal reach. Grant programs typically focus on providing start-up costs, and cannot be used for ongoing program operation. Some grant programs permit multi-year funding, while others do not.

One example of this type of grant program is Canada's Joint Emergency Preparedness Program.[4] This program is funded by the federal government, and administered by the respective provincial/territorial governments. Funding can be provided for a variety of project and program types, which have been identified and generally determined by the local community and based on that community's assessment of its needs. Funding for such programs and projects normally is divided as follows: a 55 percent share to the local community and a 45 percent share to the federal government. Funding for prototypical initiatives may be granted at the 100 percent level, and, more recently, in some cases 100 percent funding may be granted for initiatives that have specific applications in counter-terrorism.

All grant applications must meet specific criteria,[5] including an application deadline, spending requirements, the presence of a current emergency plan, and a commitment from the community for their share of the funding. Preference is given to programs and projects that meet a national priority list, which is announced annually by the government of Canada. The federal government also provides a list of program and project types that are not eligible for funding, or which have specific funding restrictions. All proposals are reviewed and prioritized, and those projects that are approved receive notification, and the community may begin implementation. The funds available for such programs are typically limited; there are more good ideas than money available, and the competition for this type of grant funding can be quite intense. Other governments in other jurisdictions may have similar programs, but will generally set their own criteria; it is up to emergency managers to learn the types and criteria of grant programs that are available in their own jurisdiction.

Private Foundations

Private foundations operate in many communities. These foundations are generally the work of either corporations or private philanthropists. Such organizations tend to focus on supporting a particular region or an aspect of community life, reflecting the priorities and beliefs of their founders. While charitable organizations and some quasi-governmental organizations such as schools and universities are certainly aware of the presence of private foundations, they are largely an untapped resource for emergency managers. To have an opportunity to receive the financial assistance of private foundations, emergency managers must undertake some advance research. It is essential that they understand exactly how such foundations work, their priorities, and their criteria for funding projects.[6] Emergency managers must be able to identify potential projects that meet the criteria of the foundation. In their application for funding, they must provide compelling arguments to support their request, including why such projects are necessary and important, and why the funding for such projects is not available from other sources.

Colleges and Universities

Grant funding is also provided to college and university research projects. Such projects are typically funded by research grants from a variety of sources, and while they may not be able to provide direct funding for an emergency preparedness project, they might be able to provide the community with additional or improved emergency preparedness resources, if such resources will assist in the conduct of the research in question. The nature of the research and the academic discipline conducting the research will often directly dictate the opportunities available. To illustrate, a geography research project on the nature of local disasters might be used to provide the community with a more comprehensive Hazard Identification and Risk Assessment (HIRA) than would normally be available, or a communications engineering research project might enhance a community's emergency communications processes during a disaster.

Colleges and universities represent another opportunity for access to resources. Most colleges and universities are constantly on the lookout for projects with real-life applications for their undergraduate and graduate students. Projects involving a whole range of academic disciplines are possible, including history, geography, earth sciences, behavioural sciences, engineering, and medicine. Collaboration with researchers, such as the gathering of data or provision of community information on such projects, allows emergency managers to provide the community with a range of planning and research information that might not otherwise be easily accessible or affordable. Such partnerships provide colleges and universities with real-life experiences to enhance the growth and learning of students. Both groups benefit substantially from the resulting programs.

Grant Criteria and Competition

In all cases of voluntary inter-organizational grant funding, certain criteria must be met. Emergency managers must understand which organizations operate in and around their community, and also the roles and priorities of those organizations. Virtually every organization that issues grants, whether governmental or otherwise, has specific rules and procedures for the grant-application process. The rules and procedures determine not only what types of grants are permissible, but also the application process, record keeping, reporting, and recognition of the organization providing the grant. It is necessary to clearly understand the rules of each grant program, and to adhere to them scrupulously.

Competition for grant funding can be fierce. Success in the process involves a number of factors, including well-written and researched grant applications, the credentials of the applicant, occasionally political support, the development of a relationship with the granting organization, and a history of success in previous grant projects. The successful writing of grant applications is a skill in itself, and one that emergency managers will derive great benefit from learning. It is important to be clear and concise, and to state your case in an effective manner. If you are unsure of your writing skills, ask others, particularly those with previous grant-application experience, to read your draft applications critically and provide advice and guidance. Above all, take the time to ensure that spelling, grammar, and punctuation are correct; there is nothing that will adversely affect the credibility of an application more than spelling and grammatical errors, and the effect is generally immediate. Taking the time to follow the rules and produce an excellent application will contribute greatly to success. First grants are typically small, and subsequent grants will grow in value as the grantee develops a track record of success. That record may not necessarily be with the same organization; success in previous grants with other organizations will also help.

Even when the project involves **in-kind contributions**, such as university student projects or research projects, a past history of successful interaction builds credibility. Success with simple projects will often lead to invitations to participate in projects that are more far-reaching and elaborate. The key is to build a positive relationship between the community and the institution, and the best means of accomplishing this is to ensure that every time an interaction of this type occurs, it benefits both parties. Reputation is important to academic institutions as well, so the public acknowledgment of their contributions to community preparedness projects is extremely important.

Service Organizations

In many communities, service organizations are an integral part of community life. They are commonly referred to in emergency management as **non-governmental organizations (NGOs)**. Some, such as the Red Cross, have a specific interest in disaster response; others, such as the Lions and Kiwanis clubs, focus on fellowship and on community improvement; while still others, such as the Salvation Army and Seventh-Day Adventists, are faith-based groups. Regardless of their primary motivation, these organizations actively work to make life better in the communities that they serve. As such, they represent an invaluable resource to emergency managers. The service organizations that are part of a community vary, so emergency managers will need to find out which service organizations operate in their community.

Service organizations can help provide community preparedness activities. They can participate in public education efforts, provide specific disaster services, or, perhaps, fundraise for the acquisition of community resources. Members of service organizations already possess a strong desire to serve the community, and with the appropriate information, can often become the allies of emergency managers. However, before any of these activities can occur, emergency managers must inform service organizations on the issues at stake. Using their public education skills, emergency managers must undertake a certain degree of consciousness raising, which can be achieved through public-speaking engagements with the organizations in question. The good news is that service organizations are almost always looking for good public speakers. Once they are made aware of the community's emergency preparedness issues, service organizations may become enthusiastic participants in the community's preparedness process.

As already mentioned, service organizations can provide added value to community emergency preparedness programs in three areas: through public education, the provision of specific disaster services, and fundraising for the acquisition of community resources. What a specific organization can do for preparedness programs depends on the size of the organization and the commitment of its members. Each of these areas is explored next.

Public Education

Service organizations can raise public awareness of emergency preparedness issues. This activity may involve public-speaking engagements or the distribution of educational materials by the organization's volunteers, and, in some cases, perhaps even the donation of funding to produce such materials. An organization's members can help with folding brochures, stuffing envelopes, and distributing educational materials at its events or door to door in the community. Many service organizations hold regular community events, such as fairs and carnivals, which can provide a suitable venue for an emergency manager's public education efforts. An organization's members are often viewed by most of the community as leaders, and therefore their influence on the preparedness level of the community can be significant.

Provision of Disaster Services

Service organizations can also provide specific services to the community during a disaster. The Red Cross is a good example; internationally, the Red Cross is one of the best and most experienced organizations at registration and inquiry. Other groups have already accepted specific disaster roles on a national or international level, including Seventh-Day Adventists, who can manage the warehousing and distribution of donated goods, and the Mennonites, who can provide skilled construction teams. Even when a local chapter of such an organization has not yet trained for such a role, with some encouragement from the emergency manager it may develop and undertake the required training.

Other service organizations, without a clear disaster response mandate, often possess other types of resources and skills that they use regularly for community fundraising for other projects. Consider the skill of the local Lions Club at organizing a community barbecue or pancake breakfast and how that might be developed into the provision of mass-feeding operations for both victims and rescue workers. Enlisting the participation of voluntary and service organizations is often a question of considering what might be possible, and asking the right people for help. Emergency managers may find that a service organization has never been approached before.

Service organizations can provide an entirely new dimension to the preparedness of the local community. The cost of their participation in emergency preparedness activities to the community tax base is minimal or non-existent. Many service organizations require minimal donations, and some will either self-fund or do their own community fundraising, and in doing so provide added value for their organization in the community.

Fundraising and Acquisition of Community Resources

Service organizations can help emergency preparedness through fundraising and the acquisition of community resources. This expectation might seem extreme for a service organization, but it is not. Local service organizations have managed to build parks, community centres, and libraries in many communities. They have also performed fundraising to purchase community resources such as new fire trucks, wheelchair vans, and ambulances. In many cases, service organizations are extremely good at such fundraising activities and are motivated to improve the quality of life in the community. In some cases, such organizations can even be persuaded to compete to see who can raise the most funds for a needed project. They can often be persuaded to take on such projects, and rarely ask much in return other than that their organization's logo be placed on the donated equipment in a reasonably prominent way.

To achieve a good level of response from the community, service organizations must understand the issues. As well, emergency managers must be specific in what they ask for—an organization's efforts might be wasted. Whatever the emergency manager asks for, it should be viable, reasonable, and achievable. Above all, the time frame associated with acquisition should be reasonable. Service organizations can fundraise effectively, but they rarely have large amounts of money immediately available. Asking an organization to immediately provide an expensive hazardous materials response truck (or for that matter, any other piece of equipment) is generally out of the question, but asking an organization to fundraise a specific amount to acquire such a truck for the community within a year or 18 months might be reasonable.

When service organizations contribute to alternative program funding, emergency managers actually achieve several important objectives. The first of these is cost-effectiveness. Emergency preparedness programs may be able to occur, even when conventional community funding is limited or unavailable. To illustrate, even if a community can afford to produce a preparedness brochure, the presence of volunteers to distribute it might make a significant difference in cost, allowing the program to go forward. The same may be true for other types of program resources as well.

The second objective is raising the community's consciousness regarding emergency preparedness and emergency management in general. A community with greater awareness of emergency matters is often a better-prepared community.

The third objective is raising awareness of and the profile of emergency preparedness and emergency management among key decision-makers. Service organizations are, after all, the constituency of the elected officials. Any issue that attracts the awareness and fundraising activities of community service organizations is clearly important to members of the community, and is more likely to be viewed as important by key decision-makers who have conflicting or competing priorities. In pursuing this course of action, emergency managers demonstrate fiscal responsibility, creativity, and community commitment. As a direct result, they are likely to be seen by key decision-makers as holding a value-added position within the community, which increases emergency managers' subsequent influence.

Public–Private Partnerships

Public–private partnerships are often overlooked as opportunities to develop community preparedness programs. Most communities are host to major employers, including, in some cases, some of the production facilities that may generate community risk in the first place. Many such companies are acutely aware of public perception of the risks posed by their operations, and most wish to be seen as good corporate citizens within the community. This is particularly true in smaller communities, where such companies tend to be conspicuous. In larger communities, such interactions regarding emergency and preparedness activities, and on public education, will often occur through industry organizations. Whether such businesses operate individually or collectively, the potential exists for an emergency management "partnership" between the industries in the private sector, and the public sector's emergency manager. When properly identified and developed by the emergency manager, such programs may provide the emergency manager and the community with information, risk-specific expertise, physical resources, or even program and project funding.

Developing Relationships

Dialogue and interaction with major employers will almost certainly occur as a regular part of an emergency manager's activities. For example, emergency managers must understand their business operations as a part of the community's HIRA process. Positive interaction between emergency managers and companies can help build a positive business relationship; once major employers understand that their operations are being scrutinized for legitimate planning purposes and not for a "witch hunt," it is likely that many doors will open, and that opportunities for public–private cooperation will present themselves. Emergency managers should bear in mind that companies may be somewhat sensitive initially; it is not uncommon for companies to have previous experience with special interest groups, such as ratepayers or environmental groups, who may have challenged their right to operate within the community.

Emergency managers must make it clear that they are involved in a legitimate community planning process, not a special interest group, and that the company is being viewed in the same light as any other community business—as a valued part of the community with a role to play in it. It may be most effective for emergency managers to establish contact with a company representative through the assistance of the community's economic development officer (who probably already possesses a positive and ongoing relationship with companies in the community). Once an emergency manager becomes known in the business life of the community, the use of intermediaries is unlikely to be required.

An emergency manager's previously positive interactions with major employers will serve as their own introduction; the key players in these companies often discuss such matters among themselves. Emergency managers should seek to develop a positive reputation in the business community. Once this foundation has been laid, they can work to enhance the relationship from one of simple contact, exchange of information, and consensus to one of true collaboration between the company and the community. The goal of emergency managers is to encourage such companies to become legitimate partners in the community preparedness process.

Some industries have a more established relationship with emergency managers and the community than others. In Canada, for example, the Community Awareness Emergency Response (CAER)[7] program partners the local chemical and petroleum industries with both emergency managers and first-responder agencies to enhance community preparedness for emergencies involving the manufacture or transportation of potentially hazardous materials.

CAER groups, which typically operate at a local community level, conduct joint planning, joint exercises, and community education efforts. In many cases, the funding for such endeavours comes from the industrial partners, and there have even been cases in which industrial partners have directly funded the acquisition of response resources, such as decontamination equipment, for local communities. CAER groups have funded community exercises and provided expertise resources to the community's emergency preparedness process without the costs normally associated with the use of expert consultants. This program is highly effective and highly regarded in the communities where it operates. Emergency managers should study the CAER program closely, as the potential for the use of a similar program exists within other industries.

Corporate Motivation

Some companies simply wish to be good corporate citizens, or are motivated to enhance the quality of life in a community in order to attract skilled workers. Such companies regularly make donations or fund programs for hospitals and other community services. There are countless examples in which a large local employer has substantially funded the construction of a new hospital wing, or even purchased and donated emergency response resources for the community in which they operate. In addition, some large companies operate their own foundations, which are specifically tasked with the provision of services to the community. A good public image is good business, and prudent emergency managers will be constantly alert to such potential program-funding opportunities.

Canadian Tire Corporation provides a spectacular illustration of this idea. Canadian Tire is one of the largest hardware and automotive retail organizations in Canada, with more than 1,000 stores and gas bars across Canada. This company operates Foundation for Families, which in turn operates a Regional Disaster Recovery Program.[8] This program focuses on larger-scale disasters, and support includes use of the company's transportation network for the large-scale movement of disaster supplies, and the coordination of the collection of monetary donations for disaster relief at their stores and outlets. While the focus of this program is Canada, its activities during the 2004 Indian Ocean Tsunami included a sizable disaster relief donation, and the shipment of more than 1,500 urgently needed first-aid kits to the affected area.

Exchange of Resources and Services

Another area for positive interaction between a community's businesses and emergency managers is the exchange of resources and services. Prudent businesses and industries require their own contingency plans, and also appropriate training for their staff. Emergency managers may be able to trade services (such as emergency management lectures, the review of contingency plans, and first-aid instruction) for the services or resources of a company. To illustrate, an emergency manager might agree to conduct a detailed review of a company's business continuity plan and provide recommendations in exchange for the company's agreement to permit the use of some of that company's surplus warehouse space to store community disaster response supplies. Both parties, the community and the business, obtain something they need, without any impact on their budgets.

Public–private partnerships can provide a range of resources that might not otherwise be affordable to emergency managers. The involvement of industrial and business interests in the life of the communities in which they operate provides benefits to both groups. Communities benefit by having more robust emergency arrangements and access to resources that might not have been available otherwise. Industrial and business interests benefit by being able to function in a stronger and more resilient community and by receiving substantial positive public recognition for their participation in preparedness activities. Wise emergency managers recognize that such partnerships ensure that companies participate more fully in the life of the community, and that the community is better prepared for an emergency as a result.

Conclusion

The funding of emergency management and preparedness programs is both complex and challenging. Communities must cope with both limited resources and competing priorities when funding such programs. While an emergency manager's initial program and position funding will probably come from the community tax base, they may be challenged to obtain the funds to fully cover other special programs and projects, as well as capital costs. Emergency managers must meet this challenge with knowledge and creativity. They must identify and understand alternative sources of funding and must function, to some extent, as an emergency preparedness ambassador and fundraiser on behalf of the community.

This reality, while inconvenient and challenging, is not necessarily negative. In the process of finding alternative sources of funding for the community's preparedness programs, emergency managers will develop a broad range of relationships across the community. The potential exists for corporate entities, such as business and industry, and also service organizations, academic institutions, and even individual philanthropists to become more aware of the community's emergency preparedness issues and to participate directly in their resolution. This process not only provides much-needed funding, but also builds partnerships with key organizations and individuals across the community. In this manner, emergency management as a whole, and emergency preparedness in particular, moves from the efforts of a single emergency manager to increased community consensus and then to a realm of community collaboration in the preparedness process. A community that truly collaborates on emergency preparedness issues will ultimately be better prepared for and, therefore, more resilient to any emergency that might occur.

KEY TERMS

capital budget

grant

in-kind contribution

non-governmental organizations (NGOs)

operating budget

special appropriation

LEARNING CHECK

Take a few minutes now to test your knowledge of emergency management funding. Select the best answer in each case. Any score of less than 16 out of 20 (80 percent) indicates that you should re-read this chapter.

1. While emergency management programs are important, they are subject to the same budgetary and funding processes as
   a. senior levels of government
   b. other community services
   c. local service groups
   d. private enterprise

2. Approval and funding for emergency management programs and activities normally compete with
   a. other community priorities
   b. the priorities of individual elected officials
   c. the priorities of other municipal services
   d. mandates from senior levels of government

3. Even in the presence of a legal mandate from a senior level of government, communities are often challenged to find
   a. sufficient funding for emergency management programs
   b. sufficient funding for infrastructure projects
   c. political support for emergency management
   d. qualified personnel for emergency management

4. Programs intended to enhance the emergency management and preparedness processes may often operate under the banner of
   a. regional government
   b. federal government
   c. economic welfare
   d. another municipal department

5. Emergency managers may be able to provide added value for their position in the community if they are able to successfully exploit
   a. the resources of other communities
   b. political situations in the community
   c. media reporting on the subject
   d. alternative sources of program funding

6. Effective emergency managers may be able to exploit alternative sources of program funding, such as grants and public–private partnerships, to
   a. enhance the image of the funding organization
   b. keep program costs under control
   c. construct a new EOC
   d. build the community's image in the business sector

7. Funding for the construction of a new fire station for the community would typically be a part of the community's
   a. capital budget
   b. operating budget
   c. funding allotment from senior government
   d. grantsmanship process

8. Funding to provide a community-wide, full-scale emergency exercise would typically be a part of the community's
   a. capital budget
   b. operating budget
   c. funding allotment from senior government
   d. grantsmanship process

9. Transfer payments from the federal government aimed at permitting the community to operate specific programs would typically be a part of the community's
   a. capital budget
   b. operating budget
   c. funding allotment from senior government
   d. grantsmanship process

10. Funding obtained from a private foundation for a community preparedness education program would typically be the result of the community's
    a. capital budget
    b. operating budget
    c. funding allotment from senior government
    d. grantsmanship process

11. While local service organizations may not have the financial resources to directly fund emergency preparedness programs, they may be able to provide in-kind contributions through
    a. agreeing to accept specific roles during an emergency
    b. providing volunteers to assist with preparedness activities
    c. fundraising to purchase specific resources
    d. all of the above

12. Public–private partnerships in emergency preparedness may be possible when they
    a. receive sufficient public support
    b. are subject to media pressure
    c. benefit all involved parties
    d. are mandated by government

13. The involvement of private enterprise, such as manufacturers, in the community's preparedness programs is often motivated by a desire for
    a. service to the community
    b. compliance with local laws
    c. a positive public image
    d. both (a) and (b)

14. Colleges and universities will often participate in programs to improve community preparedness when those programs
    a. generate local funding
    b. provide learning experiences for students
    c. are specified in the institution's charter
    d. reduce taxes

15. Special appropriations for emergency management programs will normally originate
    a. outside of the normal budget process
    b. with other levels of government
    c. from public donations
    d. from colleges and universities

16. In a normal municipal budget process, costs are monitored closely. Cost overruns or underspending are typically reported as
    a. exceptions
    b. special cases
    c. deviations
    d. variances

17. To be successful in obtaining grant funding from private organizations, emergency managers must first understand
    a. the internal politics of the organization
    b. the funding priorities of the organization
    c. the specific rules for grant applications
    d. both (b) and (c)

18. Prior to presentation to the local elected council for approval, emergency management budgets are normally subject to both internal review and
    a. public consultation
    b. committee approval
    c. auditing
    d. approval from senior levels of government

19. The receptiveness of service organizations and local businesses to participate in the community's emergency preparedness process will often be generated by the _____ of the emergency manager.
    a. credibility
    b. reputation
    c. authority
    d. both (a) and (b)

20. The intent of a truly good local emergency preparedness program is not only to prepare the community for emergencies, but also to stimulate the development of
    a. media interest
    b. a culture of preparedness
    c. funding from senior levels of government
    d. both (a) and (c)

CASE STUDIES

A. You are the emergency manager in a medium-sized community. As the result of a great deal of work and negotiation by the business and development officer and the chamber of commerce, a new chemical plant has been attracted to the community. Most members of the community are pleased, because the new plant will provide much-needed additional employment for community members and additional tax revenue for the municipality. As the emergency manager, you are aware that the average member of the community has never been exposed to this new risk, and will require specific education on emergency procedures. In addition, the community's fire department has never been trained or equipped to deal with the specific hazards that will be generated by this new community employer.

   1. Describe the type of public education program that will be required for individual members of the community. What form will it take? What is it likely to cost?
   2. Describe the equipment and training that is likely to be required by the local fire department. Where would you find information on training requirements? What is the required training and equipment likely to cost?
   3. Prepare a brief for council, outlining the programs and funding required. Describe the process for obtaining council approval and budget allocations for the project.
   4. Describe the various strategies that might be available to fund these programs, if funding from the community tax base were not available.

B. You are the emergency manager for a relatively small community. Your emergency plan has just been approved by council. In that plan, you have specified the use of the community's recreation centre as an emergency evacuation centre in the event of an emergency. You have reviewed community demographics, and have concluded that such a centre must be able to provide emergency shelter accommodations for approximately 150 residents, and a mass-feeding operation for at least twice that number. When you approached council to fund the acquisition of the resources required to make this plan a reality, you were told that no funding was immediately available, and that, given current fiscal projections, it was unlikely that funds could be made available for the next three years for this project.

   1. Describe the amount and type of physical resources that would be required to support the emergency evacuation centre.

2. Describe the amount and type of physical resources that would be required to support the mass-feeding centre.

3. Describe any grant-funding processes that might be available to the community to pay for these operations. Begin with preparedness grant programs from other levels of government, but also consider the potential for grants from private organizations or foundations.

4. Describe a process by which the community's major businesses, employers, and service organizations might be persuaded to support these projects, making community funding unnecessary.

TO LEARN MORE

1. Pick a local community and talk to its emergency manager. Find out which service organizations operate in that area, and whether or not they play a designated role in community emergency response. Consider what roles might be filled by those organizations that do not currently participate, and what efforts might be needed to persuade them to accept those roles.

2. Find out whether or not a federal government grant program for emergency preparedness activities exists in your jurisdiction, and take the time to learn its requirements and how the grant-application process works.

NOTES

1. Ray H. Garrison, *Managerial Accounting*, 3rd ed. (Plano, TX: Business Publications, 1982), p. 291.

2. "Zero-Based Budgeting," *Wikipedia*, <http://en.wikipedia.org/wiki/Zero_Based_Budgeting>.

3. Richard Brealey and Stewart Myers, *Principles of Corporate Finance*, 2nd ed. (New York: McGraw-Hill, 1983).

4. Government of Canada website, <http://www.publicsafety.gc.ca/prg/em/jepp/index-eng.aspx>.

5. Jacob Kraicer, *The Art of Grantsmanship*, <http://www.utoronto.ca/cip/sa_ArtGt.pdf>.

6. Susan L. Golden, *Secrets of Successful Grantsmanship: A Guerilla Guide to Raising Money* (New York: Jossey-Bass, 1997).

7. CAER website, <http://www.caer.ca>.

8. Canadian Tire Corporation Foundation for Families website, <http://www2.canadiantire.ca/CTenglish/foundation.html>.

Conclusion

Prepared communities are resilient communities, and the creation of a preparedness process is the most important task of emergency managers. Only communities that are fully prepared for the worst will be sufficiently resilient to absorb and address the issues and impacts of a disaster, and to quickly return to normal operations and their residents to normal life. Preparedness does not simply involve projects conducted at the community level. Real preparedness is an ongoing process of continual assessment, identification of issues, mitigation of those issues, planning for the events that cannot be mitigated against, and reassessment. The process is one of continual refinement and improvement, of learning lessons and improving performance in a never-ending cycle. This work never really stops.

Emergency managers must conduct these processes in an environment of limited resources and competing priorities; as a result, the task is rarely easy. Effective emergency managers require subject knowledge; local knowledge; and teaching, research, and writing skills. They also require well-developed people skills, political savvy, and creativity. Emergency managers will work constantly to identify needs and opportunities, to influence political processes, and to find the means with which to make the preparedness process a functioning reality. There have been cases where emergency managers have created an effective community preparedness project with no more public funding than their own salary, managing to work with and develop voluntary and financial support for needed programs and processes from service organizations, granting agencies, businesses, and even individuals, and to broker these contributions into an emergency management program.

Effective emergency managers rarely have complete authority over the community's preparedness process. They will need to work constantly with elected officials, emergency services, senior municipal staff, and community leaders to influence change. However, when they are skillful, emergency managers will develop and build both consensus and collaboration for preparedness within a community. Emergency managers will influence key decision-makers and other community leaders, will become the community's local authority on preparedness, and in doing all of these things, will lead the community to true preparedness. A prepared community will be better able to protect both its residents and public infrastructure and business interests. Ultimately, the protection of people, their activities, and their communities is really what emergency management is all about.

Glossary

After action report: A formal document prepared at the conclusion of an emergency event, in which the community's or organization's response to the event is described in detail, problems and issues arising from response are identified, and recommendations to improve response and preparedness are made.

All-hazards approach: An approach to emergency planning that attempts to create an emergency response that is sufficiently generic to be applied to all emergencies, but sufficiently adaptable and flexible to be able to respond to the specific needs of various emergency types.

Annex: A component of an emergency plan that is not necessarily intended for public distribution. Such documents are typically case-specific or functional sub-plans that are subordinate to the main body of a more generic emergency plan. An example of a case-specific annex is a sub-plan for a community to deal with the derailment of a train carrying hazardous materials. An example of a functional annex is the specific instructions for the assembly and activation of the Emergency Operations Centre.

Appendix: A component of an emergency plan that is not intended for public distribution with the main body of the plan. It usually includes lists of 24-hour contact information for elected officials, key staff members, and suppliers. It may also include "back channel" telephone numbers (numbers that are unpublished and not routed through the main telephone system) for other agencies, communities, or levels of government.

Black Death: A term commonly applied to the outbreaks of plague (*yersinia pestis*) that occurred in Europe during the Middle Ages and the Renaissance.

Bloom's taxonomy: A leading educational theory that addresses the manner in which people achieve different types of learning at different points in their lives.

Bronze Age: A time reference used in the study of human cultures and other areas of science. It is generally regarded as the period from 4500 BC to about 1200 BC.

Bylaws: Statutes enacted by the local level of government that regulate many aspects of how the local community will operate. Such laws are only applicable in the local community in which they have been passed, and are generally subordinate to legislation enacted by the regional or federal levels of government.

Capital budget: That portion of a budget allocated for the acquisition or construction of new permanent or long-term facilities, such as buildings, equipment, or vehicles.

Case study exercise: A type of emergency exercise, usually consisting of the review of an emergency event that has actually occurred, followed by facilitated round-table discussion. It is used most commonly for the identification of potential issues affecting emergency response.

Casualties: Living but injured individuals who have experienced the effects of a hazard event.

Census: A periodic collection of data related to community composition and demographics. Usually conducted by a national government.

Census tract: A small, relatively permanent statistical subdivision in a community.

Chief controller: Sometimes called "chief umpire." The individual in charge of the exercise control group. This individual is charged with the management of the exercise script and the coordination and direction of all subordinate exercise controllers to ensure that the exercise flows smoothly and meets its intended objectives.

Civil defence: The precursor of modern emergency management. This was a function of government whose primary focus was the protection of the civilian population from the effects of enemy attack in times of war, instead of protection against the physical effects of natural or technological disasters.

Commodities: Items produced by a community as its means of wealth generation for residents. These may include both raw materials and finished products, and, more recently, services and information.

Community Emergency Response Team (CERT): A voluntary organization operating in some communities, tasked with supplementing the community's emergency response resources during major emergencies.

Control cell: A location near the emergency exercise site, staffed by exercise controllers, responsible for providing inputs in the form of radio transmissions, telephone calls, faxes, or emails to make the exercise experience as real as possible for participants.

Critical infrastructure: Those physical elements in the composition of a community without which continued operation of the community would be difficult or impossible.

Critical path: A project management tool. All essential steps for the completion of a project are listed in the critical path, along with the time to complete each, and any dependencies between the various steps. The longest path of planned activities needed to end the project is then calculated and plotted temporally. Each essential step is then plotted both temporally and in sequence of dependency, starting at the earliest possible time at which it will be complete by the end of the project timeline, without making the project longer. This tool allows project managers to manage the timely performance of and problem-solve each discrete step of the project process to ensure the timely completion of the project.

Decision matrix: A logic-based decision-making tool that allows users to consider several variables to determine whether a particular course of action is required. For example, this tool could be used by junior staff to determine whether to notify key decision-makers when an incident occurs outside of normal business hours.

Declaration of emergency: A formal process by which a given level of government indicates to a senior government in the hierarchy that the community has exceeded its local resource base and requires assistance to respond to an emergency. The precise process for making the declaration varies from one jurisdiction to another.

Demographics: The study of various aspects of human populations, such as birth and death rates, age, socio-economic status, residency, and mobility, which is useful in helping to determine community composition, relative vulnerability, and disaster resource requirements.

Disaster: An event that has actually occurred and that has negative impacts for a community or an organization. This term may be used interchangeably with the terms *crisis, emergency,* and *hazard event.*

Discoverability: A component of the root cause analysis process in which hypotheses are subjected to repeated questioning and challenging to determine their validity as a root cause.

Due diligence: A legal concept. To satisfy due diligence in the emergency management context, a community or individual must be able to demonstrate that they have taken every reasonable measure within their power to identify, mitigate against, and prepare for a given type of event.

Emergency: An event that has actually occurred and that has negative impacts for a community or an organization. This term may be used interchangeably with the terms *disaster*, *crisis*, and *hazard event*.

Emergency Medical Services (EMS): Ambulances and paramedics.

Emergency Operations Centre (EOC): The designated location within a community or an organization where key decision-makers will meet to support the response to an emergency, and to guide the community or organization until the end of an emergency.

EOC support staff: A group of staff members providing such services as clerical support, security, information technology, and telecommunications support to the Emergency Operations Centre and those working within it, usually under the control of an emergency manager.

Evacuation: The physical removal and relocation or all or part of a community's population to reduce their vulnerability to a hazard event.

Exercise: The controlled simulation of an emergency event for the purposes of testing emergency plans and procedures, identifying related issues, and training staff.

Exercise controller: One of a group of individuals working under the direction of the chief controller to provide emergency exercise inputs and to ensure that the exercise flows correctly and learning outcomes are achieved.

Federal: A country's national level of government (for our purposes, regardless of how that government is constituted). It focuses on national and international issues, and on coordination at a national level.

Federal Emergency Management Agency (FEMA): An agency within the US government, part of the Department of Homeland Security, tasked with the development of emergency preparedness at the federal, state, and local levels through the development of policy, federal legislation, and training programs. This agency is also tasked with spearheading the US federal government response to local emergencies through the provision of federal response resources and funding that occur as a result of Presidential Disaster Declarations.

Filler input: An element of discrete information used in emergency exercises to provide logical background information, contribute to the realism of the exercise, or help facilitate exercise flow.

Frequency: The incidence of the occurrence of a given type of hazard event.

Full-scale exercise: A type of emergency exercise in which actual response resources and staff are deployed in a physical simulation of a real emergency event to provide as broad and comprehensive testing as possible of community emergency response arrangements.

Functional exercise: A type of emergency exercise that is usually a smaller, scaled-down version of a full-scale exercise, in which one or more discrete elements of the community's overall emergency response are tested and evaluated.

Gantt chart: A project management tool. A bar chart that describes a project schedule. The major elements of the project are included in this chart, along with the anticipated completion time. In some applications, the dependencies among project elements are also identified. It is often used in conjunction with the critical path model of project management.

Grant: A monetary gift, usually provided by a government, a private foundation, or a business organization. Such gifts are used to fund research, equipment acquisition, and special programs and projects.

Hazard: An event that has a potentially negative impact on a community or an organization.

Hazard event: An event that has actually occurred and that has negative impacts for a community or an organization. This term may be used interchangeably with the terms *disaster, emergency*, and *crisis*.

Hazard Identification and Risk Assessment (HIRA): A process that allows emergency managers to differentiate meaningfully and effectively between the risks posed by very disparate types of events. It also allows them to rank and prioritize risks to address each appropriately, in order of severity.

Hazard profile: A formal research document prepared by an emergency manager that provides a detailed description of each type of hazard event, its rate of occurrence, its likely impact in the community, the resources required to manage the event, and potential opportunities for mitigation.

Heavy Urban Search and Rescue (HUSAR): A trained interdisciplinary team consisting of police officers, firefighters, paramedics, heavy equipment operators, and structural engineers tasked with the rescue of individuals from collapsed buildings and structures.

"Hot-wash" debriefing: A method used for the debriefing of emergency exercise participants immediately following an exercise, while they are still feeling the effects of stress from the exercise.

Improvised input: An element of information that is not included in the original exercise script. During an exercise, a controller or controllers will create an unforeseen activity for exercise participants to respond to that will keep them on track to the successful completion of the exercise.

Incident Management System (IMS): A command-and-control model used by many communities to respond to, analyze information on, and coordinate response resources for major emergencies.

Incident manager: A key role in the Incident Management System, this role is also sometimes referred to as "incident commander." This person is in overall charge of the community's management of the emergency incident site.

In-kind contribution: The provision of an emergency resource or service provided without cost to the community, usually from a voluntary service group or business organization. The provision of such a service may be used to reduce community costs associated with preparedness programs.

Input: A discrete element of information provided to emergency exercise participants that is intended to elicit a particular response, conclusion, or learning outcome. Inputs may include the introduction of elements of information in a communicated form, changes in the physical environment, or even the addition of individual "victims."

International Association of Emergency Managers (IAEM): A US-based professional group that operates around the world. It acts as an information clearinghouse and point of professional certification for those tasked with the practice of emergency management.

Iron Age: A time reference used in the study of human cultures and other areas of science. Generally regarded as the period after 1200 BC.

Laws: The rules of conduct by which a given society agrees to operate.

Lessons learned: A concept in which the issues generated by a given event, either real or simulated, are shared so that they can be resolved and not occur in subsequent real emergencies or simulations.

Local authority: A community-level tier of government. Local authority, as the name suggests, is focused on both the governance of a single, local community and local issues. An elected city or town council would be an example of this.

Logic Tree: A method of diagramming or charting the root cause analysis process and the resulting information.

Magnitude: The degree to which the adverse effects of a given type of hazard event would be experienced by a community or an organization, or some subset of either, were that event to occur. Usually expressed in terms of a worst-case scenario.

Mitigation: Measures taken to reduce the likelihood of occurrence for a given type of risk event, or of reducing its effects, if it were to occur.

Municipal Control Group (MCG): A body of key decision-makers, usually headed by the mayor or elected head of local council, that is tasked with the guidance of the community throughout a major emergency and the provision of support to the incident manager. The members of this group usually include the chief administrative officer, the department heads of emergency services, and the heads of any other municipal organization with a key role to play in disaster response. It is usually located in the Emergency Operations Centre.

Municipal Support Group (MSG): A body of secondary decision-makers and support staff, usually headed by the deputy mayor or someone in a similar position, that is tasked with the provision of information gathering, communications, expertise, or secondary resources in support of the Municipal Control Group. This group may consist of other senior officers from emergency services, the heads of departments with a less direct role to play in disaster response, public utilities, and, in some cases, volunteer agencies. It is usually located somewhere near, but not in, the Emergency Operations Centre.

"Murphy" input: A type of exercise input that is not aimed at the satisfaction of a particular objective, but which may be provided at the discretion of the chief controller to slow the play of participants who are proceeding through an exercise too quickly to achieve all learning outcomes.

Neolithic period: A time reference used in the study of human cultures and other areas of science. It is generally regarded as the period before 4500 BC, and is sometimes called the *Stone Age*.

Non-governmental organization (NGO): A group or agency that plays a voluntary role in the community's response to disasters. Some of these organizations might have specific roles as a national mandate, while others will be local service, fraternal, or faith-based organizations that have agreed to play a role in community response. Examples of such organizations include the Red Cross, the Lions Club, and the Salvation Army.

Observer: One who participates in an emergency exercise, not through the provision of inputs or exercise play, but by observing and critiquing responses, events, and procedures as part of the data-collection process.

Operating budget: That portion of a budget allocated for variable operating expenses, such as staff salaries, fuel, and expendable items.

PERT chart: Project Evaluation and Review Technique chart. A project management tool related to the critical path model of project management.

Planned communities: A process that began in Europe at the start of the 20th century, but gained momentum in North America during the second half of the 20th century. In planned communities, some land is designated for specific uses, such as residential, commercial, or industrial, and other land is set aside for services such as schools, parkland, and transportation corridors. Formal plans and timelines for land use are generated in advance, and development is only permitted in designated areas and at designated times. The intent is to improve both the environment of the community and the quality of life of residents. Such plans usually involve a fairly extensive public consultation process.

Preparedness: Those activities performed in a community to prepare it for the occurrence of a hazard event, and to ensure that the response to that event will be effective.

Primary input: A discrete element of information provided to emergency exercise participants to help achieve one of the exercise's stated objectives.

Provincial: Refers to a level of regional Canadian government that exists between the federal and local authority levels. Governments at this level have their own elected legislature, the authority to enact laws for their region, and a specific mandate for areas of responsibility.

Quantitative: A measurement dealing with the volume or amount of a given item (for example, quantitative plotting, as in graphs or charts).

Ranking exercise: The process of arranging a series of different types of hazard events by quantity, in terms of frequency, magnitude, or overall risk exposure.

Recovery: Those activities performed in a community or organization following the occurrence of a hazard event that are directed at restoring normal or near-normal operations.

Redundancy: The provision of backups for any critical system, resource, or procedure to ensure that even in the event of a primary system failure for any reason, operation of the system or

procedure can continue. In the case of technological systems, each system should possess a backup that is technologically independent of the primary system.

Regulations: Specific instructions regarding what constitutes compliance with a particular law.

Repatriation: The formal process by which the victims of a disaster and other evacuees are returned to their community following the resolution of a disaster event. It is a part of the recovery process.

Resiliency: The ability of a community or organization to absorb the effects of a hazard event, and return to normal or near-normal operations. It is usually treated as a paired concept with vulnerability.

Resilient: See *resiliency*.

Response: Those activities performed in a community or organization to address a hazard event while it is occurring.

Risk: A community's or organization's degree of exposure to a given hazard event. It is usually expressed as the product of frequency × magnitude.

Risk acceptance: A risk management option in which the community or organization is aware of the risk exposure, but makes a conscious decision to proceed with the high-risk activity.

Risk avoidance: A risk management option in which the community or organization makes a conscious choice to discontinue or not participate in an activity that is known to generate risk.

Risk based: An approach to emergency planning in which risks to the community or organization are identified and planning primarily focuses on those events most likely to occur and with the greatest impact; other events are addressed in order of decreasing frequency and magnitude.

Risk mitigation: See *mitigation*.

Risk score: A numeric value assigned to a given event, expressed in terms of the value assigned for frequency of occurrence × the value assigned to event magnitude. These values are used to rank various risks and set priorities for other emergency management activities.

Risk tolerance: Similar to risk acceptance. The community is aware of the existence of a given risk, but has grown to accept it, usually due to economic necessity.

Risk transference: A risk management option in which the community or organization is aware of the risk exposure, but makes a decision to transfer that exposure either through the relocation of the high-risk activity or the acquisition of insurance coverage.

Root cause analysis: A logic-based method of examining various types of disaster events to be able to diagnose the underlying root causes of vulnerability to the event, and to identify opportunities for mitigation.

Secondary input: A discrete element of information provided to the participants of an emergency exercise to help achieve the objective of another stakeholder group participating in the exercise or the unstated objective of an emergency manager.

Sheltering-in-place: Choosing to leave a group of people, usually the residents of a hospital or some other type of building, in a sealed environment where they will be relatively safe from the effects of a hazard event. This is an alternative to evacuation, and usually occurs primarily when evacuation would present greater risk exposure.

Situation report (sitrep): A formal document used by the Municipal Control Group (MCG) to record and report progress in the management of the emergency. Generally completed by an emergency manager and signed by the head of the MCG, this document is used to provide information to other agencies, communities, and levels of government.

Social consequence: A concept that attempts to evaluate both the community's perception of risk exposure and the political will to address that risk exposure. In this model the greater the public's perception of risk and desire to address the problem, the lower the risk exposure is likely to be.

Social distancing: A public health practice consisting of limiting or eliminating gatherings of large groups of people in order to prevent the spread of disease. This is possibly the oldest public health practice, dating from a period when the actual methods of transmitting diseases were not understood.

Socio-economic status: The relative level of wealth or purchasing power of an individual or family within a society, generally expressed in census data as "combined family income."

Spatial: The physical distribution of an item within a given space (for example, spatial plotting such as mapping of the geographical distribution of risk exposures within a community).

Special appropriation: A sum of money allocated outside the normal budgeting process. As with all municipal funding, it must be approved by elected officials. It may be used as one-time funding to acquire resources or to fund the start-up costs of new programs. Ongoing costs are generally subject to regular budget approval processes.

Standards: Describe best practices or expected minimum performance, and provide the basis on which a product or a service may be judged. They have no legal force.

State Emergency Services (SES): A voluntary organization operating in Australian communities that is tasked with supplementing the community's emergency response resources during major emergencies, and providing support services to mainstream emergency response resources during normal emergencies.

Supply chain: The mechanisms and distribution systems that provide critical resources to both communities and organizations on a day-to-day basis, and also during an emergency.

Surge: An increase in demand for services, usually following the occurrence of a hazard event.

Tabletop exercise: A type of emergency exercise in which participants gather around a map, floor plan, three-dimensional model, or some other visual reference source. It contains elements of both case study and full-scale exercises; participants consider response issues and physical aspects of the disaster scene, practise deployment of resources, and conduct experimental problem-solving in a safe environment, without the resource demands of a full-scale exercise.

Tactical Exercise Without Troops (TEWOT): A type of emergency exercise in which key decision-makers, operating with or without a scenario, conduct a "walk through" of the community or other site to determine the advance placement of response resources and the logistical supports that those resources will require.

Technological independence: A principle of emergency management in which any element of technology used in emergency response must have a backup system that does not use the same technology as the primary system. Used to provide a functional option in case the primary system fails.

Temporal: The time component of an event (for example, temporal plotting involves diagramming the chronological component of inconsistent risk exposures using charts or graphs).

Variance: Exception reporting as a part of a budget process. Usually the result of overruns or underspending.

Victims: Uninjured individuals who have been exposed to, displaced by, or suffered some form of loss as the result of the effects of a hazard event.

Vulnerability: The susceptibility to the adverse effects of a given event, should it occur. This term may be applied to communities, organizations, individual elements of community structure, critical infrastructure, the population, or some subset of the population. It is usually treated as a paired concept with resiliency.

Answer Key for Learning Check

Chapter 1

1. b. to protect communities
2. c. change and evolve
3. a. human activity
4. d. both (a) and (c)
5. a. the military
6. b. oral tradition
7. d. elders or shamans
8. c. of divine origin
9. c. war
10. a. the fall of the Roman Empire
11. a. civil defence
12. d. nuclear attack
13. c. federal training programs
14. c. social sciences
15. c. those from the traditional emergency services and emergency medical services
16. d. certificate programs
17. b. certified emergency manager
18. a. every five years
19. b. sophisticated generalists
20. d. business continuity planning

Chapter 2

1. a. duty
2. d. the individual
3. b. response activities
4. c. scale
5. c. local authority
6. a. facilitation
7. c. provide centralized decision making on administrative matters
8. a. democracy
9. a. regional
10. d. directive
11. b. fails to provide a clear mandate
12. a. program enhancement funding
13. c. assisting with actual response costs for actual emergencies
14. b. issue a formal declaration of emergency
15. b. no longer has the ability to cope
16. c. the regional government
17. c. the training of emergency managers
18. a. the provision of funding to enhance emergency management programs
19. d. both (b) and (c)
20. d. both (a) and (b)

Chapter 3

1. c. provide opportunities to generate wealth
2. b. community safety issues
3. a. physical location
4. b. generation of wealth
5. d. possible areas of risk exposure
6. d. both (a) and (b)
7. a. external attack
8. d. the Neolithic period
9. c. flax
10. b. access to resources
11. a. surplus resources
12. b. hunters

13. a. access to trade/transportation routes
14. d. both (a) and (b)
15. b. loss of the single source
16. d. both (a) and (b)
17. b. resilient
18. c. improved understanding of risk
19. b. how risk has evolved
20. a. community planning

Chapter 4

1. b. community composition
2. d. both (a) and (c)
3. a. community planning
4. a. at different times in their lives
5. d. two-thirds
6. b. the type and amount of emergency resources required
7. a. 10 percent
8. c. socio-economic status
9. a. access to useful resources
10. c. communication skills
11. d. a census
12. a. census tracts
13. d. every five or ten years
14. c. predict future tax revenue levels
15. a. determine future service requirements
16. c. federal
17. a. municipal-planning departments
18. c. a local university or college
19. d. both (a) and (b)
20. b. risk and vulnerability

Chapter 5

1. c. areas of potential hazard
2. a. areas of human settlement
3. a. the generation of wealth
4. b. risks remain
5. c. reduced risk exposure
6. d. preventing risk exposure from occurring
7. a. economic activity
8. b. resources and defence

9. a. Indus valley
10. c. market towns
11. b. provided mitigation opportunities
12. c. access to resources
13. b. water routes
14. c. large volumes of goods could be moved
15. c. zoning regulations and building permits
16. c. transportation corridors
17. b. move to areas more distant from risk exposure
18. a. the vulnerabilities within delivery systems
19. b. safety and affluence are not mutually exclusive, they should be addressed concurrently
20. d. all stakeholders within the community

Chapter 6

1. b. are essential to community welfare or prosperity
2. a. economic components
3. b. the less likely a single resource is to be critical
4. a. time to critical loss
5. b. interconnected
6. c. the loss of one or more elements of critical infrastructure
7. a. impact on the local community
8. d. both (a) and (b)
9. d. all of the above
10. c. a major employer
11. a. critical
12. a. of their role in the community supply chain
13. d. both (a) and (b)
14. b. proximity to potential hazards
15. d. all of the above
16. d. all of the above
17. d. the generation of wealth
18. d. all of the above
19. c. physically visit the site
20. a. hospitals

Chapter 7

1. d. universal
2. b. acquire response resources
3. b. a hazard
4. a. a risk
5. d. all of the above
6. c. magnitude
7. c. vulnerability
8. b. an all-hazards approach
9. a. the next event may have little in common with the last
10. b. socio-economic
11. d. all of the above
12. a. manufacturing
13. a. the access model
14. c. decreased
15. b. assumptions that may be inaccurate
16. d. all of the above
17. c. the effects on people are inadequately addressed
18. b. ranking
19. c. risk from individual events
20. a. people centred

Chapter 8

1. d. all of the above
2. a. events that generate a surge in demand for services
3. b. events that disrupt supply chains
4. c. events that disrupt normal business operations
5. d. all of the above
6. d. all of the above
7. b. indefinitely
8. d. both (b) and (c)
9. a. enabling demonstration of due diligence
10. c. the emergency plan is based on the best information available
11. a. risk differentiation is poor
12. d. all of the above
13. c. public perception and risk

14. d. frequency × magnitude × social consequence
15. a. identify the need for public education
16. b. damage to reputation
17. a. added together to produce a final score
18. a. trends and patterns can be more easily seen
19. b. resiliency
20. a. transference

Chapter 9

1. b. vulnerability
2. c. resiliency
3. a. community resiliency
4. d. mitigation
5. d. both (a) and (c)
6. b. major local employers
7. a. major transportation corridors
8. b. critical
9. b. elements without which emergency response would degrade
10. d. all of the above
11. d. both (a) and (b)
12. a. industrial engineering
13. b. failure mode analysis
14. c. Logic Tree
15. b. facts only
16. c. discoverability
17. d. both (a) and (b)
18. b. contributing causes
19. d. both (a) and (c)
20. b. reasons for critical infrastructure failure

Chapter 10

1. b. paired
2. c. less vulnerable
3. a. lower response/recovery costs
4. c. 5, 2, 4, 3, 1
5. a. physiological
6. b. access to assets
7. b. access to assets/wealth

8. a. generate wealth
9. c. buffering
10. a. flatness
11. b. omnivory
12. d. redundancy
13. a. high flux
14. d. homeostasis
15. a. people
16. d. both (a) and (b)
17. b. requirements for implementation
18. d. both (a) and (b)
19. c. beyond mandate/control
20. a. community/organizational mitigation plan

Chapter 11

1. d. objectives
2. c. are most likely to occur in the community
3. b. less common
4. a. stakeholder input
5. b. buy-in for the plan
6. a. an ongoing, dynamic process
7. b. terms of reference
8. a. what it is not intended to accomplish
9. c. the practices to be used in the creation of the plan
10. d. tested
11. a. continuous improvement
12. b. a wider range of expertise
13. a. Project-planning skills
14. c. a wide range of perspectives
15. c. creating specialized subcommittees
16. a. conducting orientation and training
17. b. identifies planning implications for the other groups
18. c. may have associated budgetary implications
19. d. provide the resources specified in the plan
20. d. all of the above

Chapter 12

1. c. a good emergency plan
2. d. key components
3. a. satisfy legal requirements
4. c. facilitate plan maintenance
5. a. the information is accessible
6. b. intended for general distribution
7. a. restore normal or near-normal operations
8. d. competence
9. b. the effectiveness of the emergency plan
10. c. satisfy due diligence requirements
11. a. case specific
12. d. both (b) and (c)
13. a. make amendments without republishing the whole document
14. c. place boundaries on where the plan will operate
15. d. the glossary of terms
16. b. governing authority
17. d. both (a) and (b)
18. b. the details of operations
19. a. the roles and responsibilities
20. c. an appendix

Chapter 13

1. b. services
2. c. an effective EOC
3. a. an improvised space
4. d. design
5. b. poor EOC design
6. d. both (a) and (c)
7. b. focus on scene-related issues
8. a. Municipal Control Group
9. b. Municipal Support Group
10. c. EOC support staff
11. a. poor lighting
12. d. noise levels
13. b. convergence
14. d. full-spectrum fluorescent lighting
15. a. choice of flooring materials

16. b. pull system
17. a. push system
18. a. set objectives
19. c. ensure completion
20. c. a situation report

Chapter 14

1. b. hub
2. a. information
3. c. degrade
4. b. possess inherent vulnerability
5. a. a low-technology alternative
6. d. their own knowledge
7. b. multiple layers of redundancy
8. c. technologically independent of the primary system
9. d. telecommunications systems
10. b. 20 percent
11. c. Access Overload Control
12. b. fee-generating services
13. a. are incompatible
14. d. both (b) and (c)
15. c. are increasingly automated
16. c. router
17. b. better value
18. d. all of the above
19. d. will not work when Internet access fails
20. c. such services are not particularly secure

Chapter 15

1. c. doing or feeling
2. a. directly relevant
3. b. threatening
4. b. credible
5. c. train
6. d. both (a) and (c)
7. a. judgment skills
8. c. nonformal
9. c. auditory
10. b. cognitive

11. d. test the emergency plan
12. c. set objectives
13. c. filler
14. b. exercise objectives
15. d. both (a) and (c)
16. b. enhance the learning process
17. c. gaps, errors, and omissions in the emergency plan
18. d. are still subject to exercise stress
19. a. the low return rate
20. d. all of the above

Chapter 16

1. a. a variety of goals
2. b. not necessarily the most effective type
3. c. exercise objectives
4. b. need not be complex or expensive
5. a. as much of the organization or community as possible
6. c. they are part of a comprehensive program
7. d. issues requiring resolution
8. b. guided, not manipulated
9. d. all of the above
10. d. all of the above
11. b. experimental problem-solving
12. d. both (a) and (b)
13. a. enhancing the emergency plan
14. c. functional exercise
15. b. functions or procedures
16. b. test overall emergency response
17. a. comprehensive testing of the emergency plan
18. d. all of the above
19. a. only for confirmation
20. d. all of the above

Chapter 17

1. a. individual members
2. b. resiliency
3. c. self-interest

4. b. safety concerns
5. c. motivation to change
6. a. community partnerships
7. c. sufficient grounding in the principles of adult education
8. b. retained, valued, and acted on
9. a. some degree of interaction
10. c. lead to more comprehensive educational sources
11. b. a communications strategy
12. a. a visitor's ability to interact with it
13. c. tracked and reported
14. d. facilitated discussion boards
15. b. interact and demonstrate
16. d. both (a) and (b)
17. b. their parents
18. b. both groups may potentially benefit from the arrangement
19. c. voluntary exchange of services
20. b. a "focal point" for preparedness education efforts

Chapter 18

1. b. framework
2. a. context
3. d. both (a) and (b)
4. c. emergency management activities will be judged
5. a. degree of influence
6. b. a point of significant power
7. b. the need may not be immediately evident
8. c. exerting influence
9. a. could displace a proposal produced by his or her department
10. a. result in new resources for those departments
11. c. standards

12. a. directive
13. d. only within that jurisdiction
14. c. voluntary
15. b. knowledge similar to that of the average citizen
16. d. both (a) and (b)
17. b. it provides an opportunity to apply and retain information
18. d. both (a) and (b)
19. b. influence
20. c. a win–win situation

Chapter 19

1. b. other community services
2. c. the priorities of other municipal services
3. a. sufficient funding for emergency management programs
4. d. another municipal department
5. d. alternative sources of program funding
6. b. keep program costs under control
7. a. capital budget
8. b. operating budget
9. c. funding allotment from senior government
10. d. grantsmanship process
11. d. all of the above
12. c. benefit all involved parties
13. c. a positive public image
14. b. provide learning experiences for students
15. a. outside of the normal budget process
16. d. variances
17. d. both (b) and (c)
18. b. committee approval
19. d. both (a) and (b)
20. b. a culture of preparedness

Index